The International Migration of the Highly Skilled

CCIS Anthologies, 1
Center for Comparative Immigration Studies
University of California, San Diego

CONTRIBUTORS

Rafael Alarcón

A. Aneesh

Robert L. Bach

Monica Boyd

Paula Chakravartty

Wayne A. Cornelius

Thomas J. Espenshade

Jessica C. Gurcak

Mahmood Iqbal

Magnus Lofstrom

B. Lindsay Lowell

Martha Paskoff

Marc Rosenblum

AnnaLee Saxenian

Aaron Sparrow

Margaret L. Usdansky

Christian Zlolniski

This volume was published with the assistance of the
UCSD Division of Social Sciences and the
UCSD Civic Collaborative.

The International Migration of the Highly Skilled

Demand, Supply, and Development Consequences in Sending and Receiving Countries

edited by

Wayne A. Cornelius

Thomas J. Espenshade

Idean Salehyan

LA JOLLA

CENTER FOR COMPARATIVE IMMIGRATION STUDIES
UNIVERSITY OF CALIFORNIA, SAN DIEGO

Cover photo: Information technology workers of Mexican, British, and Filipino origin, at a communications software company in San Diego, California. — Photograph by Idean Salehyan.

Cover design by Sirious Design.

Printed in the United States of America

ISBN 0-9702838-0-6 (paper)

Contents

PART 1

INTRODUCTION

1

The International Migration of the Highly Skilled: "High-Tech *Braceros*" in the Global Labor Market

Wayne A. Cornelius and Thomas J. Espenshade

Advanced industrial economies of the twenty-first century have an apparently insatiable demand for immigrant labor, at both the top and bottom of the occupational skill hierarchy. The governmental response to this bimodal distribution of demand has been to leave the back door open to unauthorized, mostly low skilled immigrants, while flinging open the front door to legally admitted, ostensibly temporary, high-skilled foreign workers, dubbed by some scholars as "high-tech *braceros*" (Smith 1999) or "*cerebreros*" (Alarcón, this volume).

Foreign-born scientists and engineers constitute the most rapidly growing segment of the labor force in the computer, software, biomedical, and telecommunications industries in the United States, Canada, and Western Europe (Koser and Salt 1997). As the number of highly skilled foreign workers employed by these industries has increased, their presence and employers' calls for many more of them have provoked heated debate in the receiving countries.[1] Nevertheless, with economies booming and under increasing pressure from labor-short employers, the U.S. and West European governments have moved de-

---

[1] Foreign-born scientists and engineers are also contributing to the growth of these industries by starting their own high-tech firms. For example, Chinese and Indian engineers were running one-quarter of Silicon Valley's high-technology businesses in 1998 (Boxall 2001; Saxenian, this volume). Immigrant entrepreneurs are important employers of high-skill foreign workers. Of the top 100 U.S. companies that employed such workers on short-term H–1B visas in 1998, 60 percent had chief executives with South Asian surnames (*Migration News*, July 2001, p. 9 of the electronic edition).

cisively in recent years to increase legal access to their labor markets for highly skilled foreigners.

Liberalization of restrictions on high-skill immigration was the only major immigration policy issue on the agenda for action in the U.S. congressional session ending in December 2000. Other labor-importing countries around the world, unable to produce or retain enough native-born computer programmers, engineers, scientists, and other professionals to maintain economic growth and global competitiveness, have recently announced plans to liberalize their immigration and/or tax laws to attract larger numbers of highly skilled workers. The list includes Canada, the United Kingdom, Ireland, Germany, Austria, Israel, South Africa, Australia, New Zealand, Malaysia, Singapore, Hong Kong, and Japan. All of these government-orchestrated recruitment efforts, coupled with the proliferation of aggressive, technologically sophisticated private-sector labor brokerage operations, have led to the emergence of an intensely competitive, globalized market for high-tech labor.[2]

Several of the labor-importing countries—most notably, Canada, Germany, and Hong Kong—are also striving to staunch the loss of native-born high-skill workers to other countries and to induce expatriates to return. Controversy surrounds the question of whether Canada is really experiencing a brain drain to the United States. In 2000, Prime Minister Jean Chretien's Advisory Council on Science and Technology warned that this was a major problem for the high-tech sector and for universities. A recent study by Industry Canada, however, argues that Canada is merely "loaning" skilled manpower to the United States and, further, that these migrants will return with additional managerial and technical skills that will benefit the Canadian economy. Academic research shows that while between 18,000 and 30,000 foreign skilled workers enter Canada each year, offsetting the brain drain, those who leave for the United States are likely to be the highest-skilled, highest-earning people (DeVoretz 2001). Meanwhile, Canada is trying to attract H–1B visa holders in the United States whose visas are about to expire, and the federal government has announced a sweeping liberalization of immigration rules affecting highly skilled workers. A new "temporary worker" program will whisk foreigners into Canada within a few

---

[2] Some of the U.S.–based brokerage operations (commonly known as "consulting firms") specialize in recruiting highly skilled workers from India and are owned and operated by Indian-Americans. Acting as employment agencies, they file an application for the H–1B visa with the Immigration and Naturalization Service, provide housing for the visa-holders when they arrive in the United States, place them as contract employees in software development projects, and take a cut of their pay. Clusters of such firms have developed in Silicon Valley, central New Jersey, Pittsburgh, Detroit, and other cities (Fernández 2001).

weeks after a labor shortage has been identified by the private sector (working with the federal human resources department), expedite the recognition of their credentials by professional licensing bodies, and enable them to apply for permanent residence after just two years (Beauchesne 2000; Kirby 2000; Thompson 2001).

Echoing the arguments made by Canadian advocates of an expansionary high-skill immigration policy, Austrian experts recently warned that Austria is facing a skills shortage that could put a brake on the country's relatively advanced "new economy" unless the government relaxes immigration rules for high-tech workers. The Institute for Economic Research reported that Austria will have 13,000 unfilled information technology (IT) positions by 2003. The Austrian government is reacting by expanding efforts to draw in those with the necessary skills. Processing delays are being shortened, and the country's annual quota of 1,000 immigrant IT experts (in the past reserved for heads of businesses that set up shop in Austria) is now being extended to foreign IT workers generally (Padieu 2000; Reuters News Service 2000a).

Responding to concerns that Japan is unable to keep up with the world in information technology, the Japanese Posts and Telecommunications Ministry has recommended the easing of standards for foreign technicians and experts. In 1999, 108,000 individuals entered Japan for working purposes; fewer than 4,000 of these were technicians (Karasaki and Fujitani 2001; *Economist* 2000). New agreements signed by the Japanese government with India and other sources of foreign computer engineers recognize their qualifications as sufficient to work in Japan. The trend is clearly toward increased reliance by major Japanese companies on foreign high-skilled workers (Fuess 2001; Harney 2001).

In Germany, despite an official unemployment rate that has hovered at about 10 percent for a decade, the Federation of German Employers claims a national shortage of 1.5 million high-skilled workers. In the United Kingdom, with nearly three-quarters of British companies reporting shortages of various types of high-skill workers, the Confederation of British Industry has joined forces with the Labor government's Home Office Minister, the Treasury, and the Trade Department to promote an "honest debate" on changing the immigration laws to help close the country's skills gap. In the United Kingdom, as in other countries seeking to boost their intake of foreign high-skilled workers, there is strong pressure to broaden eligible occupational categories beyond the IT sector (*Daily Telegraph* 2000; Taylor 2000).

In the United States, high-tech trade organizations have issued estimates of the nationwide shortage of computer programmers, systems analysts, and computer scientists ranging from 269,000 to 843,000. Moreover, the number of U.S.–born students embarking on high-technology-related careers is declining. Since 1996, high-tech employers have been lobbying the U.S. Congress intensively to secure major increases in the number of H–1B visas (for temporary, highly skilled foreign workers). In 1998, Congress and the White House agreed to double the annual allotment of such visas from 65,000 to 115,000, but demand was so strong that the new quota was exhausted by June 1999. In the 2000 fiscal year, the allotment of 115,000 visas was exhausted by mid–March.

Major new legislation, entitled "The American Competitiveness in the Twenty-First Century Act of 2000," was approved by Congress in October 2000, with overwhelming bipartisan support (the Senate vote was 96–1; the House approved it on a voice vote). The bill raised to 195,000 the ceiling on the number of H–1B visas that can be granted in fiscal years 2001, 2002, and 2003. Without this change, the ceiling would have declined from 115,000 in FY 2000 to 107,500 in FY 2001 and to 65,000 in subsequent years. But the legislation contains several important exemptions. Not counted toward the cap are the following: (1) anyone employed (or who has an offer of employment) at a college or university or a related nonprofit entity; (2) foreign workers employed by nonprofit research organizations or a government research organization; and (3) anyone for whom a petition is filed not more than 90 days *before* and not more than 180 days *after* the person has attained a master's or doctor's degree from a U.S. institution of higher education (Palmer 2000). The law also includes provisions to eliminate the backlog of approved H–1B petitions and start with a clean slate. In particular, the caps for FY 1999 and FY 2000 would be raised to grant H–1B visas to all additional workers whose petitions had been approved in FY 1999 or before September 1, 2000, but which could not be granted because of statutory caps. This provision protects the fresh FY 2001 supply of visas from being consumed by the backlog.

The steady expansion of visa allotments for high-tech immigrants to the United States is just one element of an emerging legal regime that facilitates the international mobility of the highly skilled, even while the legal and bureaucratic barriers to low-skilled migration are preserved or even strengthened. At the insistence of the United States and over the fleeting objections of Mexico, the North American Free Trade Agreement (NAFTA), implemented in January 1994, includes no provisions concerning general labor mobility. However, it provides so-called NAFTA visas for businessmen and professionals in finance, accounting, and law, enabling them to work indefinitely in any of the three member countries (Canada, Mexico, and the United States). World Trade Organization regulations also promote the movement of professional workers in telecommunications, finance, and other services across national borders. Critics of such provisions note that governments have taken the course of least political resistance, folding labor migration mechanisms discreetly into trade liberalization agreements, rather than debating them openly and incorporating them into national immigration law and policy (see, for example, Sassen 2000).

The Politics of Liberalizing High-Skill Immigration

Much of the policy debate concerning the immigration of highly skilled workers, especially in the United States, is driven by the question of whether a skilled-labor shortage truly exists. High-tech employers insist that present and foreseeable supplies of native-born workers with the necessary skills and experience are totally inadequate to meet their needs, and that they must have greater access to the global pool of high-tech workers to prevent crippling labor shortages. Immigration lawyers and leaders of high-tech industry argue that a "global war for talent" is emerging and that the United States needs to have access to the best and brightest workers anywhere in the world to maintain its global competitive edge (Judy 1999; Burdette 1999). This view is supported by the Hudson Institute's report on the implications of an aging population for the supply of highly skilled workers (Judy and D'Amico 1997) and by widely publicized reports from the U.S. Commerce Department (Office of Technology Policy 1997) and the Information Technology Association of America (1997).

On the other hand, some legislative critics and interest groups favoring lower levels of immigration dispute the need for further increases in visas for foreign high-skilled workers and blame labor shortages, if any, on employers' preferences for younger, lower-paid, more "flexible" workers. They argue that employers have an idiosyncratic, non-market concept of labor shortages—namely, that a shortage is presumed to exist whenever leaders of high-tech industry are unable to find sufficient workers of the type they want *at a wage they are willing to pay*. Skeptics of the industry view advocate greater investment in science and technology education for native-born workers and schoolchildren. Moreover, some professional engineering societies contend that the high-tech industries that are complaining about skilled-labor shortages are often the same ones responsible for many of the layoffs of American workers (Federation for American Immigration Reform 1998).

The facts of the widely debated high-tech labor shortage remain in dispute. The U.S. General Accounting Office (1998) has reported that the Commerce Department's study alleging a shortage of information technology workers is so methodologically flawed that its conclusions cannot be taken seriously (Espenshade 2001). Previous studies that projected a shortfall of skilled labor have been contradicted by subsequent developments (Fechter 1994). For example, the number of permanent resident visas issued since fiscal year 1992 in the employment-preference categories has fallen short of the allocated quota (Papademetriou and Yale-Loehr 1996), and more than 40,000 of these visas (out of 140,000) went unused during FY 1998 (Burdette 1999). From FY 1994 through FY 1998, a period of rapid growth in H–1B visa admissions, the number of permanent resident visas issued to immigrants for employment/job-skill reasons fell from 123,000 to 78,000 (including the workers and their immediate family members).[3]

Evidence of across-the-board shortages of highly skilled workers in the United States is far from conclusive, according to independent experts (Gurcak, Espenshade, Sparrow, and Paskoff, this volume; Lowell, this volume). For example, there is little indication of the upward pressure on wages that genuine shortages would be exerting. Indeed, real wages for scientists and engineers in the U.S. labor market actually fell by about 10 percent between 1970 and 1997 (Espenshade, Usdansky, and Chung 2001). A committee of experts assembled by the U.S. National Research Council has identified labor shortages in particular segments of the IT industry, especially of "high-end" (uniquely skilled and highly educated) workers (National Research Council 2001).[4] Foreign H–1B workers are more likely than native-born U.S. workers in IT occupations to have a master's degree or better; therefore, "highly educated H–1B workers are a quick solution to production bottlenecks at the upper end" (Lowell, this volume).[5] More generally, however, the National Research Council concluded that foreign-born IT workers have probably depressed wages in the IT labor market in the sense of

---

[3] *Migration News,* July 2001, p. 10 of the electronic edition.

[4] The NRC committee itself chose to use the term "tightness" rather than "shortage" to describe the high-skill labor market. It characterized that labor market as follows: "Today, the IT labor market is tight, though the nature and extent of such tightness vary by employer, by type of IT work involved, and by geographic locale.... The data suggest that the IT labor market is highly segmented, and that certain segments experience much higher degrees of tightness [than] the overall market" (National Research Council 2001: 109). For a detailed critique of the NRC study, see Matloff 2001.

[5] Researchers in the Immigration and Naturalization Service's Statistical Branch found that this did not apply to H–1B workers in general, at least those whose visa applications were approved during the 1999 fiscal year. Among this more diverse sample of H–1B workers, just 56 percent had earned the equivalent of a U.S. bachelor's degree, and only 8 percent had a doctoral degree or equivalent (Bach, this volume). Also, audits and investigations conducted by the inspector general of the U.S. Department of Labor "have routinely shown that the individuals allowed into the United States under this program typically lack the specialized skills training necessary for meeting the requirements for H–1B visas" (U.S. Department of Labor 2000: 38).

keeping wages from rising as fast as might be expected in a tight labor market (National Research Council 2001: 155). What cannot be questioned is that, in the United States and virtually all other major labor-importing countries today, the political process invariably operates to legitimize employer demand for high-skilled foreign labor while maintaining the illusion that low-skilled immigrants are superfluous to the "objective" needs of the high-tech, knowledge-intensive, twenty-first-century economy.[6]

The United States has a long history of legislation—dating back to the Chinese Exclusion Act of 1882 and the Immigration Act of 1917—designed to exclude low-skill immigrants while creating exceptions for more highly skilled workers. But as Usdansky and Espenshade (this volume) observe, over the last 150 years Congress has gradually shifted away from barring low-skill workers and toward recruiting the highly skilled, even while imposing numerical caps on the immigration of such workers.

The 1990s were marked by rising support in Congress for a more "skills-based" immigration policy—that is, a formula for legal immigrant admissions that gives greater weight to occupational skills and educational attainment than to kinship ties with U.S. citizens. The Immigration Act of 1990 was a modest shift in this direction, more than doubling the number of employment-based visas but leaving largely intact the system of family-based immigration. During the remainder of the decade, most legislative battles over immigration issues dealt with control of illegal immigration and denial of access to tax-supported services for unauthorized immigrants (Gimpel and Edwards 1999); but the issue of the "skill mix" in U.S. legal immigrant admissions gained in salience. Restrictionist advocacy groups and members of the Republican congressional leadership argued that the proportion of skilled immigrants had declined in recent decades because of the emphasis on family reunification in U.S. immigration law as well as an uncontrolled influx of illegal immigrants.

---

[6] U.S. academic immigration specialists—mostly labor economists—who are strongly wedded to this position include George Borjas of Harvard University (Borjas 1999); Georges Vernez and Kevin McCarthy of the RAND Corporation (McCarthy and Vernez 1997); Vernon Briggs of Cornell University (Briggs 2000); and David North (North 1995). Skeptics—mostly sociologists and political scientists—emphasize the structural character of demand for both high- and low-skilled workers in today's labor-importing nations. They include Wayne Cornelius at the University of California, San Diego (Cornelius 1998; Cornelius and Kuwahara 1998); Alejandro Portes at Princeton (Portes 1995); Saskia Sassen at the University of Chicago (Sassen 1999); and Demetrios Papademetriou of the Migration Policy Institute (Papademetriou and Hamilton 2000).

While calls for more employment-based immigration resounded in the political arena, U.S. employer demand for highly skilled immigrants remained modest until the late 1990s. The cap of 65,000 H–1B visas per year set by the Immigration Act of 1990 was not reached until fiscal year 1997, fueled by a burst of economic growth. But the U.S. economic boom continued to the end of the decade and beyond, and major corporations—led by Microsoft and other IT giants—began to lobby for greater access to the worldwide pool of high-tech labor. The stage was set for a significant expansion of high-skill immigration.

The drive to raise the cap on H–1B visas was nearly derailed in the summer of 2000, when the proposed legislation bogged down in election-year politics. Democratic congressional leaders, the White House, and Latino leaders both within and outside of Congress insisted on linking the expansion of the H–1B program to: (1) the granting of a "late amnesty" to as many as 750,000 illegal immigrants who had resided in the United States since before 1986; (2) the expansion of an amnesty approved by Congress in 1996 for Nicaraguans and Cubans (considered "victims of Communism") to include four other nationalities of refugees arriving in the 1980s and early 1990s that had not benefited from the 1996 law (Haitians, Guatemalans, Hondurans, Salvadorans); and (3) a proposal to enable undocumented immigrants already established in the United States to seek adjustment to permanent legal-resident status without returning to their home countries. These provisions were presented to backers of the H–1B expansion as an essential quid pro quo.

The attempt at issue linkage failed, however, when the business community exerted such intense pressure on both members of Congress and the president that the provisions of interest to Latinos were severed and lumped together as the "Latino and Immigrant Fairness Act" (still pending). Congress then moved swiftly to approve the increase in H–1B visas. "Many CEOs made calls," reported the head of a Silicon Valley–based lobbying group, "and the message was the same: 'We don't care about the partisanship, and we don't care about who gets to claim credit. We just care that it gets done' [before Congress adjourns]" (in Puzzanghera 2000).

In West European countries as well, governments are proving susceptible to the same basic argument used so effectively by U.S. high-tech employers: Relatively unfettered access to the global IT talent pool is essential to avoiding bottlenecks in economic growth and maintaining national economic competitiveness. The Internet economies of the early twenty-first century are being driven by highly skilled workers, and the domestic supply of them is not only inadequate but being depleted constantly through brain-drain emigration. "U.S. companies go around the world cherry-picking the best skills," said a London-based analyst of international labor mobility recently. "Now the rest of the world wants to do the same" (in Zachary 2000).

If You Build It, Will They Come?—And Stay?

Given the tightness of the global labor market for highly skilled workers, there is no guarantee that a nation that liberalizes its immigration laws to attract more of them will be successful—unless it is the United States. All labor-importing countries today are competing for highly skilled workers against the United States and, to a lesser extent, Britain. Most of them are likely to lose in this competition.

An excellent case in point is Germany. In August 2000, the center-left government of Chancellor Gerhard Schroeder launched a new program to issue short-term visas—curiously referred to as "green cards" despite their temporary character—to about 20,000 non–European Union information technology specialists in the first two years of the program.[7] The actual implementation of the program was preceded by three months of worldwide publicity aimed at producing a large, immediate pool of applicants. By June 2001, however, only about 8,000 of Germany's new "green cards" had been issued. Many of the applicants did not meet the program's educational and financial requirements (a university degree in a high-tech field and an assured salary of at least 100,000 marks, about $44,250 per year) or could not speak German or English. Equally disappointing to German companies is the fact that only about one in five of the "green cards" issued to date have been claimed by the globally-much-sought-after, English-speaking, and technically skilled Indians (most of the successful "green card" applicants were from Russia, Romania, and the former Yugoslavia).

German officials initially seemed stunned by the tepid response of qualified foreign IT workers, especially considering that recipients of "green-card" visas are permitted to bring family members, who can also apply for temporary work permits. But the bureaucrats had been forewarned by academic experts that much more would have to be done to induce potential "green card" applicants to choose Germany over the United States and other attractive suitors. The disincentives to locate in Germany are not difficult to discern: high income taxes (the top rate paid by even middle-income workers is 48.5 percent); persistent acts of anti-immigrant violence and harassment by right-wing ex-

---

[7] According to German immigration experts, the introduction of a "green card" for high-skilled foreign workers represented "a dramatic change in German immigration policy, which has concentrated thus far on the regulation of the immigration of ethnic Germans from Eastern Europe, family migrants, and asylum seekers" (Bauer, Lofstrom, and Zimmermann 2000: 1).

tremist groups (up by 59 percent in 2000, according to government figures); conservative politicians and political parties, most notably the Christian Democratic Union (CDU), that rail against more liberalized immigration policies;[8] a procedure for obtaining German citizenship that, despite recent reforms, is still too stringent; and a relatively low level of general-public tolerance for non–EU foreign workers.[9]

In addition, the terms of the "green card" itself are restrictive: Visa recipients are limited to a five-year stay and have no right to petition for permanent residency. Besides demanding tax reform and a more vigorous crackdown on right-wing violence, Germany's 300 largest high-tech employers have begun to lobby the government to dispense with the five-year limit for "green card" holders. As a senior executive of the Siemens industrial group put it, "We can't order highly qualified employees to leave the country in five years [time]" (in Reuters News Service 2000b). According to a recent national survey of German employers, 71 percent would hire more non–EU skilled foreign workers if the immigration rules were liberalized (Winkelmann et al. 2001).

This highlights one of the incongruous features of "temporary" foreign worker programs, whether they are aimed at high- or low-skilled migrants, and irrespective of national or historical context. Such programs are ostensibly designed to satisfy a demand for short-term, even seasonal labor, and they require both employers and international migrants to conform to this "strict rotation" principle. But the labor market realities are that many, if not the majority, of the jobs filled by "temporary" workers are in fact permanent, year-round jobs, and neither employers nor the migrants they employ have any incentive to terminate the arrangement. In the absence of an effective, nationwide bureaucratic and police apparatus that politicians are committed to enforcing, systematic violations of the terms of "temporary" worker programs can be anticipated, and "temporary" workers eventually become de facto permanent additions to the labor force.

Whether they remain legally or illegally depends on the ease with which holders of short-term work permits can obtain permanent, legal-resident status. In most cases, the supply of permanent-resident visas will be greatly exceeded by the demand of "temporary" workers seeking to adjust their status. For example, H–1B visas in the United States

---

[8] For example, in one recent state-level election, the CDU campaigned under the slogan, *"kinder statt Inder"* ("children rather than Indians"), arguing that government money should be spent on educating native-born computer experts rather than importing them from India.

[9] In the most recent national survey, by the EMNID Research Institute, two-thirds of Germans believed that the country already accepts too many immigrants (Agence France Presse 2000). Seventy-one percent of residents of the former East Germany held this view, compared with 64 percent in the West.

are valid for three years and can be renewed for an additional three years, but most of those entering with this type of visa would like to remain permanently. Based on past behavior of H–1B visa holders, Lindsay Lowell (this volume) has estimated that under the legislation just approved, the number of H–1Bs who will seek permanent-resident visas will rise sharply to 74,000 in 2004. Yet the existing U.S. system of permanent legal immigration will absorb only about 25,000 H–1Bs annually, and the large backlog of applications to adjust to permanent-resident status ensures lengthy processing delays.[10]

Assuming a still-buoyant U.S. economy, we can anticipate strong political pressures a few years from now to modify the permanent legal immigration system to enable a much higher percentage of H–1B visa holders to adjust, and to drastically reduce the time for approving their permanent visas, which can now take from four to six years. Thus the short-term political expediency that resulted in a step-level increase in the cap for "temporary" high-skilled foreign workers in the 2001–2004 period is likely to force more sweeping and enduring changes in U.S. immigration law and policy.[11]

In West European countries having less expansionist immigration regimes and more culturally driven public hostility toward large-scale immigration than in the United States (see Fetzer 2000; Bauer, Lofstrom, and Zimmermann 2000), the dilemmas posed by high-skilled immigration will be more acute. Both general publics and political classes are still very uneasy about becoming more dependent on foreign labor, regardless of skill level. Accordingly, there is considerable ambivalence about using immigration policy proactively to offset skill deficits, despite the rising clamor from large corporations and business organizations to do exactly that.

Neither in Germany nor in other West European labor-importing countries does one find a sufficiently broad national consensus on immigration to allow the political process to forge coherent immigration policies and institutional mechanisms. Again, Germany provides the best example. Despite having absorbed over 20 million immigrants

---

[10] According to a recent report by the U.S. General Accounting Office (2001), there were 1.5 million such applications pending in 2000—more than three times as many as in 1994.

[11] Already, under pressure from the business community, the U.S. Immigration and Naturalization Service has signaled its willingness to give H–1B visa holders who have lost their jobs in the recent IT downturn a grace period—perhaps up to 60 days—in which to find a new job and stay in the United States (Bredemeier 2001). Under existing regulations, if an H–1B visa holder loses the job for which he was recruited and cannot find another one within a few days, he cannot legally remain in the country and is subject to deportation. To date, however, the INS has not deported any H–1B worker who has lost his job due to the economic slowdown.

since World War II, many of whom were "guestworkers" admitted on short-term labor contracts during the 1960s and early 1970s, Germany still has no national immigration law. In July 2001, a government commission initiated the debate on such a law by proposing that Germany admit 50,000 skilled foreign workers annually, of whom only 20,000 would immediately receive permanent resident status (Cohen 2001). Immigration at this level would be a drop in the bucket compared with the 7.3 million foreigners now living in Germany (9.1 percent of total population) and considering the massive contraction in the German labor force projected over the next fifty years due to population aging. Indeed, most politicians have continued to deny that that Germany *is* a "country of immigration" (Marshall 2000; Rubio-Marín 2000). Germany's recent thrust toward importing larger numbers of ostensibly temporary high-skill foreign workers will only prolong this exercise in denial.

An Agenda for Further Research

Economic development in the world's advanced industrial democracies—and, in particular, the gradual transition to economies requiring higher amounts of human and intellectual capital—has transformed the nature of the immigration debate. No longer do we argue mainly about effective mechanisms for restricting the flow of low-skilled workers. The spotlight in the policy debate has swung around to discussions of how to attract sufficient amounts of high-skilled talent from abroad to supplement the talent that countries produce from their own populations.

Because research and policy attention to "high-end" immigration is a relatively recent phenomenon, there is much spadework to be done. Some of the outstanding questions are dealt with in the chapters that follow, but many issues require further exploration. First, the decade of the 1990s saw a rapid expansion in worldwide demand for talented knowledge workers. Most the demand originated in the United States, but the swift spread of IT industries in the global economy meant that many countries were competing for the same workers. What will these trends mean for those who worry about a "race to the bottom" in terms of domestic wages for IT workers? (See Rosenblum, this volume.) Is it possible that what may develop is rather a "race to the top," as more and more countries compete among themselves for a limited supply of talent?

There is already some evidence that this is happening, and it is a topic that deserves further attention. The regional director of New Zealand's Immigration Service for Asia and the Middle East recently observed, "We are competing with Australia, Canada, Germany and other countries for skilled migrants" (Parasher 2000). Hong Kong finds itself in intense competition for highly skilled workers not only with Western countries but also with nearby Singapore and Malaysia (Chand 2000; Lam 2001). A major Canadian think tank, the C.D. Howe Institute, warns of an impending global shortage of skilled workers within the next twenty years, predicting that continued economic expansion in the industrial countries, coupled with shrinking workforces as populations age, will leave these countries scrambling for skilled professionals (Monchuk 2000).

Second, the labor market consequences of rapid growth in highly skilled international migration in the United States and other major immigrant-receiving countries cannot be fully appreciated until the 2000 round of decennial census data is analyzed. Many of these datasets, containing individual-level records, will become available in the next few years. Census public-use data provide samples "thick" enough to produce detailed and reliable estimates of, for example, the impacts of skilled international migrants on the employment and earnings of native workers. These new data need to be fully exploited.

Third, there has been a tendency in immigration debates, and even in the immigration research literature, to be overly preoccupied with the number of immigrants and to pay insufficient attention to immigrant characteristics. For example, the recent United Nations (2000) report on *Replacement Migration* focuses attention on the volume of immigration required in the United States, Japan, and several European countries to maintain selected demographic targets and forestall population aging and decline. The present volume helps to refocus energies on the need to pay more attention to migrant characteristics.

Finally, what happens when the current boom cycle in demand for IT workers ends? There is strong evidence that a slowdown is already under way. Dot.com companies have been disappearing at surprisingly high rates. Layoffs of IT worker—something unheard of and barely anticipated just a year or two ago—are now routine occurrences at Compaq, Dell, Intel, Yahoo, Cisco, Motorola, Nortel, and other well-known knowledge-based companies. The United States has been absorbing a growing volume of foreign high-skilled workers, many of whom are here on temporary visas but have a preference for long-term residence, if not permanent settlement. What happens to these individuals when the global economic miracle of the 1990s begins to fade and unemployment rates—even in IT—begin to rise? Will a backlash against foreign IT workers materialize, just as it has historically against immigrants in general when the U.S. economy performs badly?

Employers argue that there is still a shortage of IT workers with the right "skill sets," despite the slowing of U.S. economic growth. While fragmentary, the available evidence suggests that the majority of H–1B workers who have lost their jobs since the beginning of the downturn have been those with lower-level skills, especially those employed in subcontracting operations ("body shops" and the like). According to the U.S. Immigration and Naturalization Service, the number of visas sought by employers for foreign IT workers has continued to rise during the economic slowdown. A "Premium Processing Program" initiated by the INS in July 2001 promises to shorten the H–1B visa processing time to no more than fifteen days (as compared with the normal time of sixty to ninety days), making it more likely that U.S. employers will file for H–1B workers, particularly once the economic outlook improves.[12] Moreover, the economic slowdown in the United States that now seems to be spreading across the globe does not necessarily translate into diminished efforts by other countries to recruit highly skilled workers from abroad. No labor-importing country has yet abandoned its plans or programs to boost high-skilled immigration. In fact, government recruitment efforts seem to be proliferating.

In short, rich opportunities await the immigration researcher who focuses on high-skilled migration. The welter of competing claims about the demand, supply, and development consequences of such migration for both sending and receiving countries can only be clarified through new empirical research. We hope that this volume will be a stimulus.

References

Agence France Presse. 2000. "Poll: Germans Think Country Accepts Too Many Immigrants," October 9.

Bauer, Thomas K., Magnus Lofstrom, and Klaus F. Zimmermann. 2000. "Immigration Policy, Assimilation of Immigrants, and Natives' Sentiments towards Immigrants: Evidence from 12 OECD Countries." Discussion Paper No. 187. Bonn, Germany: Institute for the Study of Labor (IZA).

Beauchesne, Eric. 2000. "Canada Merely Loaning Its Brightest to the U.S.: The Brain Drain is Relatively Small and Many Canadians Will Return," *Vancouver Sun*, August 23.

Borjas, George J. 1999. *Heaven's Door: Immigration Policy and the American Economy*. Princeton, N.J.: Princeton University Press.

Boxall, Bettina. 2001. "Asian Indians Remake Silicon Valley," *Los Angeles Times*, July 6.

Bredemeier, Kenneth. 2001. "INS to Grant Immigrants Some Grace: Laid-Off Visa Holders Get Time to Find Jobs," *Washington Post*, June 27.

---

[12] Under this program, employers will pay an additional $1,000 for expedited processing of each H–1B visa, on top of the regular fee of $1,110 charged by the INS.

Briggs, Vernon M., Jr. 2000. "Why Clinton Should Veto 'H–1B,'" *Ithaca Journal,* September 4.

Burdette, Rebecca. 1999. "Testimony of Rebecca Burdette." Testimony to the U.S. House Judiciary Committee, Subcommittee on Immigration and Claims, Oversight Hearing on the Benefits to the American Economy of a More Educated Workforce, Washington, D.C., March 25.

Chand, N. 2000. "The Tug of War for Asia's Best Brains," *Far Eastern Economic Review,* November 9.

Cohen, Roger. 2001. "Germany Ponders Opening Door, Just a Crack, to Immigration," *New York Times,* July 5.

Cornelius, Wayne A. 1998. "The Structural Embeddedness of Demand for Mexican Immigrant Labor: New Evidence from California." In *Crossings: Mexican Immigration in Interdisciplinary Perspective,* edited by Marcelo Suárez-Orozco. Cambridge, Mass.: Harvard University Press/David Rockefeller Center for Latin American Studies.

Cornelius, Wayne A., and Yasuo Kuwahara. 1998. *The Role of Immigrant Labor in the U.S. and Japanese Economies: A Comparative Study of San Diego and Hamamatsu, Japan.* La Jolla: Center for U.S.–Mexican Studies, University of California, San Diego.

Daily Telegraph (London). 2000. "Firms Go Abroad to Plug the Skills Gap," September 28.

DeVoretz, Don J. 2001. "Triangular Human Capital Flows between Sending, Entrepot, and Rest of the World Destinations: Lessons from Canada and Germany." Paper presented at the conference "Host Societies and the Reception of Immigrants," Weatherhead Center for International Affairs, Harvard University, May 11–12.

Economist. 2000. "The Door Opens, a Crack," September 2–8.

Espenshade, Thomas J. 2001. "High-End Immigrants and the Shortage of Skilled Labor," *Population Research and Policy Review* 20 (1–2).

Espenshade, Thomas J., Margaret L. Usdansky, and Chang Y. Chung. 2001. "Employment and Earnings of Foreign-Born Scientists and Engineers in U.S. Labor Markets," *Population Research and Policy Review* 20 (1–2).

Fechter, Alan. 1994. "Future Supply and Demand: Cloudy Crystal Balls." In *Who Will Do Science? Educating the Next Generation,* edited by Willie Pearson, Jr. and Alan Fechter. Baltimore, Md.: Johns Hopkins University Press.

Federation for American Immigration Reform. 1998. "Congress Passes H–1B Foreign Worker Increase," *FAIR Immigration Report* 18 (8).

Fernández, Bob. 2001. "A Profitable Business: Tech-Worker Imports," *Philadelphia Inquirer,* February 25.

Fetzer, Joel S. 2000. *Public Attitudes toward Immigration in the United States, France, and Germany.* Cambridge: Cambridge University Press.

Fuess, Scott M., Jr. 2001. "Highly Skilled Workers and Japan: Is There International Mobility?" Paper presented at the workshop "The International Mobility of Highly Skilled Workers," Institute for the Study of Labor (IZA), Bonn, Germany, March 25–26.

Gimpel, James G., and James R. Edwards, Jr. 1999. *The Congressional Politics of Immigration Reform.* Boston: Allyn and Bacon.

Harney, Alexandra. 2001. "Tokyo to Lure Foreign IT Skills," *Financial Times* (U.K.), May 31.

Information Technology Association of America. 1997. *Help Wanted: The IT Workforce Gap at the Dawn of a New Century.* Arlington, Vir.: ITAA.

Judy, Richard W. 1999. "Immigration Policy and America's Workforce Needs: Re-establishing the Connection." Testimony to the U.S. House Judiciary Committee, Subcommittee on Immigration and Claims, Oversight Hearing on the Benefits to the American Economy of a More Educated Workforce, Washington, D.C., March 25.

Judy, Richard W., and Carol D'Amico. 1997. *Workforce 2020: Work and Workers in the 21ˢᵗ Century.* Indianapolis, Ind.: Hudson Institute.

Karasaki, Taro, and Takeshi Fujitani. 2001. "Foreigners Now Seen as an Economic Engine," *Asahi News Service*, January 12.

Kirby, Carrie. 2000. "Can't Get Action from INS? Canada Has a Deal for You," *San Francisco Chronicle*, August 25.

Koser, Khalid, and John Salt. 1997. "The Geography of Highly Skilled International Migration," *International Journal of Population Geography* 3: 285–303.

Lam, Joanna Kit-Chun. 2001. "Shortage of Highly Skilled Workers in Hong Kong and Policy Responses," *Journal of International Migration and Integration* 1 (4): 405–25.

Marshall, Barbara. 2000. *The New Germany and Migration in Europe.* Manchester: Manchester University Press/Palgrave.

Matloff, Norman. 2001. *A Missed Opportunity: Pro-Industry Report Defends "Temporary" H–1B Visa Usage.* Backgrounder Series. Washington, D.C.: Center for Immigration Studies.

McCarthy, Kevin F., and Georges Vernez. 1997. *Immigration in a Changing Economy: California's Experience.* Santa Monica, Calif.: RAND Corporation.

Monchuk, Judy. 2000. "Think-Tank Warns of Skilled Labour Shortage," *Canadian Press*, September 21.

National Research Council. 2001. *Building a Workforce for the Information Economy: A Report by the Committee on Workforce Needs in Information Technology.* Washington, D.C.: National Academy Press.

North, David S. 1995. *Soothing the Establishment: The Impact of Foreign-Born Scientists and Engineers on America.* Lanham, Md.: University Press of America.

Office of Technology Policy. 1997. *America's New Deficit: The Shortage of Information Technology Workers.* Washington, D.C.: U.S. Department of Commerce, September 29.

Padieu, Anne. 2000. "Austria Woos Foreigners to Cover Its High-Tech Deficit," Agence France Presse, October 4.

Palmer, Elizabeth A. 2000. "Well-Timed Push on H–1B Bill Gives Businesses All They Asked," *CQ Weekly—Labor and Employment*, October 7.

Papademetriou, Demetrios G., and Kimberly Hamilton. 2000. *Reinventing Japan: Immigration's Role in Shaping Japan's Future.* Washington, D.C.: Carnegie Endowment for International Peace.

Papademetriou, Demetrios G., and Stephen Yale-Loehr. 1996. *Balancing Interests: Rethinking U.S. Selection of Skilled Immigrants.* Washington, D.C.: Carnegie Endowment for International Peace.

Parasher, Paritosh. 2000. "New Zealand Wants Indian IT Professionals," *India Abroad News*, September 7.

Portes, Alejandro, ed. 1995. *The Economic Sociology of Immigration*. New York: Russell Sage Foundation.

Puzzanghera, Jim. 2000. "High-Tech Victory on Visas," *San Jose Mercury News*, October 4.

Reuters News Service. 2000a. "Consultants Say Austrian Economy Needs More Immigrants," September 7.

————. 2000b. "Response to German Green Card IT Visas Disappoints," October 13.

Rubio-Marín, Ruth. 2000. *Immigration as a Democratic Challenge: Citizenship and Inclusion in Germany and the United States*. Cambridge: Cambridge University Press.

Sassen, Saskia. 1999. *Guests and Aliens*. New York: New Press.

————. 2000. "Unstoppable Immigrants," *The Guardian* (U.K.), September 12.

Smith, Michael P. 1999. "The New High-Tech *Braceros*: Who Is the Employer? What is the Problem?" In *Foreign Temporary Workers in America: Policies That Benefit the U.S. Economy*, edited by B. Lindsay Lowell. Westport, Conn.: Quorum.

Taylor, Robert. 2000. "Shortage of Skilled Staff Worsens Employment," *Financial Times* (U.K.), October 18.

Thompson, Allan. 2001. "Ottawa to Open Door for 'Temp' Workers," *Toronto Star*, June 27.

United Nations. 2000. *Replacement Migration: Is It a Solution to Declining and Ageing Populations?* New York: Population Division, Dept. of Economics and Social Affairs, United Nations Secretariat, ESA/P/WP.160, March 21.

U.S. Department of Labor, Office of the Inspector General. 2000. *Semiannual Report to the Congress, April 1, 2000–September 30, 2000* (vol. 44). Washington, D.C.: U.S. Department of Labor.

U.S. General Accounting Office. 1998. *Information Technology: Assessment of the Department of Commerce's Report on Workforce Demand and Supply*. Report No. B-278899, GAO/HEHS-98-106R. Washington, D.C.

————. 2001. *Immigration Benefits: Several Factors Impede Timeliness of Application Processing*. Report No. GAO-01-488. Washington, D.C.

Winkelmann, Rainer, et al. 2001. "IZA Studie 'Internationale Mobilität hochqualifizierter Arbeitskräft'—Erste Ergebnisse." Paper presented at the workshop "The International Mobility of Highly Skilled Workers," Institute for the Study of Labor (IZA), Bonn, Germany, March 25–26.

Zachary, G. Pascal. 2000. "People Who Need People; With Skilled Workers in High Demand, Employers are Hunting Them Down—No Matter Where They Live," *Wall Street Journal*, September 25.

PART 2

RECEIVING COUNTRY EXPERIENCES:
THE UNITED STATES AND CANADA

2

The Evolution of U.S. Policy toward Employment-Based Immigrants and Temporary Workers: The H–1B Debate in Historical Perspective

Margaret L. Usdansky and Thomas J. Espenshade

Concern about what kinds of immigrants and temporary workers come to the United States has traditionally focused on excluding those viewed as least desirable—the uneducated, unskilled, and illegal. Most research regarding immigration has shared this focus. But increasingly since the mid–twentieth century, and especially since the late 1980s, the scope of the U.S. immigration policy debate has expanded to encompass questions about the desirability of attracting highly skilled immigrants and temporary workers. These high-skilled newcomers boast education, training, and talent that could benefit the United States economically. But some members of the public, political activists, and policymakers fear that this same social and economic capital may threaten U.S. interests by creating competition with American-born workers.

This tension between dual goals—attracting immigrants who can contribute economically, and ensuring that they do not displace or otherwise harm U.S. workers—was reflected in congressional wrangling over the number and kind of permanent visas to be issued for employment-based immigration under the Immigration Act of 1990 (Congressional Quarterly, Inc. 1991). It arose again in debate over the Immigration Act of 1996, which initially included ultimately unsuccessful proposals to curtail both employment-based permanent immigration and visas for temporary workers (Congressional Quarterly, Inc. 1997).[1]

We gratefully acknowledge support received from the Alfred P. Sloan Foundation and the Population Research Center.

[1] The sponsors of the original legislation that led to the 1996 Act, Senator Alan Simpson (R–Wyoming) and Representative Lamar Smith (R–Texas), fought hard but ultimately unsuccessfully for a variety of measures that would have restricted

But nowhere has this tension been more evident than in the ongoing congressional debate over the H–1B program, which allows high-tech and other skilled workers into the United States for stays of several years. The H–1B debate has pitted business leaders, who argue that the United States is suffering from an economically damaging shortage of qualified workers in critical fields like information technology, against labor representatives, who counter that the United States is caving into the demands of employers who would rather hire cheap foreign labor than train or retrain available U.S. workers (Congressional Quarterly, Inc. 2000).

This chapter contributes to the understanding of contemporary immigration debates by tracing the history of federal policy toward foreigners coming to work in the United States on a permanent or temporary basis. Although U.S. immigration policy has long been known for its orientation toward family-based admission of immigrants, concern about the economic impact of the labor force participation of immigrants and temporary workers has been a critical force in shaping immigration policy since the passage of the earliest federal immigration laws in the late nineteenth century. "It would in fact be difficult to determine where immigration policy ends and labor policy begins, the two are so closely interrelated," wrote immigration law expert E. P. Hutchinson (1981: 492).

In this chapter, we outline the history and socioeconomic context of U.S. legislation regarding employment-based immigration and the admission of foreign-born temporary workers. Our focus is on legislation explicitly intended to affect the numbers and types of employment-based immigrants and temporary workers coming to the United States. We gauge such intent based on language contained in the legislation we cite, and on contemporary statements by members of Congress and other proponents and opponents of the legislation.[2] Because many pieces of legislation address and distinguish between high- and low-skilled workers, we examine the evolution of U.S. policy toward both groups. We cover the period from the mid–nineteenth century to

---

legal, employment-based immigrants and temporary workers. These included plans to decrease the number of permanent, employment-based visas, to charge employers for using these visas to bring immigrants into the United States, to require employers to pay H–1B workers 110 percent of the going rate for comparable U.S. workers, and to adopt harsher penalties for employers who violated the intent of the H–1B program by hiring foreign workers at low wages to displace higher-paid U.S. workers (*Congressional Quarterly* 1997).

[2] Although we recognize that many other motives, particularly fear of the changing racial and ethnic composition of the United States, shaped the legislation we discuss, a full analysis of the relative weight of these concerns is beyond the scope of this chapter.

the end of the twentieth. We conclude that concern about employment-based immigrants and temporary workers has played a far greater role in U.S. federal immigration policy since the 1850s than is commonly recognized.

Industrialization and Immigration

The period of selective immigration restrictions that began in the 1880s had its roots in fear of the impact of foreign-born laborers on the native workforce. U.S. industrialization proceeded at a rapid-fire pace over the course of the second half of the nineteenth century, and its advance made immigrants a desirable commodity in the eyes of big business. Increasing mechanization made the employment of unskilled workers both possible and profitable. European immigrants provided a large and fast-expanding source of unskilled workers, who were willing to work grueling hours at low wages without the threat of unionization posed by native workers (Calavita 1984).

Between 1820 and 1880, more than 10 million Irish, German, English, Scandinavian, and other mainly northern and western European immigrants arrived in the United States, providing an ample pool of low-wage labor (Dinnerstein and Reimers 1999: 18–19). A smaller stream of immigrants came from Asia, including Chinese immigrants who came to California beginning in the 1850s to work in gold mines, and Japanese immigrants, who came to work in agriculture in the 1890s (Dinnerstein and Reimers 1999: 73–76).

Despite the development of a strong nativist movement that peaked during the 1850s, efforts in the U.S. Congress to restrict immigration proved unsuccessful. The lack of a strong labor movement, industry's need for labor, and the growing dominance of slavery over other political issues contributed to this lack of success (Hutchinson 1981: 37; Calavita 1984: 33–34).

The start of the Civil War curtailed immigration. The need for new workers was felt all the more sharply as some immigrants left factory jobs for more lucrative employment in the Union army, and others took advantage of the Homesteading Act and went into farming (Calavita 1984: 36). In December 1863, President Lincoln appealed to Congress to pass legislation to address "a great deficiency of laborers in every field of industry, especially in agriculture and our mines" (Hutchinson 1981: 48). Congress responded by passing the Act to Encourage Immigration in 1864. The Act allowed companies to engage immigrant laborers abroad under binding contracts, which specified that the companies would pay the immigrants' passage to the United States and deduct this cost from the immigrants' wages. The 1864 Act also created a federal commissioner of immigration and established the United States Emigrant Office in New York, which was charged with helping immigrants make their way to their U.S. destinations as quickly and cheaply as possible (*An Act to Encourage Immigration*, 13 *Statutes-at-Large* 385, 1864).

Big business and many states took an even more active role in encouraging immigration during the second half of the nineteenth century. Railroad and steamship companies and many U.S. states actively recruited immigrant laborers, sending representatives to court immigrants abroad as well as new arrivals in New York. South Carolina went so far as to offer immigrants a five-year exemption from taxes on any property they purchased (Higham 1981: 16–18).

But pro-immigrant sentiment in Congress proved short-lived. The conclusion of the war brought an end to acute labor shortages. Immigration resumed its rapid pace as northern and western European immigrants were first joined and then outnumbered by immigrants from southern and eastern Europe. Between 1881 and 1930, 27.6 million immigrants came to the United States. Italy, Austria-Hungary, Russia, and the Baltic States were among the largest sending countries (Dinnerstein and Reimers 1999: 18–19). By 1870, one of every three manufacturing and mechanical workers was an immigrant (Higham 1981: 16). Concern about immigration fraud and alleged dumping of foreign criminals contributed to a successful effort to repeal the Act to Encourage Immigration in 1868 (Hutchinson 1981: 53).

In the eyes of most native-born Americans, the new southern and eastern European immigrants were of even lower status than the preceding groups of unskilled Irish and Germans, and the new arrivals were widely perceived to pose a greater threat to the United States' national identity and to the average working man. Strong prejudice against Italians, Jews, and Poles contributed to anti-immigrant sentiment, which was further enflamed by the widespread use of immigrants as strike breakers during a period of violent conflict between labor and big business following the Civil War (Calavita 1984: 47–48). Economic depression from 1873 through 1878 also contributed to anti-immigrant feeling. Finally, the growth of the eugenics movement in the early part of the twentieth century promoted claims of marked racial and ethnic differences, not only in intelligence, but also in a broad range of mental and physical characteristics that held implications for the suitability of would-be Americans (Higham 1981: 150–53). These factors fostered the rise of restrictive immigration policies that began in 1875 and culminated in the quota laws of the 1920s, which dramatically curtailed immigration to the United States.

The rapid growth of organized labor during the final quarter of the nineteenth century played an important role in promoting congressional passage of labor-related, anti-immigrant legislation during this period. Although attitudes toward foreign workers varied among the different labor organizations, most labor organizations viewed immigrant workers, particularly Asian workers, as competitors (Foner 1964: 123–25).[3] Labor leaders commonly blamed immigrants for reducing or keeping down wages and for weakening unions through strike breaking. The American Federation of Labor (A.F. of L.) played a particularly prominent role in pushing anti-immigration legislation in Congress. A.F. of L. president Samuel Gompers strove successfully to transform the A.F. of L. from a weakly pro-immigrant organization in the 1890s to a virulently anti-immigrant one by the first decade of the twentieth century, by which time many A.F. of L. unions imposed special requirements—such as extra initiation fees, proof of competency, and even intent to become a U.S. citizen—on immigrants applying for membership (Foner 1964, vol. 2: 362–64, vol. 3: 261–64).

Selective Immigration Restriction, 1875–1917

Several of the selective immigration laws passed after the onset of the depression of 1873 were designed with an eye toward discouraging the immigration of unskilled workers. The first of these was the 1882 Chinese Exclusion Act. The passage of this law marked the culmination of rising anti-Chinese sentiment in California, where by 1880 Chinese immigrants accounted for almost one in ten residents (Brinkley 1997: 458–59).

Although local politicians and the public had initially welcomed the almost exclusively male Chinese immigrants who arrived to work in the gold mines in the 1850s, anti-Chinese feeling rose rapidly. Anger mounted as a California law taxing foreign miners succeeded only in moving Chinese workers from mine labor to railroad work, and California politicians began pressing Congress for action. The completion of the transcontinental railroad and the depression of the 1870s fostered fear that Chinese immigrants depressed wages and took jobs that rightly belonged to native-born Americans (Brinkley 1997: 459–60; Dinnerstein and Reimers 1999: 73–75). In an 1876 House resolution calling for the prohibition of further Chinese immigration, a California congressman stated that such immigration "directly brings American free labor in competition with that which is semi-servile" (Hutchinson 1981: 68). The growing U.S. labor movement played an important role in organizing political support for restriction of Chinese immigration. Both

---

[3] The Industrial Workers of the World, known as the "Wobblies," were a prominent exception, supporting and organizing immigrant workers enthusiastically (Le Blanc 1999: 64–67).

the Knights of Labor and the American Federation of Labor actively lobbied Congress to ban Chinese workers from the United States (Foner 1964, vol. 2: 204–205; Gutman et al. 1992: 114).

The first Chinese Exclusion Act barred Chinese from naturalizing and suspended the immigration of Chinese laborers to the United States for a period of 10 years (*An Act to Execute Certain Treaty Stipulations Relating to Chinese*, 22 *Statutes-at-Large* 58, 1882). Notably, the act targeted Chinese laborers, creating an exemption that allowed Chinese teachers, students, merchants, and tourists entry into the United States. Political commitment to this exemption was underscored in 1884 when Congress amended the Chinese Exclusion Act to address unforeseen loopholes believed to have allowed some Chinese laborers to continue to make their way to the United States. Among other measures, the amendment tightened standards for proof of exempt status to curtail alleged evasion of the law by laborers posing as members of the higher classes (Hutchinson 1981: 85–86). The fact that the exemption for non-laborers remained in place testifies to Congress's desire to admit better-off, higher-skilled Chinese immigrants while denying entry to Chinese laborers; it would have been simpler and more effective to bar all Chinese from the United States. The Chinese Exclusion Act was extended and remained in effect until 1943 (Hutchinson 1981: 430–33).

A related congressional concern arose over the impact of foreign contract labor on U.S. workers. Labor organizations were among those lobbying for laws to prohibit the recruitment of foreign workers under contract, an effort that gained increasing support during the depression of the early 1880s. The resulting Contract Labor Law of 1885 prohibited any person or company from pre-paying or otherwise assisting a foreigner's passage to the United States to perform "labor or service of any kind" (*An Act to Prohibit the Importation and Migration of Foreigners and Aliens Under Contract or Agreement to Perform Labor in the United States, its Territories, and the District of Columbia*, 23 *Statutes-at-Large* 332, 1885) In 1887 an amendment to the Contract Labor Law was passed in response to complaints of poor enforcement. The new law charged the secretary of the treasury with enforcing the Contract Labor Law and specified that persons caught in violation of it would be deported at the expense of the owners of the steamships on which the immigrants had arrived (*An Act to Amend An Act to Prohibit the Importation and Immigration of Foreigners and Aliens Under Contract or Agreement to Perform Labor in the United States, its Territories, and the District of Columbia*, 24 *Statutes-at-Large* 332, 1887).

These laws responded to demands from the country's growing labor movement for protection of U.S. workers. The Knights of Labor, by then well over half a million strong, lobbied actively for the Contract Labor Law from the time of its introduction in Congress in 1884

(Gutman et al. 1992: 118). However, loopholes in these laws were large enough to render them largely ineffective, a demonstration of the relative sway of big business in Congress (Calavita 1984: 52–55). Americans with relatives or friends abroad were allowed to pay these immigrants' passage to the United States, and a large group of immigrants was exempt from the contract labor laws, including domestic and personal servants, artists, lecturers, professional actors, singers, and a broad category of skilled workers in unspecified industries "not at present established in the United States" (*An Act to Prohibit the Importation and Migration of Foreigners and Aliens Under Contract or Agreement to Perform Labor in the United States, its Territories, and the District of Columbia*, 23 *Statutes-at-Large* 332, 1885).[4]

Even as Congress attempted to strengthen the contract labor laws, which were widely viewed as ineffective, not only did the distinction between laborers and members of other classes remain, but it was reinforced as new groups of workers were made exempt. In 1891, ministers, professors, and "persons belonging to any recognized profession" joined the list of exempt workers (Hutchinson 1981: 428). The contract labor provisions were revised again in 1907, 1910, and 1917. Each time, the distinction between unskilled laborers and other workers was reaffirmed (Hutchinson 1981: 429).[5]

During the first decade of the twentieth century, concern about competition from immigrant workers focused on a new group of Asians—Japanese laborers—who began coming to the United States in increasing numbers after Chinese laborers were excluded in 1882. Most Japanese immigrants settled in California and worked in agriculture, where they were widely seen as "too successful," a concern that gave way to the fear of a "yellow peril" (Dinnerstein and Reimers 1999: 75–76).

By 1904, the American Federation of Labor was vigorously lobbying Congress to extend the Chinese Exclusion Act to Japanese laborers (Foner 1964, vol. 3: 270–71). Anti-Japanese feeling was so strong in California that the state legislature threatened to pass anti-Japanese measures, and in 1906 the San Francisco Board of Education ordered the segregation of the small number of Japanese among its student body (Ng and Wilson 1995: 495–97).

---

[4] Calavita argues that the contract labor law was largely symbolic because contract immigration was a relatively rare means of recruiting immigrant workers by this time (Calavita 1984: 50–51).

[5] The prohibition on contract labor remained in effect until 1952 when Congress adopted a new tactic for limiting competition from foreign workers (Hutchinson 1981: 430). This change is discussed later in this chapter.

The school board action greatly angered Japan, and President Theodore Roosevelt had to intercede, brokering an agreement in which the San Francisco school district dropped its segregation requirement and the California legislature stopped threatening to pass anti-Japanese legislation.[6] In return, the Japanese government agreed to stop issuing passports allowing Japanese laborers to come to the United States (Ng and Wilson 1995: 495–97). To ensure that Japanese laborers could not circumvent this "Gentlemen's Agreement" by coming to the United States by way of a third country, Congress added a passage to its 1907 immigration law. The new measure authorized the president to exclude from the country any alien attempting to enter via an American possession or third country. In March 1907, President Roosevelt issued an executive order refusing admission to any Japanese or Korean laborer, skilled or unskilled, who attempted to enter the United States from Mexico, Canada, or Hawaii (Ng and Wilson 1995: 495–97).[7]

World War I and the Quota Laws

World War I heightened worry about foreign radicals and gave increased impetus to the continuing wave of anti-immigrant legislation, some of it clearly motivated by fear of competition from foreign-born workers. The Immigration Act of 1917 codified and expanded previous immigration laws and created a literacy test requiring that newcomers over the age of 16 be able to read between 30 to 40 words "in ordinary usage" in English or their native tongue (*An Act to Regulate the Immigration of Aliens to, and the Residence of Aliens in, the United States*, 39 *Statutes-at-Large* 874, 1917).[8]

Congress had passed legislation incorporating a literacy test on three previous occasions between 1897 and 1915 but had been unable to override a series of presidential vetoes until 1917 (Hutchinson 1981:

---

[6] Roosevelt favored tougher immigration laws that would screen potential newcomers to ensure that they were capable of earning a living that measured up to U.S. standards. "This would stop the influx of cheap labor and the resulting competition which gives rise to so much bitterness in American industrial life," Roosevelt told Congress in 1901 (Hutchinson 1981: 127–28).

[7] Under the Gentlemen's Agreement, the Japanese government could still issue passports to parents, wives, and children of Japanese laborers already living in the United States, and to Japanese laborers who had previously resided in the United States before returning to Japan (Kim 1986: 257).

[8] The 1917 Immigration Act exempted the wives, mothers, grandmothers, and unmarried or widowed daughters of immigrants from the literacy test, as well as fathers and grandfathers over age 55.

167).[9] The literacy test was aimed in part at excluding low-wage foreign laborers. As early as 1891, Representative Henry Lodge, a strong proponent of the test, argued that it would "reduce in a discriminating manner the total number of immigrants, and would thereby greatly benefit the labor market and help to maintain the rate of American wages" (Hutchinson 1981: 465).

Samuel Gompers and the American Federation of Labor played an important role in fostering support for a literacy test. In 1896, Gompers proposed that the A.F. of L. formally endorse a literacy test bill before Congress, and he continued to push hard for the measure, distributing literacy test literature from the Immigration Restriction League to A.F. of L. members. Still, the A.F. of L. rank and file did not agree to support the measure until 1897 (Foner 1964, vol. 2: 362–64). In 1910, when a congressionally appointed immigration commission issued a report arguing that the employment of eastern and southern European immigrants in mining and manufacturing had weakened labor unions in those industries, the A.F. of L. intensified its anti-immigrant campaign, giving local chapters around the United States copies of a petition to Congress in support of a literacy test (Foner 1964, vol. 3.: 261–64).

In addition to the literacy test, the 1917 law also created the "Asiatic barred zone," which prohibited immigration from India and other areas of South Asia not previously covered by the Chinese Exclusion Act and the Gentlemen's Agreement with Japan (Auerbach and Harper 1975: 10; Hutchinson 1981: 431–32). Even in creating the barred zone, however, Congress made an exception for certain groups of skilled workers, including government officers, ministers and missionaries, lawyers, doctors, chemists, engineers, teachers, authors, artists, and merchants. Students and tourists were also exempt (*An Act to Regulate the Immigration of Aliens to, and the Residence of Aliens in, the United States, 39 Statutes-at-Large 874*, 1917).

The 1917 law also contained a provision addressing the nation's need for unskilled labor. It allowed the admission of temporary workers (who would otherwise be inadmissible) if approved by the commissioner general of immigration and the secretary of labor. When labor shortages arose during World War I, railroad and agricultural employers pushed for the use of this provision to bring more than 76,000 temporary Mexican laborers to the United States between 1917

---

[9] Presidents Cleveland, Taft, and Wilson all vetoed the test. It became law in 1917 after Congress overrode another veto by President Wilson, who argued that the test unfairly excluded would-be immigrants on the basis of their past opportunities (Hutchinson 1981: 167).

and 1923, prevailing over the objections of labor organizations (Briggs 1984: 97–98; Tucker, Keeley, and Wrigley 1990: 126–27).[10]

Fear that the end of World War I would spur European immigration to unprecedented levels—exacerbated by worry over a perceived Communist threat from immigrant infiltrators following the Russian Revolution—quickly prompted additional legislation (Brinkley 1997: 655–56, 671–73). The quota laws of 1921 and 1924 went far beyond previous immigration restrictions, imposing the first numerical limits on immigration and dramatically curtailing the flow of southern and eastern Europeans to the United States. Concern about immigrants' race and nationality played by far the most important role in the passage of the quota laws, but the 1921 and the 1924 acts contained a handful of provisions regarding immigrants coming to work in the United States.

The 1921 law established the principle of national-origin quotas, capping the number of potential immigrants from each Eastern Hemisphere country at 3 percent of the number of persons from that country who had been living in the United States in 1910 (Dinnerstein and Reimers 1999: 180–81). The 1921 law also made some special allowances for relatives of immigrants already in the United States, foreshadowing the preference for family-based immigration that would come to dominate U.S. immigration policy later in the century (Auerbach and Harper 1975: 11–12). Consistent with past legislation, Congress made certain groups of immigrant workers exempt from these quotas. Most of these groups consisted of skilled workers who had also been exempt from the contract labor laws and the Immigration Act of 1917. Professional actors, artists, lecturers, singers, nurses, ministers, professors, members of "any recognized learned profession," and domestic servants were not subject to the caps (*An Act to Limit the Immigration of Aliens into the United States*, 42 *Statutes-at-Large* 5, 1921).

Differential treatment of particular groups of immigrant workers was also evident in the 1924 quota law, which curtailed immigration even further, imposing a total cap on immigration from the Eastern Hemisphere of approximately 150,000 new arrivals annually (Auerbach and Harper 1975: 12–14). But the number of exempt groups of workers was reduced to two, reflecting the increasing restriction of immigration in almost every aspect of the 1924 law. Ministers and college professors (and their wives and children) retained non-quota status under the 1924 law, but performers, members of the "learned professions," and domestic servants lost this privilege (*An Act to Limit the Immigration of Aliens into the United States, and for Other Purposes*, 43 *Statutes-at-Large*

---

[10] Many of these workers would have been inadmissible because of inability to pay the head tax or pass the literacy test required by the 1917 law (Briggs 1984: 97–98).

153, 1924). Within the quotas, skilled agricultural workers and their families were given preference, alongside the immediate relatives of U.S. citizens. Up to 50 percent of all visas under this quota were designated for these two groups. This was the first time that Congress singled out a particular group of workers and gave them priority among would-be immigrants through the creation of a special preference category, a tactic that would be used increasingly over the course of the twentieth century.

The 1924 law also distinguished immigrants from temporary visitors, such as government officials, tourists, and business travelers, creating the category of "non-immigrants" that would be broadened in 1952 and again in 1990 to allow foreign-born temporary workers into the United States under H visas. Finally, the 1924 law also barred the immigration of any alien ineligible for U.S. citizenship, effectively prohibiting all Asian immigration. The American Federation of Labor, unhappy with the continued migration of some Japanese workers from Hawaii to the West Coast, had lobbied actively for this provision (Briggs 1981: 45).

The quota laws, coupled with the Great Depression, succeeded in curtailing immigration rapidly and dramatically (Calavita 1984: 150). Even so, concern about the potential impact of immigration on U.S. employment remained high during the Depression, generating some changes in immigration law. In the area of labor and immigration, the contract labor laws, which had stirred little interest for most of the early twentieth century, attracted renewed attention. In 1932 Congress passed legislation making it more difficult for instrumental musicians to qualify for an exemption to the contract labor prohibition and doubled funding for enforcement of the contract labor laws to $200,000 annually (Hutchinson 1981: 222–23). Later that same year, Congress passed a law specifying that businessmen were qualified to come to the United States under the 1924 quota law only if they conducted international—not local—commerce (Hutchinson 1981: 223).

Some Easing of Restrictions: World War II through 1952

Like the Civil War and World War I, World War II created labor shortages, and big business responded with petitions to Congress for new temporary workers. During World War II, agricultural concerns dominated the lobbying for imported labor (Reimers 1985: 41–48). The resulting "bracero program" provided for the importation of Mexican contract laborers to work in agriculture beginning in 1942, and it was extended repeatedly until 1964. At the peak of this program in 1956, more than 445,000 braceros (Mexican agricultural workers) came to work in the United States on a seasonal basis (Briggs 1984: 98–102; Dinnerstein and Reimers 1999: 131–32). In addition, a 1944 law provided for the importation of temporary labor from other Western Hemisphere countries in order to aid the war effort, but Mexicans accounted for the vast majority of World War II and post–World War II temporary workers (Reimers 1985: 41–48; INS 1997: A.1–9). Although labor organizations opposed the bracero program, their protests were unsuccessful until growing mechanization of agriculture, rising concern about the bracero program's impact on low-wage U.S. workers, and plans to revamp immigration law reduced congressional enthusiasm for the bracero program in the early 1960s (Briggs 1981: 62–63; Reimers 1985: 41–48; Tucker, Keely, and Wrigley 1990: 128–29).

By the late 1940s, growing postwar prosperity had set the stage for some easing of immigration policy (Dinnerstein and Reimers 1999: 99). This trend was visible in the Displaced Persons Act of 1948. Besides authorizing the temporary resettlement, over a two-year period, of up to 205,000 Europeans displaced by World War II, the Displaced Persons Act continued the practice of taking labor qualifications into account when assigning preferences to various groups of potential immigrants. The Act gave first preference to agricultural workers and their families, and second preference to a variety of other workers, including household, construction, and garment workers, as well as professionals and technical workers (*Displaced Persons Act of 1948*, 62 *Statutes-at-Large* 1206, 1948). Subsequent amendments to the 1948 Act in 1950 and 1951 extended the displaced persons program through 1951 and increased the number of persons eligible for admission to 415,744, while combining the two preferences into a joint first-preference category (Auerbach and Harper 1975: 16–17; Hutchinson 1981: 497).[11] The vast majority of displaced persons entering the United States came in under the employment-based preferences (INS 1948–1951).

By the time Congress began working to revise and codify the nation's numerous immigration laws in 1952, there was growing interest in designing specific provisions to attract highly skilled immigrants, rather than merely exempting some groups of them from legal requirements, as the 1921 and 1924 quota laws had done. The goal, as expressed by members of Congress, was to assure that those immigrants admitted to the United States would be able to contribute to the nation's economic and social progress.

Representative Francis E. Walter (D–Pennsylvania, chairman of the Immigration and Naturalization Subcommittee of the House and co-

---

[11] Visas for displaced persons were "chargeable" to existing and future quotas, and thus did not necessarily increase the number of immigrants eligible to come to the United States from Southern and Eastern Europe (INS: 1948–1951).

author of what became the Immigration and Nationality Act) put it as follows: "We are still operating under the formula of 'first come, first served.' This formula serves the intending immigrants all right, but it does not serve the needs of our hospitals, our universities, and our industrial and defense establishments" (U.S. Congress 1951: 4). Representative Emmanuel Celler (D–New York) agreed that "our present quota system, operating under the formula of 'first come, first served,' deprives our defense and industrial establishments, our hospitals, our laboratories, research and educational institutions, of the services of many highly desirable skilled specialists who have much to contribute to our industry, social welfare, and our scientific development" (U.S. Congress 1951: 7).

This heightened interest in immigrants' skills appears to have reflected concern that U.S. population growth, and thus the future supply of American labor, was dwindling just as the Cold War increased pressure to remain competitive with Russia (U.S. Congress 1953: 1750–51). "[W]e must recognize that our rapid rise to world power during our 176–year history was based upon our population growth from 4 million to 150 million, and this growth was largely the result of immigration," Cellar said, going on to compare projected U.S. population growth with more rapid increases expected for Russia (U.S. Congress 1953: 1750–51).

Passed in 1952, the Immigration and Nationality Act, also known as the McCarran-Walter Act, retained the national-origins quota system established in the 1920s, but it eliminated immigration and naturalization prohibitions based on race (Auerbach and Harper 1975: 21–23). The 1952 Act also contained several employment-related provisions. At least half of the approximately 154,700 visas for Eastern Hemisphere immigrants arriving under the quota were reserved for workers "whose services are determined by the Attorney General to be needed urgently in the United States because of high education, technical training, specialty experience, or exceptional ability of such immigrants and to be substantially beneficial prospectively to the national economy, cultural interests, or welfare of the United States" and their spouses and children (*Immigration and Nationality Act, 66 Statutes-at-Large* 163, 1952). The remaining quota visas were designated for relatives of U.S. citizens and permanent residents. Although this was not the first time that Congress had singled out skilled immigrants by setting aside a portion of quota visas for them, it was the largest such setaside in a major immigration law and the first one to focus on immigrants with high levels of education and technical training.[12] On paper,

---

[12] The 1924 Immigration Act gave preference to skilled agriculturalists, while the 1948 Displaced Persons Act gave preference to a range of agricultural and other workers, including some professional and technical workers.

this measure appeared to represent a large and unprecedented commitment to skill-based immigration, but the reality proved quite different.

Immigrants admitted on the basis of their high skill levels constituted only a tiny share of quota-based immigration during the 1950s and 1960s (Papademetriou and Yale-Loehr 1996: 38–39, 81–87). The preference never accounted for more than about 7,000 immigrants in any given year between 1952 and 1965, and spouses and children of skilled workers often accounted for half or more of these immigrants (see table 2.1)

The largest number of skilled workers—3,941 immigrants accompanied by 3,179 family members—entered in fiscal year 1958. Nowhere near the approximately 77,000 workers and family members allowed to enter under the first preference category, these immigrants accounted for just under 7 percent of the 102,153 quota immigrants who entered the United States in 1958, and less than 3 percent of the total of 253,265 quota and non-quota immigrants combined (INS 1957–1965).

The explanation for the rare use of the skilled worker preference rested in the larger design of the immigration system. First, the vast majority of immigration during this period took place outside the quotas, involving newcomers from the Western Hemisphere and the immediate relatives of U.S. citizens. Second, within the quota system, a small group of countries accounted for the vast majority of the allocated quota visas, but many of these countries regularly failed to use most of their quota. This circumstance not only sharply reduced the number of Eastern Hemisphere quota visas actually put to use, but it also enabled most immigrants from countries with large quotas, such as Great Britain, Ireland, and Germany, to enter as non-preference immigrants rather than qualify under the preferences for workers or relatives of U.S. citizens and permanent residents (INS 1959). In 1959, for example, 80 percent of the 102,153 quota immigrants who entered the United States did so outside the preference system.

Another important change incorporated within the 1952 law was the end of the prohibition against contract laborers. By then widely seen as obsolete, this prohibition was replaced by a provision creating a new class of excludable workers. This provision gave the secretary of labor the power to declare skilled or unskilled would-be immigrant workers inadmissible if a sufficient supply of such workers already existed in the worker's stated destination within the United States, or if the person's employment would threaten the wages or working conditions of similar U.S. workers (Hutchinson 1981: 430). The Department of Labor, however, lacked staff to enforce this authority and exercised it only in response to outside complaints or in extreme cases, such as when immigrants were used as strike breakers. The certification power was invoked only 10 times between 1952 and 1962, and only about 12 times per year between 1962 and 1965, after the certification process was revised (Briggs 1981: 59).

The 1952 McCarran-Walter Act also expanded the classes of eligible non-immigrants to the United States, creating the H category of workers, which would come to play a central role in the debate over the impact of skilled immigrants on the U.S. labor force during the 1990s (see table 2.2). The H temporary visas made two quite different groups of workers eligible to come to the United States on a temporary basis. The first group consisted of immigrants "of distinguished merit and ability" coming to the United States "to perform temporary services of an exceptional nature requiring such merit and ability." The second group consisted of immigrants coming "to perform other temporary services or labor, if unemployed [native] persons capable of performing such service or labor cannot be found" (*Immigration and Nationality Act*, 66 *Statutes-at-Large* 163, 1952). This measure was intended to provide a way for the United States to import agricultural workers, industrial laborers, and other less highly skilled workers during labor shortages (U.S. Congress 1952: 1698). For both groups of workers, the nature of the work, as well as the length of stay, had to be temporary.

Ministers and their immediate family members retained their non-quota status under the 1952 Act, and this privilege was extended to another small group of workers—longtime employees of the U.S. government abroad and their families (*Immigration and Nationality Act*, 66 *Statutes-at-Large* 163, 1952).

A year later, the Refugee Relief Act echoed the McCarran-Walter Act's employment preferences. The 1953 Refugee Relief Act, which authorized the admission of an additional 214,000 refugees as permanent residents, gave first priority for visas to refugees "whose services or skills are needed in the United States" (Hutchinson 1981: 498).

The End of the National-Origins System

More than a decade later, the 1965 Immigration and Nationality Act Amendments marked the end of the era of immigration based on national origin, which had lasted almost half a century. In an attempt to rectify past discrimination, the 1965 Act eliminated the national-origins quota system. In its place, it established a seven-category preference system for the allocation of 170,000 visas annually for immigrants from the Eastern Hemisphere, of which no more than 20,000 could come from any single country, and it established the first cap (120,000 an-

Table 2.1. Employment-based Immigration to the United States, 1950 to 1998

	1950	1955	1960	1965	1970	1975	1980	1985	1990	1995	2000
Immigration Quotas											
Annual quota, Eastern Hemisphere[a] Annual ceiling, worldwide	154,206	154,657	154,887	158,561	170,000	170,000	280,000	270,000	270,000	675,000[b]	675,000[b]
Quota or ceiling for employment-based immigrants	NA	77,329[c]	77,444[c]	79,281[c]	34,000	34,000	56,000	54,000	54,000	140,000[b]	140,000[b]
Immigration Admissions											
Total of immigrants admitted	249,187	237,790	265,398	296,697	373,326	386,194	530,639	570,009	1,536,483[d]	720,461	660,477
Total of immigrants admitted under quotas or ceilings	197,460[e]	82,232	101,373	99,381	172,547	160,460	289,479	264,208	298,306	593,234	314,517
Total of quota immigrants admitted under employment-based preferences	751	3,012	7,066	4,986	34,016	29,334	44,369	50,895	58,192	85,336	77,517
Total of quota immigrants admitted under employment-based preferences as a proportion of the quota for employment-based immigrants	NA	0.04	0.04	0.04	1.00	0.86	0.79	0.94	1.08	0.61	0.55
Total of quota immigrants admitted under employment-based preferences as a proportion of all quota immigrants	0.004	0.04	0.07	0.05	0.20	0.18	0.15	0.19	0.20	0.14	0.25
Total of quota immigrants admitted under employment-based preferences as a proportion of all immigrants	0.003	0.01	0.03	0.02	0.09	0.08	0.08	0.09	0.08[f]	0.12	0.12

Immigrants Admitted under Specific Employment-based Preferences

Category											
1924 Act (Eastern Hemisphere only)											
Skilled agriculturalists	751										
1952 Act (Eastern Hemisphere only)											
Immigrants of special skill or ability		1,776	3,385	2,376							
Their spouses and children		1,236	3,681	2,610							
1965 Act (Eastern Hemisphere FY 1970, 1975; worldwide, FY 1980-1990)											
3rd preference, professional or highly skilled immigrants					10,142	8,363	8,238	10,947	11,879		
6th preference, needed skilled or unskilled workers					8,786	6,724	12,599	11,425	10,753		
Families of 3rd and 6th preference immigrants					15,088	14,247	23,532	28,523	31,097		
1990 Act (worldwide)[g]											
1st employment preference, priority workers										17,339	21,408
2nd employment preference, professional or highly skilled immigrants										10,475	14,384
3rd employment preference, skilled workers, professionals, other workers										50,245	34,317
Skilled and professional workers										42,361	28,062
Unskilled workers										7,884	6,255
4th employment preference, special immigrants									4,463	6,737	6,584
5th employment preference, employment creation										540	824

Category								
Total Nonquota Immigrants Admitted	51,727	155,558	164,025	197,316	86,043	104,633	241,160	305,801
Employment-based nonquota immigrants								
Ministers and their families	833	307	485	494	1,497	1,231	1,529	1,853 [h]
Employees of U.S. government abroad and their families		9	27	75	290	1,622	1,354	479 [h]
Professors and their families	603							

[a] Western Hemisphere cap of 120,000 for FY 1970 and 1975 not shown since preferences did not apply to immigrants from this region.

[b] Number is approximate.

[c] Number is approximate, based on half the quota.

NA = Not applicable because the 1924 law did not specify the number of first preference visas for skilled agriculturalists.

[d] Includes 880,372 formerly illegal immigrants who adjusted to legal status under IRCA. Of these, 56,668 were special agricultural workers.

[e] The number of quota immigrants admitted this year was increased by the admission of almost 96,000 displaced persons.

[f] The denominator for this percentage is the 656,111 non-IRCA immigrants in 1990.

[g] Each category includes spouses and children.

[h] Under the 1990 Act, these immigrants were admitted under the 4th employment-based preference.

A blank space indicates that the relevant visa category was not in existence that year.

Source: U.S. Immigration and Naturalization Service, Annual Reports and Statistical Yearbooks, 1950 to 1998.

Table 2.2. Employment-Based Temporary Migration to the United States, 1950 to 1996

	1950	1955	1960	1965	1970	1975	1981[a]	1985	1990	1996[b]
Total of non-immigrants admitted	385,934	559,504	1,042,841	1,872,732	3,938,358	6,283,986	11,756,903	9,539,880	17,574,055	24,842,503
Selected non-immigrant workers[c]	73,760	114,924	221,522	366,698	504,478	710,379	1,434,042	2,201,671	3,252,630	4,598,721
Selected non-immigrant workers as a proportion of all non-immigrants	0.19	0.21	0.21	0.20	0.13	0.11	0.12	0.23	0.19	0.19
Temporary visitors for business (B-1 visas)	67,984	68,696	108,130	175,500	324,810	527,387	1,135,422	1,796,819	2,661,338	3,770,326
Treaty traders and investors and their families (E visas)	766	1,203	3,803	7,639	19,209	35,031	80,802	96,489	147,536	138,568
Representatives of international organizations and their families (G visas)	5,010	6,003	7,398	14,026	23,766	32,624	54,223	57,203	61,449	79,528
Exchange visitors (J-1 visas)		16,077	25,233	33,768	50,817	46,001	80,230	110,942	174,247	215,475
Intracompany transferees (L-1 visas)					188	12,570	38,595	65,349	63,180	140,457
Professional workers, NAFTA (TN visas)[d]									5,293	26,987
Total of temporary workers and industrial trainees (H visas)		22,945	38,479	67,869	85,688	56,766	44,770	74,869	139,587	173,470
Workers of distinguished merit and ability/workers in specialty occupations (H-1 visas)[e]			7,431	8,295	11,096	15,550	NA	47,322	100,446	146,504
Registered nurses (H-1A visas)										2,046
Workers in specialty occupations (H-1B visas)										144,458

Other workers performing services unavailable in the U.S. (H-2 visas)	28,084	56,654	69,288	37,460	24,544	35,973	23,980
Agricultural workers (H-2A visas)					NA	18,219	9,635
Nonagricultural workers (H-2B visas)					NA	17,754	14,345
Industrial trainees (H-3 visas)	2,964	2,920	5,304	3,756	3,003	3,168	2,986
Workers with extraordinary ability and achievement (O visas)							9,289
Internationally recognized athletes or entertainers (P visas)							33,573
Workers in international cultural exchange programs (Q-1 visas)							2,056
Workers in religious occupations (R-1 visas)							8,992
Bracero workers	116,052	337,996	427,240	100,876			

[a] Non-immigrant data are provided for fiscal year 1981 because they are not available for fiscal year 1980.

[b] 1996 is the most recent year for which non-immigrant data are available.

[c] Family members are included only where data for principals are not available separately. Examples of other non-immigrant categories that include workers are representatives of foreign governments, foreign news media, and NAFTA officials. The largest categories of non-workers are tourists and students, although some students are permitted to work part time. NA signifies "not available."

[d] From January 1989 through December 31, 1993, this category consisted of professional workers entering under the U.S.-Canada Free Trade Agreement (TC visas). Visas under the North American Free Trade Agreement, including Mexico, went into effect on January 1, 1994.

[e] The H-1 visa category, created by the 1952 Act, was for workers of distinguished merit and ability. In the 1990 Act, this category was revised and designated for workers in specialty occupations.

[f] These workers are not included in INS totals for non-immigrants and thus are not included here among the total number of selected non-immigrant workers. A blank space indicates that the relevant visa category was not in existence that year.

Source: U.S. Immigration and Naturalization Service, Annual Reports and Statistical Yearbooks, 1950 to 1997.

nually) on admissions from the Western Hemisphere.[13] The preference system gave 80 percent of visas to immigrants with family members in the United States, bolstering Congress's primary immigration policy objective of encouraging family reunification and providing what turned out to be false reassurance to conservative organizations that mistakenly believed that an emphasis on family-based, rather than employment-based, immigration would maintain the then current racial and ethnic makeup of the United States (INS 1975; Briggs 1981: 68–69).

However, the preference system also allowed a place for employment-based immigration, allocating the remaining 20 percent (34,000) of Eastern Hemisphere visas to two groups of workers—10 percent to foreigners who were "members of the professions or who because of their exceptional ability in the sciences or the arts will substantially benefit prospectively the national economy, cultural interests, or welfare of the United States," and 10 percent to "qualified immigrants who are capable of performing specified skilled or unskilled labor, not of a temporary or seasonal nature, for which a shortage of employable and willing persons exists in the United States" (*An Act to Amend the Immigration and Nationality Act, 79 Statutes-at-Large* 911, 1965).

In an effort to assuage labor organizations' opposition to employment-based preferences, Congress specified that Eastern Hemisphere immigrants applying for employment-based visas and Western Hemisphere immigrants who sought to work in the United States and who were not immediate relatives of U.S. citizens or residents could be admitted only with certification from the secretary of labor. This certification had to specify that the future immigrants would work in occupations where the supply of U.S. labor was inadequate, and that their arrival would not adversely affect the wages and conditions of native-born workers (*An Act to Amend the Immigration and Nationality Act, 79 Statutes-at-Large* 911, 1965). This was a significant shift from the 1952 Act, which merely allowed the secretary of labor to exclude immigrant workers deemed likely to compete with their U.S. counterparts. The new law placed the burden of proof of non-competitiveness on would-be immigrants and on the U.S. companies seeking to employ them.

Both the cap on Western Hemisphere immigration and the labor certification requirement reflected congressional concern that increased immigration could adversely affect the wages and unemployment levels of U.S.–born workers. This fear was fresh in the minds of members of Congress who, a year earlier, had ended the bracero program, due in part to fears about its impact on native workers (Briggs 1981: 62–63). In its final form, the 1965 Act placed less emphasis on skilled immigration

---

[13] Parents, children, and spouses of U.S. citizens were not subject to the caps.

than did the original version of the legislation proposed in Congress, which would have given first preference to highly skilled immigrants. This change came in response to lobbying from labor organizations, which opposed the employment-based visas (Gimpel and Edwards 1999: 102–103).

In contrast to the situation after the passage of the 1952 Immigration Act, most of the employment-based visas established under the 1965 law were used. In 1970, for example, 34,016 immigrants entered the United States under employment-based preferences (INS 1971). Of these entrants, 18,928 were workers, and 15,088 were their spouses or children. Within the scheme of total immigration to the United States, employment-based immigration continued to play a relatively minor role, representing only about 20 percent of all quota immigrants and just 9 percent of all 373,326 new immigrants in 1970 (INS 1971). But a growing backlog of new applications for employment-based visas from certain oversubscribed countries created demands from corporate America that Congress relax a number of employment-based provisions (U.S. Congress 1971: 2750–55).

The 1970 Immigration Act eased several requirements that directly affected non-immigrant workers and indirectly affected employment-based immigrants. The Act dropped the requirement that the work performed by non-immigrants of distinguished merit and ability be temporary, allowing companies to use temporary workers to fill permanent jobs (*An Act to Amend the Immigration and Nationality Act to Facilitate the Entry of Certain Nonimmigrants into the United States*, 84 *Statutes-at-Large* 116, 1970).[14] This change was particularly important to universities, many of which had resorted to bringing foreign visiting professors to the United States under exchange visas for non-immigrants, a disadvantage because holders of these visas could not apply to convert to permanent residency without first leaving the country (U.S. Congress 1971: 2750–55).[15]

The 1970 Act also enabled temporary workers coming to the United States under H visas to bring their spouses and minor children with them, and it created a new non-immigrant L visa for intra-company transferees. The creation of the L visa was a response to complaints from international businesses facing long waits for permanent employment-based visas for workers temporarily transferred to the

---

[14] The so-called double temporary requirement had demanded that the job itself—as well as the length of stay of the non-immigrant—be of a temporary nature. This double temporary requirement remained in effect for other workers entering under H visas.

[15] The 1970 Act lifted this requirement for certain holders of exchange (J–type) visas (U.S. Congress 1971: 2750–55).

United States. Members of Congress agreed that this use of permanent visas for temporary workers reduced the number of such visas available for their intended purpose (U.S. Congress 1971: 2750–55).

Less than a decade later, Congress passed two more laws that would significantly affect the skill levels of immigrants. The Immigration and Nationality Act Amendments of 1976 extended the seven-category preference system and the 20,000 per country cap to immigrants from the Western Hemisphere, while the Act of October 5, 1978, combined the previously separate hemispheric quotas into one world-wide ceiling (INS 1999: A.1-16-17). A growing belief that fairness dictated applying the same immigration regulations to both hemispheres, along with a desire to limit immigration from large sender countries in the Western Hemisphere (particularly Mexico), motivated these laws passed during the economic doldrums of the 1970s (Gimpel and Edwards 1999: 113–24). But the laws also had the effect of increasing from 34,000 to 58,000 the total number of visas allocated to employment-based immigrants and their family members.[16] At first, few Western Hemisphere immigrants made use of the employment-based permanent visas, but by the early 1980s almost the full quota was claimed each year (INS 1987).

However, the proportion of all immigrants entering the United States via employment-based visas remained about where it had been under the 1965 Immigration Act because the number of immigrants eligible to come to the United States under quota and the total number of immigrants grew as well. In 1985, for example, 50,895 immigrants entered the United States under employment-based preferences, accounting for about 19 percent of numerically limited immigration and 9 percent of total immigration (INS 1987).

To the surprise of those who believed the 1965 Act's emphasis on family-based immigration would safeguard the nation's racial and ethnic makeup, the 1965 Act not only increased total annual immigration levels to more than 600,000, but it also shifted the source of that immigration dramatically (Dinnerstein and Reimers 1999: 103). The share of new immigrants of European origin fell from an overwhelming 90 percent of all immigrants in 1965 to just 10 percent in 1985 (Brinkley 1997: 935). By the end of the same period, Hispanic and Asian immigrants accounted for about two-thirds of all legal immigrants. This shift meant that new immigrants increasingly came from countries where education levels were considerably lower than in the United States. At the same time, the end of the bracero program contributed to an in-

---

[16] Subsequent laws reduced the worldwide ceiling slightly, lowering the number of employment-based visas from 58,000 in 1978 to 56,000 in 1980, and to 54,000 in 1981 (Michael D. Hoeffer, personal communication).

crease in the number of low-skilled, illegal immigrants to the United States (Espenshade et al. 1997: 769–70). This influx of relatively less skilled legal and illegal immigrants and their impact on the U.S. economy became an increasingly important issue in immigration debates in Congress during the 1980s and 1990s (Borjas 1999: 8–10, 39–61).

Developments in Immigration Policy, 1980–1998

The Immigration Reform and Control Act of 1986 (IRCA) grew out of recommendations by the 1981 Select Commission on Immigration and Refugee Policy for a crackdown on illegal immigration. Committee members worried that rising numbers of unauthorized immigrants, many coming from Mexico and Central America after the end of the bracero program, would taint perceptions of legal immigrants as well. The commissioners hoped that providing amnesty to illegal immigrants would reduce the likelihood of their being exploited by employers and thus driving down wages (Gimpel and Edwards 1999: 135–56).

The main components of IRCA consisted of increased enforcement of U.S. borders, the imposition of sanctions on employers who hired undocumented aliens, and a large-scale amnesty program for illegal immigrants who had been living in the United States since 1982 (INS 1999: A.1-19). But the law was almost derailed by a congressional battle over whether to bring large numbers of temporary agricultural workers to the United States, a proposition sponsored by supporters of agriculture and opposed by supporters of labor. The legislation was rescued through a compromise that gave temporary legal status to up to 350,000 workers already living in the United States who could prove that they had previously performed seasonal agricultural work here, and it made these workers eligible to apply for permanent legal status under certain conditions (Gimpel and Edwards 1999: 170–74).

By the late 1980s, congressional attention had shifted to legal immigration. Driving this renewed interest was a sense that the 1965 and 1976 laws had tipped too heavily in favor of family-based immigration and took too little account of U.S. economic needs in the face of what was widely perceived as a growing mismatch between the education and training levels of U.S. workers and the business sector's increasing demand for high-skill and specialty workers (U.S. Congress 1991: 6721). A number of government-sponsored reports issued in the late 1980s and early 1990s raised concern about this potential mismatch; these included the Hudson Institute's "Workforce 2000" and the Report of the President's Council of Economic Advisors of 1990 (U.S. Congress 1991: 6721). Congress was also responding to mounting complaints from the business community that not only was the number of perm nent, employment-based visas inadequate, but the requirements placed on employers seeking to bring immigrants to the United States under these provisions were too onerous and time-consuming. There was an 18-month wait for immigrants seeking to enter the United States under the third preference (for professional and high-skilled workers), and a two-and-a-half-year delay for those attempting to enter under the sixth preference (for other skilled and unskilled workers) (U.S. Congress 1991: 6721).

In the area of temporary visas for employment-based non-immigrants, Congress also faced employer complaints that the qualification process was overly cumbersome and that the visa categories for non-immigrants discouraged the admission of certain groups of high-tech workers and managers (U.S. Congress 1991: 6723). But these concerns were tempered by rising controversy over alleged abuse of the H–1 visa for temporary workers of distinguished merit and ability, the use of which had grown from about 47,000 admissions annually in 1985 to more than 100,000 admissions in 1990 (INS 1991). Labor organizations alleged that some workers who did not meet the definition of distinguished merit and ability were coming to the United States under the H–1 program, and that the program put certain groups of U.S. workers at a competitive disadvantage with foreign-born workers.

The Immigration Act of 1990 represented the first comprehensive reform of legal immigration in a quarter-century and the culmination of congressional efforts begun in 1988. It substantially increased immigration, setting a flexible, worldwide cap of approximately 700,000 immigrants annually for fiscal years 1992 through 1994 and about 675,000 thereafter (INS 1997). The biggest changes in employment-based immigration involved a large increase in employment-based visas, coupled with the allocation of an increased share of those visas to highly skilled workers. The total number of employment-based visas grew from 54,000 in 1991 to approximately 140,000 in 1992, while the number of those visas devoted to highly skilled immigrants and their spouses and children rose from 27,000 to approximately 110,000. The 1990 Act set aside a maximum of 10,000 visas for unskilled immigrants and their families (INS 1997).

The number of employment-based preferences also grew, from two to five. The 1990 Act set aside about 40,000 visas for "priority workers," the highest skill group, including persons of "extraordinary ability," prominent academics, and multinational executives (*Immigration Act of 1990*, 104 *Statutes-at-Large* 4978, 1990). The second employment-based visa category established by the 1990 Act devoted 40,000 visas to professionals and workers of "exceptional ability." The third visa category allocated another 40,000 visas to skilled workers, professionals, and "other workers," no more than 10,000 of whom could be unskilled.

Another 10,000 visas were allocated to a miscellaneous assortment of workers, including several groups that had previously been eligible to enter the United States outside of quotas, such as ministers and former government employees abroad. Finally, the 1990 Act reserved the last 10,000 employment-based visas for foreign investors coming to the United States to start a new business (*Immigration Act of 1990*, 104 *Statutes-at-Large* 4978, 1990).

The 1990 Act required that most immigrants in the second and third employment-based preference categories receive certification from the secretary of labor. As had been true since 1965, this certification involved a determination by the secretary of labor that these workers were needed in the United States and that their arrival would not adversely affect the wages and conditions of U.S. workers performing similar jobs (Papademetriou and Yale-Loehr 1996: 48). However, the 1990 Act introduced a new pilot program allowing some groups of immigrant workers in a few industries in which a shortage of U.S. workers had been established by the Labor Department to receive automatic certification (*Immigration Act of 1990*, 104 *Statutes-at-Large* 4978, 1990).

Employment-based immigration initially rose sharply after implementation of the 1990 Act. The number of employment-based immigrants grew from 59,525 in 1991 to 116,198 in 1992, and it peaked at 147,012 in 1993 (INS 1999: 32). After this initial rise, however, the number of employment-based immigrants fell, fluctuating between 85,000 and 120,000 annually before reaching a nadir of 77,517 in 1998 (INS 2000: 16). About 34,000 (or 44 percent) of these visas went to workers, with the remainder admitting their spouses and children. In 1998, employment-based immigration accounted for roughly one-quarter of all numerically limited immigration and about 12 percent of total immigration. In comparison, at its historical high in 1993, employment-based immigration represented only 20 percent of numerically limited immigration but 16 percent of total immigration (INS 2000).

The 1990 Act also made important changes in U.S. policy toward high-skilled temporary workers. The 1990 Act created a new nonimmigrant category, the H–1B visa, for workers in specialty occupations who held at least a bachelor's degree or its equivalent in their field. This new category replaced the former H–1 visas for workers of distinguished merit and ability.[17] The 1990 law further established an annual cap of 65,000 on H–1B visas and a maximum six-year stay for

---

[17] The "B" in H–1B visas derived from a 1989 law creating the H–1A visa for registered nurses. Congress established the H–1A visa category in 1989 for a limited (five-year) period to address temporary nursing shortages (U.S. Congress 1990: 1894–98).

workers arriving under these visas. The Act also required employers to pay H–1B workers the prevailing wage. Unlike the cap on employment-based permanent immigration, the H–1B quota applied only to workers, not to their family members (*Congressional Quarterly* 1991).

In addition, the 1990 Act placed an annual limit of 66,000 on H–2B visas for nonagricultural temporary workers, and it created three additional visa categories for skilled temporary workers—O and P visas for prominent scientists, educators, artists, athletes, and entertainers, and R visas for religious workers (*Immigration Act of 1990*, 104 *Statutes-at-Large* 4978, 1990).[18]

However, the 1990 Act did not end the controversy over high-skilled temporary workers. Throughout 1998, representatives of the high-tech industry lobbied hard for an increase in the size of the H–1B program. Their position was strengthened by several new developments. In September 1997, for the first time, the annual 65,000 ceiling for H–1B workers was reached, halting H–1B admissions for the remainder of the fiscal year and providing the computer industry with new evidence of unmet demand for high-tech workers (Mittelstadt 1998). That same month, the U.S. Department of Commerce (1997) issued a report predicting a coming shortage of high-tech workers. Although the U.S. General Accounting Office sharply criticized the report's methodology in a March 1998 assessment for Congress, the findings allowed industry representatives to argue that official government statistics supported their claims of unmet demand for high-tech workers (Koch 1998; U.S. General Accounting Office 1998). In addition, the year 2000 computer bug raised the specter of technological breakdown affecting sectors as diverse as airlines, banks, electricity providers, and the federal Social Security system unless enough workers could be found to reprogram computers to allow them to function into the coming millennium (*Congressional Quarterly* 1998a).

Still, opponents of H–1B expansion, particularly professional organizations for engineers, continued to argue that high-tech employers were taking advantage of the H–1B program to avoid hiring native workers. Opponents of H–1B expansion emphasized that H–1B workers needed to remain with their employers in order to retain their temporary visas or to apply for permanent residency. They contended that this dependency on the employer gave H–1B workers little bargaining power and was a powerful incentive to put up with low wages and relatively poor working conditions (*Congressional Quarterly* 2000).

Bills to expand the H–1B program from 65,000 to 115,000 workers were introduced in both the House of Representatives and the Senate,

---

[18] The "B" in the H–2B visas stemmed from the H–2A visa category for temporary agricultural workers created in IRCA (INS 1988).

but the legislation was quickly bogged down in a dispute over measures to protect U.S. workers from potential H–1B competition. In the House, a coalition of Republicans favoring tighter controls on immigration and Democrats concerned about protecting U.S. workers refused to support any bill without strong worker protections, such as a requirement that H–1B employers demonstrate prior attempts to recruit native-born workers (Carney 1998).

A compromise bill to apply the worker protection provisions only to firms depending heavily on H–1B workers passed the House in September 1998, but it was blocked from consideration in the Senate. Prospects for expanding the H–1B program looked slim (Carey 1998), but a last-minute tactical move to incorporate the H–1B bill into the omnibus spending bill prevailed. As signed by President Clinton on October 21, 1998, the legislation increased the number of H–1B visas from 65,000 to 115,000 in 1999 and 2000, then reduced them to 107,500 in 2001 and to 65,000 in 2002 and beyond. A group of worker protection provisions passed by the House remained in the bill but applied only to companies whose workforce included a high proportion of H–1B workers (*Congressional Quarterly* 1998b).

Industry demand for high-tech workers quickly overwhelmed the temporary expansion in H–1B visas, however. For fiscal year 1999, the supply of H–1B visas was exhausted by June, a precursor of even more rapid events the following year. In March 2000, only halfway through the fiscal year, the U.S. Immigration and Naturalization Service stopped accepting new H–1B visa applications because the agency already had sufficient pending applications to meet the 115,000 cap for that year (INS 2000). Various proposals for additional expansion of the H–1B program were stalled in Congress over the summer of 2000 due to wrangling over a number of issues. These included not only the merits of H–1B expansion itself, but also proposals to incorporate H–1B expansion into a broader immigration bill granting permanent legal status to certain groups of Central Americans, Haitians, and others residing in the United States illegally or holding only temporary legal status (Palmer 2000a). By late summer, legislative watchers predicted that a provision for H–1B expansion would be inserted into one of the end-of-year appropriations bills if a compromise on separate legislation could not be reached sooner (Taylor 2000). This tactic did not prove necessary. Congress reached a last-minute agreement in October that gave the high-tech industry virtually everything it wanted (Palmer 2000b). The Senate and the House passed legislation to raise the H–1B cap to 195,000 workers annually for a three-year period, while charging H–1B employers a $500 fee to be used toward a program to train U.S.

workers and educate U.S. children in the area of high technology.[19] President Clinton was expected to sign the legislation, which did not include new protections for workers and dealt only with the status of H–1B workers. It did not address the previously proposed amnesty for certain Central American and Haitian immigrants (Palmer 2000b).

Conclusion

Congressional concern about employment-based immigration and temporary workers has played a far larger role in shaping immigration policy than is usually recognized. Congress has regularly taken into account the potential labor force effects of these groups not only in crafting legislation regarding legal immigrants and authorized temporary workers, but also in designing policy toward illegal immigrants. Recent examples include the Immigration Act of 1990, which more than doubled visas for employment-based immigrants while establishing the first cap on highly skilled temporary workers, and the 1986 Immigration Reform and Control Act, which attempted to raise barriers against illegal immigration in response to fear that unauthorized immigrants from Mexico and Central America threatened labor prospects for low-skilled U.S. workers.

Several, sometimes conflicting, goals have been evident in congressional policy-making regarding employment-based immigrants and temporary workers since the mid–nineteenth century. First, Congress has enacted legislation aimed at barring low-skilled immigrant workers from the United States. Many of these laws have prohibited the entry of particular groups of laborers, while making concomitant exceptions for more highly skilled workers. Examples include the Chinese Exclusion Act, the contract labor laws, and the Immigration Act of 1917.

Second, Congress has adopted measures specifically designed to attract highly skilled workers by creating special visa and preference categories for them. Examples of this tactic include the 1952 Immigration and Nationality Act, the 1965 and 1990 amendments to that act, and the H–1B visa increase in 1998. Over the century and a half discussed in this chapter, Congress has gradually shifted from barring low-skilled workers to recruiting the highly skilled. Along with this shift, Congress has increasingly imposed stiffer labor certification requirements and numerical caps on highly skilled workers.

---

[19] The legislation exempted H–1B visa holders employed by universities, government, and non-profit organizations from the cap, as well as H–1B employees admitted after the H–1B cap was reached in fiscal years 1999 and 2000.

Third, at the behest of big business, particularly agriculture, Congress has actively recruited low-skilled workers, especially during war-induced labor shortages but also during peacetime. These efforts include the 1864 Act to Encourage Immigration, the bracero programs initiated during World Wars I and II, the visas for temporary laborers in the 1952 Immigration and Nationality Act and its 1990 amendments, and the provisions for seasonal agricultural workers in the 1986 Immigration Reform and Control Act.

Fourth, most legislation involving employment-based immigrants and temporary workers has incorporated measures designed by Congress to protect U.S. workers from foreign competition. In some cases, this goal was the main focus of the legislation, as in the Chinese Exclusion Act and the contract labor laws. In other cases, this protection took the form of various types of labor certification, a check that has been widely used since the mid–twentieth century. Over the last 60 years, Congress has increasingly passed legislation allowing the recruitment of low-skilled immigrants and temporary workers during peacetime, but such legislation has also become more likely to include stricter requirements for labor certification and numerical caps.

In pursuing the four goals outlined above, Congress has sought to juggle the often competing interests of U.S. industry and organized labor. Given legislative history and the recent congressional battles over the H–1B visa ceiling, employment-based immigrants and temporary workers are likely to remain a key issue in U.S. immigration policy for the foreseeable future.

References

Auerbach, Frank L., and Elizabeth J. Harper. 1975. *Immigration Laws of the United States.* 3d ed. New York: Bobbs-Merrill.

Borjas, George J. 1999. *Heaven's Door: Immigration Policy and the American Economy.* Princeton, N.J.: Princeton University Press.

Briggs, Vernon M., Jr. 1984. *Immigration Policy and the American Labor Force.* Baltimore, Md.: Johns Hopkins University Press.

Brinkley, Alan. 1997. *The Unfinished Nation: A Concise History of the American People.* 2d ed. New York: Knopf.

Calavita, Kitty. 1984. *U.S. Immigration Law and the Control of Labor: 1820–1924.* London: Academic Press.

Carey, Mary Agnes. 1998. "Compromise Revives Measure to Increase Visas for Highly Skilled Workers," *Congressional Quarterly Weekly Report*, October 17.

Carney, Dan. 1998. "Immigration Bill's Fine Print Sends Industry into High-Tech Turmoil," *Congressional Quarterly Weekly Report*, May 2.

Congressional Quarterly, Inc. 1966 through 1997. *Congressional Quarterly Almanac*, vols. 13–52. Washington, D.C.: Congressional Quarterly, Inc.

————. 1998a. "The Year 2000 Problem: Titanic Disaster or Big Yawn?" *Congressional Researcher* 8 (16): 374–75.

————. 1998b. "Legislative Summary: Government Regulations," *Congressional Quarterly Weekly Report*, November 14.

————. 2000. "Debate Over Immigration: Does the U.S. Admit Too Many Newcomers?" *Congressional Quarterly Researcher* 10 (25): 569–92.

Dinnerstein, Leonard, and David M. Reimers. 1999. *Ethnic Americans: A History of Immigration*. 4th ed. New York: Columbia University Press.

Espenshade, Thomas J., et al. 1997. "Implications of the 1996 Welfare and Immigration Reform Acts for U.S. Immigration," *Population and Development Review* 23 (4): 769–801.

Foner, Philip S. 1964. *History of the Labor Movement in the United States*. Vols. 2–4. New York: International Publishers.

Gimpel, James G., and James R. Edwards, Jr. 1999. *The Congressional Politics of Immigration Reform*. Boston: Allyn and Bacon.

Gutman, Herbert G., et al. 1992. *Who Built America? Working People and the Nation's Economy, Politics, Culture, and Society*. Vol. 2: *From the Gilded Age to the Present*. New York: Pantheon.

Higham, John. 1981. *Strangers in the Land: Patterns of American Nativism, 1860–1925*. New York: Atheneum.

Hutchinson, E. P. 1981. *Legislative History of American Immigration Policy, 1798–1965*. Philadelphia: University of Pennsylvania Press.

INS (U.S. Immigration and Naturalization Service.) 1948 through 1980. *Annual Report of the Immigration and Naturalization Service*. Washington, D.C.: U.S. Government Printing Office.

————. 1980 through 1999. *Statistical Yearbook of the Immigration and Naturalization Service*. Washington, D.C.: U.S. Government Printing Office.

————. 2000. World Wide Web at http://www.ins.usdoj.gov, August 30.

Kim, Hyung-Chan, ed. 1986. *Dictionary of Asian American History*. New York: Greenwood.

Koch, Kathy. 1998. "High-Tech Labor Shortage: The Issues," *Congressional Researcher* 8 (16): 363–71.

Le Blanc, Paul. 1999. *A Short History of the U.S. Working Class from Colonial Times to the Twenty-first Century*. New York: Humanity Books.

Mittelstadt, Michelle. 1998. "INS to Cap Skilled Immigrant Visas," Associated Press, May 8.

Ng, Franklin, and John D. Wilson, eds. 1995. *The Asian American Encyclopedia*. New York: Marshall Cavendish.

Palmer, Elizabeth A. 2000a. "House Leaders Weigh Strategy as Panel Approves H–1B Visa Bill with Provisions Despised by Business," *Congressional Quarterly Weekly*, May 20, p. 1186.

————. 2000b. "Well-Timed Push on H–1B Gives Businesses All They Asked," *Congressional Quarterly Weekly*, October 7, p. 2331.

Papademetriou, D. G., and S. Yale-Loehr. 1996. *Balancing Interests: Rethinking U.S. Selection of Skilled Immigrants*. Washington, D.C.: Carnegie Endowment for International Peace.

Reimers, David M. 1985. *Still the Golden Door: The Third World Comes to America*. New York: Columbia University Press.

Taylor, Andrew. 2000. "It's All Endgame as Lawmakers Hold Lawmaking Political Hostage," *Congressional Quarterly Weekly,* July 29, p. 1860.

Tucker, Robert W., Charles B. Keely, and Linda Wrigley, eds. 1990. *Immigration and U.S. Foreign Policy.* Boulder, Colo.: Westview.

U.S. Congress. 1951. Subcommittees of the Committees on the Judiciary. *Revision of Immigration, Naturalization, and Nationality Laws: Joint Hearings before the Subcommittees of the Committees on the Judiciary,* 82nd Congress, First Session, March–April. Washington, D.C.: U.S. Government Printing Office.

———. 1953. *United States Code Congressional and Administrative News.* 82nd Congress, Second Session, 1952. Vol. 2, Legislative History. St. Paul, Minn.: West Publishing.

———. 1971. *United States Code Congressional and Administrative News.* 91st Congress, Second Session, 1970. Vol. 2, Laws and Legislative History. St. Paul, Minn.: West Publishing.

———. 1990. *United States Code Congressional and Administrative News.* 101st Congress, First Session, 1989. Vol. 3, Legislative History: Public Laws 101–189 to 101–239. St. Paul, Minn.: West Publishing.

———. 1991. *United States Code Congressional and Administrative News.* 101st Congress, Second Session, 1990. Vol. 8, Legislative History: Public Laws 101–625 to 101–650, Proclamations, Executive Orders, Tables and Index. St. Paul, Minn.: West Publishing.

U.S. Department of Commerce. 1997. *America's New Deficit: The Shortage of Information Technology Workers.* Washington, D.C.: Department of Commerce.

U.S. General Accounting Office. 1998. "Information Technology Workers." Washington, D.C.: General Accounting Office.

3

Immigration of Scientists and Engineers to the United States: Issues and Evidence

Jessica C. Gurcak, Thomas J. Espenshade, Aaron Sparrow, and Martha Paskoff

The United States is in the vanguard of one of the world's greatest social experiments. Around the globe people are on the move. An estimated 125 million persons—or roughly 2 percent of the world's population—are now living outside their countries of birth, and the number increases by several million each year (Martin and Widgren 1996). A limited number of countries comprise the destination choices for these migrants and refugees. In the mid–1990s, for example, the United States accepted for permanent settlement roughly half of the world's immigrants (Martin and Midgley 1994).

Since records were first kept beginning in the 1820s, more than 60 million legal permanent residents have been admitted to the United States (INS 1996). After a drop in the mid-twentieth century, immigration to the United States accelerated in the last quarter of the century. According to data from the March 1995 Current Population Survey, there are an estimated 23 million foreign-born persons living in the United States (Hansen 1996). Nearly one-quarter of these migrants came to the United States in the 1990s, and another 35 percent arrived during the 1980s. The rising tempo of international migration has lifted the proportion of the foreign-born among the U.S. population from less than 5 percent in 1970 to nearly 9 percent today (Hansen 1996), and net immigration now accounts for nearly 30 percent of annual U.S. population growth (Hansen and Bachu 1995). Newcomers to the United States represent a great variety of countries of origin. In contrast to the beginning of the twentieth century, when 90 percent of immigrants to the

Support for this research was provided by a grant from the Alfred P. Sloan Foundation.

United States arrived from Europe, 85 percent of all legal immigrants during the 1980s came from Latin America and Asia.

International migration poses challenges and opportunities for receiving countries, although it is the challenges that are most frequently emphasized. Can the major Western industrial democracies that are the new homes for many of the world's migrants accommodate such large numbers of newcomers, finding productive employment for family members while at the same time enabling migrants to move into the social and political mainstream? These concerns sharpen when, as now seems to be the case in the United States, the skill level of international migrants is declining relative to U.S.–born members of the labor force (Borjas 1994, 1995). Under these circumstances it becomes commonplace to hear complaints that immigrants are taking jobs from lower-skilled native workers and, on the fiscal front, using more public services than they are able to pay for in taxes (Rothman and Espenshade 1992).

Most of the research on the consequences of U.S. immigration has focused either on the bottom end of the education and skill distribution or on immigrants in general (Abowd and Freeman 1991; Borjas and Freeman 1992). One reason for this concentration is that U.S. immigrants are disproportionately represented among the adult population with less than a high school education (Hansen 1996). Immigrants today are only half as likely as natives to have finished high school (Martin and Midgley 1994). What is not so well appreciated, however, is the fact that immigrants are also overrepresented among the best-educated segments of the U.S. population. Holding an advanced degree, for example, is more common among the immigrant population than among natives, especially for immigrants arriving in the 1990s (Hansen 1996).

This "high-end" segment of the foreign population has received much less attention, but to ignore it would produce a biased impression not only of the composition of U.S. immigration streams, but also of the impact that immigrants have on the labor force and U.S. society more generally. The Immigration Act of 1990 gives these issues greater significance because the Act attempted to upgrade the skill distribution of the U.S. workforce by allotting proportionately more visas to skilled migrants. We do know that foreign-born individuals represent a rising share of graduate students enrolled in U.S. Ph.D.–granting institutions (Espenshade and Rodríguez 1995) and that immigrants, especially scientists and engineers, are receiving a more prominent share of high-technology jobs (Regets 1995).

This chapter is concerned with the educational and labor market implications of high-skill immigration to the United States. Is the growing presence of foreign-born scientists and engineers good or bad from the standpoint of U.S. institutions of higher education and for the American economy? The current literature suggests that in some fields immigrants fill a niche for which natives seem not to compete. While these fields benefit from immigration, others may have had more mixed results. Additionally, foreign-born graduate students in science and engineering provide a large labor force with the asset of U.S. training. Therefore, a nation experiencing labor shortages that might otherwise choose to encourage science education from an early age, may instead look to the foreign-born workforce to meet its needs.

Rising levels of U.S. immigration raise questions about the labor market impacts of immigrant professionals, the fairness of these implications for native workers, whether foreigners work for lower pay than comparably skilled natives and therefore benefit employers, and what the implications of high-skilled immigration are for the international competitiveness of the U.S. economy. Although many of these issues have been addressed in the context of overall immigration, there is no reason to expect the same answers when the focus is directed toward scientists and engineers.

Policy Issues

Contemporary legislation and policy debates have addressed many of the issues outlined above. First, in 1992, George Bush signed the Soviet Scientists Immigration Act into law, allowing scientists from the former Soviet Union to immigrate without labor certification or an offer of employment. This act was limited to 750 employment-based visas per year (Hart 1993). Second, the U.S. Commission on Immigration Reform (1995) proposed, along with provisions eliminating unskilled immigration and restricting family-based immigration, an extensive reworking of current legislation pertaining to skilled immigration. Under their proposals, a limit on skill-based immigration would be set at 100,000 per year (as a reference point, total skill-based immigration in fiscal year 1994 was 90,134). The Commission also proposed a division of the skill-based immigration pool into those who needed labor certification and those who would be exempt. The latter category included individuals at the very top of their field, multinational executives, entrepreneurs, and religious workers. The skill-based immigration pool would be restricted to those with at least a bachelor's degree or highly specific skills, and with at least five years of experience. The Commission also proposed that those entering under skill-based immigration be given a conditional permanent resident status, to be made permanent only if the worker can prove employment at set wage levels after two years. These wage levels would be set at 105 percent of the prevailing wage, not 95 percent as in current law. Additionally, the Commission recommended that every time a company hired a foreign worker, it would have to make a contribution to a private-sector initiative to increase U.S. native worker competitiveness. Lastly, recent legislation has been introduced to expand the number of temporary work visas offered to high-skilled foreign workers (H–1B visas). H–1B visas allow foreigners to work up to six years in the United States. A recent bill expanded the ceiling on the annual number of such visas from 115,000 to 195,000.

Demographic Overview

Immigration of scientists and engineers, while perhaps not as controversial as unskilled or illegal immigration, has nonetheless been a subject of debate within the academic community as well as among corporations and scientific personnel. Much of the literature, clouded by politics, argues that immigrants are either all good or all bad for the science and engineering population. It seems likely that neither is the case.

Most current immigration literature focuses on the period since 1965, when the U.S. government changed immigration laws, dropping quotas on immigrants from Asian countries. Other legal changes in 1965 made indirect immigration (adjustment of status from a temporary visa to a permanent one) more attractive and feasible. The demographic characteristics of the immigrant population changed greatly after these acts were passed. For example, professional Asian workers immigrated at higher rates after the Immigration Act of 1965, while a downward trend began for European-born workers (Keely 1975). The Eilberg Act of 1976 further modified immigration laws by requiring employers to demonstrate that hiring an alien would not negatively impact U.S. workers, and required that any foreign employee have skills exceeding those of natives. (For universities, this requirement was modified to require a demonstration of equivalence with natives.) The final major modification of immigration regulations in recent years was the 1990 Immigration Act, which considerably loosened regulations on skilled immigration and increased the ceiling on employment-based visas.

As a result of the Immigration Act of 1990, employment-based immigration increased considerably in the early 1990s, from less than 60,000 to well over 120,000. The number of immigrants admitted under employment preferences increased by 95 percent from fiscal year 1991 to fiscal year 1992 alone. Permanent visa admissions for science and engineering also significantly increased over the period 1990–1993.

Overall, in the four-year period, science and engineering admission nearly doubled, from 12,659 to 23,277. While the number of immigrants in mathematics and computer science, the natural sciences, and the social sciences all increased steadily in this period, engineering experienced a slight drop from 1992 to 1993. Though consistently the largest group in high-skilled immigration, engineering declined in its share of admissions, dropping from 73 percent in 1990 to 62 percent in 1993.

The differences between foreign-born and native-born scientists and engineers in levels of educational attainment are striking. Forty-one percent of foreign-born engineers, mathematicians, and computer scientists, and almost two-thirds of foreign-born natural scientists have advanced degrees. Less than one-fifth of native engineers, mathematicians, and computer scientists, and just over one-third of native natural scientists have advanced degrees (NSF 1996a; Bouvier and Martin 1995). Consequently, while 10 percent of scientists and engineers with a bachelor's degree are foreign-born, 23 percent of those with doctorates, and 28 percent of doctoral scientists and engineers in research and development are immigrants (Regets 1995). However, many of these high-skilled immigrants were educated in the United States. Stephan and Levin (1995) found that 93 percent of highly skilled engineers, whether native or foreign-born, and 94 percent of highly skilled scientists graduated from a U.S. college.

Level of educational attainment explains much of the income differentials among immigrants by ethnicity. For instance, while Hispanic engineers have, on average, been in the United States much longer than Asians, Asians earn considerably more (Bouvier and Martin 1995). However, among Asian engineers, the Japanese earn the most, although Chinese, Indians, and Koreans have higher levels of educational attainment (Tang 1993a). This apparent inconsistency may owe to differences in the degree of transferability of education from different countries.

The share of science and engineering immigrants from different countries has shifted in the past two decades. A majority of scientists and engineers now enter the United States from Asia, with a growing share coming from Eastern Europe as well. In this period, science and engineering immigration from the rest of the world dropped. From 1988 to 1990, the top five sending countries for mathematicians and computer scientists (Taiwan, India, the People's Republic of China, Hong Kong, and Iran, in that order), natural scientists (India, Taiwan, the PRC, Iran, and Hong Kong), and engineers (India, Taiwan, the Philippines, the PRC, and Iran) were Asian (Kanjanapan 1995).

The prevalence of Asians has changed the pattern of high-skilled immigration to the United States. While overall, family preferences and other non-occupational visas represented the greatest sources of science and engineering immigration, almost half of all immigrant Asian engineers from 1988 to 1990 entered on occupational visas (NSF 1993a; Kanjanapan 1995). Further, a large share of those entering on occupational visas did so through visa adjustment. According to Huang (1987), indirect immigration accounts for half of all professional immigration to the United States. This trend is a concern to those who wish to limit high-skilled immigration. If a large share of temporary visa holders adjusts their status, then temporary residency may be merely a backdoor source of permanent immigration. Visa adjusters, primarily students or temporary workers, represented two-thirds of Asian engineers who entered on occupational visas from 1988 to 1990 (Kanjanapan 1995).

Lastly, most sciences are heavily male-dominated disciplines. Women are only one-tenth of all engineers, one-fourth of natural scientists, and just over one-third of mathematicians and computer scientists (Bouvier and Martin 1995). Moreover, several researchers (Bouvier and Martin 1995; North 1995) have noted the higher proportion of women among native-born than foreign-born scientists and engineers. The income differentials between the sexes have also remained large for all groups (Barringer et al. 1990). Consequently, some have argued that high-skilled immigration should be reduced to allow native-born minorities and women, who are currently underrepresented in science and engineering, to pursue such careers.

Issues in the Immigration of Scientists and Engineers to the United States

Many issues surround the immigration of foreign-born scientists and engineers. The chief one, of course, is the effect that this population has on employment. Several lobbying groups made up of scientists and engineers, such as the Young Scientists' Network, have voiced objections to laws that allow large numbers of foreign-born scientists and engineers to come to the United States. Equally vociferous on the other side of the argument are firms that employ scientists and engineers, such as Microsoft, which have lobbied against restrictions on the hiring of foreign-born scientists and engineers. As an illustration of the latter group's power, their lobbying made the U.S. Senate drop plans to cut skilled immigration slots in half in 1996 (McDonnell and Pitta 1996).

Those who support the immigration of foreign-born scientists and engineers often maintain that these immigrants, because of their skills, create jobs through product innovation, and they therefore facilitate the employment of enough Americans to compensate for the jobs taken by foreign-born workers. Others point out that immigrants help to support

American workers by virtue of being consumers in the U.S. economy. As Glassman (1996) states, "When an engineer from Russia moves here to work for a software firm, the U.S. economy wins—both because the engineer's family buys goods and services and because the engineer's brain power creates more jobs."

Opponents of immigration charge that foreign-born scientists and engineers, especially those in computer programming, are taking jobs that could be filled by older, native-born workers, many of whom have been laid off due to cuts in the defense industry. While many industry leaders charge that retraining older workers is inefficient and not their responsibility (McDonnell and Pitta 1996), lobbyists for American scientists and engineers maintain that these workers represent a source of talent that can be retrained quickly (Matloff 1996) and would be wasted otherwise.

Another possibility is that a sort of dual labor market exists for scientists and engineers. Foreign-born persons, who generally have higher rates of Ph.D.–level education, may be needed to fill teaching positions and other jobs requiring a doctorate. However, native-born scientists and engineers might be quite content to terminate their studies after receiving a bachelor's or master's degree and be employed in a different type of position. Because salary differentials between advanced and bachelor's degree holders are often not great, especially in engineering, the choice to pursue a Ph.D. may only depend on the type of job one wishes to have. This theory holds that the United States needs both sorts of workers for growth, with an increase in one leading to an increase the other.

For several years a debate has raged over whether an undersupply of scientists and engineers exists. Certainly, credible anecdotal evidence suggests that some middle-aged native-born scientists and engineers have experienced lengthy spells of unemployment and/or stagnant wages (*American Prospect* 1999). However, equally compelling evidence supports the notion that potentially severe labor shortages exist within certain segments of the science and engineering labor market (*Chronicle* 1999a). Most likely, the wide disparity in reports of labor market conditions is attributable to widely varying definitions of the science and engineering labor market. An American physicist is not likely to be in competition for a job with a foreign-born biologist. Studies that assess the labor market conditions in science and engineering need to recognize the diversity of fields that fall under this broad heading.

If an undersupply should exist, and if the native supply of scientists and engineers does not rise to meet demand, then many would feel that the immigration of scientists and engineers is necessary. One potentially severe example of an undersupply is the "seed-corn" problem. In other words, as innovative researchers join the ranks of information technology entrepreneurs, many computer science departments worry that there are not enough academics left to teach a new generation of computer scientists. However, others agree with the Young Scientists' Network, who often refer to the "myth of undersupply." Taking yet another view are those who argue that an oversupply is necessary to maintain fierce competitiveness in U.S. science and engineering (Greenberg 1993a).

Complementary to the concern that foreign-born scientists are taking jobs that would otherwise belong to natives is the worry that the immigration of high-skilled workers depresses wages. This concern has been addressed by legislation designed to repeal the requirement that an employer must pay a foreign worker at least 95 percent of the prevailing wage for that field, which is set by the Department of Labor. Some have suggested that this amount is inadequate and that the salary should be set at 100 or 105 percent of the prevailing wage. Also, even if foreign-born workers receive salaries comparable to those of native workers, a large influx of workers in any industry loosens the labor market and may drive down wages. Those who are unable to find work, whether native or foreign-born, make lower salary demands while providing the same skills, thereby lowering wages.

Although examining current wages is important, the comparative wage trajectories of native and foreign-born scientists and engineers are also relevant to a study of the impacts of immigration. While the earnings of the foreign-born may initially be lower, the true earning power of a foreign-born scientist or engineer may emerge after adjusting to a new country and perhaps a new language as well. Alternatively, foreign-born scientists and engineers may initially earn more than their native-born counterparts, but their earnings may stagnate after a few years and therefore not keep up with native scientists' earnings growth.

In short, the debate over the economic benefits of high-skill immigration comes down to whether the innovation and job-creating skills that immigrants provide outweigh potential losses to the native population. Immigration advocates often accuse their opponents of using the "lump of labor" fallacy—in other words, the assumption that a fixed number of jobs exist and any job given to a foreigner represents a loss for a native. Clearly this is not the case; through job creation, it is possible that immigrants do much more good than harm. However, rates of entrepreneurship and innovation must be established before conclusions can be drawn. The following sections give an overview of the literature that addresses the concerns mentioned in the preceding paragraphs.

Does the Immigration of Scientists and Engineers Increase Unemployment?

Scientists and engineers have always enjoyed unusually low unemployment rates. After a brief period of rising unemployment during the early 1990s, unemployment has tapered off again, leading to a widespread characterization of the high-skilled labor market as tight. Evidence suggests that skilled U.S. workers enjoy higher rates of employment than their immigrant counterparts. In October 1994, before the current economic expansion reached full swing, the unemployment rate among immigrant college graduates was 3.9 percent, compared to 2.2 percent among native college graduates in the labor force (U.S. Dept. of Labor 1995a).

Despite the favorable overall labor market conditions for high-skilled natives, some groups of frustrated native scientists have petitioned the U.S. government to reduce immigration of scientists and engineers. For example, in a 1996 letter to Senator Ted Kennedy, Eric Weinstein quoted the American Mathematical Association as saying that new mathematics Ph.D.s have unemployment rates between 23 and 49 percent at the end of their first temporary employment (presumably a postdoctoral appointment). However, other sources present a different story. The National Science Foundation (NSF 1996b) gives the following April 1993 rates for those who had received their mathematics Ph.D.s in 1988–1992: 1.2 percent unemployed, 4.9 percent involuntarily out of field, 3.8 percent in postdoctorates, and 15.0 percent in non–tenure track or adjunct positions. The same study quotes the American Mathematical Society as giving the rates of new mathematics Ph.D.s still looking for work in the autumn after their graduation (i.e., four to six months later) as 10.7 percent in 1994. While this rate is higher than in previous years, it still does not approach the rate Weinstein quotes. Additionally, doctoral scientists and engineers graduating between 1990 and 1992 had an overall unemployment rate of only 2 percent and an underemployment rate of 4.5 percent (Wilkinson 1995).

Although companies may save money indirectly by hiring a foreign-born worker with greater skills and efficiency, laws prohibit them from doing so directly. However, the literature suggests that U.S. companies may have found ways to get around these problems. The simplest way, of course, is to ignore the requirement on the assumption that punishment is unlikely. Evidence shows that it is rare; Andersen (1996) reports only seven cases of H–1B wage violations in the period 1991–1995. Most of these cases involved outsourcing, the dismissal of a native worker and subcontracting his or her share of the work to another company.

Matloff (1996) claims that large companies such as Sun and Hewlett Packard openly admit that cheapness is a factor in hiring foreign-born workers. He states that mid-career computer professionals are fired for being obsolete and immigrants are hired in their places because they have a more up-to-date skill set. However, he feels that, given the lack of formal computer education among even computer magnates such as Bill Gates and Steve Jobs, educational qualifications should not be a factor. Matloff suggests that an emphasis on creativity, not on paper credentials, would be advisable. In his opinion, computer workers can quickly be retrained if they lack the necessary skills for a certain job.

North (1995) suggests that some companies bring in software professionals on B–1 visas for short-term employment. These non-immigrants are poorly paid, he states, but also difficult to catch by the nature of their visas. While these allegations are possibly true, they are also difficult to verify because B–1 is a business visitor visa and therefore not monitored for employment violations. North suggests that the legal H–1B visa is also being exploited in terms of wage violations.

North suggests several other possible abuses of H–1B wage regulations. One is the use of foreign postdoctoral students, paid at low rates, to fill needed research positions. North proposes that this is a large source of cheap foreign labor that others have not noticed because it is hidden within the university system. The proportion of the foreign-born in postdoctoral positions is quite high. From 1980 to 1991, non–U.S. citizens held approximately 60 to 75 percent of engineering postdoctorates, and 35 to 50 percent of science postdoctorates (NSF 1993c).

Even if immigrants do not work for lower wages than natives, a glut of any group in the marketplace may lower wages and increase unemployment, as the equally qualified unemployed will be willing to work for less. Therefore, although immigrants may receive comparable wages, their presence still might lower salaries (*Scientific American* 1988). However, it is not clear that higher rates of immigration hurt the native economy. Kanjanapan (1995) quotes Borjas and Tienda as saying that while immigration rates might be up, the absorptive capacity of the United States is growing faster. Borjas and Tienda (1987) also state that for all workers, not just scientists and engineers, immigrants have a very small negative impact on native workers. Using cross-sectional analysis, Kposowa (1993) found that overall immigration in the period 1970–1980 had positive effects on native earnings. Using an instrumental variables approach to control for potential spurious correlation between immigrant inflows and favorable labor market conditions, Card (1997) finds little or no effect of recent high-skilled immigration on employment or wages of high-skilled natives and earlier immigrants. Additionally, there is little historical evidence that even large inflows of immigrants have had any more than a minimal impact on wages (Borjas 1994).

Is There a Labor Shortage in Science and Engineering?

In recent years, high-tech industry lobbyists and their political backers have become increasingly concerned about the prospect of a high-skilled labor shortage. Arguing that a shortage of labor could threaten the competitive edge held by U.S. high-tech companies, these groups have continually called for fewer restrictions on high-skilled immigration. Meanwhile, organizations representing scientists and engineers in the United States have argued that, in fact, there are plenty of qualified high-skilled workers at home who are unable to find employment while U.S. companies continue to import labor from abroad.

Greenberg (1990) and the National Science Foundation found a shortage, as did the Information Technology Association of America (1997), and the Office of Technology Policy (1999). However, other researchers (North 1995, among others) have found flaws in these calculations. Moreover, Matloff (1996) presents figures stating that in computer science and engineering, there are currently 525,000 workers but only 378,000 jobs. Teitelbaum (1996) argues that most scientists and engineers are experiencing declining wages and that the undersupply found by others never existed. This complete lack of agreement among different studies is due in no small part to differences in the definition of the science and engineering labor market. Studies that assess the labor market conditions in science and engineering need to recognize the diversity of fields that fall under this broad heading.

Most of the debate regarding a high-skilled labor shortage has focused specifically on information technology (IT) workers. While a number of science and engineering backgrounds offer suitable training for IT careers, most IT workers have backgrounds in computer science, programming, software, or electrical engineering. The first step in determining whether or not there is a shortage of IT workers is defining the appropriate pool of potential IT workers. While Matloff (1996) finds a glut of such workers, the Office of Technology Policy (1999) and the Information Technology Association of America (1999) find just the opposite. The OTP report finds that, while unemployment and wage growth among engineers have merely kept pace with professional workers as a whole, unemployment is particularly low and wage growth moderately high for computer scientists, systems analysts, and programmers, suggesting a labor shortage. Moreover, for particular "hot skills"—those jobs that have shown the strongest growth in IT departments—wage growth has been especially high. However, it is not clear that older American workers could not be trained to acquire these hot skills.

Espenshade (1999) notes that long-term labor shortages can only exist if "some artificial mechanism ... prevents wages from rising to a market-clearing wage." So far there is little evidence of such a mechanism. The *Chronicle of Higher Education* (1999a) notes that there has been exceptional growth in the number of computer science majors at U.S. universities, implying that the domestic supply is responding to the increased demand for IT workers. Ironically, one market for which a shortage may truly exist is that of computer science professors. Universities simply cannot meet the rising wages paid to computer scientists in private industry; similarly, graduate schools have a difficult time retaining computer science students. There is some concern that a seed-corn problem may exist, whereby there are not enough faculty members available to train the next generation of computer scientists (*Chronicle* 1999a; Freeman and Aspray 1999).

Wage Comparisons

Among all foreign-born workers except Hispanics, income is on average greater than that of native U.S. workers. However, the income distribution within the foreign-born is more uneven than among the native-born (U.S. Dept. of Labor 1995a). In a cross-sectional study of foreign-born scientists and engineers, Bouvier and Martin (1995) found that immigrants earned more than natives in engineering, mathematics and computer science, and the natural sciences. Interestingly, this pattern held despite differences in the age distributions of natives and the foreign-born by field. Foreign-born mathematicians and computer scientists were younger on average than natives, while foreign-born natural scientists were older. Of course, other factors are equally important, such as levels of education.

Espenshade, Usdansky, and Chung (2000) use regression analysis to identify the effect of variables such as education, location of residence, and English proficiency, along with a host of demographic variables, on the earnings of scientists and engineers. They find that the unconditional earnings advantage held by the foreign-born disappears when these other factors are considered. In particular, education and location of residence alone more than account for the higher average earnings of foreign-born scientists and engineers. After controlling for all of the above-mentioned variables, the authors find no statistically significant difference between the earnings of foreign-born and native scientists and engineers. However, recent immigrants do earn less than others, presumably because of a lack of English language proficiency as well as an incomplete initial transferability of skills.

Other studies have examined differences in pay by ethnicity as well as nativity status. Tang (1993a) finds that Asians earn less and have lower employment status than comparably trained Caucasians. After controlling for demographic variables, training, specialty, and government/nongovernment employment, recently arrived Asians earned 18 percent less than native Caucasians, a difference that remained for the first 6 to 11 years in the workforce. Barringer et al. (1990) found that among Ph.D.s whites earned the highest salaries. Of those with a bachelor's degree or the equivalent, Japanese led, followed by whites. They quote the U.S. Commission on Civil Rights as saying that minorities and women were not receiving the same returns on educational investment. Additional years of schooling also raised earnings more for natives than for the foreign-born (Chiswick 1978).

Does an Earnings Gap Exist?

While the evidence cited above suggests that there is no earnings gap between foreign-born and native scientists and engineers, certain groups, recent immigrants in particular, do earn less than others. This difference need not merit concern as long as the earnings trajectory of immigrants is such that their wages eventually catch up with natives' wages. If the lower wages of newer immigrants is indeed due to lack of English language proficiency and an incomplete initial transferability of skills, then over time the earnings gap should disappear.

Several researchers, using cross-sectional data, have found that immigrants, while making less than natives immediately after immigration, are able to close this earnings gap after several years, often exceeding the earnings of natives. In a cross-sectional study of all immigrants using the 1970 census, Chiswick (1978) found that earnings of immigrants are initially less than those of natives, rise to equal them after 10 to 15 years, then surpass them. This trajectory was seemingly unrelated to the citizenship status of the immigrant. Other researchers (Bouvier and Martin 1995; Sehgal 1985) have also found support for the hypothesis that income rises with a longer stay in the United States and eventually resembles native earnings. However, Barringer et al. (1990) found that, of all Asian immigrant groups, only the Japanese eventually approach income parity with whites, after controlling for education. This is especially interesting because, as a group, Japanese have been here longest. This finding suggests that the duration of a group in the United States may have an effect on the group's earnings.

In several papers, Borjas cast doubt on the findings that immigrant earnings trajectories catch up with native earnings. Borjas (1994, 1995) claimed that cross-sectionality distorted the data used to establish this earnings profile of immigrants. Using data from the 1970, 1980, and 1990 censuses, he tracked immigrant cohorts over time and found that earlier cohorts had higher skills and earnings that had never been far below those of natives. Later cohorts possessed considerably lower skills, and their earnings did not catch up with those of natives. Rather than telling a story of rapid assimilation, Borjas's findings suggest that immigrant skills, relative to native skills, are in decline.

More applicable to the science and engineering population, Borjas (1989) analyzed the 1972–1978 Survey of Natural and Social Scientists and Engineers. He found a decline over time in the productivity of immigrants, and he projected that the earnings of then-recent immigrants would take longer to catch up compared with previous cohorts. However, the latest data were from the 1970 census, making predictions for current recent immigrants difficult.

More recent surveys indicate that immigrant earnings may well catch up over time. In a survey of engineers, Waldinger et al. (1995) compared initial and current earnings for graduates in an engineering master's program at the University of California, Los Angeles from 1970 to 1990, eliminating possible cross-sectional biases. They found a similar pattern to that established in previous cross-sectional analyses: in their first jobs, foreign students earned significantly less (natives $41,464, immigrants $38,792, foreign students $33,171); but the gap closed in current jobs (foreign students $83,801, natives $83,521, immigrants $80,855). In addition, Duleep and Regets (1997) find evidence that the lower earnings of immigrants at entry have more to do with decreased transferability of skills than with declining immigrant quality.

Differences by Job Type

The types of science and engineering jobs likely to go to immigrants are different from those going to natives, and they vary along ethnic lines as well. For example, several studies have found that Asians are significantly less likely than Caucasians to move into managerial positions, although they may achieve pay equity. One explanation for this tendency is the "glass ceiling" hypothesis. However, in this case the glass ceiling blocks power, not pay. Another explanation is that American culture teaches leadership roles for those in the sciences, while other cultures may not. Therefore, an American engineer may be more likely to be ready to move into management than one trained in Asia. Others have hypothesized that Asian immigrants have trouble attaining top positions because of linguistic barriers. Additionally, because engineers tend to work in teams, objective measures of an individual's influence on the success of a project are difficult to make. Therefore, prejudices rather than actual evaluations of performance might be influential in deciding which engineers advance to managerial positions.

Waldinger et al. (1995) find little support for the glass ceiling hypothesis. The authors found that Asian engineers were more, not less, likely to report autonomy. However, this finding may be distorted by the higher rate of self-employment among foreign engineers. Immigrants also reported less stability than natives, which supports the latter theory, given that stability is lower for those who are self-employed than for those in managerial positions at large firms.

Other surveys have found underrepresentation of some groups in management. Among college graduates in the United States, 62 percent of the foreign-born are in managerial positions, compared with 67 percent of natives. Asians, both native and foreign-born, are also less likely to hold managerial positions than native and foreign-born Caucasians. While prejudice is one explanation for the underrepresentation of some groups in management, there are other factors as well. Asians, for instance, tend to concentrate in fields where there are fewer managers. Further, newly arrived Asian engineers are more likely to hold management positions than their older counterparts (Tang 1993a). However, one study of employee performance evaluations found clear favoritism toward whites—although no pattern of active antagonism towards non-whites or females (Smith et al. 1994).

One explanation for the underrepresentation of foreign-born scientists and engineers in management positions is that, in certain fields, immigrants are more likely than natives to go into teaching. This is especially true of engineering, where few natives obtain the doctoral degrees necessary for teaching at a university level (NSF 1993b). As a result, by the mid–1980s over 50 percent of young assistant professors of engineering were foreign-born, up from 10 percent in 1972 (Walsh 1988). As noted above, immigrants are also much more likely to work in research and development than are natives. Almost 60 percent of all foreign-born scientists and engineers work in research and development, compared to less than half of the native-born (Regets 1995).

Entrepreneurship and Innovation

One of the arguments noted above in favor of increasing high-skilled immigration is the job-creating effects of immigrants, particularly those engaged in entrepreneurship or innovation. Waldinger et al. (1995) observe higher rates of self-employment among foreign-born engineers compared with the native-born. Indeed, immigrants started 12 percent of companies in 1995's Inc. 500, an index of fast-growing corporations. Additionally, immigrants have played a key role in the development of notable high-tech companies such as Cypress Semiconductor, whose manufacturing division founder was an immigrant, and Sun, which was founded by foreign nationals and whose influential SPARC system was developed by two other immigrants (Andersen 1996).

Stephan and Levin (1995) found that immigrants in the life and physical sciences were more likely to be cited in scientific journals than natives, indicating a greater innovation rate. Over one-fifth of the members of the National Academy of Science (NAS), an honor society of scientists, in each field except earth and environmental sciences, were born abroad. NAS members were also more likely than scientists as a whole to have been trained abroad. The highest proportion of the foreign-born (one-third) was in mathematics and computer science. Similar results were noted for the National Academy of Engineering, an honor society of engineers. The authors also found that research and development innovators were more likely to have been born abroad than highly skilled scientists and engineers on the whole, an unsurprising result given the prevalence of immigrants in research and development.

Education

U.S. graduate schools are among the main sources of foreign-born scientists and engineers in the United States. Only one-third of immigrants with science and engineering doctorates received their degrees from foreign schools (Regets 1995). In addition, foreign students comprise a growing share of doctoral students in these fields. In 1995, foreign students received almost 40 percent of the doctoral degrees awarded by U.S. universities in science and engineering (Chronicle 1996). However, the current growth rate of foreign students in doctoral programs is not as high as in previous years. During the 1970s, the number of foreign students in doctoral programs increased 10 to 20 percent on average per year. After a slowdown in the mid–1980s, the growth of foreign students picked up again, averaging approximately 4 percent per year in the late 1980s and early 1990s.

The overall growth in the number and percent of foreign-born students in U.S. schools masks significant changes in the composition of the foreign-born student body by sending region. The most noticeable change is the considerable growth in the number of foreign students from Asia. By 1991, 10 of the top 12 sending countries were Asian, and

65 percent of total foreign graduate student enrollment was Asian (NSF 1993c). U.S. colleges and universities educate one-fourth of all Asian Ph.D. recipients, and they train more Indians than India and more Taiwanese than Taiwan. Half of South Korea's graduate students and a third of China's are educated in the United States.

In addition to changes in the composition of the foreign student body by sending region, there has been differential growth in the number of foreign students by type of visa. From 1980 to 1991, the share of science and engineering doctorates earned by those on temporary visas grew from 15 percent to 32 percent (NSF 1993c). This pattern reversed itself in the early 1990s, as temporary residents accounted for 12 percent of the overall doctorate growth from 1990 to 1995, and permanent residents for 63 percent (mostly from the People's Republic of China as a result of the Chinese Student Protection Act). Table 3.1 shows the distribution of students earning degrees in the various science and engineering subfields by nativity and visa type. While the percent foreign-born varies widely, in each field the number of students on temporary visas far outweighs the number on permanent visas.

Table 3.1
Distribution of Science and Engineering Doctorate Degrees by Nativity and Visa Type

	U.S. Citizens (%)	Permanent Residents (%)	Temporary Residents (%)	Number of degrees awarded in 1992
Engineering	38.7	7.5	50.3	5,437
Physical sciences	54.2	5.5	37.7	6,498
Life sciences	65.7	4.9	26.9	7,108
Social sciences	74.3	4.5	16.7	6,205

Source: Data are from Ries and Thurgood 1993.

Some have expressed concern that foreign-born students are taking places that would have otherwise gone to equally qualified Americans. Of particular concern is that graduate enrollment of minorities and women may be lagging, due in part to the substantial presence of foreign students in U.S. graduate programs. The rapid growth of foreign students in science and engineering has come as doctoral participation by U.S. minorities has increased slowly or not at all.

Alternatively, some professors and others argue that many graduate schools, especially smaller ones, would not exist if foreign-born students did not come to the United States (Brezenoff 1992). They cite the decline in the college-age population as creating a void that foreign students must fill if the schools are to stay open. This argument is countered, however, by those who suggest that there is an oversupply of Ph.D.s, and therefore, fewer doctorates should be produced, even if it means closing schools.

The stay rates of foreign students are also an issue in the debate on science and engineering immigration. Some foreign students leave the United States after graduation, creating few benefits for this country (*New York Times* 1995). Some believe that this exodus of U.S.–trained foreign workers will increase as Asian economies continue to grow, making trading competitors out of U.S.–educated Asians (Daly 1993; Greenberg 1993a). Meanwhile, the presence of foreign students who do stay has sparked the same debate on foreign workers outlined above, although it should be noted that the job market for doctorates is typically considered among the tighter labor markets.

Are Foreign Graduate Students Taking Natives' Places?

One reason for the scarcity of domestic students in science and engineering is that an intelligent student can make much more money with an MD, JD, or MBA than with a science or engineering Ph.D. Salary levels and rates of increase are higher in medicine, law, and business than in science or engineering. In the period 1987–1992, salaries increased 20 percent for natural sciences and engineering and 28 percent for mathematics and computer science (North 1995). However, in the same time period physicians had an average salary increase of 44 percent and lawyers, 33 percent.

While native-born students continue to study science and engineering at the undergraduate level, they shy away from graduate school (North 1995). In 1990, students with temporary visas earned 5.4 percent of science and engineering bachelor's degrees, compared to 27.0 percent of master's degrees and 32.4 percent of Ph.D.s. Even those natives who do choose to pursue a science or engineering career may decide that the short-run financial benefits of going to work after college outweigh the long-run salary increase a Ph.D. provides. This is especially true in engineering, which has a lower rate of domestic enrollment than all science programs. Over a lifetime, after-tax earnings of those with Ph.D.s in engineering are only about $93,000 higher than for those with only a bachelor's degree. Accounting for the potential savings of the latter group during the time it would have taken to get a Ph.D., those with bachelor's degrees make only about $28,000 less (North 1995).

Of course, the lack of great financial rewards for earning a Ph.D. in science and engineering begs the question of why so many foreign-born students choose that path. North argues that foreign students may find more benefits in a Ph.D. than do domestic students, because obtaining a U.S. Ph.D. is well regarded worldwide and because it provides access to U.S. residency through a student visa and ultimate adjustment of status. Additionally, the culturally specific nature of law, business, and, to a lesser degree, medicine may explain the low enrollment of foreign students in these areas.

One concern about the prevalence of foreign-born students in U.S. graduate programs is that these students may be taking spots that might otherwise go to native-born minority students. Neither domestic minorities nor women are well represented in science and engineering (Pearson 1990; Lorimer 1992). Some fear that these underrepresented groups are not being recruited as aggressively as they could be because foreign graduate students are in such abundance (North 1995). In the period 1983–1991, when graduate student enrollment by the foreign-born grew by 5 percent, underrepresented minorities experienced a slower growth rate than graduate students as a whole (NSF 1993b). The number of blacks earning doctoral degrees decreased 9 percent from 1982 to 1992, although it should be noted that the number of degrees earned by white males also declined by 9 percent, while degrees earned by white U.S. females rose 30 percent (Martin 1994). More recently, women and minorities alike have been growing in numbers in doctoral programs during the early 1990s. However, U.S. citizens were responsible for just 25 percent of such growth from 1990 to 1995.

Despite the relatively slow growth of minorities in U.S. graduate schools, both acceptance and enrollment rates are higher for minority applicants than for non–U.S. citizens. A 1990 study of 43 university Ph.D. programs found that they preferred U.S. citizen applicants, but the pool of such applicants was too small (Andersen 1996). North (1995) also found that graduate schools show a preference for citizens, with schools of a lower quality generally accepting more foreign students. He found that the high proportion of non–U.S. enrollees was explained by their greater application rate, not because graduate schools preferred them. North quotes Finn as estimating that graduate schools rejected one native-born applicant for every four foreign-born students they accepted. There was no evidence of affirmative action policies benefiting foreign-born scientists and engineers, and no displacement of minority graduate school applicants.

Given the lack of a demonstrated preference for foreign-born students, some have argued that the prevalence of foreign students is irrelevant to the shortage of minority students; they maintain that any doctoral shortage is merely a result of fewer minority students in the science and engineering pipeline (Zinberg 1992). Others have countered this argument by suggesting that without foreign scientists and engineers, a shortage would force the entire educational system to be revamped, starting in elementary grades. North (1995) has contended that without a ready supply of foreigners to fill research and development positions, the United States would have already felt the pinch of its short domestic supply and improved its science education starting in elementary levels, leading to more science majors (and a distribution more reflective of the ethnic and gender mix in the United States) as well as more domestic graduate students in science. As Bouvier and Martin (1995) point out, if native-born minorities and women participated in graduate education in science and engineering to their share of the population, no vacancies would be left for foreigners to fill. However, nothing is likely to remedy this shortage of qualified Americans in the near future.

Stay Rates of Foreign-Born Graduate Students

To some extent the United States is educating foreign-born scientists and engineers who subsequently return home. To many, this seems like a waste of U.S. educational resources. Moreover, there is some evidence that the rate of departure may increase, especially for Asian countries experiencing continued economic growth. For example, Moore (1988) gives anecdotal evidence of greater returns home by Taiwanese who find new opportunities as their country develops. However, currently only 30 percent of Taiwanese studying outside Taiwan return home after their studies. Other countries subsidize research in the United States and elsewhere, which increases rates of return for students. France gives full salaries while scientists employed in the Centre Nationale de la Recherche Scientifique and the Institut National de la Santé et de la Recherche Médicale go abroad to study; virtually all French who go abroad return. Tang (1993b) has hypothesized that development in the Pacific Rim might encourage those of Asian descent to return, pointing out that older immigrants who have American passports as political insurance can return without fear to take advantage of growth opportunities, departing again if the political climate turns inhospitable. Gaillard and Gaillard (1998) note that such decreases in stay rates may leave host countries such as the United States vulnerable, since many of them have come to depend on a large supply of foreign-born high-skilled labor.

In contrast, Kwok and Leland (1982) have theorized that many foreign students, even those who would receive the same wages at home and who would prefer to go back home, inevitably stay in the United States after graduation because of asymmetric information. This comes about because employers in the country of origin cannot closely evaluate individual students abroad and therefore must offer a wage consistent with the average productivity of all students studying abroad, based on other workers who have returned. Therefore, workers who are more productive than average get better job offers in the United States. Because U.S. work experience is a valued asset to employers in the country of origin, workers who do remain abroad "signal" their productivity to their home countries. However, as the home countries become more aware of these workers' high productivity, the workers become more accustomed to living abroad and therefore are more likely to stay. To remedy this, Kwok and Leland suggest that a "return clause" be built into home country scholarships, as is the case in Japan, or that the home country subsidize returns, like Taiwan.

Pernia (1976) also hypothesizes that for countries with a low level of economic progress, an exodus of highly skilled workers is inevitable. Because emigrants come from the top of the working pool in their home country (Portes 1976), this drain can have serious consequences for the development of a nation. For example, a large proportion of biotechnology leaders in the United Kingdom have been lost to the United States and Canada (Kidd 1986). However, Gaillard and Gaillard (1998) point out that as countries grow economically and increase the size of the research community at home, many expatriates either return or are brought into contact with scientists from their home country, especially in light of the extraordinary recent advances in information technology.

Currently, around 60 percent of foreign students earning doctorates in science and engineering stay in the United States (North 1995). The retention rate has been increasing over the past two decades, from 27 percent in 1972 and 40 percent in 1982 (Martin 1994). However, only 30 percent of students receive firm offers of employment by the time they graduate, mainly in academic or postdoctoral positions. Many more plan to stay without having a guaranteed job (NSF 1996b). For example, though only 50 percent of Chinese have firm offers, 75 percent stay.

As table 3.2 indicates, stay rates vary considerably by field and by type of visa. Permanent residents earning degrees in engineering or the life sciences are much more likely to remain in the United States than are temporary residents. However, the difference is considerably smaller among students in the physical sciences (Ries and Thurgood 1993).

Table 3.2

Distribution of New Science and Engineering Doctorate Recipients with Definite Plans upon Graduation (percents)

	U.S. Employ-ment	U.S. Study	Foreign Employ-ment	Foreign Study
Engineering				
Permanent residents	16.1	76.0	1.0	6.8
Temporary residents	21.3	38.1	6.5	34.1
Physical sciences				
Permanent residents	44.4	43.9	5.6	6.1
Temporary residents	44.8	27.2	12.6	15.4
Life sciences				
Permanent residents	66.2	20.5	4.6	8.7
Temporary residents	53.0	7.8	11.2	28.0

Source: Data are from Ries and Thurgood 1993.

Stay rates also vary by region and country of origin. Fifty percent of students from North and South America stay, compared with 56 percent of those from Europe and 62 percent of those from Asia. Development seems to affect stay rates, at least for Asian countries; less developed nations such as China and India had the highest stay rates, while the more developed Taiwan and South Korea had the lowest (NSF 1993b). Borjas (1994) quotes Bratsberg as saying that, as might be expected, foreign students whose native countries have high rates of return to schooling and are wealthy have a greater likelihood of returning. Other studies have found that family- and U.S.–financed students are more likely to stay than those financed by their home country (Huang 1987), and that students are less likely to stay when visa adjustment is difficult.

One study that followed a cohort of doctoral recipients found that less than one-half of foreign students who earned Ph.D.s in the 1980s in science and engineering were in the United States in 1992 (Finn and Pennington 1995). Using a sample from the 1991 Survey of Doctoral Recipients longitudinal file, Finn and Pennington studied Ph.D. recipients in the period 1981–1986 who were temporary residents at the time of receipt of their Ph.D. and who were in the United States in 1987, examining who had left and who had stayed as of 1991. Average salary in 1987 was lower for leavers, and growth of salary from 1987 to 1991 was also slower. Degree field accounted for some of the difference; leavers were more likely to have studied marine, earth, environmental, or social sciences and less likely to have studied engineering. Employers were also a factor, especially in academia, as those without tenure or not on a tenure track were more likely to leave. Leavers were also less likely to be married or to have children, and on average they obtained degrees later in life and completed them more rapidly. However, the only statistically significant variable in explaining propensity of departure was employment type. Foreign-born scientists and engineers were more likely to leave if in government or nonprofit jobs, and less likely to leave if receiving government support for their work.

Table 3.3
Foreign-born Students, with Doctorates Earned in 1984, Living in the United States in 1992 (percents)

	Permanent Residents	Temporary Residents
Engineering	85	55
Physical science	85	45
Life science	79	33
Social science	63	26

Source: Data are from Finn and Pennington 1995.

The stay rates vary widely by field, country of origin, and type of visa held. Table 3.3 presents the stay rates of the 1984 graduating cohort by field and visa type. Engineers had the highest stay rate, social scientists the lowest. Predictably, permanent residents in each field are considerably more likely to remain in the United States than are temporary residents. The authors also found that many temporary residents who, at the time of their graduation did not indicate that they had plans to remain in the United States, did in fact end up working in the United States in 1992. The authors speculated that the high stay rates among those who had planned to be abroad were partially due to political unrest in China.

Graduate Student Funding

Funding of foreign students is also a source of controversy. The U.S. government provides direct financial support for less than 1 percent of foreign students (*Chronicle* 1999b). However, this does not include the large number of fellowships and other indirect sources of funding provided by universities or students themselves. Agarwal and Winkler (1984) note that a student's funding source is an important factor in the decision to emigrate, since students receiving support from U.S. and home governments usually cannot adjust status.

Table 3.4
Primary Funding Sources for Students, by Nativity and Visa Type (percents)

	U.S. Students	Permanent Residents	Temporary Residents
Research assistantships	29.0	40.9	47.4
Own earnings	16.3	12.1	2.9
Teaching assistantships	16.1	20.9	23.5
Federal fellowships	8.0	1.7	0.2
University fellowships	5.0	4.4	4.5
Other federal support	4.8	1.9	2.5
Other university funding	1.6	1.4	0.8

Source: Data are from NSF 1993a.

Foreign students are more likely to receive funding than are natives, and temporary visa holders are more likely than permanent residents to receive funds (North 1995). Citizens are more likely to be teaching assistants than research assistants, while the reverse is true for foreign students. As table 3.4 indicates, for U.S. citizens, permanent residents, and temporary residents, a larger percentage of primary funding comes from research assistantships than any other source (29.0 percent, 40.9 percent, and 47.4 percent, respectively) (NSF 1993c). Temporary residents are the least likely to use their own earnings to finance their education. However, U.S. citizens and permanent residents are permitted a wider range of work options than are temporary residents.

Conclusions

The data presented above show clear trends for specific careers. For example, compared with other disciplines, proportionally fewer doctoral degrees in life sciences are awarded to foreign citizens, and a smaller than average proportion of those degrees that do go to foreign citizens go to those on temporary visas. Comparatively fewer foreign students in the life sciences planned to be in the United States after receiving their doctoral degrees. And when measured after several years, comparatively fewer students in the life sciences had stayed, whether they had held permanent or temporary visas when they graduated. In short, they are less likely to study in the United States and less likely to stay if they do. For engineering, all the trends outlined above were reversed, with physical, mathematical, and computer sciences generally falling in the middle.

Why do some fields encourage foreign-born participation at every level, while others discourage it? Can the explanation lie in salary levels, comparative quality of U.S. education in those fields, or relative availability of jobs? One suggestion might be that since engineering Ph.D.s are rare among the U.S. population, foreign students find it easier to carve out a niche for themselves in engineering. Additionally, proportionally more blacks and women participate in the life sciences than in other science and engineering fields (North 1995), further supporting a competition model for underrepresented minorities and immigrants.

Gaps in Current Research

Although many questions about the impact of foreign-born scientists and engineers have already been answered, many more remain. For example, no concrete model exists for wage trajectories of foreign-born scientists and engineers compared to the native-born, and cohort trends, if they exist, still have not clearly been explained. Additionally, the scope of the brain drain from the United States, stay rates of those educated here, and the impact of these figures are still unclear. More research into these questions would help to establish the effect of the foreign-born in the U.S. labor market and help to make well-informed policy decisions in the future.

Emigration rates for scientists and engineers, both native- and foreign-born, are crucial in understanding the implications of an increasingly international technology workforce. Simply looking at immigration is not enough; the stock of scientists and engineers in the United States, as well as the flow of talent worldwide, is clearly influenced by both immigration and emigration rates. However, more information on emigration of older foreign-born recipients of U.S. science and engineering degrees, as well as those who received their doctorates overseas, is largely absent from current literature and must be tracked before a full picture of foreign-born scientists and engineers can be complete.

Migratory patterns, both within the United States and to other countries, have been largely undocumented. Although little research has been done on the migratory effects of immigrant scientists and engineers on their native-born counterparts, foreign-born scientists and engineers might cause native scientists and engineers to relocate more frequently. If they were positively correlated, however, this would suggest that growth attracts both immigrants and natives, indicating that both groups are important to development.

Another dimension of U.S. science and engineering that has been largely ignored in the literature thus far is that of second-generation Americans. Given the large number of immigrants currently in the United States, second-generation Americans will most likely be a strong presence in science and engineering in the years to come. Therefore, it is important to know what patterns this group has followed in the past. Do those scientists and engineers whose parents immigrated behave like first-generation immigrants, or are they more like those who have been in the United States for three or more generations?

Additionally, even topics for which a fairly adequate current picture exists, such as demographic breakdowns and wages, need to be explored in the long term. While the current situation is clearly important, the past reactions of foreign-born scientists and engineers to U.S. legislation, availability of graduate education, and situations in their homelands, among many other factors, need to be documented in order to predict future patterns. Therefore, a historical perspective on foreign-born scientists and engineers is needed if this population is to be treated in the most mutually beneficial way possible.

Foreign-born scientists and engineers have clearly had a strong influence on the course of science and engineering in the United States. Their patterns of immigration, as well as their demographic makeup and choice of career, have varied greatly, showing that not all foreign-born scientists and engineers can be lumped together and classified as good or bad for the United States. However, much more needs to be researched, both about their impact on the United States and the

United States' impact on them, before the portrait of foreign-born scientists and engineers in this country will be complete.

References

Abowd, John M., and Richard B. Freeman, eds. 1991. *Immigration, Trade, and the Labor* Market. Chicago: University of Chicago Press.

Agarwal, Vinod B., and Donald R. Winkler. 1984. "Migration of Professional Manpower to the United States," *Southern Economic Journal* 50 (3): 814–30.

American Prospect. 1999. "High Tech Migrant Labor." December 20.

Andersen, Stuart. 1996. *Employment-Based Immigration and High Technology: Issues and Recommendations.* Washington, D.C.: Empower America.

Barringer, Herbert R., et al. 1990. "Education, Occupational Prestige, and Income of Asian Americans," *Sociology of Education* 63 (1): 27–43.

Borjas, George J. 1989. "Immigrant and Emigrant Earnings: A Longitudinal Study," *Economic Inquiry* 27 (1): 21–37.

———. 1994. "The Economics of Immigration," *Journal of Economic Literature*, 32 (4): 1667–1717.

———. 1995. "Assimilation and Changes in Cohort Quality Revisited: What Happened to Immigrant Earnings in the 1980's?" *Journal of Labor Economics* 13 (2): 201–45.

Borjas, George J., and Richard B. Freeman, eds. 1992. *Immigration and the Work Force: Economic Consequences for the United States and Source Areas.* Chicago: University of Chicago Press.

Borjas, George J., and Marta Tienda. 1987. "The Economic Consequences of Immigration," *Science*, February 6 (235), pp. 645–51.

Bouvier, Leon F., and John L. Martin. 1995. *Foreign-Born Scientists, Engineers, and Mathematicians in the United States.* Washington, D.C.: Center for Immigration Studies.

Brezenoff, Henry. 1992. Letter, *New York Times*, May 12.

Card, David. 1997. "Immigrant Inflows, Native Outflows, and the Local Labor Market Impacts of Higher Immigration." NBER Working Paper 5927. Cambridge, Mass.: National Bureau of Economic Research.

Chiswick, Barry. 1978. "The Effect of Americanization on the Earnings of Foreign-Born Men," *Journal of Political Economy* 86 (5): 897–921.

Chronicle of Higher Education. 1996. "'In' Box." June 7.

———. 1999a. "Computer Scientists Flee Academe for Industry's Greener Pastures." September 24.

———. 1999b. "Foreign Students Continue to Flock to the U.S." December 10.

Daly, William A. 1993. "Asian Students in U.S. Are the Future of the Pacific Rim," *San Diego Union-Tribune*, September 4.

Duleep, Harriet Orcutt, and Mark C. Regets. 1997. "The Decline of Immigrant Entry Earnings: Less Transferable Skills or Lower Ability?" *Quarterly Review of Economics and Finance* 37: 189–208.

Espenshade, Thomas J. 1999. "High-End Immigrants and the Shortage of Skilled Labor." Manuscript.

Espenshade, Thomas J., and Germán Rodríguez. 1995. "Foreign Graduate Students in U.S. Doctoral Programs in Sciences and the Humanities: Final Report to the Alfred P. Sloan Foundation." Princeton, N.J.: Office of Population Research, Princeton University.

Espenshade, Thomas J., Margaret L. Usdansky, and Chang Y. Chung. 2000. "Employment and Earnings of Foreign-Born Scientists and Engineers in U.S. Labor Markets." Manuscript.

Finn, Michael G., and Leigh Ann Pennington. 1995. "Foreign Nationals Who Receive Science or Engineering Ph.D.'s from U.S. Universities: Stay Rates and Characteristics of Stayers." Oak Ridge, Tenn.: Oak Ridge Institute for Science and Education.

Freeman, Peter, and William Aspray. 1999. *The Supply of Information Technology Workers in the United States*. Washington, D.C.: Computer Research Association.

Gaillard, Anne Marie, and Jacques Gaillard. 1998. "The International Circulation of Scientists and Technologists," *Science Communication* 20 (1): 106–15.

Glassman, James K. 1996. "Meet Our 'Jose,'" *Washington Post*, March 12.

Greenberg, Daniel S. 1990. "Derelict State of Education: America's Low on Brainpower," *San Diego Union-Tribune*, September 27.

———. 1993a. "World's Science Students Flock to U.S. Classrooms," *Sacramento Bee*, July 5.

———. 1993b. "Asia Advances: U.S.–Trained Scientists Making Great Strides," *San Diego Union-Tribune*, August 26.

Hansen, Kristin A. 1996. "Profile of the Foreign-born Population in 1995: What the CPS Nativity Data Tell Us." Paper presented at the annual meetings of the Population Association of America, New Orleans, May 9–11.

Hansen, Kristin A., and Amara Bachu. 1995. "The Foreign-Born Population: 1994," *Current Population Reports*. Series P20-486. Washington, D.C.: U.S. Bureau of the Census.

Hart, David J. 1993. Letter, *New York Times*, January 26.

Huang, Wei-Chiao. 1987. "A Pooled Cross-Section and Time-Series Study of Professional Indirect Immigration to the United States," *Southern Economic Review* 54 (1): 95–109.

INS (U.S. Immigration and Naturalization Service). 1996. *1994 Statistical Yearbook of the Immigration and Naturalization Service*. Washington, D.C.: U.S. Department of Justice, February.

Kanjanapan, Wilawan. 1995. "The Immigration of Asian Professionals to the United States: 1988–1990," *International Migration Review* 29 (1): 7–32.

Keely, Charles B. 1975. "Effects of U.S. Immigration Law on Manpower Characteristics of Immigrants," *Demography* 12 (2): 179–91.

Kidd, Charles V. 1986. "International Mobility of Bioscientists: Trends and Perceptions, Country by Country," *Perspectives in Biology and Medicine* 29 (3:2): s21–s31.

Kposowa, Augustine J. 1993. "The Impact of Immigration on Native Earnings in the United States, 1940 to 1980," *Applied Behavioral Science Review* 1 (1): 1–25.

Kwok, Viem, and Hayne Leland. 1982. "An Economic Model of the Brain Drain," *American Economic Review* 72 (1): 91–100.

Lorimer, Linda Koch. 1992. "Women Can Help U.S. Close 'Science Gap,'" *Atlanta Journal and Constitution*, December 21.

Martin, John. 1994. "Displacement of U.S. Students at the Doctoral Degree Level?" *Immigration Review* 18 (Summer): 7–11.

Martin, Philip, and Elizabeth Midgley. 1994. "Immigration to the United States: Journey to an Uncertain Destination," *Population Bulletin* 49 (2): 2–45.

Martin, Philip, and Jonas Widgren. 1996. "International Migration: A Global Challenge," *Population Bulletin* 51 (1): 2–48.

Matloff, Norman. 1996. "A Critical Look at Immigration's Role in the U.S. Computer Industry." At ftp://heather.cs.ucdavis.edu/pub/svreport.html.

McDonnell, Patrick J., and Julie Pitta. 1996. "'Brain Gain' or Threat to U.S. Jobs?" *Los Angeles Times*, July 15.

Moore, Jonathan. 1988. "Taiwan's New Breed: U.S. Trained Engineers Find Homecoming a Profitable Turn," *Far Eastern Economic Review*, July 2.

New York Times. 1995. "Evaluating U.S. Universities," September 19.

North, David S. 1995. *Soothing the Establishment: The Impact of Foreign-Born Scientists and Engineers on America*. Lanham, Md.: University Press of America.

NSF (National Science Foundation). 1993a. *Immigrant Scientists and Engineers: 1990*. Detailed Statistical Tables. NSF 93-317. Arlington, Va.: NSF.

———. 1993b. *Science and Engineering Indicators 1993*. NSB 93-1. Arlington, Va.: NSF.

———. 1993c. *Foreign Participation in U.S. Academic Science and Engineering: 1991*. NSF 93-302. Arlington, Va.: NSF.

———. 1996a. *Characteristics of Doctoral Scientists and Engineers in the United States: 1993*. NSF 96-302. Arlington, Va.: NSF.

———. 1996b. *Science and Engineering Indicators 1996*. NSB 96-21. Arlington, Va.: NSF.

Office of Technology Policy. 1999. *The Digital Work Force*. Washington, D.C.: U.S. Dept. of Commerce Technology Administration.

Pearson, Willie, Jr. 1990. "How Best to Honor Memory of King? Attract Blacks to Sciences, Engineering," *Orlando Sentinel Tribune*, January 15.

Pernia, Ernesto M. 1976. "The Question of the Brain Drain from the Philippines," *International Migration Review* 10 (1): 63–72.

Portes, Alejandro. 1976. "The Determinants of the Brain Drain," *International Migration Review* 10 (4): 489–508.

Regets, Mark C. 1995. "Immigrants Are 23 Percent of U.S. Residents with Science and Engineering Doctorates." Science Resources Studies Division Data Brief. Arlington, Va.: NSF.

Ries, P., and D. H. Thurgood. 1993. "Summary Report 1992: Doctorate Recipients from United States Universities." Washington D.C.: National Academy Press.

Rothman, Eric S., and Thomas J. Espenshade. 1992. "Fiscal Impacts of Immigration to the United States," *Population Index* 58 (3): 381–415.

Scientific American. 1988. "Embarrassment of Riches: Foreign-Born Students Fill U.S. Science Programs." Vol. 258, no. 5, p. 22.

Sehgal, Ellen. 1985. "Foreign Born in the U.S. Labor Market: The Results of a Special Survey," *Monthly Labor Review* 108 (7): 18–24.

Smith, D. Randall, et al. 1994. "An Examination of Bias in Performance Ratings of Scientists and Engineers."

Stephan, Paula E., and Sharon G. Levin. 1995. "Birth Origin and Educational Background of Scientists and Engineers Making Exceptional Contributions." Final Report to the Alfred P. Sloan Foundation. Atlanta: Georgia State University.

Tang, Joyce. 1993a. "The Career Attainment of Caucasian and Asian Engineers," *Sociological Quarterly* 34 (3): 467–96.

———. 1993b. "Caucasians and Asians in Engineering: A Study in Occupational Mobility and Departure," *Research in the Sociology of Organizations* 11: 217–56.

Teitelbaum, Michael S. 1996. "Too Many Engineers, Too Few Jobs," *New York Times*, March 19.

U.S. Commission on Immigration Reform. 1995. *Legal Immigration: Setting Priorities. A Report to Congress.* Washington, D.C.

U.S. Department of Labor. 1995a. "Labor Force School Enrollment and Educational Attainment Statistics for the Foreign-Born Using the October 1994 Current Population Survey." Bulletin No. 3. Washington, D.C.: Division of Immigration Policy and Research, Bureau of International Labor Affairs, U.S. Department of Labor, October.

———. 1995b. "Further Labor Force and Income Statistics for the Foreign-Born Using the March 1994 Current Population Survey." Bulletin No. 2. Washington, D.C.: Division of Immigration Policy and Research, Bureau of International Labor Affairs, U.S. Department of Labor, October.

Waldinger, Roger, et al. 1995. "In Search of the Glass Ceiling." Final Report to the Alfred P. Sloan Foundation. Los Angeles: Department of Sociology, University of California, Los Angeles.

Walsh, John. 1988. "Foreign Engineers On Rise," *Science* 239 (4839): 455.

Wilkinson, R. Keith. 1995. "For 1993, Doctoral Scientists and Engineers Report 1.6 Percent Unemployment Rate but 4.3 Percent Underemployment." Data Briefs. Arlington, Va.: NSF, March 15.

Zinberg, Dorothy S. 1992. Letter, *New York Times*, May 12.

4

Asian Immigrant Engineers in Canada

Monica Boyd

The high-skilled and professional component of immigrant flows is a major topic in current North American immigration policy developments. Such emphasis reflects the broader context of economic globalization, based on worldwide networks of communication, transportation, economic transactions, and the market and production strategies of companies (Reich 1991; Thurow 1992). Starting in the 1980s, both Canada and the United States actively sought agreements such as the General Agreement on Trade and Services (GATS) and the North American Free Trade Agreement (NAFTA) in order to regulate and institutionalize their participation in this new international system. Economic competitiveness in a knowledge-based society has thus become the mantra of the early twenty-first century, highlighting the importance of high-skilled labor in postindustrial economies.

Engineering is a professional occupation that not only plays an important role in the attempts of firms and nations to position themselves in the new world order, but it also relies on a global labor supply. In North America, exporting engineering services is a core activity for many firms. Engineers (and scientists) trained outside of North America are also frequently viewed as part of a global labor supply by high-technology firms. In the United States, the foreign-born accounted for almost 10 percent of all engineers enumerated in the 1980 census, rising to 12 percent in the 1990 census (Lim, Waldinger, and Bozorgmehr 1998). This is a minimum estimate of those with engineering training, since the data refer only to persons actually employed in engineering occupations. In Canada, the foreign-born are close to half (44.5 percent) of those in the 1995–1996 experienced labor force who are age 15 and older and who list engineering as a post-secondary major field of study. Most (97 percent) are permanent residents (unpublished tabulations from the 1996 2B census database).

Most studies of foreign-born engineers in the North American work-force adopt a supply-side perspective found in immigrant integration research. In documenting similarities and discrepancies between na-tives and the foreign-born in employment and earnings, this research frequently attributes immigrant disadvantages to human capital stock (including language knowledge and recency of arrival), as well as to ethnic or racially based discrimination. For example, U.S. studies that examine the experience of engineers, particularly those in California's "Silicon Valley," find that the skills of these workers are not always well matched to their jobs. Instead, immigrants may experience under-employment or blocked mobility. Asian (and Mexican) foreign-born engineers in the United States are more likely than their white, Ameri-can-born counterparts to be employed in technical work and less likely to move from engineering positions into the management rungs (Alarcón 1999; Fernandez 1998; Lim, Waldinger, and Bozorgmehr 1998; Tang 1993a, 1993b, 1995).

These findings generate two additional questions not systematically considered by researchers to date. First, is the experience of under-employment of Asian-born engineers unique to the United States, or are such findings also observed in other postindustrial economies, sug-gesting that foreign-trained immigrants, particularly from Asia, are by definition or design not likely to be fully utilized? Second, what do such findings of "mismatch" or under-utilization imply for immigra-tion policy debates, which often are fueled by labor demand considera-tions?

In this chapter, the first question about the uniqueness or generality of studies on the American labor force is answered by examining the employment patterns of foreign-born Asian engineers who are perma-nently residing in Canada. As a postindustrial country characterized by a growing knowledge-based economy, Canada has many similarities with the United States. Moreover, in both countries immigration from Asia increased in the last quarter of the twentieth century as a result of new immigration policies first adopted in the 1960s (Boyd 1976; Keely 1971). During the 15–year period from 1980 to 1995, migration flows from Asia represented about one-third of all foreign-born men age 25 to 64 who entered Canada as permanent residents, listed engineering as an intended occupation, and had at minimum a bachelor's degree (unpublished tabulations from Citizenship and Immigration Canada, Landed Immigrant Data System, April 2000). As in the United States, engineers from Asia are a significant share of the inflow of engineers in general. Whether foreign-born engineers also are mismatched in the Canadian labor market is the empirical question to be investigated here.

The second question asks what the implications of the answers to the first question are for immigration policy debates. This is addressed in the concluding section of the chapter. Like the United States, Canada has an immigration policy that emphasizes permanent settlement and uses economic factors as one of its three admissibility criteria (the other two being family reunification and humanitarian considerations). Compared to the non–Asian-born intending to work in engineering occupations, Asian-born engineers are more likely to be admitted on the basis of economic criteria than on humanitarian or family reunification grounds. Between 1980 and 1995, 90 percent of Asian-born men intending to enter engineering and related occupations (managerial and technical occupations) were admitted in the economic class, in contrast to 73 percent of their non–Asian-born counterparts.[1] Such trends suggest that the immigration of engineers in general, and Asian engineers in particular, reflects current Canadian labor market demands. Recent immigration policy changes also indicate continued recruitment in the near future of high-skilled labor—both permanent and temporary. At the same time, concerns are mounting over Canada's ability to retain high-skilled labor, including foreign-born and Canadian-born engineers. In contrast, such concerns are notably absent in the U.S. policy arena, where debate and controversy focus on the revisions to the H–1B visa program (see Lochhead 2000; Lowell, this volume; Krikorian 1998; Usdansky and Espenshade, this volume; Valbrun 2000).

How Do Asian-Born Engineers Differ?

Studies find that Asian-born immigrants are more likely than white, American-born engineers in the United States to be under-employed. Four explanations exist for the observed disparities between engineers demarcated by national origin and race. One explanation for disparities between groups of engineers is that specific national origin or racially

[1] The occupational categorization of "intended engineering occupations" is based on the Canadian Classification and Dictionary of Occupations (CCDO) list of occupational titles, and it includes management occupations in engineering, all engineering occupations, and related technical occupations. Data are from the Citizenship and Immigration Canada, Landed Immigrant Data System (April, 2000) for men aged 25 to 64 with bachelor's degrees or higher. Although the data are consistent with the interpretation that the admission of foreign-born engineers reflects Canada's labor market demands, flow data do not necessarily capture the entire population of immigrant residents who are engineers. Immigrants with engineering training also can enter Canada under family and humanitarian criteria, and in some instances, their occupations may not be recorded in administrative data on admissions.

defined groups lack the requisite human capital skills, represented by training, work experience, and high levels of language proficiency. A second is that these workers have fewer social capital–based resources than their white American-born colleagues. Asians and other migrants may have fewer professional networks to draw upon in their job searches, and they may be less likely to have English language–based networks. Social skills, including leadership styles, may differ as well. Researchers, however, argue that these gaps should disappear over time to the extent that "assimilation" occurs and improves access to networks, job searches, and language skills. This supposition implies that differences between Asian-born immigrants and other groups should diminish as time spent in the host society increases.

A third explanation is that immigrants face discrimination in the host society (Alarcón 1999; Fernandez 1998; Lim, Waldinger, and Bo-zorgmehr 1998; Tang 1993b, 1995, 1997). In U.S. studies, discrimination is frequently described in terms of employer decisions over hiring and promotions, negative stereotyping, and homosocial behaviors in which colleagues are selected on the basis of presumed similarities in out-looks, managerial styles, and "understandings" (Fernandez 1998; Tang 1997). In this context, "race," country of origin, or other phenotypical characteristics act as markers of presumed dissimilarities, leading to racial and country of origin–based discrimination. In such circum-stances, differences should be observed in the labor market outcomes of Asians (and other non-white groups) compared to whites.

Discrimination can also result from structural barriers. In Canada, the term "systemic discrimination" refers to rules and procedures that are not explicitly designed to produce differential outcomes but do so through their applications. Certification requirements are often de-scribed as a form of systemic discrimination, in that criteria are created that are universally applied to the Canadian-born and foreign-born alike, but that have disproportionate effects in restricting access to a trade or profession among the foreign-born (Bolaria 1992; Mata 1992, 1994, 1999; McDade 1988).

For the foreign-born who studied engineering outside Canada, the requirement of within-Canada accreditation is the fourth possible ex-planation for under-employment or occupational mismatches. The Ca-nadian engineering profession is a publicly regulated occupation with its own "reserve" title.[2] This means that, by law, no one may offer engi-neering services to the public unless they first obtain a license from one of the twelve provincial and territorial engineering associations (*ordres* in Quebec) that have been mandated by provincial/territorial law. Per-

---

[2] See www.nspe.org for information on comparable licensing in the United States by the National Society of Professional Engineers.

sons may do engineering work without accreditation, but it must be under the direct supervision of a licensed professional engineer, who is legally entitled to use the designation "P.Eng." ("Ing." in Quebec) after their name. Figures suggest that the majority of those trained as engineers are licensed. As of the year 2000, approximately 157,000 engineers were licensed.[3] According to the most recent census (1996), 262,000 persons age twenty-one and older who had at least a bachelor's degree gave engineering as their major field of study (Schwanen 2000: table 1).

These four explanations imply that engineers immigrating to Canada after receiving their degrees abroad are faced with three outcome scenarios. First, they may be less likely to be in the labor force, or they may be more likely to be unemployed as compared to Canadian-trained engineers. Second, when employed, immigrants with foreign engineering training also may be less likely to be working in engineering or engineering-related occupations than are the Canadian-born or the foreign-born who received Canadian engineering degrees. Since employment in engineering occupations often is the first rung on a ladder to management (Fernandez 1998; Tang 1993b, 1997), this scenario implies that engineers with foreign training will be less likely to be in management. Third, with increasing years of residency in the host country, immigrants should improve their labor market profiles and narrow the gaps that exist between training and occupations. This third expectation rests on two inputs. The first derives from the general literature on immigrant adaptations, observing that downward mobility and unemployment are not uncommon shortly after arrival. Researchers argue, however, that these gaps should disappear over time to the extent that language skills and job-related networks improve and knowledge about the new society increases. The second is specific to professions with accreditation requirements, emphasizing that re-accreditation takes time, during which courses must be taken, exams passed, and host-country experience obtained.

In principle, these scenarios should describe the experiences of all foreign-trained engineers. However, as found in American studies, the possible existence of discrimination implies that larger discrepancies in employment and occupational patterns may be observed for Asian-born immigrants compared to immigrants born elsewhere. Discrimination may result when race or ethnicity is used as a criterion of hiring or occupational placement. Furthermore, accreditation requirements can play a role. Knowledge of engineering programs and the Canadian Council of Professional Engineers (CCPE) list of acceptable engineering institutions is likely to favor engineering programs in the United States,

---

[3] See the Canadian Council of Professional Engineers Web site: www.ccpe.ca.

the United Kingdom, and Europe.[4] As a result, occupational gaps should be especially pronounced for the Asian-born, assuming that most obtain their degrees in their countries or regions of origin.

These considerations generate three specific questions to be answered. First, do the labor market profiles of Asian immigrants with foreign training in engineering differ from those of immigrants born elsewhere or from those of the Canadian-born? Second, do Asian immigrants with foreign engineering training have the same occupational patterns observed for the those born elsewhere, including the Canadian-born with similar credentials? Third, does increased time spent in Canada lessen the differences in employment and occupational profiles that may exist between the Asian-born and other immigrant groups, or between the Asian-born and the Canadian-born?

Data Sources and Methods

The analysis associated with these questions extends U.S. research in three ways. It examines the employment of foreign-born engineers in another country; it provides an updated analysis; and it analyzes a database that removes some of the difficulties associated with American sources of data. Insightful as it is, American research rests either on small case studies or on two data sets, notably the United States census and the Survey of Natural and Social Scientists and Engineers (SSE), collected by the Bureau of the Census for the National Science Foundation. U.S. census data provide information only on those who are employed as engineers, thus preventing any analysis of those trained as engineers but not currently in engineering occupations. The longitudinal samples in the SSE rest on a 1982 study, which, in turn, includes only those individuals who responded to the 1980 census. As a result, data on foreign-born engineers arriving after 1980 are not available from the 1984, 1986, and 1989 follow-ups. Concern also exists over the definition of scientists and engineers used in the SSE and over selective sample attrition over time (Tang 1995, 1997).

In Canada, data on the economic performance of immigrant engineers are collected by the Census of Population. Fielded on May 14, 1996, the most recent census of Canada includes a one-in-five sample of the Canadian population that answered the 2B questionnaire. As is true for U.S. census data, occupational titles can be classified into those that are managerial, engineering, those that are of a technical nature, or

---

[4] Agreements exist between accreditation bodies in Canada, the United Kingdom, Ireland, Australia, New Zealand, South Africa, and Hong Kong for recognizing accredited university bachelor degree programs in engineering (Canadian Council of Professional Engineers, www.ccpe.ca, 1/25/2000).

those unrelated to engineering skills. However, the novel contribution of the Canadian census is that it provides information on major field of study for those who have post-secondary education or higher. The census question asks: "What was the major field of study or training of this person's **highest** degree, certificate or diploma (**excluding** secondary or high school graduation certificates)?"[5] This question on major field of study permits identifying those who underwent training in engineering fields, an identification that is not possible with U.S. census data. The ability to identify those who have engineering majors broadens the scope of our investigation from a more narrow examination restricted to persons employed in engineering and related occupations.

The focus of this chapter is on the labor market experiences of men between the ages of 30 and 54 who have bachelor's degrees or higher and at least 16 years of schooling. Most engineering majors are men, and the comparatively small numbers of women constrain the analysis, particularly when examining variations by area of birth. The age parameters are chosen because the period between the ages of 30 and 54 is the core of the productive life for most people. It is also the period when they typically are well established in their careers. The focus on this age group also removes variation associated with school completion and selective early retirement. The restriction of the population under study to those with bachelor's degrees or higher and a minimum of 16 years of schooling ensures that the population analyzed corresponds to the group eligible for CCPE accreditation.

Most discussions of the immigration of highly skilled labor assume that these workers trained abroad. As previously discussed, it is this group that is most likely to face re-certification requirements in professions such as engineering or medicine, have greater language problems, face employers who are unfamiliar with their credentials, or be trained in programs that differ from those in North America. In order to better capture the group that was most likely trained outside of Canada, permanent residents[6] are restricted to those who immigrated at age 28 or

---

[5] Bold print appears on the questionnaire.

[6] "Permanent resident" is a term used by immigration authorities to denote a person who is in Canada legally and has permanent residence status. It has replaced the "landed immigrant" terminology of the 1970s and 1980s. "Non-permanent residents" refers to foreign-born who are in Canada on a temporary basis. They are a diverse group that includes students, persons on short-term work authorization permits, and refugee claimants. Non-permanent residents represented about 1 percent of the population enumerated in the 1996 census. Although overall flows may be large, the numbers in Canada at any one point in time are much smaller. Numbers of non-permanent residents who were engineers in the 1996 census were too few for analysis.

later and arrived by 1994.[7] The Canadian census currently does not ask for the geographical location of the last degree, thereby preventing a precise grouping of those who received engineering degrees from Canadian institutions or from institutions in other countries. Because education generally is completed by one's mid-twenties, it is assumed that most, if not all, of those immigrating at age 28 or later have received their degrees outside Canada. Two reasons exist for the requirement that this group legally entered Canada by 1994. First, this restriction means they are at least age 30 by the date of the 1996 census. Second, it minimizes the initial impact of arrival, which for the general immigrant population is associated with high unemployment (Badets and Howatson-Leo 1999). It is assumed that most if not all of the Canadian-born have received degrees from Canadian (or American) institutions.

In this chapter, employment states are defined as follows: out of the labor force, unemployed, or currently employed. Occupational location consists of working in one of four main types of work: managers, engineering occupations, technical occupations that are related to engineering activities, and all other occupations. This categorization follows U.S. research on engineers (Fernandez 1998; Lim, Waldinger, and Bozorgmehr 1998; Tang 1993a, 1993b, 1995, 1997). For some, engineering occupations are steps on the ladder to managerial occupations. Alternatively, some find a glass ceiling between engineering and managerial jobs that restricts such mobility. In addition to employment in managerial and engineering occupations, some individuals trained in engineering will find employment in occupations that are further removed from engineering but which are of a technical nature that may require or utilize engineering knowledge and applications. Others will find no employment at all in occupations related to engineering. Based on these outcomes, a four-category classification of over 500 occupational titles into manager, engineer, technical, and all other occupations was constructed (see Boyd and Thomas 2000: appen. A).

Because the dependent variables are categorical variables, multinomial logistic regression is used (Liao 1994). The technique relies on the computation of logits reflecting the natural logarithm of the odds (log odds) of being in each occupational category as opposed to some reference category. Key independent variables of interest are

---

[7] Another analysis of those with engineering as a major field of study (Boyd and Thomas 2000) compared the employment and occupational profiles of the Canadian-born, permanent residents immigrating as children (ages 0-18), and permanent residents immigrating at age 28 or later. The profiles for permanent residents who immigrated to Canada before age 18 were remarkably similar to the Canadian-born, suggesting that a major distinction is between degrees received from Canadian institutions and those received outside of Canada, rather than between Canadian birth and immigrant status per se.

education, defined as level of degree (bachelor's, master's, and Ph.D.) and duration in Canada for those arriving in Canada as adults. Control variables include age; residence in large Census Metropolitan Areas (CMAs, specifically Montreal, Toronto, and Vancouver) as opposed to other areas; specialized fields of study within engineering; and, for those arriving at age 28 or later, home language. This latter variable is selected as a crude measure of the extensiveness of English and/or French language use.[8]

Demographic and Human Capital Characteristics

Stock data from the 1996 census 2B form (representing one in five Canadian households) show that most permanent residents with engineering as a major field of study are recent arrivals to Canada. Over two-thirds of those born in Asia and elsewhere who have bachelor's degrees or higher have lived in Canada for less than 10 years (table 4.1). Compared to the Canadian-born, both Asian- and non–Asian-born men are on average about three years older, have much higher percentages living in the three major metropolises of Montreal, Toronto, and Vancouver, and are much less likely to speak English and/or French (Canada's two official languages) at home.

Compared to the Canadian-born population that studied engineering, immigrants with foreign training are more likely to have received master's and Ph.D. degrees rather than just bachelor's degrees. However, those who are Asian-born are more likely than immigrants born elsewhere to have only a bachelor's degree. If they have advanced degrees, they are more likely to have a Ph.D. degree than those born elsewhere (11 percent of Asian-born men have Ph.D. degrees, compared to 8 percent of those born in other countries and 2 percent of the Canadian-born).

Asian-born men are also slightly more likely than others to specialize in electrical and civil engineering (table 4.1). Electrical, mechanical, and civil engineering are the three "core" fields in engineering. Electri-

---

[8] The language variable is constructed as English and/or French spoken in the home, either solely or with another language, versus no English and/or French spoken in the home. It is an imperfect measure of language familiarity. Unlike the Australian and U.S. census questions, Canadian census questions in general do not provide good measures of linguistic skill (for further discussion, see Boyd 1999; Boyd, DeVries, and Simkin 1994). The question on knowledge of Canada's two official languages provides even less information than the question on home language. When asked the question on knowledge of Canada's two official languages, virtually all engineers in our sample indicated they speak English and/or French well enough to carry on a conversation.

Table 4.1

Selected Characteristics of Men, Ages 30 to 54, with a Bachelor's Degree or Higher, with Engineering as Their Major Field of Study, Canadian-Born and Permanent Residents, Arriving at Age 28+, Canada, 1996

| Characteristics | Canada-born (1) | Permanent Residents | |
		Asia-born (2)	All Other Birthplaces (3)
Highest degree	100.0	100.0	100.0
Bachelor's	82.2	68.1	58.3
Master's	15.4	20.7	33.8
Ph.D.	2.4	11.2	8.0
Specialization	100.0	100.0	100.0
Electrical	20.1	25.6	24.7
Mechanical	18.3	18.0	22.9
Civil	18.2	20.3	18.0
Chemical	7.2	6.3	5.1
Other	36.2	29.8	29.3
Labor force activity	100.0	100.0	100.0
Not in labor force	2.5	11.4	7.6
Unemployed	2.0	6.1	8.5
Employed	95.5	82.4	83.9
Occupational group	100.0	100.0	100.0
Manager	28.6	17.2	18.3
Engineer	41.3	29.2	33.4
Technician	11.6	16.4	16.5
Other	18.6	37.2	31.9
Place of residence	100.0	100.0	100.0
Montreal, Toronto, Vancouver	34.6	73.4	67.5
All other areas	65.4	26.6	32.5
Official language spoken at home	100.0	100.0	100.0
Yes	99.4	35.3	44.5
No	0.6	64.7	55.5
Years in Canada			
Non-immigrant	NA	100.0	100.0
2–4		34.2	35.9
5–9		37.6	32.7
10–14		9.1	14.7
15–19		8.7	10.5
20 or more		10.4	6.2
Mean age	39.7	42.7	42.5

NA = not applicable.

Source: Statistics Canada, 1996 Census 2B database.

cal engineering includes expertise in electronics which, as in the United States, has become an important sector in Canada's knowledge-based economy. Civil engineering is the area most likely to be affected by the CCPE regulations because it includes construction activities that affect public safety.

Employment Patterns by Country of Origin, Degree, and Years of Residence

In addition to the social and demographic differences discussed above, Asian-born, engineering-trained immigrants differ from the Canadian-born with respect to their employment and occupational profiles. At the time of the census, those born in Asian countries had lower employment percentages, and they were more likely than non-Asian immigrant groups to be out of the labor force (table 4.1). This relative under-employment of permanent residents who are either Asian-born or born elsewhere is consistent with the recency of arrival patterns observed for these groups and with the higher percentages speaking only a non-English/non-French language in the home. However, the permanent resident Asian-born population has other characteristics that should enhance their employment opportunities, such as higher percentages with Ph.D. degrees and residency in large urban areas.

Multinomial analysis reveals the diverse influence of these variables on being out of the labor force, unemployed, or employed. Earlier analysis found that residential location (major CMA versus other areas) and language spoken in the home had no significant effects on the likelihood of being employed, unemployed, or out of the labor force, so these two variables were excluded from the results presented in table 4.2. For Canadian-born men with engineering training, level of degree and specialization were not important predictors of the (log) likelihood of being out of the labor force or being unemployed compared to being employed. However, these other variables did significantly influence the (log) likelihood of not being in the labor force or of being unemployed versus being employed for the permanent resident population. In addition, the coefficients for place of birth indicate that, compared to non-Asian immigrants, those born in Asia have greater (log) likelihood of not being in the labor force versus being employed, but they are less likely to be unemployed than employed (table 4.2).

The analysis indicates that for those permanent residents born elsewhere, other variables—including length of stay, level of degree, age, and specialization—condition their overall employment profile. Once these factors are taken into account, what is the actual impact of being Asian-born on employment possibilities? One "common sense" way of

Table 4.2
Multinomial Logit Estimates of Labor Force Status for Men Aged 30 to 54, with Engineering as a Major Field of Study, Bachelor's Degree or Higher, Canadian-born and Permanent Residents Arriving at Age 28+, Canada, 1996

	Canada-born		Foreign-born	
	Not in Labor Force versus Employed (1)	Unemployed versus Employed (2)	Not in Labor Force versus Employed (3)	Unemployed versus Employed (4)
Intercept	−4.760***	−4.274***	−5.021***	−4.843***
Age	0.031***	−0.007	0.020*	0.022*
Highest degree				
Bachelor's	−0.150	0.659	1.054***	0.609**
Master's	−0.277	0.293	0.659**	0.447*
Ph.D.	(rg)	(rg)	(rg)	(rg)
Specialization				
Electrical	−0.042	−0.028	−0.216	−0.302*
Mechanical	−0.324	0.074	−0.022	-0.105
Civil	−0.058	0.382*	0.238	0.169
Chemical	−0.285	−0.096	0.191	-0.266
Other	(rg)	(rg)	(rg)	(rg)
Years in Canada				
2–4			1.360***	1.697***
5–9			0.927***	1.137***
10–14			0.255	0.479
15+			(rg)	(rg)
Place of birth				
Asia			0.391***	0.314**
All others			(rg)	(rg)
Parameters				
Log likelihood	1348.65		3790.37	
Chi-square	42.59		294.43	
df	14		22	

* p<.05
** p<.01
*** p<.001
(rg) = Reference group.
Source: Statistics Canada, 1996 Census 2B database.

answering this question is to calculate the probabilities of being out of the labor force, unemployed, or employed for specific combinations of characteristics, using the multinomial regression equations. This is done in table 4.3, which calculates probabilities for men age 45, whose major field of study is electrical engineering. Table 4.3 also shows the variations in employment profiles that are produced by Asian versus non-Asian region of birth, level of degree (bachelor's, master's, Ph.D.), and duration in Canada. These variations generate three conclusions regarding the employment profiles of Asian-born and other immigrants arriving at age 28 or later vis-à-vis each other and compared to the Canadian-born. First, for all levels of education and years of residence, the employment profiles of immigrants born in Asia versus those born elsewhere are not very different. As suggested by the logits (table 4.2) and data presented in table 4.3, Asian-born men have slightly higher percentages out of the labor force and slightly lower percentages unemployed or employed compared to permanent residents who are not born in Asia. The differences are minuscule, however, with advanced degrees and increasing length of time spent in Canada. In fact, a second conclusion supported by the probabilities in table 4.3 is that, after approximately 10 years in Canada, the employment profiles of both Asian and non-Asian groups are remarkably similar and correspond closely to those observed for Canadian-born men who are age 45 and have studied electrical engineering. A third conclusion is that for Asian-born and non–Asian-born permanent residents alike, advanced degrees afford some protection against being unemployed or out of the labor force.

Occupational Profiles: Birthplace, Degree, and Date of Arrival

Compared to Canadian-born men, permanent residents who immigrated at age 28 or later had lower percentages holding managerial or engineering occupations in 1996, and higher percentages employed in technical or other occupations. Again, as with employment patterns, relatively small differences exist in the actual occupational profiles observed for the Asian-born and non–Asian-born immigrants (table 4.1). The main difference is a slightly lower percentage of the Asian-born in engineering occupations and a corresponding slightly higher percentage in occupations other than managerial, engineering, or technical work compared to the occupational profile of other immigrant men. However, both Asian-born and non–Asian-born immigrants are much less likely than the Canadian-born to hold managerial occupations, and they are almost twice as likely to be employed in occupations that are

Table 4.3
Chances Out of 100[a] of Being Employed, Unemployed or Not in the Labor Force, for Men Aged 45, with Electrical Engineering as Major Field of Study, for Canadian-born and Permanent Residents Immigrating at Age 28+, by Level of Degree and Place of Birth, Canada, 1996

	Total	Currently Employed	Unemployed	Not in Labor Force
Bachelor's Degrees				
Canada-born	100.0	95.1	1.8	3.1
Foreign-born, Asian birthplace				
2-4	100.0	75.1	8.6	16.2
5-9	100.0	82.9	5.4	11.6
10-14	100.0	90.4	3.1	6.5
15+	100.0	92.9	2.0	5.2
Foreign-born, non-Asian birthplace				
2-4	100.0	76.7	12.1	11.2
5-9	100.0	84.4	7.6	8.0
10-14	100.0	91.3	4.3	4.4
15+	100.0	93.8	2.7	3.5
Master's Degrees				
Canada-born	100.0	96.3	1.3	2.4
Foreign-born, Asian birthplace				
2-4	100.0	80.4	7.9	11.7
5-9	100.0	86.9	4.9	8.2
10-14	100.0	92.8	2.7	4.5
15+	100.0	94.8	1.7	3.5
Foreign-born, non-Asian birthplace				
2-4	100.0	81.1	10.9	8.0
5-9	100.0	87.7	6.7	5.6
10-14	100.0	93.3	3.7	3.0
15+	100.0	95.3	2.3	2.4
Ph.D. Degrees				
Canada-born	100.0	95.9	0.9	3.2
Foreign-born, Asian birthplace				
2-4	100.0	87.9	5.5	6.6
5-9	100.0	92.2	3.3	4.5
10-14	100.0	95.8	1.8	2.4
15+	100.0	97.0	1.1	1.9
Foreign-born, non-Asian birthplace				
2-4	100.0	88.0	7.5	4.5
5-9	100.0	92.4	4.5	3.1
10-14	100.0	96.0	2.4	1.6
15+	100.0	97.2	1.5	1.3

(a) If divided by 100, data convert to probabilities.
Source: Table 4.2.

not engineering or technically related. The under-representation of the foreign-born in managerial occupations parallels U.S. research that emphasizes the likely existence of a glass ceiling (Fernandez 1998; Tang 1997).

Multinomial analysis confirms the similarities in the occupational profiles of Asian-born and non–Asian-born migrants (table 4.4, columns 4 to 6). Here the analysis includes language spoken at home and major CMA residence, given that these variables were found to be significantly associated with occupational outcomes along with other variables. The results show that being born in Asian countries as opposed to being born in non-Asian countries increases the (log) likelihood of holding a non-engineering occupation (other) versus an engineering occupation. However, the likelihood of being a manager or a technical worker, compared to holding an engineering occupation, does not differ between Asian-born and non–Asian-born immigrants.

Again, probabilities are calculated from multinomial regressions. These probabilities show very similar occupational profiles for Asian-born and non–Asian-born immigrants (table 4.5). Here the example is for those living in Canada's three largest cities, with electrical engineering as a major field of study, a field that leads to "Silicon Valley"–type jobs. For those with bachelor's degrees in electrical engineering, not speaking English or French in the home slightly increases the chances of being employed in technical or other occupations. But as was true for the employment profiles, the most dramatic change in the occupational profile is associated with increased residence in Canada. The longer the duration in Canada, the higher the chances that the Asian-born and non–Asian-born alike will be employed in engineering occupations. At the same time, neither group fully "catches up" to the patterns found for Canadian-born men with engineering as a major field of study. Differences are especially pronounced with respect to managerial and other (non-engineering or non-related technical) occupations. Even among those who have resided 15 years or more in Canada and who speak English or French at home, foreign-born men—regardless of area of birth—are less likely than the Canadian-born to be employed in management occupations, and they are much more likely to be working in occupations unrelated to engineering (table 4.5, rows 1, 5, and 9).

Conclusions and Policy Implications

Overall, this study, which matches field of study to employment profiles and occupational distributions, does not find the same degree of difference between Asian and non-Asian immigrants observed in U.S. studies. Several reasons may account for such divergent findings rela-

Table 4.4

Multinomial Logit Estimates of Occupations Held by Employed Men Aged 30 to 54, with Engineering as a Major Field of Study, Bachelor's Degree or Higher, Canadian-born and Permanent Residents Arriving at Age 28+, Canada, 1996

	Canadian-Born			Foreign-Born		
	Manager versus Engineer (1)	Technical versus Engineer (2)	Other versus Engineer (3)	Manager versus Engineer (4)	Technical versus Engineer (5)	Other versus Engineer (6)
Intercept	-3.384***	-1.461***	-2.002***	-4.697***	-0.960	-3.149***
Age	0.057***	0.000	0.027***	0.072***	-0.019*	0.026***
Highest Degree						
Bachelor's	0.931***	0.469**	0.642***	1.346***	0.990***	1.935***
Master's	0.994***	0.337	0.397	0.839***	0.642***	1.070***
Ph.D.	(rg)	(rg)	(rg)	(rg)	(rg)	(rg)
Specialization						
Electrical	-0.429***	0.089	-0.847***	-0.630***	0.126	-0.448***
Mechanical	-0.151**	-0.490***	-0.455***	-0.501***	-0.372**	-0.134
Civil	-0.124*	-0.349***	-0.530***	-0.011	-0.190	-0.002
Chemical	-0.085	-0.411***	-0.274**	0.005	-0.378	0.242
Other	(rg)	(rg)	(rg)	(rg)	(rg)	(rg)

continued

Table 4.4 continued

Place of Residence					
Montreal, Toronto, Vancouver	(rg)	(rg)	(rg)	(rg)	(rg)	(rg)
Other	-0.076	-0.152**	-0.157**	-0.329***	-0.151	-0.381***
Years in Canada						
2-4				0.471**	0.514**	0.927***
5-9				0.533***	0.310*	0.888***
10-14				0.264	0.174	0.469***
15+				(rg)	(rg)	(rg)
Official Language(s) Spoken at Home						
Yes				(rg)	(rg)	(rg)
No				-0.810	0.229*	0.184*
Region of Birth						
Asia				0.040	0.107	0.227**
Other				(rg)	(rg)	(rg)
Parameters						
Log Likelihood	6073.0			10453.96		
Chi-square	817.98			654.18		
df	24			39		

* p<.05
** p<.01
*** p<.001
(rg) = Reference group

Table 4.5
Chances Out of 100[a] of Employment in Manager, Engineering, Technical, or All Other Occupations, for Men Age 45, with Bachelor's Degrees and Electrical Engineering as Major Field of Study, Residing in Montreal, Toronto, and Vancouver, for Canadian-born and Permanent Residents Immigrating at Age 28+, by Language Spoken at Home and Duration in Canada, 1996

Region of Birth, Language, Years in Canada	Total (1)	Occupation Group			Other (5)
		Manager (2)	Engineer (3)	Technical (4)	
Canada-born	100.0	29.1	39.9	16.2	14.8
Foreign born, speaks English/French at home					
Asian birthplace					
2-4	100.0	17.1	21.5	19.9	41.6
5-9	100.0	18.9	22.4	16.9	41.8
10-14	100.0	18.3	28.3	18.6	34.7
15+	100.0	17.6	35.5	19.6	27.2
Non-Asian birthplace					
2-4	100.0	18.4	24.2	20.1	37.3
5-9	100.0	20.4	25.2	17.0	37.4
10-14	100.0	19.5	31.4	18.5	30.6
15+	100.0	18.4	38.7	19.2	23.7
Foreign-born, speaks no English/French at home					
Asian birthplace					
2-4	100.0	14.0	19.1	22.3	44.6
5-9	100.0	15.7	20.1	19.1	45.1
10-14	100.0	15.3	25.7	21.2	37.8
15+	100.0	14.9	32.5	22.6	30.0
Non-Asian birthplace					
2-4	100.0	15.3	21.7	22.7	40.3
5-9	100.0	17.1	22.8	19.4	40.7
10-14	100.0	16.4	28.6	21.3	33.7
15+	100.0	15.7	35.7	22.3	26.3

(a) If divided by 100, data convert to probabilities.
Source: Table 4.4.

tive to American research. First, it is possible that the mix of "Asian" engineers differs in Canada and in the United States. American researchers do not always identify the specific origins of "Asian" immigrant engineers, but discussions suggest that many of them are from India, particularly when employed in high-technology firms. Second, differences may exist among North American studies with respect to sites of employment and the population under study. This chapter focuses on the employment and occupational profiles of all immigrant men who have studied engineering as their major field. Most importantly, it is not restricted only to those who are currently employed either in engineering or management occupations or in a particular geographic area such as Silicon Valley. Finally, although further study is needed to determine its accuracy, a third possible explanation for the similar occupational profiles of Asian and non-Asian immigrant men may be differences in the United States and in Canada with respect to the impacts of employer and systemic discrimination. American labor history is fraught with racial divides and racial discrimination. Unlike the United States, Canada lacked a large black population for much of its history, and it is wrong to assume that the U.S. model of race relations accurately describes Canada. At the same time, in Canada greater emphasis may be placed on having certification as a professional engineer for employment purposes, a possibility supported by statistics suggesting that a majority of those with engineering training in Canada have a P.Eng.

Despite discrepancies between this study's findings and those of American researchers concerning Asian and non-Asian immigrant engineers, there exists one finding that is common in studies on the employment of foreign-born engineers. In both Canada and the United States, foreign-born engineers as a group are less likely than native-born engineers to be in jobs that correspond to their training (Boyd and Thomas 2000; Lim, Waldinger, and Bozorgmehr 1998; Tang 1995, 1997). These results are consistent with a large number of studies that examine the economic integration of all immigrants, not just the highly skilled. Such studies frequently find that the wage gaps between comparably educated native-born and foreign-born workers are slow to narrow, usually requiring at least 10 to 15 years of residency.

Interest in the matching of foreign-born professional workers, such as engineers, to jobs is likely to persist given policy developments aimed at procuring highly skilled labor through immigration. In both the United States and Canada, recruitment of high-skilled, permanent migrants has been a growing feature of legislative changes to immigration law. During the 1990s, immigration policy changes in both countries increased the levels of high-skilled permanent residents who may be admitted. The latest development in Canada occurred on April 6,

2000, when the Canadian minister of citizenship and immigration introduced a new Immigration and Protection Act to replace the Immigration Act of 1996. Included in this new act are provisions that will move away from an occupation-based model to a model focused on flexible and transferable skills. This will be accomplished in part by assigning more weight to education and increasing the relative weight of knowing either French or English. The intent of such changes is "to attract 'the best and the brightest' to Canada" (Citizenship and Immigration Canada 2000).

Both the United States and Canada also admit skilled workers on a temporary basis. NAFTA includes a provision for the free movement of services, thereby facilitating temporary employment of non-residents in both Canada and the United States. In the United States, the numbers of H–1B visas for temporary high-skilled foreign workers was increased in 1998 and again in 2000. In Canada, new developments include a recently completed pilot project designed to facilitate the employment of spouses accompanying high-skilled principal applicants who have been granted temporary employment authorizations. Moreover, the new Immigration and Protection Act contains provisions to increase temporary highly skilled labor and to facilitate the permanent residency of recently graduated foreign students. The purpose of such changes is to strengthen Canada's economic competitiveness. This act also will expand the Temporary Worker Program by: (1) developing a more service-oriented approach designed to facilitate the entry of temporary workers; (2) creating an in-Canada landing class for temporary workers; (3) allowing recently graduated foreign students who meet the criteria for economic integration, who have a permanent job offer, and who have been working in Canada to land from within Canada; and (4) pursuing agreements with sectors and firms to identify and meet short-term labor market needs. The intent of these initiatives is to meet the immediate needs of employers faster—to expand Canada's access to the global labor market and to attract and keep the world's "best and brightest."

In both the United States and Canada, heated debates are ongoing regarding the flows of skilled migrant labor. In the United States, temporary workers are the group of concern, and the controversy focuses firmly on immigration policy. Points of debate are whether to increase the annual number of H–1B visas and whether such legislative changes should be tied to other specific immigration changes targeted at persons seeking permanent resident rights. Such changes would give permanent residency rights (green cards) to between 1 and 2 million persons by extending amnesty to migrants who entered the United States illegally before 1986 (instead of the current 1972 cutoff date) and granting green cards to immigrants fleeing civil strife in El Salvador,

Guatemala, Honduras, and Haiti (Lochhead 2000). By August 2000, it was apparent that the H–1B issue had crept into the presidential election campaign, with both the Democratic and Republican candidates seeking business and Latino electoral support with nuanced statements about the pending H–1B legislation (Lochhead 2000; Valbrun 2000).

In Canada, little concern is voiced over policy proposals intended to increase the numbers of skilled foreign-born workers, admitted either as temporary workers or as permanent residents. Instead, the inflow and outflow of high-skilled workers has become central to a debate, not about immigration policy, but about fiscal policy, especially focused on personal taxation laws (Canadian Association of University Teachers 1999; Emery 1999; Globerman 1999). Proponents who seek to reduce tax rates at higher income levels and/or to alter rules governing the treatment of stock options emphasize both the outflow of Canadian skilled labor to the United States and the difficulty of attracting highly paid foreign CEOs. Given this stance, the debate has evolved into arguments over why Canadians move to the United States, and whether immigrant inflows replace outflows. In fact, the massive input into the debate and the intensity of media coverage have generated a Web site on the issue, including articles with opposing views.[9]

Those who seek reformulation of tax laws affecting high-income earners argue the following: (1) Canadian skilled workers are leaving for the United States because taxes are too high; (2) knowledge-based firms cannot recruit the best managers because of the Canadian tax structure; (3) high-skilled immigrants do not replace those leaving, in part because many recent arrivals lack linguistic skills and strategic knowledge about Canada's economy; and (4) the existing tax structure dampens employment opportunities and weakens the capacity to retain high-skilled workers (DeVoretz and Laryea 1998; Iqbal 1999; Schwanen 2000; Vanasse 2000; Watson 1999).

In contrast, critics of this stance argue that: (1) Canada's tax strategy is favorable compared to that of the United States; (2) taxes are not a major reason why Canadians leave for the United States (job opportunities in a larger market and higher salaries are the main reasons); (3) trend data do not support claims of an increased flow of Canadian graduates to the United States; and (4) the volume and characteristics of high-skilled immigration from elsewhere compensate both numerically and in skill level for outflows to the United States (Bank of Montreal 1999; Brown 2000; Frank and Belair 1999, 2000; Globerman 1999; Helliwell and Helliwell 2000; Nadeau, Whewell, and Williamson 2000; Zhao, Drew, and Murray 2000).

---

[9] See "Publicly Available Sites on Canada's Brain-Drain," under "Related Links and Reports," strategis.ic.gc.ca/sc_ecnmy/engdoc/homepage.html).

As in the United States, business interests are crucial elements in the debate. But unlike the United States, where high-technology firms lobby for legislative changes to increase inflows of knowledge workers, in Canada the objective is to restructure taxes so as to reduce tax burdens for those in higher income brackets. Questions about the labor market adjustment of skilled immigrants enter into this debate only to the extent that the results show that high-skilled inflows either replace or fail to substitute for the outflow of workers to the United States.

However, census-based studies of immigrant integration may not offer the best evidence for resolving replacement/substitution debates. In both Canada and the United States, the census does not collect information on class of admission (economic, family, or humanitarian criteria). As a result, analyses investigating the economic adaptation of highly skilled immigrants are not necessarily studies of immigrants recruited on the basis of labor market skills. This is an important point because discussions of substitutability of inflows to outflows often compare foreign-born permanent residents as a group to persons who have entered the United States[10] on temporary visas issued solely for economic reasons. Yet even among the highly skilled, permanent residents include those who entered on family reunification grounds or as refugees. Because census-based immigrant adaptation studies can include these groups, they may generate conservative conclusions, notably that specific occupational groups experience difficulties or delays in their labor market integration.

If Canadian replacement/substitution debates are to be resolved on empirical rather than ideological grounds, studies must satisfy at least two requirements. First, they should analyze the economic integration experiences over time of only those recruited explicitly for labor market needs. And second, they should compare results to similar studies in other countries, including the United States, in order to assess how exceptional or normal Canadian findings may be.

References

Alarcón, Rafael. 1999. "Recruitment Processes among Foreign-born Engineers and Scientists in Silicon Valley," *American Behavioral Scientists* 42: 1381–97.

---

[10] Among foreign born engineers aged 25 to 64, for example, one in five of the non–Asian-born men who were admitted between 1980 and 1995 with engineering occupations were admitted on humanitarian grounds, reflecting to a large extent the upheavals in Eastern Europe. Although only 2 percent of the Asian-born engineers were admitted in the humanitarian class during this period, earlier immigrants admitted in the aftermath of the Vietnam war also would have entered as refugees (unpublished tabulations from Citizenship and Immigration Canada, Landed Immigrant Data System, April 2000).

Badets, Jane, and Linda Howatson-Leo. 1999. "Recent Immigrants in the Work-force," *Canadian Social Trends* Catalogue No. 11–008.

Bank of Montreal. 1999. *Trends in Canada–US Migration: Where's the Flood?* Special Report, March 24 (also available at: www.bmo.economic/special/bdrain.html).

Bolaria, B. S. 1992. "From Immigrant Settlers to Migrant Transients: Foreign Professionals in Canada." In *Deconstructing a Nation: Immigration, Multiculturalism and Racism in 90's Canada*, edited by Victor Satzewich. Halifax: Fernwood.

Boyd, Monica. 1976. "International Migration Policies and Trends: A Comparison of Canada and the United States," *Demography* 13 (February): 73–80.

———. 1999. "Integrating Gender, Language and Visible Minority Groups." In *Immigrant Canada: Demographic, Economic and Social Challenges*, edited by Shiva Halli and Leo Driedger. Toronto: University of Toronto Press.

Boyd, Monica, John deVries, and Keith Simkin. 1994. "Language, Economic Status and Integration: Australia and Canada Compared." In *Immigration and Refugee Policy: Australia and Canada Compared*, edited by Lois Foster. Vol. 2. Melbourne: University of Melbourne Press.

Boyd, Monica, and Derrick Thomas. 2000. "Match or Mismatch? The Employment of Immigrant Engineers in Canada's Labor Force." Working Paper 00–02k. Princeton, N.J.: Princeton University, Office of Population Research, Center for Migration and Development.

Brown, Robert D. 2000. "The Impact of the U.S. on Canada's Tax Strategy," *ISUMA: Canadian Journal of Policy Research* 1 (Spring): 70–78.

Canadian Association of University Teachers. 1999. "Have We Lost Our Minds?" *CAUT Education Review* 1 (2). Also available at www.caut.ca/English/Publications.

Citizenship and Immigration Canada. 2000. "News Release: Caplan Tables New Immigration and Refugee Protection Act." 000–09. April 6.

DeVoretz, Don, and Samuel A. Laryea. 1998. *Canadian Human Capital Transfers: The USA and Beyond*. Toronto: C.D. Howe Institute.

Emery, Herb. 1999. "The Evidence vs. the Tax-Cutters." *Policy Options* (Institute for Research on Public Policy), September, pp. 25–29.

Fernandez, Marilyn. 1998. "Asian Indian Americans in the Bay Area and the Glass Ceiling," *Sociological Perspectives* 41: 119–49.

Frank, Jeff, and Eric Belair. 1999. *South of the Border: Graduates from the Class of '95 Who Moved to the United States*. Ottawa: Minister of Public Works and Government Services Canada, Catalogue Number MP 43-366/2-1999. Also available at: www.hrdc-drhc.gc.ca/arb.

———. 2000. "Are We Losing Our Best and Brightest to the U.S.?" *Canadian Journal of Policy Research (ISUMA)* 1 (Spring): 111–13. English version available at www.isuma.net/vol01n01.

Globerman, Steven. 1999. "Trade Liberalization and the Migration of Skilled Workers." Paper No. 13 (April 15), Perspectives on North American Free Trade Series. Economic Analysis and Statistics, Industry Canada. Aalso available at http://strategis.ic.gc.ca.

Helliwell, John F. 1999. *Checking the Brain Drain: Evidence and Implications*. Report prepared for the Expert Panel on Skills, Advisory Council on Science and Technology. Ottawa: Industry Canada Cat. No. c2-467/2000-7E-IN. Also available at http://acst-ccst.gc.ca/skills.

Helliwell, John F., and David F. Helliwell. 2000. "Tracking UBC Graduates: Trends and Explanations," *ISUMA: Canadian Journal of Policy Research* 1 (Spring): 101–10.

Iqbal, Mahmood. 1999. *Are We Losing Our Minds?* Report No. 250-99. Ottawa: Conference Board of Canada.

Keely, Charles B. 1971. "Effects of the Immigration Act of 1965 on Selected Population Characteristics of Immigrants to the United States," *Demography* 8: 157–69.

Liao, Tim Futing. 1994. *Interpreting Probability Models: Logit, Probit and Other Generalized Linear Models.* Thousand Oaks, Calif.: Sage.

Lim, Nelson, Roger Waldinger, and Mehdi Bozorgmehr. 1998. "The Subjective Side of the Glass Ceiling: Immigrant and Native Differences in Job Satisfaction." Paper presented at the annual meeting of the American Sociological Association, San Francisco.

Lochhead, Carolyn. 2000. "Plan to Boost Tech-Worker Visas is Victim of Election-Year Politics," *San Francisco Chronicle* (final edition), August 25.

Krikorian, Mark. 1998. "Captive Workers: A Disturbing Trend in Immigration Policy," *Immigration Review* (Center for Immigration Studies) 33(1): 4–8.

Mata, Fernando G. 1992. "The Recognition of Foreign Degrees in Canada: Context, Development and Issue Relevance." Paper presented at the conference "Migration, Human Rights and Economic Integration," Centre for Refugee Studies, York University.

———. 1994. "The Non-Accreditation of Immigrant Professionals in Canada." Paper presented at the annual meeting of the Canadian Sociology and Anthropology Association, Calgary.

———. 1999. "The Non-Accreditation of Immigrant Professionals in Canada: Societal Dimensions of the Problem." Paper presented at the conference "Shaping the Future: Qualifications Recognition in the 21st Century," Toronto.

McDade, Kathryn. 1988. "Barriers to the Recognition of the Credentials of Immigrants in Canada." Ottawa: Institute for Research on Public Policy.

Nadeau, Serge, Lori Whewell, and Shane Williamson. 2000. "La question de l'éxode des cerveaux," *ISUMA: Canadian Journal of Policy Research* 1 (Spring): 154–57. English version available at www.isuma.net/vol01n01.

Reich, Robert B. 1991. *The Work of Nations.* New York: Alfred A. Knopf.

Schwanen, Daniel. 2000. "Putting the Brain Drain in Context." C. D. Howe Institute *Commentary* No. 140. Also available at: www.cdhowe.org.

Tang, Joyce. 1993a. "Caucasians and Asians in Engineering: A Study in Occupational Mobility and Departure." In *Research in the Sociology of Organizations,* edited by Samuel B. Bacharach. Greenwich, Conn.: JAI Press, Inc.

———. 1993b. "The Career Attainment of Caucasian and Asian Engineers," *Sociological Quarterly* 34: 467–96.

———. 1995. "Differences in the Process of Self-Employment among Whites, Blacks, and Asians: The Case of Scientists and Engineers," *Sociological Perspectives* 38: 273–309.

————. 1997. "The Glass Ceiling in Science and Engineering," *Journal of Socio-Economics* 26: 383–406.

Thurow, Lester C. 1992. *Head to Head: Coming Economic Battles between Japan, Europe and America.* New York: Morrow.

Valbrun, Marjorie. 2000. "Immigration Foe's Reversal Bodes Well for Silicon Valley," *Wall Street Journal,* May 2.

Vanasse, Pierre. 2000. "After the Reduction in Personal Taxes: Is the Grass Still Greener on the Other Side?" *Viewpoint Report.* Ottawa: Conference Board of Canada.

Watson, William. 1999. "The Brain Drain Campaign," *Policy Options* (Institute for Research on Public Policy), September, pp. 3–4.

Zhao, John, Doug Drew, and T. Scott Murray. 2000. "Brain Drain and Brain Gain: The Migration of Knowledge Workers to and from Canada," *Education Quarterly Review* 6 (3): 8–35.

PART 3

TEMPORARY HIGH-SKILLED MIGRATION:
THE H–1B DEBATE IN THE UNITED STATES

5

New Dilemmas of Policy-Making in Transnational Labor Markets

Robert L. Bach

Politics has once again brought the United States to a consensus of sorts on immigration. In 1996, the politics of immigration pushed pro-immigration and anti-immigration advocates to virtual agreement on the need to recognize and embrace the "legitimacy of enforcement." Immigration expansionists found themselves in a difficult position, but they ultimately accepted the 1996 legislative changes targeting illegal immigration primarily because they saw it as a means to preserve exist-ing *legal* immigration rules. Immigration restrictionists, in contrast, saw the 1996 legislation as long overdue. Today, with the U.S. economy steaming steadily ahead, the two groups in the debate have reached another moment of reluctant agreement. Both pro- and anti-immigration forces are backing legislative reforms to increase the num-ber of highly skilled immigrant workers admitted to the United States.

At both of these historical junctures—1996 and 2000—it has been difficult to separate the "spin" from the "science." Both moments were election years; in 2000 both major political parties seemed determined to gain the high-tech sector's backing through proposals to expand the number of high-skilled immigrant workers. The parties' proposals ranged from a virtually open door to temporary high-skilled workers (advocated, ironically, by one of the authors of the 1996 anti-immigration legislation) to industry-sponsored plans that would essen-tially grant permanent U.S. residence to every foreign student graduat-ing with a computer degree from a U.S. university.

The author is solely responsible for the content and perspectives expressed in this chapter. They do not necessarily represent the views of any institution with which he is or has been associated.

Whipsawed by its own set of political pressures, the administration of President Bill Clinton deliberated far longer than congressional sponsors of immigration reform, but it finally announced its proposal for high-tech workers in May 2000. Unlike other proposals put forward, the Clinton administration's plan sought to establish a core set of principles for the recruitment and utilization of skilled immigrant labor. One objective of this approach was to provide an analytical benchmark against which other proposals could be evaluated. In particular, the administration sought to focus the debate on the labor market conditions underlying the current round of demands for immigrant workers. It sought to uncover the factors driving immigrant labor recruitment and, especially, to foster investments to train and integrate native-born and resident U.S. workers into expanding, better-paying jobs. The administration's proposal, thus, attempted to build a more comprehensive policy framework that incorporated the needs of both industry and the domestic labor supply, the latter through education and training.

The Administration's Proposal

The Clinton administration's proposal regarding the H–1B visa (the visa given to temporary, high-skilled, specialty workers) comprised four elements designed to make it more comprehensive than other legislative plans.[1] The administration's proposal shared with the others a recognition of the exceptional and specific demand for skilled workers that resulted from unprecedented sectoral growth in the computer software industry. The Clinton proposal recommended increasing employers' access to high-skilled workers from abroad by raising the annual numerical limit on H–1B visas to 200,000, substantially above the limit set in 1998 under the American Competitiveness and Workforce Improvement Act (ACWIA). The rationale for the increase in the visa limit under ACWIA (from 65,000 to 115,000) was the need to respond to the computer industry's anticipated special needs as it geared up to deal with anticipated Y2K computer bug modifications.

A second element in the administration's proposal was its emphasis on workplace standards and protections. The plan stipulated that any increase in H–1B visas had to be tied to the high-skill, technical jobs deemed vital to sustain growth in the high-tech sector, jobs that employers claimed they could not fill with native workers.[2] Moreover, the administration's proposal moved to set aside 10,000 visas annually for

---

[1] At the time of writing, Congress had just passed an H–1B.

[2] Alternate proposals sought to expand the types of jobs covered and to open the temporary visa regime to other economic sectors.

workers in higher education in order to maintain high standards of instruction, research, and training for future U.S. workers.

Third, the administration reiterated its position that any proposal to increase the number of immigrant workers should also expand investment in educating and training U.S. workers, as stipulated in the ACWIA. To date, efforts to attract U.S.–born and resident students into the booming high-tech sector have been generally unsuccessful. Minority and female students remain starkly underrepresented in math, science, and computer programming. In a study reported in *Investor's Business Daily*, for example, Jason Mahler, of the Computer and Communications Industry Association, concluded that women held only 29 percent of all technology jobs. He argued that "too few women seek education in fields that offer the best-paying jobs." The administration's H–1B proposal sought to overcome that underrepresentation by providing incentives and investments in educational and training opportunities to expand the participation of women and minorities in high-tech fields.

Fourth, the administration's proposal sought to put price back into the labor market debate. Although employer groups have campaigned aggressively for access to international labor pools, few have been willing to pay the full costs of recruiting, processing, and regaining overseas workers. Rather, the federal government has had to subsidize—directly and indirectly—corporate human resource actions through costly consular and immigration agencies. The ACWIA first established the principle that employers had to pay a modest $500 for each foreign worker hired in order to offset processing costs and to fund training opportunities for U.S. workers. The administration also created the concept of an "H–1B dependent" firm in an effort to distinguish companies that sought workers to meet special, immediate needs from employers who used imported workers for more traditional strategies of wage suppression.

The "user or training fee" introduced with the ACWIA, however, did not approximate the market price for skilled immigrant workers. It was also totally insufficient for meeting the educational needs of domestic workers. As a result, the administration revised its position in the year 2000 round of debates to raise the training fee to $2,000 for each H–1B worker. Even then, many inside and outside of the administration believed that the amount failed to meet the recruitment and market opportunity costs and that the fee should be much higher.

Beyond these four specific principles, the administration also insisted that this round of immigration reform not be limited to the narrow interests of employers in search of high-skilled technical workers. Especially as employers from outside the high-tech sector entered the legislative fray seeking access to foreign workers, the administration argued for a more comprehensive set of immigration reforms. In particular, it requested that Congress provide legislative parity for Central American immigrants who had been resident in the United States and who had not been included in legislation that permitted the adjustment to permanent status of similarly situated Nicaraguans and Cubans. The administration also pushed for technical updates to the 1996 immigration law (IIRIRA) which, by updating the so-called registry date, would help perhaps hundreds of thousands of Mexican immigrants who did not adjust their status under the 1986 Immigration Reform and Control Act.

The Characteristics of H–1B Workers

Unfortunately, no serious analyst believes that this current round of debate over the labor market demand and supply of high-skilled technology workers was well informed by careful analyses of reliable information. Throughout this debate, advocates from all sides of the issue made unsubstantiated claims about both the size and character of labor shortages and alleged impacts on domestic workers. A large part of the problem was simply the lack of information. The U.S. Immigration and Naturalization Service (INS), which has responsibility over much of the necessary information, was totally unable to produce reliable or valid counts of the visas issued. Only after analysts and statisticians inside INS formally requested from the INS commissioner an independent audit of the INS record systems did those responsible for the information systems respond. The subsequent audit found numerous flaws and errors, and in the end it could not independently validate the number of H–1B visas that had been approved.

The Department of Labor (DOL) had even less information on the labor market characteristics of the applicants, approved workers, or the employers who use them. With such grossly incomplete data, all sides of the debate could allege support for their positions without any fear of systematic evaluation. The debate, therefore, hinged on abstract and ideologically driven principles of labor market demand. No sustained debate occurred on the implications of policy changes that could result in the recruitment and permanent residence of over one million new workers and their families, and that could have significant impacts on the sectoral labor markets in which these newcomers would settle.

As part of the internal struggle over the integrity of the INS's dismal record-keeping systems, the INS Statistics Branch sent a group of its employees in the Fall of 1999 to count and record by hand a sample of H–1B applications. The sample represented all approved applications during fiscal year 1999 and served for the first time to provide an accurate demographic profile of the specialty occupation workers who were approved for H–1B non-immigrant status. The sample covered H–1B visa holders who were authorized to begin employment during the period from October 1, 1999, to February 29, 2000 (INS 2000).

In anticipation of congressional demands, the INS group collected information on several essential features of H–1B visa applicants, including their jobs, wages, nationality, and education. Not surprisingly, H–1B applicants' occupational skills were clearly concentrated in the computer industry. Data derived from each employer's petition, which contains a Labor Condition Application (LCA), include information on the occupation for which an H–1B worker is recruited. Computer-related occupations accounted for nearly 55 percent of the total of approved H–1B petitions. The second most frequent occupational group—categorized as Architecture, Engineering, and Surveying—also included computer and information systems engineers. They accounted for nearly 15 percent of total H–1B petitions. The third largest grouping was Administrative Specialization occupations. These jobs, which comprised 8.5 percent of the total, included accountants and management systems analysts.

Although the concentration of H–1B visa petitions in high-skill jobs matched popular perceptions, the educational backgrounds of the applicants were relatively modest, especially in the context of the widespread portrayal of these workers as exceptionally skilled and critical to the economy. On each LCA, the petitioning employer provides information on the recruited immigrant's U.S. or foreign educational degree. Unfortunately, in cases in which the degree was earned outside the United States, the employer makes his or her own evaluation of the equivalence of a foreign degree with a U.S.–earned credential. This practice probably introduces significant error in the reporting of educational skills. Still, according to the INS sample, employers who needed skilled workers reported that only slightly more than half (56 percent) of all H–1B workers had earned the equivalent of a U.S. bachelor's degree. Only 8 percent of the sample had earned the equivalent of a doctorate.

The lack of information on H–1B workers especially hampered the debate over the wage levels of recruited immigrants and their native-born counterparts. Industry representatives routinely argued that labor shortages were driving wages sharply upward, and that in some cases a worker could not be found at any wage. According to the INS sample, however, the average wages of H–1B workers were quite modest. Employers reported that the wages to be paid to H–1B workers averaged $50,000 a year. Nearly half of all H–1B workers were expected to earn between $40,000 and $65,000 per year. The median wage for occupational groups ranged from a low of $31,100 for religious workers to a high of $130,000 for fashion models. Among the leading occupations for H–1B workers, wages varied from $33,500 for jobs in education to $54,000 for occupations in architecture and engineering.

The INS data also showed that the average wage of H–1B workers increased the longer they stayed and worked in the United States. A comparison of H–1B workers who were petitioning for time extensions on previous employment with new H–1B workers showed that those who had been in the United States earned $13,000 more a year on average than their newer counterparts ($60,000 a year for extensions, compared with $47,000 for new petitions).

Finally, the INS sample documented that H–1B workers were highly concentrated in one particular nationality group: nearly 43 percent of H–1B petitions in the study were granted to persons born in India. This share far exceeded the number of workers admitted from China, the next leading country. Indian H–1B workers were concentrated even more disproportionately among those who remained in the United States and sought extensions to previous periods of employment. Indian workers taking up their H–1B jobs for the first time represented 37 percent of globally recruited high-skilled workers. Further, India was the nationality of 51 percent of H–1B workers seeking time extensions.

These figures contrast sharply with those released by one of the primary proponents of raising the H–1B visa limits. In a strongly worded denunciation of government efforts to regulate the immigrant labor supply, the Cato Institute, a Washington-based think tank, released figures showing a lower concentration of H–1B workers among Indian nationals and the prevalence of British immigrants as the second leading nationality in this category of imported workers. The significance of their figures will be argued for years and will undoubtedly add to the fierce controversy over the labor market impacts of immigration that has been ongoing for at least the last two decades. In the current round of debate, however, the INS figures raise substantial questions about the nature of the labor market demand for foreign workers, their use inside the United States, and the process through which a general visa category could result in a lopsided concentration of one or two nationality groups.

Labor Market Arguments

Unfortunately, the generally frantic and politically charged atmosphere of the debate over the need for additional high-skilled workers preempted any effort to focus serious discussion on the underlying labor market structures and dynamics. Overall, the debate was framed in relatively simple, if deeply rooted, mythologies about "open labor market" competition. In particular, the Cato Institute adopted a leadership role in advocating the repeal of any cap on the number of foreign workers. Citing the high demand for skilled workers in the information technology sector, the libertarian institute claimed that federal regulations were "distorting" the workings of the labor market by imposing quotas on the flow of high-skilled workers across international borders (Cato 2000).

Historically, the aggregate number of H–1B visas has not been a significant problem. Even when the H–1B visa category was capped at 65,000 a year in the Immigration Act of 1990, the limits were not reached until the U.S. economy entered a period of extraordinary growth in 1996. H–1B applicants increased dramatically at that time and reached the annual cap (for the first time) in early September 1997, one month before the end of the fiscal year's allocated limits. As a result, approximately 5,000 approved H–1B visa holders had to wait an additional month (until the beginning of the new fiscal year) before they could take up their new employment. The situation worsened in the 1998 fiscal year. The INS rolled the excess number of visas (5,000) from fiscal year 1997 into the 1998 annual limit, which resulted in the perception that the availability of new visas in fiscal year 1998 had actually been explicitly reduced. The rollover then combined with increasing demand to cause the annual cap to be reached even earlier than in the preceding year. By fiscal year 1999, the problems compounded, and the H–1B cap was reached still earlier.

In each of these years, a substantial number of visa applications went unfulfilled, and applicants became much more aware of the growing backlog in processing. Many advocates for H–1B applications drew the conclusion that the government was restricting visas at a time when demand was increasing exponentially. Under mounting pressure, especially due to the inflated demand for software programmers to help with anticipated Y2K problems, the annual cap was raised in 1998 to 115,000 for 1999 and 2000. Applicants again began filling the quota quickly, and the shortage of information technology workers showed no sign of abating. Both the U.S. Department of Labor and private industry sources estimated that roughly 300,000 computer technology–related positions would remain unfilled in future years.[3] The Cato Institute and others seized the moment to assert that the domestic labor supply alone could not meet the annual increase in demand for information technology, which they estimated to be 150,000 workers a year for the next eight years.

---

[3] According to an October 1999 report by the Computing Technology Industry Association, nearly 10 percent of IT service and support positions remain unfilled. These equal some 268,740 positions.

In this rapidly expanding economy, new labor market recruits exerted little downward pressure on wages or local employment rates. The CATO Institute argued that "fears that H–1B workers cause unemployment and depress wages are unfounded.... H–1B workers create jobs for Americans by enabling the creation of new products and spurring innovation." They also cited the relatively small number of reported violations of systematic underpayment and fraud in the program as evidence that there were few, if any, negative labor market effects. The Department of Labor had found only 134 violations from 1991 through September 1999, and only 7 were found to be intentional. "The lack of widespread violations," the Cato researchers argued, "confirms that the vast majority of H–1B workers is being paid the legally required prevailing wage or more, undercutting charges that they are driving down wages for native workers. Wages are rising fastest and unemployment rates are lowest in industries in which H–1B workers are most prevalent.... Congress should return to U.S. employers the ability to fill gaps in their workforce with qualified foreign national professionals rapidly, subject to minimal regulation, and unhampered by artificially low numerical quotas."

Notwithstanding these claims, analysts and policymakers failed to pursue the complexity of this labor market activity and ignored potentially negative consequences of the uneven distribution of H–1B workers and its irregular impacts on local labor markets. Similar situations in the past had led researchers to seek to understand the "mismatches" of jobs, skills, and workers. These mismatches occurred geographically and sectorally, and they typically had profound impacts on the distribution of opportunities among racial and ethnic minorities in the workforce. The way economic restructuring unfolded over time created periodic, temporary pools of unused and underutilized domestic workers. With time to adjust and some assistance, these temporarily misallocated groups could become sources of workers for the new companies and industrial sectors that were experiencing labor shortages.

Labor market mismatches have also repeatedly challenged national policymakers to choose between letting workers adjust on their own to labor market restructuring. In effect, the choice is between suffering periodic but short spells of unemployment and the recurring costs of job search, or facilitating and assisting workers to connect with new jobs. For most of the last two decades, interest in employment and job retraining programs dissipated, and the prevailing policy choice directed workers to find new opportunities on their own. That approach has had very little impact on changing the highly uneven and unequal access and capacities of low-skilled and less educated workers, minorities, and women. Labor market growth alone has not overcome structural dislocations and mismatches, and it may have actually exacerbated the social inequalities associated with them.

Part of the policy dilemma in these situations has been to gauge the extent to which economic expansion benefits workers and communities unevenly. The benefits of a strong economy are not limited to stock returns and retirement packages. For a strong economy to benefit everyone, wages and productivity must increase. Yet these achievements often result in labor market tightness and demands on employers to pay more to recruit their workers. However, if at precisely the time that this tightness begins to take hold (around 1996 and 1997 in this case), the government increases the supply of labor through overseas recruitment, the expected benefits of the increased opportunities, labor market competition, and investments made to help generate job growth will not be realized. Moments of aggregate economic expansion are opportunities to overcome past barriers and push for greater opportunities for those who have been historically excluded. To what extent, for example, can strategies designed to increase educational and training activities, and efforts to expand employment standards that benefit all workers, enlarge access to good jobs among welfare recipients, ethnic minorities, and students who historically have not participated in the economy at the same rates or with sufficient benefit?

Immigrant workers contribute to economic expansion and help achieve broad policy goals, but they do not do so in unfettered or totally beneficial ways. For example, the impacts of the recruitment of immigrant workers on the domestic labor supply may reshape future labor market dynamics, not just fill jobs in response to short-term demand. Just as skilled immigrant workers help to sustain economic growth and job expansion, they also occupy some of the very positions they create if, initially employed as temporary workers, they are able to adjust status to become permanent residents and employees.

In the current H–1B case, a future clash of recruited H–1B workers and newly trained and graduated U.S. workers may occur in the following manner. The INS estimates that at least 40 to 50 percent of H–1B temporary workers adjust their status to permanent legal resident, without first going home. This high adjustment rate could cut off the employment opportunities for U.S. workers, whom the nation has tried to create through training and education. The "cutoff" results from the collision of two cycles: H–1B workers are admitted for a three-year period that is routinely extended to a cumulative six-year period. At the end of six years, half of those admitted earlier stay to become permanent residents. The training and education of U.S. students or workers to fill the jobs for which H–1B workers are temporarily recruited occurs over a similar three-to-six-year time frame. As a result, just at the time that U.S. workers or students are prepared to take up the formerly "temporary" jobs, the H–1B workers-turned-permanent-residents could occupy the skilled positions. In a sense, the process allows H–1B "temporary workers" to become permanent occupants of the very jobs that the nation wants to create for U.S. workers.

The contributions of H–1B workers to aggregate economic growth and to filling absolute shortages of skilled workers may also be affected by the internal structure of the high-tech sector and, especially, the bifurcated demand for and utilization of skilled workers. Competition in the "new economy" is rooted squarely in the ability of a firm to develop a new idea and get it to the market before its competitors. Highly innovative research and development, timeliness, and specialty, if not uniqueness, are clear criteria of success. These are also the skills and characteristics that many H–1B workers provide to the new economy, and one of the reasons nearly all sides of the current debate agree that the number of visas should be greater than the 65,000 limit established in 1990.

Undoubtedly, some large global firms and many start-up high-tech firms operate at this sharply competitive frontier, at which profits and performance occur because of the ability to discover an idea and apply it first. Only a fraction of the high-technology sector, however, works on this innovative edge. Once discovered, a new idea or product is easily replicated, and the initial advantage disappears quickly. As it does, a firm's production advantages begin to reflect costs more than inventiveness, and the price of labor becomes a more crucial component. The value of most H–1B workers is to fulfill this latter, more traditional function—to moderate wage pressures and maximize organizational flexibility.

Previous labor market research has also documented the ways in which social networks organize the internal structure of labor markets to partially close, rather than open, competition for jobs. The figures presented earlier on the nationality of H–1B workers certainly raise the question of how labor market recruitment and immigration continue to produce such a disproportionate concentration of a single nationality in a particular industrial sector. India is clearly the leader in sending the highest number of skilled IT workers to the United States. Even open labor market advocates acknowledge this unusual concentration: "India is in a category all by itself," Dan Griswold, director of the Cato Institute's immigration studies, acknowledged to the India Abroad News Service.

Some observers, in an effort to defend the influx of immigrant workers in the face of persistent disadvantages for U.S. low-wage and minority workers, point to the value of imported labor to so-called niche labor markets. These niches form through a combination of skill and geographical mismatches and the social networks and other informal mechanisms that enable a particular group, usually defined by ethnicity or national origin, to dominate particular jobs or sectors. The agricultural labor market serves as a prototype of a niche labor market sector. These niches, however, have contradictory dimensions. While providing job opportunities for some, they function on principles of exclusion and privilege. They can also be exploitative in the sense that the worker encumbers obligations to the co-ethnic employer or recruiter that located and helped secure the job.

Researchers have been reluctant to focus on the potentially negative dimensions of niches because they believe such portrayals erode support for sustained immigration. Ironically, the social networks that help immigrants find employers willing to petition for them often lead to jobs that offer comparatively weak opportunities for subsequent advancement. The result is that immigrants are able to secure residency in the United States and a job, but they remain in insecure and comparatively low wage employment.

These analytical insights have become familiar in discussions and policy concerns about the domestic U.S. labor market. Yet few researchers or policymakers have applied them to the new "international labor markets" within which H–1B workers participate. Many international labor market connections have been created through explicit and highly structured government programs and specialized overseas corporate activities. The connections form what could aptly be called international "internal labor markets," built and linked across borders largely through protected collaboration of private industry and governments in both sending and receiving countries. While novel to scholars of labor markets and migration, this new reality follows similar rules—internal labor markets work by excluding competition, not by encouraging it. Just because it is "global" or "international" does not make it any more competitive or transparent or valuable.

A special feature of segmented transnational labor markets is the crucial role of middlemen, those who create and manage the connections between employers and potential foreign workers. Informally, these middlemen are often family members who, using immigration laws as guides, serve as recruiters and petitioners for relatives living abroad. In the agricultural labor market, these middlemen are the labor contractors. Smugglers and traffickers in people, who connect workers to jobs in the United States through illegal movements across borders, also work this "middle ground" extensively.

In the case of formal recruitments of professional and high-skilled specialty workers, as with H–1B visa petitioners, these middlemen often represent law firms or personnel management companies. Their value lies in their ability to work with federal immigration laws and regulations designed to manage the connections between employers and skilled workers abroad. Their work is intrinsically entrepreneurial, thriving on performing a service for clients at both the demand and supply side of the labor market.

In the policy debates on H–1B workers, this "middle sector" advocated fiercely for expansion of the visa category. Facing cutbacks in many other areas of immigration work, these labor market operatives found strong self-interest in expanding a system that required their service. As a group, and in partnership with corporate sponsors, they organized and lobbied Congress for a dramatic increase in the numerical limits on H–1B workers and a change in the residency rules to allow these recruited workers to remain in the United States virtually as long as it takes to acquire permanent residency. In doing so, their goals and actions at best ignored the interests and well-being of domestic workers. Some of these labor market intermediaries believed that H–1B jobs clearly were beyond the reach of domestic workers. Others simply had no interest in the domestic labor market because their own services were restricted to international recruitment. At worst, though, their actions functioned explicitly to the competitive disadvantage of U.S. workers and students who needed strong allies to gain training and educational investments to help move them into these opening areas of economic opportunity.

Comprehensive Labor Market Reform

The policy debate on the labor market has clearly expressed a one-sided interest in the high-skilled as opposed to low-wage sectors of the economy and workforce. Around the edges of the current H–1B debate, however, there has been an interest in expanding immigration reform beyond the specific needs of the high-tech sector. The administration's proposal to include parity for Central Americans and the registry update in the H–1B legislative package had less to do with the labor market than with overcoming past policy mistakes. Even if the legislation passed, parity and registry updates are not amnesties, as the H–1B debate has cast them, and they do little to reform inequality and injustice in the low-wage sectors of the labor market.

The H–1B debate—and the corporate sector's advocacy—has missed the link with and the responsibility for those who labor throughout their firm, not just those who write computer code. The policy debate has also downplayed the policy connections between the employment of the highly skilled with those of the unskilled. For example, Zlolniski (this volume) reports that by the mid–1990s the number of janitorial workers throughout Silicon Valley almost matched the number of computer engineers employed there. Many of these janitors were employed by the numerous, small cleaning companies operating in the informal sector, maintaining the buildings by night that H–1B workers and their counterparts inhabited by day.

Although employment of these two groups of workers looks very different, both face similar pressures within the labor market and serve comparable functions within firms. Employers of H–1B workers seek much more than a simple increase in the size of their computer workforce, as their needs are usually portrayed. They also seek employment contracts that are sufficiently conditional on market performance to maximize the firm's control over the flexibility, size, and costs of its workforce. Many supporters of H–1B workers also persist in promoting the fiction that these workers are only temporarily resident in the United States and, therefore, do not need the advantages and protections that would otherwise be available to established workers in skilled jobs.

The juxtaposition of H–1B reforms at the end of the 1990s with the crackdown on illegal immigration through the middle of the decade highlights how vastly different policies shape the insertion of foreign workers into the U.S. labor market. Despite different motivations, government actions have used immigration policies to weaken the position of domestic labor in general and minority workers in particular. They have undermined strategies that high- and low-wage workers alike use to gain opportunities and economic advancement. The government's H–1B policy interventions undercut—or at the very least redirected—attention from the dramatic need to improve employment and training opportunities for low-wage and less skilled U.S. workers and students. At the low-wage end, stepped-up enforcement of immigration laws increasingly undercut—or was perceived to have undercut—the rights and bargaining positions of all low-wage workers.

Concern over the impacts of immigration policies on the domestic labor force has motivated organized labor to oppose recruitment of foreign workers in general and, especially, to call for broad reforms of prevailing enforcement practices and a general amnesty for those working illegally in the United States. On February 16, 2000, the AFL–CIO Executive Council issued a statement that argued that the "current system of immigration enforcement is broken and needs to be fixed." The Executive Council alleged that current efforts to improve immigration enforcement had failed to stop the flow of undocumented workers and had resulted in a system of worksite actions that caused discrimination and left unpunished unscrupulous employers who exploited undocumented workers. Such actions, they argued, denied labor rights to all workers. The Council specifically cited the INS enforcement actions against hotel workers at the Holiday Inn Express in Minneapolis as an example of these recurring problems.

For much of the 1990s, various proposals for a general amnesty had been met with skepticism and opposition. The primary reason was a continuing, widespread disbelief in the impact that an amnesty would have on illegal immigration. Most observers believed that amnesties simply reinforced and entrenched the structural features of the illegal flow.

The potential value of the AFL–CIO call for a new amnesty is that it has less to do with immigration per se than with changing employment practices throughout the low-wage labor market. Debate over a new round of amnesty will have more to do with the bargaining power of employers and employees than with aggregate labor shortages. An initial step toward that debate would involve clearing away complicating and confusing policy issues, such as resolving the status of individuals who have been in an ambiguous position because of previous U.S. policies and programs. These include the Central Americans covered in the administration's proposal, nearly 300,000 Salvadorans and Guatemalans, and approximately 750,000 persons who could benefit from an updated registry date.

The more comprehensive labor market reform would focus on a new general amnesty, starting at a specific eligibility date in the late 1990s. For example, a reasonable eligibility date for amnesty would be January 1, 1996. The date matches the parity cutoff of December 31, 1995, for the Central Americans and reinforces the "FIX-IT 96" campaign, which tries to highlight changes in the 1996 legislation as the core reform targets. The difference between the current year (2000) and cutoff (1996) dates also matches the difference in the dates used in the 1986 legalization program (the cutoff date for eligibility was 1982).

The INS estimates that if an amnesty began in 2000, approximately 3.5 million persons were residing illegally in the United States who had entered the country before January 1, 1996. This amount is roughly the same population size that existed at the time of the 1986 legalization program. At least a third of this current pool of illegal residents belong to groups that would be covered by the parity and updated registry reforms, which have already been proposed and widely accepted. A new general labor market amnesty, therefore, would potentially add 2.5 million persons to the list of covered workers.

Although lessons from the 1986 legalization program should not be drawn uncritically, two dimensions of that earlier experience suggest that these estimates significantly overstate the number of people who would actually apply under a new amnesty program. A third of the people that the INS believed were eligible for the 1986 program did not step forward. In addition, if there had been no Special Agricultural Worker Program, which many believe was rife with fraud, the INS estimates that the number of legalization applicants would have been closer to 2 million than the 2.8 million that signed up. A more realistic estimate of the size of the population that would adjust under a new program, therefore, may be closer to 1.6 million.

Of course, the total number of persons affected by a legalization program is not limited to the applicants. As the 1986 program demonstrated, legalization leads over time to increased applications for family reunification, either directly through existing procedures (such as naturalization) or through special programs (for example, the Family Fairness legislation). The number of potential follow-on family members is difficult to estimate without knowing the social composition of the legalizing population and the cutoff date. Presumably, however, a significant share of these family members would already be living in the United States and would not represent additional new entrants to the labor force.

The number of potential legalized workers only reinforces the scale and pervasiveness of the labor market issue. Much more important would be systemic changes in labor market enforcement practices, through either immigration law or labor law. The AFL–CIO Executive Council called for two major reforms: an end to employer sanctions as a nationwide policy, and criminalization of employer behavior, targeting employers who recruit undocumented workers from abroad. According to the union's view, INS enforcement of employer sanctions has served as a surrogate for employers' bargaining power, working against the interests of workers and allowing employers to manage a labor recruitment policy that relied safely on illegal recruitment.

Zlolniski (this volume) offers a good example of how enforcement policies have aided employers in restructuring janitorial services in California, led to an increasing use of Mexican and Central American workers (rather than a reduction in the use of illegal workers), and fostered a huge corporate shift toward subcontractual labor. Throughout the 1990s, according to Zlolniski, many janitors who lacked valid work authorization lost their employment when their company tried to verify their social security numbers. Union representatives claimed that the large janitorial firms used the INS and the need to check information from the Social Security Administration to maintain a high turnover rate. The general fear caused by Proposition 187 and the 1996 immigration legislation also undercut the willingness of many workers to seek better wages and benefits. The tactic prevented many undocumented workers from gaining seniority, which would have increased their wages and given them greater stability. Zlolniski writes, "[workers] lost not only their jobs, but also all of the benefits for which they had struggled so hard.... Disheartened by this outcome, workers' reaction was a mixture of disappointment, anger, and resignation.

Many believed that everything was a [company] plot to replace them with new workers at entry-level wages."

Responding to complaints about worksite problems, the INS is developing guidelines for its regional and district officers to use "discretion" in worksite enforcement activities. The initiative is long overdue, but it also could be counterproductive. INS officials, who have long exercised enforcement discretion, could use these guidelines to help prevent local employers from drawing them into workplace organizing activities. Yet without structural reform, workers will remain dependent on the discretion of the same law enforcement officials who have been part of previous episodes. Rather than receiving a reaffirmation of discretionary authority, workers need clear rules and tight regulations that protect their rights and interests in the workplace.

Moving Forward

A progressive policy agenda needs to take advantage of periods of economic expansion to advance the goals of middle- and low-income workers and their families. These efforts include increasing access to opportunities that previously were foreclosed, expanding standards and protections embodied in the social wage, and establishing institutional rules and relationships that underwrite labor market practices. These advancements are especially crucial to solidifying wage gains that suffer from huge pressures when the economy slows, labor becomes a target, and immigrants become scapegoats, as was the case only a few years ago. Frenzied Washington policy debates about immigration, however, obscure the fundamental features of the connection with the labor market. They reduce the debate to simplistic, yet politically incisive, notions of "pro" and "anti" immigration. As one immigration advocate recently said, "If you don't agree with me, you simply don't like immigrants."

The current H–1B debate is a clear example of this misdirected controversy. It has not focused on the principles and possibilities of the U.S. or global labor markets. In a year of political horse-trading, the underlying values of economic and labor market policies have been lost. George Soros recently drew a similar conclusion upon withdrawing his hedge fund from the marketplace. He argued then that price as an underlying measure of value had been eliminated from the stock market and could no longer serve as a gauge of economic trends. The four- or five-year period of exceptional growth that has produced the current H–1B debate is no less an unpredictable gauge of the direction of labor market developments. It is a period of high risk for the labor market and, especially, for middle- and low-income workers in the United States.

The rush to import large numbers of new temporary workers may be, as Alan Greenspan has said, necessary to moderate inflation and to sustain growth in the short run. What Mr. Greenspan has not admitted, however, is that when the structural parameters of this new economy moderate, as the Federal Reserve Bank itself is trying to achieve, additional workers may no longer be needed. Who, then, will defend the temporary immigrant worker or the restructured U.S. worker?

References

Cato Institute. 2000. "The H–1B Straitjacket: Why Congress Should Repeal the Cap on Foreign-Born Highly Skilled Workers." Washington, D.C.: The Institute.

INS (U.S. Immigration and Naturalization Service). 2000. "Characteristics of Specialty Occupation Workers (H–1B): October 1999 to February 2000." April 2000.

6

The Foreign Temporary Workforce and Shortages in Information Technology

B. Lindsay Lowell

Over the past decade there has been an increasing call for a greater number of well-educated, high-skilled immigrants. The business community in particular has called for immigrants who are selected for the skills that they offer, and the U.S. Congress has responded by acting, in part, upon purported domestic shortages of scientists and engineers. At first, permanent immigrants dominated the discussion, but temporary foreign workers are now getting their due, especially from the information technology (IT) sector.

This chapter focuses on the admission of the so-called temporary specialty workers, or H–1B visa holders, that dominate today's debates. These are highly skilled individuals with at least a bachelor's degree. The majority of them work in the rapidly growing information technology occupations. Immigration law places a numerical cap on H–1Bs, a cap that IT employers claim is impeding their business growth. Considering that the IT sector has experienced unusually rapid growth over the past half-dozen years, and that it contributes to over one-third of U.S. productivity, claims of worker shortages get a serious hearing. Congress has, and is once again, considering raising the numerical cap on the permitted number of H–1B visas.

As the number of visas issued was increasing during the late 1980s, Congress imposed restrictions intended to protect domestic workers.

I would like to thank the many individuals who gave their critical input to the methods and data used to estimate the H–1B population: Susan Martin, Jeffery Passel, Rick Rogers, Jay Teachman, Jackie Bednarz, Mike Hoefer, Charles Oppenheim, Bob Warren, and Eric Larson. All assumptions and interpretations are those of the author. This research was produced with a grant from the Alfred P. Sloan Foundation.

Originally, this visa category had no numerical limitations, and visa holders had few labor protections. That changed in 1990, when employers were required to attest that they would provide working conditions that protect domestic workers. A numerical cap of 65,000 new H–1Bs per year was imposed. The numerical cap was intended to dampen the escalating demand for foreign workers and to encourage internal market adjustments that are in the best long-term competitive interests of the U.S. economy (for example, increased training, better wages and working conditions, new technologies, or innovative production strategies).

The imposition of a numerical cap as a means of limiting labor market impacts was prescient insofar as demand for H–1B visas has indeed continued to grow. Today this reflects demand in the IT sector, as well as a supply of foreign-born IT graduates from U.S. colleges, the changed nature and appeal of the visa, and procedural backlogs faced by those who would prefer admission via the permanent system but find the H–1B an easier alternative (see Lowell 1999a). The IT business community claims that they face unique shortages of skilled workers, which the H–1Bs have helped to offset, but that they need access to more foreign H–1B workers to meet continuing strong demand.

This chapter describes the evolution of the H–1B visa and presents the only available estimates of the size of the H–1B working population. It also critically reviews the debate over labor shortages in the IT sector. First, it describes the historical and legislative background of the H–1B visa. It goes on to describe the occupational composition of the population. Next, the chapter presents demographic estimates and forecasts of the H–1B working population. Integral to those estimates are equally important estimates of the population adjusting to permanent status. The chapter then discusses shortages in information technology.

Historical Trends in Visa Issuances

The number of H–1 visas issued by the State Department more than doubled in the 1970s, the 1980s, and again in the 1990s (see figure 6.1).[1] Congress first set a limit to H–1B growth in the Immigration Act of 1990 (IMMACT90) by setting a cap of 65,000 which was implemented in 1992. Given the long-running increases, the surprising drop-off in numbers shown in figure 6.1 during 1993 and 1994 can be attributed to two factors. First, beginning in 1992 the IMMACT90 further separated

---

[1] It was split after 1989 into a very targeted H-1A visa (nurses only), and the main inheritor of H-1 or the H–1B visa (specialty workers). The H-1A was short lived, averaging just fewer than 7,000 visas from 1992 to 1995.

out H–1B occupations such as entertainers and models into new visa categories (mainly O and P). These classes admitted just under 20,000 individuals per year at that time. If these new visas were recombined back into the H–1B, then the decline would essentially fill in, though a flat period would remain between 1991 and 1995.

Second, the 1990 Act was passed in part because of a growing backlog for legal admissions in the permanent employment–based classes. Accordingly, the Act nearly tripled the number of such permanent slots available. In the immediate post–IMMACT90 years, many potential H–1B applicants bypassed the temporary visa and went directly to permanent resident status. This strongly demonstrates the preference that most temporary H–1B workers and their employers have for permanent visas. The number of permanent visas processed has continued to decline markedly since 1995 due to processing backlogs at the involved U.S. agencies, which divert employer and foreign worker demand from the permanent to the temporary visa.

Continued growth in the demand for the H–1B visa is due, then, to a number of factors. These include the employers' use (or not) of the permanent system, cyclical demand in growth industries, a buoyant U.S. economy, changes in the nature of global competition which creates demand for foreign workers, growth in the supply of U.S.–educated foreign students, and the self-generating nature of migrant employment networks. In lieu of a cap, it seems reasonable to speculate that the number of H–1B visas issued would have continued to grow strongly. What natural limits the market would set are unknown. After three decades of cultivation of the H–1 program, it is well integrated with and responsive to U.S. employer demand.

Legislative History and Regulations

As originally set forth in the Immigration and Nationality Act of 1952, a temporary H–1 "non-immigrant" was "an alien having a residence in a foreign country which he has no intention of abandoning (i) who is of distinguished merit and ability and who is coming temporarily to the United States to perform temporary services of an exceptional nature requiring such merit and ability." The use of words "temporarily" and "temporary" is significant, in that the alien must be coming to the United States for a limited period to perform a task that is temporary in nature. In 1970 Congress removed the word "temporary" before "services," thus enabling an H–1 worker to come temporarily and then adjust to a permanent position. The legislative history for this change indicates that Congress felt the provision as originally written was too limiting.

The Immigration Nursing Relief Act of 1989 separated registered nurses from the rest of the H–1 visa pool by setting up the new H–1A visa. The rest of the classification became H–1B. A primary requirement for obtaining an H–1A classification was the filing of an attestation by the medical facility with the U.S. Department of Labor. In this document, the medical facility attested to both facts and commitments, including a general vacancy rate for nurses, above-average salaries, training programs, incentives, and other practices designed to alleviate the nursing shortage. The H–1A classification was limited in duration, expiring in September 1995.

The Immigration Act of 1990

During the 1980s, the U.S. Immigration and Naturalization Service (INS) came under fire from organized labor and Congress for its administration of the H–1 classification. Of particular concern was the large number of H–1 non-immigrants coming to the United States to work in entry-level positions. In response to the concerns of organized labor and Congress, the INS commissioned Booz, Allen, and Hamilton (1988) to conduct a study. The report found the use of H–1 non-immigrants in entry-level and mid-level positions to be inappropriate; such workers did not possess the skills that Congress intended these visa holders to hold. At the same time, they found no adverse impact on U.S. workers, including entertainers and professionals.

Nonetheless, the legislative history of the Immigration Act of 1990 indicates that there were several issues regarding the H–1 visa classification that concerned the drafters. Of primary concern was that there was no test for qualifications, and H–1 admissions counted by the INS had increased dramatically—from 45,000 in 1981 to 78,000 in 1988. Furthermore, according to the Report of the House Committee on the Judiciary, "the erosion of definitional lines through administrative decision making has meant that little-known entertainers and their accompanying crews qualify within this category, and aliens with nothing more than a baccalaureate degree have been deemed 'distinguished.'"

In a parallel to today's debate, some observers believed that reliance on these foreign workers was excessive and that H–1 non-immigrants had an adverse impact on U.S. wages and working conditions. In short, the INS regulations for the H–1 visa "did not reflect congressional intent" (GAO 1992: 17). Thus, in early 1990, the INS issued a regulation that significantly tightened the H–1 classification by articulating standards for qualification as a professional or a person of prominence. Going further, in IMMACT90, the Congress took aliens of prominence (such as artists and entertainers) out of the H–1 category and created the new O and P classifications. The H–1A was retained, and the H–1B was restricted to aliens in specialty occupations.

Additionally, prospective employers would now be required to file labor condition applications for the H–1B with the U.S. Department of Labor as to wages and working conditions. According to the House Committee Report, this latter was to "provide a more valid test of the employer-asserted need." Congressman Bruce Morrison, chairman of the Immigration Subcommittee, noted during the floor debate that "this law perfects the rules regarding the temporary admission of workers to this country, an area that is subject to abuse, and the rules and standards are tightened for the benefit of American workers." Temporary workers may be admitted in H–1B status for the period of time required by the employer, up to a maximum initial stay of three years. The period of stay may be extended for up to three additional years, for a maximum total period of admission of six years. Admissions of H–1B non-immigrants were limited to 65,000 a year. (No numerical limits were imposed on the H–1A or the new O and P classifications.)

And while tightening up the H–1B classification in many areas, the bill recognized that many employers hired non-immigrants with a dual intent—as temporary workers initially and as potentially permanent additions to their workforce. The legislation permitted the entry of non-immigrant H–1B workers who may possess intent both to work temporarily and to immigrate permanently at some future time. The legislation, therefore, limited the duration of H–1B status to six years (an increase of one year over the prior temporary stay). At the same time, IMMACT90 removed the language in the H–1 statutory description that required that the H–1B have "a residence in a foreign country which he has no intention of abandoning." In effect, the new legislation continued the H–1B as a temporary work authorization program; yet by removing the requirement of temporary intent, the H–1B differs from other non-immigrant visas and implicitly encourages a transition to permanent residency.[2]

Pressures on the Cap and New Legislation

The 65,000 visas permitted under the 1990 Act proved to be insufficient; the numbers of H–1Bs sought by employers exceeded that cap beginning in 1997. In the closing months of 1998, the U.S. Congress passed the "American Competitiveness and Workforce Improvement

---

[2] Indeed, employers since 1970 were permitted to employ H-1 workers in jobs that were of a permanent nature, and by 1990 just over half of the employers of H-1s reported that the job was intended to continue permanently (GAO 1992).

Act" (ACWIA) which increased the number of available H–1B visas from 65,000 per year to 115,000 per year in 1999 and 2000, and to 107,500 in 2001. The numerical limit was to return to 65,000 in the year 2002. However, even this increased number has not been sufficient to accommodate both the backlogs carried over from previous fiscal years and an ever-growing demand. Available visas under the cap ran out before year's end in 1998 and 1999. By the middle of fiscal year 2000, the INS would process no new applications.

In mid–2000, with the demand for H–1B workers exceeding even the expanded cap, Congress was again lobbied to increase the H–1B allowance. Three bills were actively being considered in Congress in 2000. The various bills would have increased visa numbers by 40 to 75 percent, introduced an unlimited number of H–1 visas for foreign graduates of U.S. schools, and imposed new fees to be used to train domestic workers. In October 2000, Congress overwhelmingly passed the American Competitiveness in the Twenty-First Century Act, raising the annual H–1B visa cap to 195,000 for three years, with unlimited numbers of H–1Bs for nonprofit research institutions. President Clinton signed the bill into law shortly thereafter.

Demographic Characteristics of Specialty Workers

The characteristics of H–1 workers have changed over time. In part, these changes have to do with the legislative shifts in the type of occupations covered by the H–1/H–1B visa. However, these changes also have to do with cyclical demand within industries with unique labor needs and within the countries of origin that supply H–1 workers.

Specialty Occupations

The vast majority of aliens in the H–1/H–1B classification are aliens in specialty occupations. As defined in INA 214, a specialty occupation is one that requires a "theoretical and practical application of a body of highly specialized knowledge." The basic statutory requirements are a bachelor's degree or higher in the specialty and a full state license if such a license is required. The statute goes on to provide for equivalence of the degree through experience, in which case there also is recognition of the alien's expertise.

Unfortunately, an account of the occupations included in specialty occupations is not part of regular INS statistics. Our knowledge of the occupations actually filled by H–1Bs comes indirectly, either from the occupations reported by employers on the Department of Labor condition attestation, or from samples taken of the INS's petition information for new H–1Bs (Lowell 1999b). The Department of Labor occupations reports (as filed on the Labor Condition Attestation [LCA]) are reliable, but they do not represent the occupations of persons who actually are petitioned for and who receive H–1B visas.

Consider instead two random samples of approved INS petitions for newly admitted H–1 visa holders taken by the General Accounting Office around the time that Congress first expressed concern regarding the H–1 program, and a more recent sample of H–1B visa holders taken by the INS to meet congressional information mandates. The occupations from a representative sample of H–1s in 1989 appear in table 6.1. At that time the leading occupations were in nursing (and medical occupations), which was later incorporated into the separate H–1A stream. Those in the entertainment, movies, and television occupations were separated out after 1992 by IMMACT90 into the O visa category.

By 1999 computer-related occupations had come to dominate the flow of H–1B visa holders (see table 6.2). In fact, even if nurses and entertainers were removed from the 1989 data, the computer and related occupations would have been no greater than 20 percent of all new H–1s in that year. If we consider the core computer occupations in 1999, along with the related engineering and computer occupations, these information technology occupations comprised 57 percent of all H–1B occupations in that year. More recent INS data place 47.4 percent of all H–1B petitions in core IT occupations.

These trends cannot be followed on an industry-by-industry basis because, although we have information on industry of employer in 1989, the INS did not collect industry data for 1999. If they had, it is likely that the changes by industry would reflect those seen in the occupational statistics. For example, in 1989 education and nonprofit science industries dominated H–1 visas (23 percent), followed by hospitals and health care (18 percent) and entertainment (13 percent). As a point of comparison, a study of the top 100 users of H–1 visas in 1998 found that 80 percent of H–1B employers are in information technology industries (Lowell and Christian 2000). It appears that the H–1 visa used to be rather diverse. Since the H–1 was split into O and P visas, demand for health occupations has declined, and information technology has led U.S. economic growth. The information technology industry has come to dominate the H–1B visa as no single industry has done previously.

Countries of Origin

The shift in H–1 occupations has been accompanied by a shift in the countries from which H–1 visa holders come. Table 6.3 presents the ten

Table 6.1. H-1 Occupations for Northern and Eastern INS Regions, 1989

Occupation	Number	Percent
Nursing, health care, medical, and related	16,689	27.7
Entertainment, movies and television, modeling, and allied	9,764	16.2
Engineering, science, and related	8,813	14.6
Computers, programming, and related	6,894	11.4
Managers and executives	10,127	3.6
Marketing and sales	1,892	3.1
Finance, law, accounting, and related	1,259	2.1
Supervisors, skilled craftsmen, and technicians	541	0.9
Other occupations	1,445	2.4
Did not respond	636	1.1
Total	**60,256**	**100.0**

Source: GAO 1992, p. 33.

Table 6.2. H–1B Occupations Nationally, 1999

Occupation	Number	Percent
Occupations in systems analysis and programming	71,700	53.3
Electrical/electronics engineering	6,500	4.9
Computer-related occupations (not elsewhere classified)	4,600	3.4
Occupations in college and university education	4,000	3.0
Accountants, auditors and related	3,800	2.8
Architecture, engineering, and surveying	3,000	2.3
Other occupations	40,800	30.3
Total	**134,400**	**100.0**

Source: INS 2000.

Table 6.3. H-1 Visas Issued by Country of Origin, 1989–1999

	1989	1990	1991	1992	1993	1994	1995	1996	1997	1998	1999
India	2,144	2,697	4,102	5,552	7,606	11,301	15,528	19,203	31,686	40,247	55,047
UK	6,663	7,174	8,794	6,726	3,993	4,230	4,771	5,601	6,928	6,343	6,665
China	837	610	1,145	894	1,031	1,256	1,887	2,330	3,214	3,883	5,779
Japan	3,678	3,791	5,167	2,767	2,152	2,217	2,070	2,411	2,929	2,878	3,339
Philippines	6,055	7,302	7,221	7,550	7,596	8,753	10,026	4,601	2,685	2,758	3,065
France	2,318	2,293	2,413	1,686	870	1,003	1,216	1,463	1,894	2,110	2,633
Germany	1,798	1,637	1,888	1,501	1,012	1,092	1,484	1,518	2,088	2,242	2,451
Mexico	2,951	3,727	3,227	2,488	1,307	1,147	1,451	1,909	2,785	2,320	2,419
Australia	872	827	1,102	990	863	1,050	1,042	1,123	1,438	1,666	1,651
Russia	2,256	3,709	3,942	1,651	1,892	1,245	1,196	1,255	1,357	1,395	1,619
Total	48,820	58,673	59,325	51,667	42,206	49,284	59,093	60,072	80,608	91,378	116,695

Source: U.S. Department of State, Visa Office.

leading H–1B source countries for 1999 and the number of H–1 visas issued in that year and for the preceding decade (including H–1As from 1990 through 1995). The Philippines was the leading country of origin for H–1s from 1989 through 1992, during the period in which medical-related occupations dominated the H–1 program. The number of Filipinos peaked in 1995, at the end of the H–1A nursing program. Indian H–1Bs grew steadily from 1989 forward, to become the largest category in 1994, and then doubling in size by 1996 and quintupling by 1999—a remarkable pattern of growth, accounting for nearly half of all visas issued in 1999 (47 percent). No other country during the lifetime of the program has so completely dominated the H–1 visa classification.

The shifting national origins of the H–1 population are clearly part of the shift from an H–1 program dominated by nursing and medical-related professions (along with teaching) to a program dominated by computer-related occupations. In this regard, India has become the dominant nation almost certainly because it has a large supply of computer-trained workers and because prior waves of Indian information technology workers have successfully established a beachhead in an industry that places them first in the demand queue.[3] The information technology industry is the leading growth sector of the U.S. economy, and it is drawing on the readily available source of trained IT engineers from India.

H–1/H–1B Population Estimates

Since the H–1 visa was created in 1952, we have had a good idea of how many H–1 workers have been entering the country, but no benchmark estimate exists of the population actually working in the country at any given time. Because the administrative data do not track H–1Bs, a demographic model was constructed to estimate the resident population working in the United States.[4] The final population does not just depend on the addition of the entering cohorts over time, but it must account for the rate at which they exit the H–1 population. The entering cohorts of H–1s are depleted by emigration, death, adjustment to permanent status, and illegal overstay of the visa (for a more com-

---

[3] For example, a study of the top 100 companies employing H–1Bs in 1998 shows that 60 percent of their CEOs had South Asian surnames (Lowell and Christian 2000).

[4] Estimates by Passel and Clark (1998) are based on the Current Population Survey (CPS) and are based on imputation of H–1B/L–1 status based on likely individual characteristics. Because this is a sample of households and "usual" residents, it generates figures in the 60,000 range that are clearly too low.

plete discussion of the derivation of the population estimates, data, and the assumptions that were made to model the current and future population, see Lowell 2000).[5]

The first year for which population estimates can be generated is 1976, at which time there were 72,000 H–1 workers in the United States.

Estimates of the Workforce Population

The H–1 population grew to 82,000 in 1981, and at the outset of IM-MACT90's implementation in 1991, the population of H–1Bs is estimated to have stood at 204,000. These rates of population growth track the changes in the underlying growth of visas issued over the same period. As of 1999, the population is estimated to have grown to 360,000, drawing upon entry cohorts that increased from 49,000 to 137,000.

Forecasts of the population are given under two scenarios. First, what would have been the population under the caps of the 1998 American Competitiveness and Workforce Improvement Act (ACWIA)? And second, what will the population be if we use low estimates of H–1Bs under the American Competitiveness in the Twenty-First Century Act (ACTFCA)? The former permits a number as high as 115,000 for a three-year period, to be phased out in 2002; the latter permits a number of at least 195,000 per year, to be phased out in 2003.[6]

The estimated population for the year 2000 is about 425,000, given ACWIA levels of admission (see figure 6.2). The ACWIA population would have reached a high of 460,000 in 2001 and then began to decline as the permitted number of H–1s under the cap dropped to 65,000, reaching a stable population of around 270,000 by 2010.

What will be the size of this population now, given that the cap has been raised to 195,000? These estimates (which also appear in figure 6.2) indicate that much larger workforce populations would occur as a result. Now that the H–1B numbers will be at 195,000 for a three-year

---

[5] The discussion below will present estimates of adjustment. Mortality is set to that of average U.S. White and Asian males (the mix of H–1B visa holders) in the modal years of their stay ages 27 to 33. Emigration rates are taken from Census Bureau estimates of all foreign-born across the 1980 and 1990 censuses. The latter set of rates may well vary much more strongly over time than these fixed rates permit, decreasing over the history of the program. Nonetheless, they produce a high number of emigrants, as might be expected with temporary populations.

[6] These estimates were originally made assuming that ACTFCA was to have gone into effect during fiscal year 2000. In other words, the dates discussed for ACT-FCA should move not quite one year into the future to be accurate given the ultimate timing of its passage.

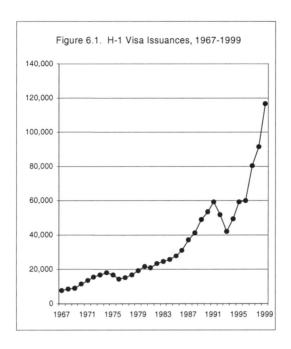

Figure 6.1. H-1 Visa Issuances, 1967-1999

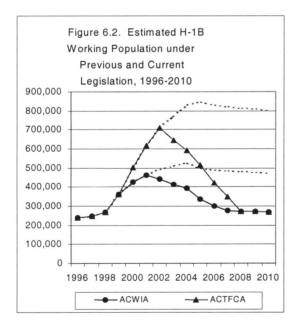

Figure 6.2. Estimated H-1B Working Population under Previous and Current Legislation, 1996-2010

period, the population will reach a high of 710,000 in 2002, after which it will decline slowly to around 270,000 by the end of the decade.

When will demand for H–1Bs decrease? Figure 6.2 demonstrates (dotted lines) the H–1B populations that would result from maintaining either the old ACWIA cap or the current ACTFCA cap into the future. These workforce populations would be just over 400,000 and 800,000, respectively. While these "what if" figures were not being actively discussed in policy debates, these forecasts show that significant and continued increases in the cap can create large H–1B workforce populations. In any event, these are rather large "temporary" populations, and the new legislation represents a substantial increase over the old cap. These levels of H–1B admissions, in turn, create pressures on the permanent admission system.

The Proportion Who Adjust to Permanent Status

We turn next to estimates of one of the main sources of "exit" from the incoming visa cohorts. Shifts from temporary to permanent status are subtracted from entrants to yield the population estimates just discussed. The H–1B workers who adjust to permanent (green card) status during their six-year stay are, obviously, no longer part of the temporary workforce. The percent of H–1Bs adjusting is a function of how many H–1Bs desire to adjust and how many are able to do so.

It can be anticipated that the proportion of H–1Bs who desire permanency has increased over time as the composition of H–1B workers has come to reflect more distant countries of origin, shifts in occupations (from occupations such as entertainers to scientists and engineers), and new expectations conditioned by a visa that supports the transition to permanency. Further, nearly one-quarter of today's H–1B labor force had changed from foreign student status (F visa) and had been in the country for many years prior to the six years permitted by the H–1B (INS 2000). This population's members have solid ties to the United States and equities that they wish to keep. It has been demonstrated that about two-thirds of foreign doctoral students express a desire to stay in the United States (Johnson and Regets 1998).[7] A nonrandom membership survey of temporary visa holders indicates that over two-thirds are in the process of adjusting to permanent status (CPAEA 2000).

---

[7] Interestingly, the 1993 National Science Foundation survey found that roughly two-thirds of doctoral students "desire to stay" and about two-thirds of these "have firm plans," yielding an actual stay rate in the low 40 percent range—which was close to the cohort adjustment rates actually observed at that time.

On the other hand, caps on the number of permanent resident slots set limitations on available adjustment opportunities, and large populations of H–1B workers will quickly exceed the numerical caps on the permanent system (notably the employment-based classes). Further limitations on adjusters have to do with the ability of the government to process the paperwork for green card approval and adjustment in a timely fashion. Today's long lead times to green card approval, in excess of the duration of stay permitted by the H–1B visa, will make it impossible for many H–1B workers who want to become permanent residents, to do so. Others will remain in a growing adjustment-of-status backlog that ACTFCA now encourages by permitting an H–1B visa holder whose green card application is pending to stay in the country until approval is granted and adjustment is final.

The cohort adjustment rates within the permitted period of stay rose from 5 percent of the entering H–1 cohort of 1972 to a high of 47 percent of the 1993 entering H–1B cohort (see figure 6.3). Estimated rates of adjustment then dip precipitously because of the long time it now takes for the government to process the paperwork required for adjustment. The longer it takes for adjustment to permanent status and the greater the size of the H–1B workforce, the fewer the number of H–1Bs who ultimately are able to adjust their status within their duration of stay.

The estimated adjustment rates dip for a period, after which forecasted rates begin to climb again (figure 6.3). Perhaps no more than one-fifth of the 1996–1998 H–1B entry cohorts adjusted within their six-year duration of stay (taking a record average of 4.6 years to adjustment). Because cohort adjustment percentages had been running more than twice as high in the three previous years, this suggests significant slowdowns in paperwork processing for green card applications. After a three-year lag, there was a forecasted resumption of adjustment rates (extrapolated from the past), reaching just over 50 percent by the end of the decade.[8] This is likely a conservative estimate of the share of those who would desire to adjust, although the numbers of potential adjusters generated by this rate of adjustment would exceed the cap on em-

---

[8] To make estimates into the future, it is assumed that the procedural backlog clears slowly over a three-year period, 2000 to 2002 (the time INS took to clear naturalization backlogs), and that by 2003 H–1Bs resume adjustment to permanent status at rates linearly extrapolated from the past. It is further assumed that no further permanent admission backlogs (caps) come into play that would, perforce, push adjustment rates back down. Thus, rates from 2003 onward are simple linear forecasts of the prevailing growth in year-to-year rates of adjustment as extrapolated from the past. If the forecast rates overstate true adjustment, then the estimated population of adjusters is overstated, but the estimated H-1 population is understated.

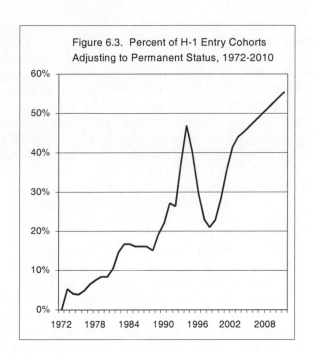

Figure 6.3. Percent of H-1 Entry Cohorts Adjusting to Permanent Status, 1972-2010

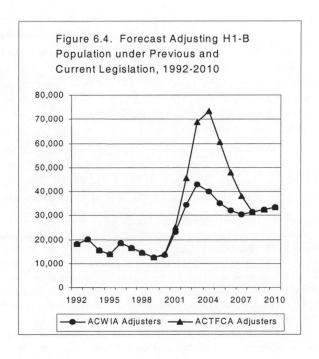

Figure 6.4. Forecast Adjusting H1-B Population under Previous and Current Legislation, 1992-2010

ployment admissions regardless of whether the old or new legislation was in effect.

The Number of "Temporary to Permanent" Adjusters

The number of adjusters in the past is known, and forecasted rates reflect the linear increase in the percentage of the H–1B labor force that desires permanent residency. The forecasted rates presume a resumption of past behaviors and an immigration system that does not impede adjustment. Applying those forecasted rates to the legislative caps on future H–1B admissions produces estimates of potential downstream adjusters. These figures can be compared to what it is believed the system will actually absorb.

Large numbers of potential adjusters are created under either of the two acts (ACWIA and ACTFCA), hitting a high of 43,000 in 2003 under the former and a high of 74,000 in 2004 under latter (see figure 6.4). The new ACTFCA cap goes on to create potential adjustment numbers that range from 22 to 85 percent above the ACWIA cap from 2004 through 2007. Once again, it is not known whether these figures will correspond to actual adjustments. That is determined by the tension between procedural time frames and ceilings created by the permanent immigration admission system. These estimates assume a braking effect due only to the speed with which a hypothetical future system actually processes H–1Bs through to green card status.

Indeed, given per-country limits and past trends, it would be likely that only about 25,000 H–1B workers would be able to adjust into the permanent system (Lowell 2000). In the first place, around 20,000 H–1B workers numbered among permanent adjusters between 1992 and 1996, when more than 100,000 employment-based immigrants were admitted yearly. Moreover, per-country caps on permanent admissions have limited possible H–1B adjusters. The nationality groups that make up the largest share of H–1Bs—Indians, Chinese, and Filipinos—have long been at their per-country maximum. But things have changed under the new legislation.

ACTFCA lifted the per-country caps, permitting unlimited numbers from any given country as long as the total employment-based cap of 140,000 is not hit in any given quarter of the year. Thus, if the processing of green card and adjustment applications occurs on a timely basis, the potential upper limit of H–1B adjusters is significantly greater than the level shown in figure 6.4. Recall that the employment cap includes principal applicants and their spouses. Thus roughly half (at most) of the 140,000 employment immigration cap are principal applicants. Of the total of "H" green card adjusters, about 60 percent are H–1B workers, and 40 percent are their spouses and families. As a conservative estimate, then, consider that if only half of the 200,000 H–1Bs wish to adjust, they and their spouses would generate about 160,000 permanent visa applicants. Clearly the H–1Bs are likely to overwhelm the permanent employment system as it is currently configured. It appears that many, if not most, of the H–1B workers who desire to adjust to permanent status will be frustrated by the realities of the immigration system.[9]

Summary of Population Estimates

The number of H–1Bs working in the United States is substantial. While "temporary" in nature, the H–1B visa permits an individual to work for up to six years. Under the new law, this allows for a labor force of well over 700,000 to be generated within a few years. If one considers the addition of tens of thousands of other working visas (O, P, selected Js and Fs), it becomes clear that any discussion that focuses exclusively on the permanent admission system misses quite a lot. This is especially the case because these estimates also demonstrate that the temporary H–1B visa is a feeder program for the permanent system.

The IT Shortage Controversy

Thus far, this chapter has described in some detail the evolution of the H–1B visa and offered hitherto unavailable estimates of the supply of the H–1B workforce. We have also established that the majority of H–1B visa holders work in information technology occupations. Of course, this will come as no surprise to observers of today's calls to increase the H–1B cap that are being led by the information technology sector, with its claims of severe labor shortages that threaten to put a "straight jacket" on economic growth (Masters and Ruthizer 2000; Spalding 2000; McLennan 2000).

The final section of this chapter evaluates that debate and, drawing upon the preceding discussion, contributes some further estimates of the role of the H–1B and the foreign-born workforce in the IT sector. The focus is on the core IT workforce that consists of computer scien-

---

[9] Lifting of the per-country limits may provide a short-term fix for nationality groups such as Indians, Filipinos and possibly the Chinese. However, the magnitude of the forecasted number of adjusters should make it evident that putting these groups first into the queue will create other problems by displacing competing nationalities and other classes of non-immigrant adjusters, to say nothing of creating expectations among future H–1Bs that may not be sustainable given current permanent admission ceilings (or resumption of per-country limits).

tists and engineers as well as computer programmers (Ellis and Lowell 1999). Core IT workers have increased from 974,000 in 1989 to 2,450,000 in 2000, for a 250 percent increase overall. What evidence supports claims of a shortage of IT labor, and how much do H–1B visa holders contribute to IT growth?

The History of Shortage Claims

For many observers of the H–1B controversy, it may seem evident that the "new economy" is being built by information technology and that the IT sector has a uniquely voracious appetite for specially trained IT experts who, naturally, are in short supply. After all, who could have imagined the full scale of the personal computer, Internet, and dot.com revolutions just a decade ago? Yet is this debate new? It is not. Warnings of dire shortages of scientists and engineers have cycled in and out of national debates regularly since the 1950s.

A "sky is falling" forecast of shortages of scientists and engineers played a major role in Congress's nearly threefold increase in the cap on employment-based permanent visas in the Immigration Act of 1990. A 1985 study by the National Science Foundation (NSF) projected a shortfall of 692,000 bachelor's degree holders in the natural sciences and engineering by 2006. It based its prognosis on demographic momentum and a declining number of 22-year-olds who, presumably, would continue to graduate at average historic rates at the same time that demand escalated (although no analysis was undertaken). The projections proved technically inept and, for the most part, wrong.

Of course, sophisticated economic models exist to forecast supply and demand, albeit the attempt remains an inherently imprecise art. These include various assumptions about exogenous changes in demand and endogenous shifts in the supply of labor and wages. An early model specifies a lag in changes in wages proportional to shortages (the gap between demand and supply; Arrow and Capron 1959). Others build in a lag parameter for supply that exhibits cyclic behavior: supply fluctuates in a "sticky" manner as if caught in a cobweb. A preliminary theoretical model of IT shortages includes a parameter for the supply of H–1B workers and specifies a dynamic wage and supply response (Radner 2000). Unfortunately, these "rough and ready" estimates generate a population of H–1Bs and average wages that are substantially greater than those observed.

Although these formal models admit to lags in supply, many economists are skeptical about claims of shortages. More precisely, they ask about shortages "at what wage" (Lerman 2000). If wages go up, supply will follow. In fact, if wages are not rising, there is a good chance that shortages do not exist. Yet there are constraints on wage increases having to do with company bottom lines and the fact that increased wages for one class of worker may spill over to others in the organization. At the same time, technology can substitute for wage labor, or labor can be outsourced. Even if employers increase wages, there are constraints on supply that have to do with time lags in training new workers or (as some observers insist) employer preferences that exclude perfectly acceptable workers (typically minorities or older workers). All of this leaves us with the question of how to establish the existence of shortages.

Job Vacancies

One way to measure the existence of a labor shortage is to ask employers about positions that are unfilled. Reports on the IT workforce issued by the Information Technology Association of America (ITAA) cite vacancy rates as evidence of serious shortages. The ITAA's first report estimated a total of 191,000 vacancies for 1996. Total core IT employment in 1996 was 1,654,000, indicating that one in every ten positions was vacant. A problem with the ITAA's findings is that they were based on a sample survey of employers that had a return rate of only 13.6 percent, rendering the results suspect due to potential response bias.

The second ITAA study was similar to the first, reporting shortages of about 340,000 workers for 1997. Response rates improved to 35.6 percent of the employers sampled, but weighted extrapolations of the data led to an estimate of well over 3.3 million core IT workers in the United States, nearly double the number counted by the Bureau of Labor Statistics (BLS) at the time. At any rate, as Lerman (2000) points out, if IT job growth runs about 10 percent, with job turnover of about 20 percent on average, while typical job vacancies take four months to fill, then the equilibrium percentage of vacancies would be about 10 percent of that which ITAA estimates suggest. Unfortunately, the sample characteristics of the ITAA 2000 vacancy estimate of 800,000 are unavailable and the reliability of the survey estimate is unknown (Crouse 2000). The definition of IT workers appears to have been broadened.

Job Growth and Graduation Rates

One of the simplest indicators of possible shortages is job growth. It is important to remember that IT is already the fastest-growing employment sector in the United States. There has been little growth in the number of computer programmers since the mid–1980s, while growth in the number of computer scientists and engineers has been strong for many years. Since 1995, the number of core IT jobs (which precisely match the positions defined by ITAA) has grown 10 percent per year—exactly the level that the ITAA vacancy figures suggest. Recent Bureau of Labor Statistics forecasts put the future growth of computer scientists and engineers at about the same rapid pace through 2008 (Braddock 1999). Computer science jobs are projected to grow 99 percent and programming jobs 30 percent, compared to 14 percent for the labor force overall.

At first glance, it appears reasonable that shortages exist because the supply of new graduates in the computer sciences has been too small in the face of this strong employment growth. Between 1987 and 1992, new computer science and engineering graduates declined in number from 51,000 to 38,000. Computer science bachelor degrees show marked declines through the mid–1990s, although master's degrees and doctorates evidenced slow but steady growth.

It appears that the educational marketplace is now responding to IT demand, and increases in new graduates are in the offing. There are reports that enrollments in computer science programs increased by about 46 percent in 1996 and 35 percent in 1997 (Lerman 2000). The Taulbee surveys, conducted by the Computing Research Association, show that the number of computer science majors effectively doubled in 1996 and 1997 (Freeman and Aspray 1999). And the end of the baby-bust effect on university enrollments generally reinforces the trend. For the first time in a decade, colleges are admitting rising numbers of high school graduates. Large numbers of future IT workers may come from two-year programs and the growing number of persons who become qualified through company or industry certification programs (Lerman 2000).

Furthermore, focusing on IT graduates misses the fact that non–IT graduates from the natural and social sciences are a significant source of IT labor (Ellis and Lowell 1999). Otherwise, a third of the people trained in IT professions would not be employed in these fields. To be sure, some of these persons work in closely allied jobs, as computer science professors or managers of IT companies (either status is counted outside the IT specialty per se). Even so, more than a quarter of a million persons with degrees in IT disciplines were not employed in such fields in 1995. Some of these individuals might be persuaded to return to the industry. And a sizable future source of IT workers will continue to be non–IT graduates who qualify for IT jobs through experience and special training.

Seeking Labor Abroad

An alternative supply of IT specialists comes from the outsourcing of work to shops in India, Russia, and elsewhere. This strategy evokes mixed reactions. Some observers are concerned that outsourcing may undermine internal labor market response, dampening incentives for domestic workers to enter the IT field. At the same time, the business community often argues that IT outsourcing cannot be done effectively, downplaying outsourcing as an effective solution to domestic shortages anyway. Businessmen go further and argue that, if forced to outsource because H–1B workers are unavailable, the United States will lose a hometown advantage and its innovative edge.

Still, the ITAA survey suggests that 16 percent of IT firms already outsource. The president of California's Regional Technology Alliance reports that 10 percent of the state's companies outsource, up from just 1 percent two years ago (Ballon 2000). And rather than offsetting the trend toward outsourcing, the supply of H–1B workers may actually facilitate that trend. A study of Indian H–1B workers and the IT industry suggests that they serve as intermediaries for U.S./Indian outsourcing. Moreover, the best and brightest Indian IT workers increasingly see advantages to staying in India, a country that is developing its own IT industry, a development that reinforces the value of outsourcing to India (Salzman and Biswas 2000).

A measure of the magnitude of growth in outsourcing IT work to foreign job shops is provided by import statistics from the Department of Commerce. The dollar value of U.S. purchases of offshore computer, data-processing, database, and other information services increased nearly eightfold in the eleven-year period between 1986 and 1997, to reach $434 million. While still a relatively small dollar figure, the growth and level of work implied is impressive when one notes that the cost of using the services of people with Ph.D. degrees in electrical engineering in India is about one-tenth the cost of hiring workers in the United States. Rather than being a bogeyman, globalization and market forces are likely to increase the use of offshore labor. Still, shortages may occur until IT enrollments generate new graduates, non–IT graduates switch fields, or outsourcing grows.

Market Indicators of Demand

Fortunately, shifts in labor demand that exceed available labor supply should be reflected in commonplace labor market indicators. The most straightforward indicators for IT were proposed by Barnow, Trutko, and Lerman (1998) and updated through a comprehensive literature review by Lerman (2000). These indicators are as follows. Trends in employment levels are indicative of escalating demand. Trends in unemployment rates are indicative of tight labor markets. And trends in wages are indicative of attempts to increase the attractiveness of unfilled jobs.

The higher-level core IT occupations—computer scientists, computer engineers, and systems analysts—grew from less than 300,000 workers in 1983 to over 1.5 million workers by the end of 1998. Growth for programmers was less rapid, but the numbers of those workers also increased during this 15–year period, from about 450,000 to over 600,000. This growth has continued; averaged over 1999, it has generated a core IT labor force of 2.1 million workers. Simply on the basis of rapid growth, there is reason to closely examine other indicators of shortages in the IT labor market.

Increased levels of unemployment suggest weak demand. Despite rates of unemployment that historically have been lower than those prevailing throughout the labor market, unemployment among experienced IT workers has been rising since 1997. The levels of unemployment are still not especially high, standing at 2.1 percent in the last quarter of 1999. Even so, the increases in joblessness undermine the conclusion that the overall growth in IT employment might be a signal of serious shortages.

Wages are the most popular indicator of shortages (at least for the short term). "Rapidly rising wages within an occupation suggest that at least a temporary imbalance exists between the labor supply and the demand" (Barnow, Trutko, and Lerman 1998: 65). The major difficulty with wage data is that nationally representative government sources show moderate wage growth, while special-purpose surveys of select populations suggest more rapid growth.

Data from the Bureau of Labor Statistics' Current Population Survey (CPS) show that, during the ten years from 1988 through 1997, changes in the earnings of core IT workers were similar to those for all professionals, and only marginally higher than those for the entire civilian labor force (Barnow et al. 1998). Since then, professionals as a whole experienced a 3.2 percent wage growth from 1997 to 1999, about the same as the 3.3 percent for programmers but exceeded by the 4.7 percent growth experienced by computer scientists and engineers. Yet data from the National Compensation Survey indicate that three out of four IT occupations experienced less wage growth than other professionals (Lerman 2000). If arguments are to rest solely on these data, there is little evidence of a shortage of IT workers.

However, private surveys evidence stronger growth than do government surveys (see Ellis and Lowell 1999; Lerman 2000). For example, the U.S. branch of the Institute of Electrical and Electronics Engineers (IEEE-USA) has conducted biennial compensation surveys of its members for over a quarter-century. The 1995, 1997, and 1999 editions of these surveys show higher wage rates and a strong salary growth of 6 percent for IT specialists. But private sources such as the IEEE include a membership with specialties in computer software or hardware that represent an elite subset of IT workers. We can expect that individuals captured in such private surveys should earn more.

Another source of difference between government and private surveys, and one often cited to dismiss the value of the government data, is the addition of irregular contributions (such as bonuses and stock options) to income. Bonuses are one of the components of the primary incomes tracked by IEEE. Since 1994, their importance as contributors to the total income of IEEE's electrical and computer engineers has risen slightly, from 3.8 to 6.4 percent of overall earnings for those employed full time in their areas of professional competence. These increases are not large enough to make bonuses a major component of overall pay. Similar findings apply to the effects of income from profit-sharing plans, which rose from 2.8 to 4.4 percent of total earnings.

Data on the impact of stock options are less easily assessed, given that the value of options fluctuates from day to day. Both the share of IEEE members who reported options and the estimated value of those awards did rise between 1996 (when 16.1 percent of these engineers and computer scientists reported options with a median value of $7,100) and 1998 (when 27.5 percent reported options with a median value of $10,000). These values were highly skewed; about 10 percent of those who got options accounted for more than 80 percent of the aggregated value of these rewards. Another 10 percent viewed their options as worthless, estimating present values of zero.

More convincing data on wage increases are for new graduates in information technology fields (Kuh 2000). Bachelor degree recipients actually experienced a fall in wages from 1989 through 1994–1995, followed by a growth in wages through 1999. Computer programmers experienced about a 9 percent increase in yearly salary (to approximately $39,000), while computer scientists and engineers experienced an increase in salary of roughly 20 percent, to about $45,000. These data reflect the greater evident demand for computer scientists and engineers which, once again, outstrips the demand for programmers. This suggests that the reason enrollments are up may be linked to the demand for new graduates, while demand has generally not driven strong wage increases on average for established workers.

The Supply of H–1B Workers

The available data lead most academics and nonpartisan observers to conclude that the evidence for across-the-board shortages is rather weak. However, the evident demand for H–1B workers is very strong, at least as gauged by increases in the number of H–1B workers being hired by the IT industry and as suggested by IT firms' persistent lobbying for an increase in (or abolishment of) a cap on their future availability. Consider a couple of different ways for evaluating the supply of H–1B workers.

The changing shares between 1994 and 2000 of IT workers who are native born versus foreign born, along with an estimate of those who are H–1B workers, appear in figure 6.5. The native-born and foreign-born shares come from the March 2000 Current Population Survey of 45,000 households nationally (the CPS first collected information on nativity beginning in 1994).[10] These figures are highly reliable.

The INS petitions data indicate a near quintupling of the share of H–1Bs in core IT occupations, from 11 percent in 1989 to 53 percent in 1999 (see tables 6.1 and 6.2). In order to estimate the share of H–1Bs in intervening years, the rate of growth in visas issued to Indian nationals was used to fit the trend in the share of all H–1Bs in IT. However crude this first approximation may be, almost all Indian H–1Bs are IT workers, and the increase in their visa numbers is strongly correlated with IT demand during the decade (see table 6.3). In turn, the known and estimated share of all H–1Bs in IT occupations is applied to the population estimates discussed above.

From 1994 to 2000, native-born IT workers fell from 90 percent of the IT labor force to just under 80 percent, while the total share of foreign-born IT workers increased to 20 percent (figure 6.5). Of course, foreign-born workers make up at least one-fifth or more of many occupations in the natural sciences and engineering. But this is a significant, almost unheard of, gain in a seven-year period. The estimate of H–1B temporary workers, who are a subset of the total foreign-born IT labor force, rises from under 3 percent to over 8 percent of all IT workers. Clearly, almost all of the growth of foreign-born workers in IT occupations can be attributed to the H–1B visa program.[11]

---

[10] Tabulations made by the author on the Census Bureau's ferret website. Note that these March estimates differ from the more typically seen 12–month CPS average estimates (Ellis and Lowell 2000).

[11] As noted in footnote 4 above, the CPS most likely undercounts H–1Bs and, in turn, underestimates the total foreign-born IT labor force. There is no way to know at this time how significant that error may be, but it is likely that it results in an understatement of the contribution of the H–1B workforce to IT labor force growth.

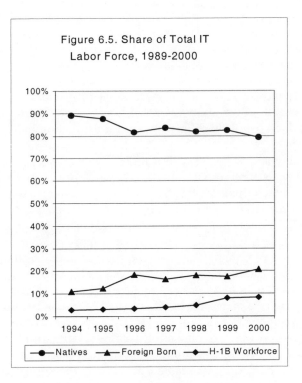

Figure 6.5. Share of Total IT Labor Force, 1989-2000

Legend: Natives, Foreign Born, H-1B Workforce

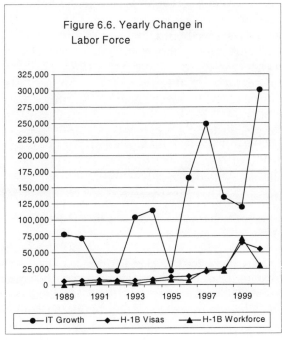

Figure 6.6. Yearly Change in Labor Force

Legend: IT Growth, H-1B Visas, H-1B Workforce

Another aspect of the supply of H–1Bs is their contribution to year-to-year growth in the IT labor force. Using the same method of estimating H–1Bs in IT occupations discussed above, figure 6.6 shows: (1) the net year-to-year growth in the size of the total IT labor force, (2) net year-to-year changes in the size of the estimated IT workforce who are H–1Bs, and (3) the estimated new visas issued to H–1Bs for use in IT occupations. Again, numerical increases in the IT labor force are known from the nationally representative CPS data. The estimated net change in the H–1B workforce and the number of new visas issued track each other closely.

The results of these comparisons indicate that there has been a two-year to four-year growth-and-bust cycle in the IT labor force over the past decade. On the other hand, the estimate of the number of new H–1B workers in IT occupations, while fluctuating in response, has been on more of an upward trend. This means that the share of new IT workers who are H–1Bs fluctuates strongly, comprising as much as half or more during down cycles and being under one-tenth during up-swings. Estimates for 1989 and 1999, dates for which the shares are known, are most reliable. At the outset of that ten-year span, H–1Bs made up between 4 and 7 percent of IT labor force growth. In 1999, following Congress's unprecedented increase in visas, the H–1Bs made up 54 to 60 percent of IT labor force growth. Over the entire ten years, the core IT occupations grew 7.4 percent on average, to which H–1Bs contributed 20 percent on average.

Summary Observations on Shortages

In short, there is no strong evidence that shortages pervade the IT labor market, and there is little evidence that H–1Bs have been hard to hire. The National Research Council (NRC), commissioned by Congress to assess shortages, reached more or less the same conclusion (NRC 2000). Nor, despite some conflicting data, did the NRC conclude that older workers are systematically pushed out of the IT labor force as younger, cheaper, and harder working individuals are preferred. Nor did the NRC conclude that IT employers systematically inflate their expectations as to the skills that new workers bring to the job, thereby creating artificial shortages.

Conclusions

The H–1B visa for temporary skilled workers has clearly come of age. In the 1970s and 1980s, the numbers of workers admitted were relatively small, and no single industry or country of origin dominated the use of the visa. That has changed. Today, use of this visa category is primarily driven by employer demand for information technology services. India and other Asian nations send the greatest numbers of H–1B visa holders. These changes were set into play by the global labor marketplace, the rapidly growing IT sector, a pool of English-speaking Indian engineers, and—despite the claims of some critics—government policies that have facilitated use of the H–1B visa.

Indeed, the H–1B visa is, with few exceptions, rather easy to obtain. The labor attestation requirement is easy to meet, and despite recent slowdowns in processing, the time needed to procure the visa is relatively short. Furthermore, legislation has created a temporary visa that most observers would hesitate to call "temporary." The visa holders can stay in the United States for up to six years, and they and their employer are led to expect that they may stay on as legal permanent residents. While not a focus of this chapter, this set of expectations can lead to problems when H–1B workers confront a permanent admission system that takes four to six years for visa approval, to say nothing of the fact that caps on permanent admissions will exclude most H–1B applicants (Lowell 2000). In other words, evaluating the H–1B visa within the context of the entire U.S. immigration system as it is currently configured should lead one to conclude that the system will malfunction in the future.

As far as the critical question of market performance, the reality of absolute shortages is questionable; yet it should be clear that H–1B workers are truly major players in the growth of the IT labor force. In fact, and despite the claims of IT lobbyists, the evidence of across-the-board shortages of IT workers is highly questionable, for two reasons. First, data on wages do not suggest shortages. Second, the market appears to be rebounding as enrollments, as well as domestic or outsourced supplies, may be starting to pick up the slack. But this is not to say that employers are completely wrong. Indeed, as the National Research Council concluded, the rapid growth of the IT sector places unique demands on particular segments of the IT industry, especially for uniquely skilled workers (NRC 2000). Until the number of new IT graduates begins to rise, there is one way in which the demand for foreign workers remains clear: over one-third of native-born workers in core IT occupations do not even have a college degree, while 40 percent of foreign-born IT workers hold a master's degree or doctorate (compared to just one-seventh of natives; Ellis and Lowell 2000). Indeed, 40 percent of H–1B workers also hold a master's degree or better. With escalating demand, highly educated H–1B workers are a quick solution to production bottlenecks at the upper end.

A generous number of H–1B admissions clearly seems to be in order, but an expansionary program of H–1B admissions does not. Minority workers who are under-represented in IT have already demonstrated their opposition to continued expansion of the H–1B cap. An expansionary regime of H–1B admissions threatens to hold down opportunities for domestic labor, and, equally important, it will create admission problems in the permanent system. The data presented here indicate that, at current levels, the H–1B already provides a significant source of year-to-year increases in the IT workforce. Generosity should be tempered by a concern that domestic labor get its due, considering that the 3 to 4 percent increase in wages of IT workers in the past couple of years is dwarfed by the 8 percent increase in lawyers' wages. A generous but non-expansionary cap on H–1Bs provides an incentive for domestic industries to reach out to domestic labor, as well as to actively implement tomorrow's competitive solutions using the innovations for which IT is well known, through advances in technology, human resources, and capital investment.

References

Arrow, K. J., and W. M. Capron. 1959. "Dynamic Shortages and Price Rises: The Engineer-Scientist Case," *Quarterly Journal of Economics*, May, pp. 292–308.

Ballon, Marc. 2000. "U.S. High-Tech Jobs Going Abroad," *Los Angeles Times*, April 24.

Barnow, Burt, John Trutko, and Robert Lerman. 1998. "Skill Mismatches and Worker Shortages: The Problem and Appropriate Responses." Final report to the Office of the Assistant Secretary for Policy, U.S. Department of Labor. Washington, D.C.: The Urban Institute.

Booz, Allen, and Hamilton, Inc. 1988. *Characteristics and Labor Market Impact of Persons Admitted under the H–1 Program*. Bethesda, Md., June.

Braddock, Douglas. 1999. "Occupational Employment Projections to 2008," *Monthly Labor Review*, November, pp. 51–77.

CPAEA (Chinese Professionals and Entrepreneurs Association). 2000. Member Survey, at http://cpaea.org/immigration/index.asp.

Crouse, Douglass. "Competition from Abroad Increasing Visas for High-Tech Workers Criticized," *Bergen Record*, May 2.

Ellis, Richard, and B. Lindsay Lowell. 1999. *The IT Workforce Project*, United Engineering Foundation, at http://www.uefoundation.org.

Endelman, Gary E., and Robert F. Loughran. 1993. "The Reality of Reliance: Immigration and Technology in the Age of Global Competition," *Immigration Briefings* No. 93-7.

Freeman, M., and William Aspray. 1999. "The Supply of Information Technology Workers in the United States." Washington, D.C.: Computing Research Association.

GAO (U.S. General Accounting Office). 1992. *Immigration and the Labor Market: Nonimmigrant Alien Workers in the United States*. GAO/PEMD-92-17. Washington, D.C.

INS (U.S. Immigration and Naturalization Service). 2000. "Characteristics of Specialty Occupation Workers (H–1B)." Washington, D.C., February.

Johnson, Jean M., and Mark C. Regets. 1998. "International Mobility of Scientists and Engineers to the United States—Brain Drain or Brain Circulation?" National Science Foundation, *SRS Issues Brief*, September 23.

Kuh, Charlotte V. 2000. "Information Technology Workers in the Knowledge-Based Economy." In *Building a Workforce for the Information Economy*. Washington, D.C.: National Academy Press.

Lerman, Robert. 2000. "Information Technology Workers and the U.S. Labor Market: A Review and Analysis of Recent Studies." In *Building a Workforce for the Information Economy*. Washington, D.C.: National Academy Press.

Lowell, B. Lindsay. 1999a. "Skilled Temporary and Permanent Immigration to the United States." In Research on Immigration and Integration in the Metropolis, at http://riim.metropolis.globalx.net/ Virtual%20Library/ 1999/wp99S2.pdf, January.

———.1999b. "Foreign-Origin Persons in the U.S. Information Technology Workforce." Report III of the IT Workforce Data Project, at www. uefoundation.org, March.

———. 2000. "H–1B Temporary Workers: Estimating the Population." A Report for the Institute of Electrical and Electronic Engineers, at http://www.ieeeusa.org/grassroots/ immreform/h1breport.pdf.

Lowell, B. Lindsay, and Bryan Christian. 2000. "The Characteristics of Employers of H–1Bs." Institute for the Study of International Migration, Georgetown University.

Masters, Suzette Brooks, and Ted Ruthizer. 2000. "The H–1B Straightjacket: Why Congress Should Repeal the Cap on Foreign-Born Highly Skilled Workers." CATO Institute Trade Briefing Paper No. 7.

McLennan, Kenneth. 2000. "Skills Shortages: Is the Solution Reforming the Immigration, H–1B, and Employment-Based Visa Programs?" *Policy Review Manufacturers' Alliance*, PR-148.

NRC (National Research Council). 2000. *Building a Workforce for the Information Economy*. Washington, D.C.: National Academy Press.

Passel, Jeffrey S., and Rebecca L. Clark. 1998. "Immigrants in New York: Their Legal Status, Incomes, and Taxes." Washington, D.C.: The Urban Institute.

Radner, Roy. 2000. "A Simple Model of Aggregate IT Labor Market Dynamics." In *Building a Workforce for the Information Economy*. Washington, D.C.: National Academy Press.

Salzman, Hal, and Radha Roy Biswas. 2000. "The Indian IT Industry and Workforce: Perspectives from the U.S." In *Building a Workforce for the Information Economy*. Washington, D.C.: National Academy Press.

Spalding, Elizabeth J. 2000. "Shortage of IT Service and Support Workers Costs America Billions Annually," CompTIA, at http://www.comptia. org/newspr.

PART 4

IMMIGRANT ENTREPRENEURSHIP AND ETHNIC NICHES

7

Self-Employment and Earnings among High-Skilled Immigrants in the United States

Magnus Lofstrom

The current policy debate about immigration in the United States focuses almost entirely on high-skilled workers. The debate regarding an increase in the number of temporary visas given to high-skilled workers, particularly in the information technology (IT) sector, is not unique to the United States. In Germany, for example, the government recently approved Chancellor Gerhard Schroeder's "green card" plan. The law gives 20,000 high-skilled immigrants 5;nd-year temporary work permits in order to ease the perceived shortage of IT workers. Similar proposals of making temporary work permits more easily available for high-skilled immigrants are being advanced in Great Britain, Ireland, and even Sri Lanka.

Although the H–1B visa debate concerns only "temporary" immigration, the European experience—in particular, the German guest worker program—shows that immigrants who are given temporary work permits are very likely to stay permanently (Dustmann 1996). This means that we need to have an understanding of how these so-called temporary immigrants affect the economy in the long run. One crucial determinant is the success, or lack thereof, of immigrants in the U.S. labor market. That is, how do *high-skilled* immigrants perform in the U.S. labor market relative to high-skilled natives? No previous study in the economics of immigration literature has analyzed this issue for this group of immigrants. Instead, an implicit assumption has been made that highly educated immigrants are relatively successful, as

I am grateful to Jörgen Hansen, Mark Regets and participants at The Center for Comparative Immigration Studies conference on "The International Migration of the Highly Skilled" in San Diego and the annual meeting of the European Society for Population Economics in Bonn for helpful comments.

compared to natives, in the labor market. Furthermore, about one in five high-skilled males are self-employed in the United States. This is true for both natives and immigrants. Therefore, to get an accurate picture of the labor market performance of high-skilled immigrants, it is necessary to include the self-employed and to analyze their decision to become self-employed.

This chapter looks closely at the labor market performance of the group of immigrants currently in the United States who are most likely to resemble the inflow of immigrants under the H–1B visa—that is, high-skilled immigrants. To obtain an accurate prediction of this group's performance in the labor market, it is necessary to use a large representative sample containing detailed individual background information on variables such as education, occupation, geographic location, age, time of arrival in the United States, and earnings. The only currently available data set that satisfies these criteria for this minority group of immigrants—high-skilled immigrants—is the U.S. census.

This chapter uses data from the 1980 and 1990 U.S. censuses to show in which occupations the high-skilled immigrants work, their self-employment rates, and differences in the proportion of high-skilled immigrants by national origin group. I also construct a model of the self-employment decision, taking into account differences in socioeconomic background, occupation, regional differences in immigrant population proportions, national origin, and ethnicity. The data shows that immigrants are more likely than natives to be working in one of the high-skill occupations, but the gap between the two groups decreased in the 1980s. It also shows that high-skilled natives are more likely than high-skilled immigrants to be entrepreneurs. Self-employment rates for high-skilled immigrants appear to vary less between national origin groups than they do among immigrants overall. Higher proportions of co-nationals or co-ethnics in an area, so called "enclaves," seem to increase the probability that a highly skilled individual selects self-employment. The estimates from the self-employment decision model are used to control for self-selection into self-employment and wage/salary work in the estimated earnings functions.

The estimated earnings functions are used to generate sector-specific measures of labor market assimilation. I find that among the high-skilled, both self-employed and wage/salary immigrants are likely to reach earnings parity with natives, although the results vary somewhat between immigrant country of origin. However, earnings of self-employed immigrants appear to be higher throughout most of their work life when compared to the earnings of both wage/salary and self-employed natives. Furthermore, there appears to be very little difference in predicted earnings across national origin group of self-employed immigrants. For example, high-skilled Mexican entrepreneurs, though a small group of Mexican immigrants, are predicted to do as well as European self-employed immigrants in the U.S. labor market. The low variation in predicted earnings across country-of-origin groups is not found for wage/salary immigrants.

The chapter is organized as follows. The first of the following sections describes the data used. The next outlines and compares traits of immigrants and natives in the two sectors. This is followed by a section in which the self-employment decision model is described, and another which shows the empirical results. Earnings equations are presented next, along with age-earnings profiles. The conclusion summarizes the results of the study.

The Data

The data used in this paper are drawn from the 1980 5% A Sample and the 1990 5% Sample of the U.S. Census of Population. The study includes males between the ages of 22 and 64 who are not residing in group quarters, who are not in military service or enrolled in school, and who reported working in the year prior to the census. Given this extremely large data set, I extracted a 20 percent randomly selected subsample of native-born Americans from the 5% Sample, but kept all immigrants. Given that the 1990 census is not a random sample of the population, sampling weights were used. These were set to the appropriate constants for the 1980 Censuses. All weights were then adjusted accordingly because not all observations for natives were used.

The sample described above includes 1,320,091 observations. From this sample a subsample consisting only of individuals in high-skill occupations was created. The occupations were chosen based on the propensity of individuals in the occupation to be highly educated, where highly educated is defined to be at least a college graduate. The high-skill occupations were then grouped into eight groups: Management and Finance, Architecture, Engineering, Computer Sciences, Mathematical and Natural Sciences, Health and Medicine, Social Sciences, and Law. The average number of years of schooling for this subsample was 16.65 years in 1980 and 16.7 years in 1990. The number of observations for high-skill occupations is 106,908.

The earnings regressions in this chapter use logarithm of weekly total earnings as the dependent variable, where weekly earnings is defined to be the sum of earnings from wage/salary work and self-employment divided by reported weeks worked. This restricts the sample to include only males who reported positive earnings in the year prior to the census. Because entrepreneurs may report negative earnings and would hence be excluded from the wage regressions, I also estimated the earnings function using weekly earnings as the dependent variable. The general results that are reported here also hold for this measure of earnings. It should be noted that earnings and income reported in the census refers to year prior to the census—that is, 1979 and 1989 in this chapter. Earnings and income have been realized to 1989 dollars by using the consumer price index (CPI).

It is interesting to note that the selection process that determines who migrates or not, and hence the labor market performance of immigrants, is believed to be determined by relative conditions in the host and the source country (see for example, Borjas 1987). However, the majority of studies on immigrant performance have been done based on *ethnic* groups and not on *country of origin*. In this chapter I try to create 10 relatively homogenous groups based on countries' geographic location and cultural and economic conditions, while maintaining a large enough sample size for each group.

It should be noted that any attempt to create homogenous groups will be scarred by compromises. It is quite clear that there *are* substantial differences in characteristics such as self-employment rates and educational attainment between immigrant groups (Lofstrom 1999). If the group is defined too widely, the impact of variations in these variables may not be accurately estimated. If the group is too narrowly defined—by country, for example—the sample size will be small for some of the countries. This is particularly true when studying the sub-group of high-skilled immigrants. However, if different ethnic groups face different labor market constraints, such as discrimination, creating groups based on national origin may not be the best way to compose groups.

The national origin groups used in this chapter are Mexico, Central/South America, South East Asia, North East Asia, India/Pakistan, Europe/Canada/Australia/New Zealand, Africa, Caribbean, Cuba, and lastly all other countries of origin. Table 7.A-1 in the appendix describes the countries represented in each national group discussed in this chapter. Although immigrants are a heterogeneous group, Lofstrom (1999) shows that the national origin groups defined here are quite homogenous internally, at least in terms of educational attainment and ethnicity, and they appear to be reasonably defined groups.

Descriptive Statistics of High-Skilled Natives and Immigrants

The proportion and distribution of workers in high-skill occupations among natives and immigrants changed in the 1980s. The proportion of male natives in high-skill occupations increased from 7.3 percent in 1980 to 8.5 percent in 1990 (see table 7.1). Although the proportion of workers in high-skill occupations is higher for immigrants than natives in both census years, there appears to be a downward trend among immigrants. In 1980, 9.7 percent of immigrants worked in one of the high-skill occupations. This figure dropped to 9.2 percent in 1990. There are also more high-skilled individuals working in management and finance (a 1.5 percent increase for natives and a 2.5 percent increase for immigrants between 1980 and 1990) and law (0.7 percent natives and 0.2 percent immigrants). The most dramatic increase, not surprisingly, was in computer sciences, where the proportion of high-skilled immigrants more than doubled (from 4.1 percent to 9.1 percent). The proportion of high-skilled natives in this occupational category also increased (from 5.6 percent to 8.6 percent) but not as dramatically as for immigrants.

Self-employment rates among high-skilled natives and immigrants are substantially higher than overall self-employment rates (see table 7.2). Approximately one-fifth of all individuals in high-skill occupations are self-employed. Not surprisingly, self-employment rates vary considerably across occupational groups. Nevertheless, it appears that self-employment rates do not differ very much between immigrants and natives within occupational groups. Also, the overall self-employment rates are quite similar for immigrants and natives. However, *high-skilled* natives are more likely than high-skilled immigrants to be self-employed. The observed increase in overall self-employment rates for both immigrants and natives is due to an increase in the self-employment rates of the relatively less skilled individuals (table 7.2).

Previous studies of immigrant labor market performance have found that skill levels vary across immigrants of different countries of origin, as do self-employment rates (see, for example, Borjas 1994; Fairlie and Meyer 1996). Skill levels vary substantially across national origin groups (see table 7.3). For example, only about 1 percent of Mexican immigrants in 1990 were reported as working in a high-skill occupation, while in the same year nearly one-third of immigrants from India and Pakistan were high-skilled. Although there is large variation in the proportions of high-skilled workers between countries of origin, there is substantially less variation in self-employment rates of the high-skilled across national origin groups. According to the 1990 data, if we exclude Cubans (of whom 30 percent of the high-skilled are self-employed), self-employment rates vary from 13.7 percent for high-skilled African immigrants to 20.6 percent for the Central/South American and Middle Eastern national origin groups.

Immigrants in the United States have been found to be less successful than natives in the labor market in the 1980s (Betts and Lofstrom

Table 7.1
Proportions of Natives and Immigrants in High-Skilled Occupations, Males Ages 22-64

Occupation:	1980		1990		Change 1980-1990	
	Natives	Immigrants	Natives	Immigrants	Natives	Immigrants
High-skilled overall	7.3%	9.7%	8.5%	9.2%	1.2%	-0.5%
		Distribution of High-Skilled Occupations				
Management and finance	23.0%	16.2%	24.5%	18.7%	1.5%	2.5%
Architecture	2.4%	2.9%	2.4%	3.0%	0.0%	0.1%
Engineering	32.5%	37.8%	28.5%	34.8%	-4.0%	-3.0%
Computer sciences	5.6%	4.1%	8.6%	9.1%	3.0%	5.0%
Mathematical and natural sciences	6.5%	7.3%	6.0%	6.9%	-0.5%	-0.4%
Health and medicine	15.8%	25.9%	15.0%	21.7%	-0.8%	-4.2%
Social sciences	3.4%	2.8%	3.5%	2.6%	0.1%	-0.2%
Law	10.9%	3.0%	11.6%	3.2%	0.7%	0.2%

Source: Data drawn from 1980 and 1990 Public Use Samples of the U.S. census.
Note: Number of observations in high-skilled occupations is 106,908.

Table 7.2
Self-Employment Rates by High-Skilled Occupations, Males Ages 22-64

Occupation:	1980		1990		Change 1980-1990	
	Natives	Immigrants	Natives	Immigrants	Natives	Immigrants
All occupations	12.8%	12.5%	12.9%	13.0%	0.1%	0.5%
Less-skilled overall	12.1%	11.9%	12.2%	12.5%	0.1%	0.6%
High-skilled overall	21.0%	18.6%	20.7%	18.4%	-0.3%	-0.2%
Management and finance	14.9%	11.5%	18.3%	17.6%	3.4%	6.1%
Architecture	43.6%	32.0%	34.7%	31.3%	-8.9%	-0.7%
Engineering	3.0%	3.0%	3.6%	3.6%	0.6%	0.6%
Computer sciences	3.2%	2.8%	6.2%	5.8%	3.0%	3.0%
Mathematical and natural sciences	4.5%	3.4%	5.7%	3.7%	1.2%	0.3%
Health and medicine	57.4%	48.4%	50.6%	48.0%	-6.8%	-0.4%
Social sciences	10.0%	11.2%	19.4%	14.2%	9.4%	3.0%
Law	52.3%	49.7%	45.3%	42.5%	-7.0%	-7.2%

Source: Data drawn from the 1980 and 1990 Public Use Samples of the U.S. census.

Table 7.3
Self-Employment Rates and Proportions of Immigrants in High-Skilled Occupations by National Origin Groups, Males Ages 22-64

National Origin Group	Proportion (and sample size) in High-Skilled Occupations			Self-Employment Rates		
	1980	1990	% change, 1980-90	1980	1990	% change 1980-90
Mexico	1.0% (279)	0.9% (492)	-0.1%	24.4%	19.5%	-4.9%
Central/South America	7.0% (779)	5.3% (1,385)	-1.7%	15.6%	20.6%	1.0%
South East Asia	15.3% (1,357)	12.6% (2,496)	-2.7%	20.9%	14.6%	-6.3%
North East Asia	19.0% (1,941)	16.9% (3,296)	-2.1%	13.8%	14.7%	0.9%
India, Pakistan	42.9% (1,953)	31.4% (2,921)	-11.5%	13.5%	18.9%	5.4%
Middle East/Egypt	17.8% (776)	19.0% (1,933)	1.2%	23.1%	20.6%	-2.5%
Europe,CAN,AUS,NZ	9.6% (5,877)	11.8% (6,201)	2.2%	19.1%	20.0%	0.9%
Africa	18.0% (311)	16.5% (673)	-1.5%	17.4%	13.7%	-3.7%
Caribbean	5.1% (389)	4.7% (550)	-0.4%	15.7%	16.2%	0.5%
Cuba	7.7% (648)	7.5% (763)	-0.2%	23.3%	30.4%	1.1%
Other	8.3% (801)	5.5% (507)	-2.8%	21.3%	15.0%	-6.3%

Source: Data drawn from the 1980 and 1990 Public Use Samples of the U.S. census.

2000; Borjas 1995). Notably, the self-employed are excluded from these studies. However, my earlier work (Lofstrom 1999) includes the self-employed and finds that self-employed immigrants do better in the labor market than wage/salary immigrants, and they are also likely to reach earnings parity with self-employed natives.

The relative success of self-employed immigrants, compared to natives and wage/salary immigrants, also appears to hold for high-skilled immigrant entrepreneurs (see table 7.4). High-skilled native entrepreneurs reported 12 percent lower annual incomes than their self-employed immigrant counterparts in 1989. Wage/salary natives in high-skill occupations reported an income disadvantage of 2 percent in 1989, relative to wage/salary immigrants. Furthermore, self-employed immigrants in less-skilled occupations also reported similar, or slightly higher, income levels to those of natives in 1989. Wage/salary immigrants in the relatively less skilled occupations earned 22 percent less than natives in the same occupations.

Wage/salary and self-employed immigrants in both high-skill and less-skilled occupations displayed lower relative income, compared to natives, in 1989 than they did in 1979. It appears that the decline in immigrant labor market performance relative to natives is not unique to the less-skilled immigrants. However, the relative income decline of high-skill immigrants in the 1980s did not take place in all occupation groups (table 7.4). For example, immigrant computer scientists reported improvements in relative income in the 1980s.

The next two sections of this chapter outline a model of the self-employment decision and report the results from estimating the model using the data described above. Mean characteristics for the dependent and independent variables appear in table 7.5.

The Self-Employment Decision

This section outlines the model of a person's choice regarding whether to become self-employed or to work in the wage/salary sector, and it details the explicit assumptions made by the model. Individuals choose between participation in the wage/salary sector of the labor market and self-employment. The decision will depend on several factors that-determine expected utility in each sector. In this chapter, I assume that the utility function is a function of expected earnings, y_i^{s-e} for self-employment work and $y_i^{w/s}$ for work in the wage/salary sector, and that the function also indicates preferences for the characteristics of work in the two sectors, denoted z_i . Further, earnings in each sector will depend

Table 7.4
Total Annual Income (in $1989) and Ratio of Average Total Annual Income, Natives/Immigrants, by High-Skilled Occupations, Males Ages 22–64

	1980						1990					
	Wage/Salary			Self-Employed			Wage/Salary			Self-Employed		
Occupation:	Natives	Immigrants	Natives/ Immigrants	Natives	Immigrants	Natives/ Immigrants	Natives	Immigrants	Natives/ Immigrants	Natives	Immigrants	Natives/ Immigrants
Less-skilled overall	29,347	25,997	1.13	31,312	34,733	0.90	29,503	24,270	1.22	32,881	33,378	0.99
High-skilled overall	43,676	46,478	0.94	73,765	85,858	0.86	49,875	50,747	0.98	84,059	95,838	0.88
Management and finance	39,063	36,865	1.06	57,835	51,817	1.12	45,045	42,777	1.05	53,602	55,640	1.05
Architecture	36,950	37,570	0.98	45,018	44,983	1.00	43,171	41,531	1.04	49,863	53,886	0.93
Engineering	44,036	44,227	1.00	55,330	57,120	0.97	45,679	47,042	0.97	52,911	54,257	0.98
Computer sciences	42,089	42,698	0.99	43,677	41,364	1.06	43,531	44,271	0.98	52,730	51,561	1.02
Math and natural sciences	40,338	43,876	0.92	66,645	74,536	0.89	42,015	42,989	0.98	53,817	55,768	0.97
Health and medicine	54,441	65,135	0.84	87,007	100,471	0.87	74,387	81,457	0.91	106,134	123,225	0.86
Social sciences	43,890	50,779	0.86	57,272	55,838	1.03	45,749	51,531	0.89	67,649	58,297	1.16
Law	52,127	53,815	0.97	72,953	63,645	1.15	73,329	64,136	1.14	92,670	85,547	1.08

Source: Data drawn from the 1980 and 1990 Public Use Samples of the U.S. census.

Table 7.5

Mean Characteristics for Natives and Immigrants in High-Skilled Occupations, Males Ages 22-64

Variable	Natives	Immigrants
Self-Employed	0.208	0.185
Weeks Worked	49.52	48.90
Hours per Week	44.60	44.88
Log Weekly Wage	6.74	6.80
Age	39.49	40.04
Years of Schooling	16.59	17.32
Northeast	0.234	0.301
Midwest	0.234	0.167
West	0.222	0.301
Disability	0.034	0.015
Married	0.763	0.799
SMSA Resident	0.899	0.968
Period Effect 1980	0.447	0.389
Years Since Migration	N/A	17.33
Limited English Proficiency	N/A	0.021
Proportion of Natives of the Same Ethnicity in SMSA	0.767	N/A
Ratio of S-E earnings to W/S earnings by SMSA and Ethnicity	0.659	N/A
Proportion of Immigrants from Same Country of Origin Group in SMSA	N/A	0.010
Ratio of S-E earnings to W/S earnings by SMSA and National Origin Group	N/A	0.703
Number of Observations	71,888	35,020

Source: Data drawn from the 1980 and 1990 Public Use Samples of the U.S. census.

on a vector of observable characteristics, X_i and unobserved characteristics ε_i. Note that the characteristics z_i are assumed to affect utility but not earnings in each sector. Assuming that individuals maximize expected utility, a person will choose self-employment if the expected utility from self-employment, denoted $E(u_i^{s\text{-}e})$, is greater than the expected utility in the wage/salary sector, represented here by $E(u_i^{w/s})$. Expected utility in the two sectors can be defined as:

$$E(u_i^{w/s}) = z_i^{w/s}\lambda^{w/s} + y_i^{w/s} = z_i^{w/s}\lambda^{w/s} + X_i\beta^{w/s} + \varepsilon_i^{w/s} \tag{1}$$

$$E(u_i^{s\text{-}e}) = z_i^{s\text{-}e}\lambda^{s\text{-}e} + y_i^{s\text{-}e} = z_i^{s\text{-}e}\lambda^{s\text{-}e} + X_i\beta^{s\text{-}e} + \varepsilon_i^{s\text{-}e} \tag{2}$$

where $\varepsilon^{w/s}$ and $\varepsilon^{s\text{-}e}$ are jointly normally distributed with mean zero and variances $\sigma_{w/s}^2$ and $\sigma_{s\text{-}e}^2$. An individual chooses self-employment if:

$$I_i^* = E(u_i^{s\text{-}e}) - E(u_i^{w/s}) > 0 \tag{3}$$

Clearly the index function I_i^* is unobservable. However, from equations (1), (2) and (3) I_i^* can be defined as:

$$
\begin{aligned}
I_i^* &= E(u_i^{s\text{-}e}) - E(u_i^{w/s}) \\
&= X_i\beta^{s\text{-}e} - X_i\beta^{w/s} + z_i^{s\text{-}e}\lambda^{s\text{-}e} - z_i^{w/s}\lambda^{w/s} + \varepsilon_i^{s\text{-}e} - \varepsilon_i^{w/s} \\
&= W_i\pi + e_i
\end{aligned}
\tag{4}
$$

If we set $I=1$ if $I_i^* > 0$, if self-employment is chosen, and $I=0$ if $I_i^* \leq 0$, if the wage/salary sector is selected, then equation (4) can be seen as a probit model of sectoral choice of self-employment.

Estimating the self-employment decision in equation (4) has two main benefits. The first is that it will give us insight into the role of the different characteristics in the choice of sector. The questions that can be answered through this process are: What are the reasons for the differences in self-employment rates between immigrants and natives, and what are the roles of the factors? The second advantage is that from the probit estimates, when the instruments z_i are included in the model, the inverse Mills ratio can be calculated. This will help to correct for self-selection problems when estimating the earnings functions through use of the Heckman two-step procedure.

Estimation Results: The Self-Employment Decision

The sectoral choice—wage/salary or self-employment—that an individual makes will depend on several factors. As explained above, an individual is assumed to compare the expected utility from work in the self-employment sector to the expected utility from employment in the wage/salary sector. If this difference is positive, the individual chooses to be self-employed. The model to be estimated by probit is:

$$I_i^* = W_i \pi + e, \quad \text{where} \quad e \sim N(0,1)$$

The probability an individual chooses self-employment is:

$$\text{Prob}[I_i = 1] = \Phi(W\pi)$$, where $\Phi(\cdot)$ is the standard normal cumulative density function. The probability a person chooses the wage/salary sector is then simply:

$$\text{Prob}[I_i = 0] = 1 - \Phi(W\pi)$$

The choice of sector will likely depend on socioeconomic characteristics such as age, education, marital status, disability, and geographic location. If there are differences in the impact that any of these variables has on earnings, we would expect these variables to affect the self-employment decision. Factors that may affect the expected utility of an individual, but not an individual's earnings directly, will also influence the self-employment decision and need to be controlled for. The estimated marginal effects for different variations of the model above described are presented in table 7.6. The marginal effects are calculated based on the sample means for continuous variables and for a discrete change of indicator variables from 0 to 1.

High-skilled natives are on average about 2 percent more likely than high-skilled immigrants to be self-employed (table 7.5). To test whether this difference is due to observable socioeconomic characteristics, a model including the above discussed traits, a period effect dummy variable for 1980, and an indicator variable for immigrants was estimated. The results are presented as Model 1 in table 7.6. The estimated difference between immigrants and natives increases to 5.7 percent when these observable characteristics are taken into account. Given the estimated results suggesting that age and education affect the self-

Table 7.6

Probit Models of Self-Employment for High-Skilled Males Ages 22-64

Variable:	Model 1	Model 2	Model 3	Model 4
Immigrant	-0.0569	-0.1288	0.2876	0.2044
	(0.0023)	(0.0057)	(0.1006)	(0.0947)
Age	0.0300	0.0300	0.0335	0.0318
	(0.0011)	(0.0011)	(0.0017)	(0.0016)
Age2/100	-0.0263	-0.0264	-0.0300	-0.0289
	(0.0013)	(0.0013)	(0.0019)	(0.0018)
Years of Schooling	0.0530	0.0530	0.0519	0.0091
	(0.0006)	(0.0006)	(0.0009)	(0.0009)
Northeast	-0.0067	-0.0068	0.0049	0.0014
	(0.0036)	(0.0036)	(0.0055)	(0.0050)
Midwest	-0.0065	-0.0067	-0.0032	-0.0083
	(0.0038)	(0.0038)	(0.0057)	(0.0052)
West	0.0070	0.0068	0.0077	0.0173
	(0.0038)	(0.0038)	(0.0056)	(0.0054)
Disability	0.0206	0.0205	0.0330	0.0241
	(0.0084)	(0.0084)	(0.0130)	(0.0118)
Married	0.0188	0.0191	0.0160	0.0158
	(0.0036)	(0.0035)	(0.0051)	(0.0047)
SMSA Resident	-0.0684	-0.0682	-0.0685	-0.0389
	(0.0053)	(0.0053)	(0.0079)	(0.0072)
Period Effect 1980	0.0114	0.0134	0.0691	-0.1226
	(0.0027)	(0.0029)	(0.0574)	(0.0479)
Years since Migration		0.0064	0.0071	0.0086
		(0.0010)	(0.0011)	(0.0010)
Years since Migration2/100		-0.0030	-0.0047	-0.0086
		(0.0022)	(0.0022)	(0.0020)
Arrival Cohort Pre-1950		-0.0510	-0.0410	-0.0596
		(0.0212)	(0.0238)	(0.0168)
Arrival Cohort 1950-59		-0.0132	-0.0155	-0.0445
		(0.0196)	(0.0206)	(0.0149)
Arrival Cohort 1960-64		0.0003	-0.0051	-0.0332

Continued...

Table 7.6 continued

Variable:	Model 1	Model 2	Model 3	Model 4
		(0.0188)	(0.0192)	(0.0146)
Arrival Cohort 1965-69		0.0004	0.0126	-0.0127
		(0.0169)	(0.0182)	(0.0149)
Arrival Cohort 1970-74		0.0340	0.0580	0.0029
		(0.0170)	(0.0185)	(0.0144)
Arrival Cohort 1975-79		0.0408	0.0479	0.0106
		(0.0158)	(0.0159)	(0.0133)
Arrival Cohort 1980-84		0.0456	0.0547	0.0253
		(0.0174)	(0.0174)	(0.0154)
Limited English Proficiency			0.0915	0.0480
			(0.0248)	(0.0204)
Years of Schooling*Immigrant			-0.0109	-0.0049
			(0.0016)	(0.0011)
Proportion of Immigrants from Same			0.1901	0.0926
Country of Origin Group in SMSA			(0.0690)	(0.0507)
Proportion of Natives of the Same			0.0206	0.0318
Ethnicity in SMSA			(0.0123)	(0.0113)
Ratio of S-E earnings to W/S earnings			0.0329	0.0213
by SMSA and National Origin Group			(0.0124)	(0.0086)
Ratio of S-E earnings to W/S earnings			0.0579	0.0412
by SMSA and Ethnicity			(0.0112)	(0.0099)
Model Interacted with Immigrants and Census Year	No	No	Yes	Yes
Model Includes Controls for Country of Origin and Ethnicity	No	No	Yes	Yes
Model Includes Controls for Occupation	No	No	No	Yes
Number of Observations	106,908	106,908	105,545	105,545
Log Likelihood	-45,364	-45,310	-44,691	-38,357

Note: The table shows marginal effects and robust standard errors in parentheses.
Source: Data drawn from the 1980 and 1990 Public Use Samples of the U.S. census.

employment probability positively and the observation that immigrants in these occupations are on average older and more educated, it is not surprising that the difference between the two groups increases.

It is quite clear that there are other variables not included in Model 1 that will have an effect on an individual's self-employment decision. For example, for immigrants it is likely that the number of years in the United States and the time of arrival in this country will also influence this decision. Pooling data from the two census years allows for identification of the effect of both years since migration and arrival cohort. In other words, we can estimate differences in self-employment probabilities across cohorts controlling for years spent in the United States. Model 2 in table 7.6 shows the results when these factors are included. Interestingly, it appears that immigrants who arrived in the 1970s and early 1980s are the most likely of the high-skilled immigrants to select self-employment, holding all other traits constant. Furthermore, as expected, time spent in the United States has a positive effect on the probability of choosing self-employment.

The models discussed so far are quite restrictive in the sense that they do not allow for different effects of the observable characteristics on the self-employment decision for immigrants and natives. Furthermore, one of the reasons for estimating the probits of the self-employment decision is to derive a selection correction term for choosing self-employment—that is, to calculate the inverse Mills ratio. The objective in doing so is to reduce the possible selection bias that may arise in the estimated earnings models. The goal is to include in the probit model variables that will influence the self-employment decision, but that will not affect earnings—that is, some characteristics z_i from the self-employment decision model above. It is highly desirable, but not necessary, for the probit model to include instruments that help to predict self-employment but which do not belong directly in the earnings function. Models 3 and 4 in table 7.6 include the instruments used in this chapter and also allow for different marginal effects of the observables for immigrants and natives. In addition, these models control for any changes in the estimated parameters over the decade studied by interacting all variables with the 1980 period effect. Controls for country of origin group and ethnicity are also incorporated. Model 4 adds indicator variables for occupations. The role and the estimated results of the instruments tried in this chapter are discussed below.

The first instrument is a variable to test whether immigrants living in areas where a relatively large number of co-nationals reside—so-called enclaves—may be the reason we observe higher self-employment rates for some immigrant groups. The sociology literature commonly speaks of ethnic resources as a determinant in an individual's decision whether or not to choose self-employment (see, for example, Aldrich and Waldinger 1990; Light 1984). Examples of ethnic resources are skills or knowledge to provide services or goods to other co-ethnics or co-nationals, availability of low-wage labor, and social support networks that assist an individual in obtaining necessary start-up capital or in transferring managerial skills. Aldrich and Waldinger (1990) describe "opportunity structures" as market conditions that may favor goods or services oriented toward co-ethnics or co-nationals. Immigrants who are living in areas with relatively high proportions of co-nationals may have a comparative advantage in providing certain goods or services (food or restaurant services, for example) to their co-nationals compared to natives or other immigrants. The result, according to this theory, is higher self-employment rates among immigrants living in enclaves. To allow for the possibility that native co-ethnics may also have an advantage similar to that of immigrant co-nationals, a native ethnic enclave variable is also included in the analysis.

The enclave variables are added to Models 3 and 4 in table 7.6. The immigrant enclave variable represents the proportion of immigrants in the census year of the total population by the Standard Metropolitan Statistical Area (SMSA) and country of origin. This is calculated by adding up the number of male immigrants in the sample from a particular country in the SMSA and then dividing this by the total male population in the sample in the SMSA. For immigrants living in a non–SMSA area, the proportion is calculated based on the state's non–SMSA immigrant population. Given the definition above, it follows that the value of this variable is zero for all natives. The enclave variable for natives is calculated in the same fashion, but using the five ethnic groups: whites, blacks, Asians, Hispanics, and others. The variable is set to zero for all immigrants.

The estimated coefficients of the enclave variables are positive and significant. This indicates that immigrants' residence in an area where a greater proportion of co-nationals live increases the probability of self-employment. Model 4 shows that although the effect is significantly positive for natives as well, it is only about one-third of the effect for immigrants. The results suggest that, on average, an increase in the proportion of co-nationals in the SMSA where the immigrant resides increases the probability of choosing self-employment by about 0.1 percent. The effect for natives from an increase in the pro-portion of co-ethnics is about 0.03 percent. It appears that both immigrants and natives are positively influenced by a concentration of co-nationals and co-ethnics.

These results suggest that positive enclave effects also hold true for high-skilled individuals. That is, not only are small shops and restaurants created by the inflow of immigrants to a specific area, but high-skilled firms are positively affected as well.

It is also possible that individuals are affected by their co-nationals' and co-ethnics' success as entrepreneurs in deciding whether or not to become self-employed. To control for this possibility, two instruments measuring the ratio of self-employment earnings to wage/salary earnings are included. The first variable is calculated by dividing the average native self-employment earnings in the SMSA in a given census year by the average native wage/salary earnings in the same SMSA, by natives' ethnicity. The second variable measures the same ratio, but for immigrants by SMSA and national origin group. The latter variable is set to zero for all natives, and the former is set to zero for all immigrants. It is expected that higher self-employment earnings to wage/salary earnings ratios are associated with higher self-employment rates, given a set of individual characteristics, since it essentially measures the relative success of the self-employed in the area.[1] The signs of both of the estimated coefficients are positive, as expected, and significant. However, the impact of a change in the earnings ratio on the probability of self-employment appears to be stronger for natives than immigrants.

Light (1984) argues that differences in traditions of commerce among immigrants from different countries help explain differences in self-employment rates among immigrants in the United States. This may be one of the reasons for variations in self-employment rates over countries of origin that is not captured by the observable traits in the model. Also, if immigrants experience discrimination in the labor market and if discrimination varies over source countries, this needs to be controlled for in the model. To attempt to incorporate these country-specific unobservables, dummy variables for the national origin groups are included in Models 3 and 4. The estimated coefficients on the national origin group variables (not shown for sake of space) indicate that there is virtually no difference in the probability an individual selects self-employment across national origin groups, holding all observable characteristics constant. The exception is that high-skilled immigrants from South East Asia are slightly less likely to choose to become entrepreneurs compared to statistically similar immigrants from the Middle East. Furthermore, there is no statistical difference in the self-

---

[1] One concern with incorporating these variables into the self-employment decision models is that they may be determined endogenously and consequently lead to inconsistent estimators. However, given that the ratios are relative group characteristics by SMSA and not individual characteristics, this seems somewhat unlikely. The earnings ratio is not clearly endogenous, but may simply reflect entrepreneurial conditions or opportunities in an area.

employment probability of high-skilled whites, blacks, Asians, and Hispanics.

These results should not be interpreted to mean that there are no differences in self-employment propensities between immigrants from different countries or across individuals of different ethnicity. It means that once we *condition* our sample on being *highly skilled*, there are only small differences across these groups. Several earlier studies have shown, using population representative samples, that both self-employment rates and earnings vary across national origin groups (Camarota 2000; Fairlie and Meyer 1996; Lofstrom 1999; Yuengert 1995). It is very interesting, however, to note that there is very little variation across high-skilled immigrant and ethnic groups.

As mentioned above, one of the advantages of estimating a model of the self-employment decision is that the estimates can be used to control for self-selection in the earnings models. The consistent estimates obtained from the earnings models can then be used to derive age-earnings profiles. From these profiles, we may determine whether immigrants' earnings are likely to converge with the earnings of natives over the work life. The specification in Model 4 is used for the two-step Heckman selection correction models estimated, and it is described below.

Estimation Results: Labor Market Assimilation

Immigrants' earnings in the wage/salary sector have been found not to converge with natives' earnings (Borjas 1985, 1995) over the work life. Earnings of immigrants start out at a lower point and rise more rapidly over time than natives' earnings. However, parity is not reached. The labor market performance of immigrant entrepreneurs, who are excluded from Borjas's studies, have been found to be significantly different from wage/salary immigrants. Lofstrom (1999) finds that earnings of self-employed immigrants is predicted to converge with native wage/salary earnings at around age 30 and with native self-employed earnings at around age 40. This section will look at the labor market success of high-skilled immigrants in both the wage/salary and self-employment sectors.

The earnings models estimated in this chapter use as the dependent variable log of weekly earnings. To try to take into account the possibility that self-employed workers earn a return on physical capital, I also estimate models using as the dependent variable the log of weekly income, which includes any earnings from wage/salary work and/or self-employment earnings and, in addition, any interest, rental, or dividend income. If an individual is deciding between a wage/salary job or self-employment, he can keep his assets in, for example, savings accounts, the stock market, bonds, or real estate, and work in the wage/salary sector. Alternatively, he can use all or some of his assets to start a business. In the former case, returns to physical capital will be observed in terms of interest, rental, or dividend income. If self-employment is chosen, returns may show up both in increased earnings and in interest, rental, or dividend income. Therefore, as an alternative outcome measure, I use log income, where income is the sum of total earnings and interest, rental, or dividend income. With this measure, both groups are put on "par," and this measure of income can be compared reasonably between the two sectors. As stated above, the models estimated in this chapter were also estimated using weekly earnings, as opposed to log weekly earnings. It appears that the results are not very sensitive to whether log earnings, log income, or weekly earnings are used. In light of this, I use the log of weekly earnings as the dependent variable in all wage regressions presented and discussed in this chapter. Furthermore, all earnings are deflated to 1989 dollars using the consumer price index.

One convenient way to analyze labor market assimilation is to estimate earnings equations and use the estimated coefficients to trace out age-earnings profiles. The wage models are estimated separately for the self-employed and the wage/salary workers. The regressions are specified as:

$$\log y_i^{s-e} = \mathbf{X}_i \beta^{s-e} + \mathbf{A}_i \delta^{s-e} + \mathbf{YSM}_i \gamma^{s-e} + u_i^{s-e}, \quad \text{for the self-}$$
employed

$$\log y_i^{w/s} = \mathbf{X}_i \beta^{w/s} + \mathbf{A}_i \delta^{w/s} + \mathbf{YSM}_i \gamma^{w/s} + u_i^{w/s}, \text{for wage/salary}$$
workers

where $\mathbf{X}$ is a vector of socioeconomic and geographic characteristics, including dummy variables for immigrant status, national origin group, and arrival cohort, $\mathbf{A}$ is a vector of age variables (that is, age and age^2), and $\mathbf{YSM}$ is a vector of years since migration variables (that is, YSM and YSM^2). The vector $\mathbf{A}$ also includes the age variables interacted with an immigrant dummy variable. The years since migration variable is equal to zero for all natives.

The models described above were estimated both by ordinary least squares with no selection correction and by heteroskedastic robust ordinary least squares using the inverse Mills ratio to correct for selection bias. The estimated coefficients from the earnings models are presented in tables 7.7 and 7.8, where Models 1, 2, and 3 are the equations without selectivity correction, and Model 4 includes the correction term calculated based on estimation of Model 4 in table 7.6.

Immigrant entrepreneurs report higher weekly earnings than natives even when age and education are controlled for, as shown in Model 1 of table 7.7. However, the estimated coefficient, 0.07, of the immigrant dummy shows that differences in observable characteristics explain about two-thirds of the earnings advantage of self-employed immigrants (the observed difference between the two groups is about 21 percent). Model 2 in the same table shows that only the most recent immigrants in 1989 earned less than natives. It also appears that there is no significant difference in weekly earnings across all other arrival cohorts, holding years since migration constant. The higher observed earnings of wage/salary immigrants, compared to natives, can be explained by the variables included in Model 1 of table 7.8. In fact, the observed immigrant earnings advantage of about 5 percent turns into an earnings gap favoring natives by approximately 7 percent when differences in age, education, marital status, and geographic location are accounted for. The results in Model 2 indicate that the estimated initial earnings upon arrival in the United States do not differ between arrival cohorts.

The last two models in tables 7.7 and 7.8 are more flexible than Models 1 and 2 in the sense that they allow for differences in the effect of the included variables for immigrants and natives. In addition, they also include controls for national origin and occupation. The last model, Model 4, adds a control for self-selection. The results do not appear to be very sensitive to the inclusion of the selection correction term. The discussion will therefore focus on the results for Model 4 in tables 7.7 and 7.8.

Immigrants have been found to earn lower returns to schooling than natives (Betts and Lofstrom 2000). The estimated coefficient on the variable interacting years of schooling with the immigrant indicator variable allows us to test if this also holds for high-skilled immigrants. The estimated coefficients on this variable is negative but statistically insignificant for both self-employed and wage/salary workers. It appears that high-skilled immigrants earn similar returns to education when compared to natives.

The sign of the coefficient on the inverse Mills ratio variable tells us whether there is an overall positive or negative selection into each sector. Not surprisingly, the correction term indicates that there is positive selection into both wage/salary work and self-employment. That is, individuals who choose self-employment are better suited for self-employment, at least in terms of earnings, than are the persons who choose to work in the wage/salary sector and vice versa. However, the

Table 7.7
Linear Earnings Models of Log Weekly Total Earnings, <u>Self-Employed</u>
High-Skilled Males Ages 22-64

Variable	Model 1	Model 2	Model 3	Model 4
Constant	1.7401	1.7665	2.0256	1.9339
	(0.1422)	(0.1429)	(0.2396)	(0.2433)
Immigrant	0.0662	-0.2938	-0.1625	-0.1561
	(0.0138)	(0.0816)	(0.3123)	(0.3123)
Age	0.1243	0.1236	0.1204	0.1229
	(0.0064)	(0.0072)	(0.0102)	(0.0114)
Age2/100	-0.1319	-0.1311	-0.1285	-0.1308
	(0.0072)	(0.0072)	(0.0113)	(0.0114)
Years of Schooling	0.1185	0.1180	0.0925	0.0932
	(0.0033)	(0.0033)	(0.0060)	(0.0060)
Northeast	0.0361	0.0368	0.0459	0.0463
	(0.0182)	(0.0182)	(0.0279)	(0.0279)
Midwest	0.0035	0.0031	-0.0697	-0.0702
	(0.0189)	(0.0189)	(0.0288)	(0.0288)
West	0.0042	0.0053	-0.0076	-0.0059
	(0.0188)	(0.0188)	(0.0283)	(0.0282)
Disability	-0.3208	-0.3208	-0.3582	-0.3567
	(0.0468)	(0.0469)	(0.0721)	(0.0720)
Married	0.2964	0.2960	0.2865	0.2883
	(0.0212)	(0.0212)	(0.0309)	(0.0308)
SMSA Resident	0.1341	0.1346	0.1861	0.1834
	(0.0209)	(0.0209)	(0.0305)	(0.0305)
Period Effect 1980	-0.0307	-0.0319	0.0514	0.0402
	(0.0133)	(0.0143)	(0.2857)	(0.2859)
Limited English Proficiency		-0.3387	-0.3403	-0.3397
		(0.1136)	(0.1064)	(0.1061)
Years of Schooling*Immigrant			-0.0083	-0.0090
			(0.0066)	(0.0066)
Years Since Migration		0.0024	0.0042	0.0041
		(0.0052)	(0.0052)	(0.0052)
Years Since Migration2/100		-0.0024	-0.0034	-0.0040
		(0.0101)	(0.0102)	(0.0103)
Arrival Cohort Pre-1950		0.2906	0.2778	0.3026
		(0.1441)	(0.1424)	(0.1425)

Continued...

Table 7.7 continued

Variable	Model 1	Model 2	Model 3	Model 4
Arrival Cohort 1950-59		0.3020	0.2753	0.2922
		(0.1189)	(0.1167)	(0.1167)
Arrival Cohort 1960-64		0.3451	0.3344	0.3460
		(0.1101)	(0.1084)	(0.1084)
Arrival Cohort 1965-69		0.3801	0.3360	0.3480
		(0.1018)	(0.0994)	(0.0993)
Arrival Cohort 1970-74		0.3762	0.2995	0.3044
		(0.0949)	(0.0936)	(0.0936)
Arrival Cohort 1975-79		0.3644	0.3104	0.3157
		(0.0903)	(0.0880)	(0.0880)
Arrival Cohort 1980-84		0.2653	0.2277	0.2328
		(0.0967)	(0.0936)	(0.0936)
Correction Term				0.0226
				(0.0152)
Model Interacted with Immigrants and Census Year	No	No	Yes	Yes
Model Includes Controls for Country of Origin, Ethnicity and Occupation	No	No	Yes	Yes
Model Controls for Self- Selection	No	No	No	Yes
Number of Observations	21,663	21,663	21,663	21,598
R-squared	0.1579	0.1586	0.1797	0.1797

Note: The table shows robust standard errors in parentheses.
Source: Data drawn from the 1980 and 1990 Public Use Samples of the U.S. census.

Table 7.8
Linear Earnings Models of Log Weekly Total Earnings, <u>Wage/Salary</u>
High-Skilled Males Ages 22-64

Variable	Model 1	Model 2	Model 3	Model 4
Constant	3.3657	3.3703	3.0306	3.0457
	(0.0353)	(0.0354)	(0.0569)	(0.0571)
Immigrant	-0.0716	-0.2181	0.0691	0.0890
	(0.0043)	(0.0146)	(0.0774)	(0.0785)
Age	0.0901	0.0900	0.0930	0.0915
	(0.0017)	(0.0021)	(0.0025)	(0.0032)
Age2/100	-0.0902	-0.0905	-0.0940	-0.0928
	(0.0021)	(0.0021)	(0.0032)	(0.0032)
Years of Schooling	0.0660	0.0661	0.0749	0.0745
	(0.0010)	(0.0010)	(0.0017)	(0.0017)
Northeast	0.0619	0.0617	0.1010	0.1009
	(0.0055)	(0.0055)	(0.0082)	(0.0083)
Midwest	0.0115	0.0111	-0.0103	-0.0099
	(0.0057)	(0.0057)	(0.0086)	(0.0086)
West	0.0316	0.0315	0.0413	0.0398
	(0.0057)	(0.0057)	(0.0082)	(0.0083)
Disability	-0.1552	-0.1549	-0.1822	-0.1827
	(0.0163)	(0.0163)	(0.0258)	(0.0259)
Married	0.1205	0.1214	0.1229	0.1217
	(0.0052)	(0.0052)	(0.0075)	(0.0075)
SMSA Resident	0.1447	0.1449	0.1606	0.1642
	(0.0077)	(0.0077)	(0.0110)	(0.0110)
Period Effect 1980	-0.0635	-0.0619	0.4590	0.4622
	(0.0041)	(0.0044)	(0.0682)	(0.0684)
Limited English Proficiency		-0.1613	-0.1521	-0.1592
		(0.0340)	(0.0340)	(0.0349)
Years of Schooling*Immigrant			-0.0020	-0.0018
			(0.0021)	(0.0021)
Years Since Migration		0.0144	0.0132	0.0132
		(0.0015)	(0.0016)	(0.0016)
Years Since Migration2/100		-0.0158	-0.0171	-0.0169
		(0.0035)	(0.0036)	(0.0036)
Arrival Cohort Pre-1950		-0.0646	0.0129	0.0051
		(0.0407)	(0.0430)	(0.0436)

Continued...

Table 7.8 continued

Variable	Model 1	Model 2	Model 3	Model 4
Arrival Cohort 1950-59		-0.0509	-0.0046	-0.0071
		(0.0293)	(0.0304)	(0.0309)
Arrival Cohort 1960-64		-0.0300	0.0535	0.0521
		(0.0263)	(0.0270)	(0.0275)
Arrival Cohort 1965-69		-0.0266	0.0480	0.0440
		(0.0233)	(0.0238)	(0.0243)
Arrival Cohort 1970-74		0.0114	0.0832	0.0796
		(0.0203)	(0.0206)	(0.0210)
Arrival Cohort 1975-79		0.0134	0.0481	0.0455
		(0.0182)	(0.0182)	(0.0185)
Arrival Cohort 1980-84		-0.0131	0.0116	0.0102
		(0.0192)	(0.0189)	(0.0192)
Correction Term				-0.0440
				(0.0029)
Model Interacted with Immigrants and Census Year	No	No	Yes	Yes
Model Includes Controls for Country of Origin, Ethnicity and Occupation	No	No	Yes	Yes
Model Controls for Self- Selection	No	No	No	Yes
Number of Observations	84,965	84,965	84,965	83,688
R-squared	0.2319	0.2339	0.2550	0.2551

Note: The table shows robust standard errors in parentheses.
Source: Data drawn from 1980 and 1990 Public Use Samples of the U.S. census.

coefficient on the correction term for the self-employed is not statistically significant from zero.

The estimated coefficients and correction terms from the earnings equations—Model 4 in tables 7.7 and 7.8—can be used to predict earnings that individuals who chose self-employment would have earned if they had instead chosen wage/salary work, and vice versa. This can be done by applying the estimated coefficients from the wage/salary model, for example, to each self-employed individual's observed characteristics and estimated correction term. Predicted average earnings can then be calculated separately for immigrants and natives. The exercise gives us insight to "the returns to self-employment." Given that there appears to be positive selection into the wage/salary sector, we expect predicted wage/salary earnings for self-employed individuals, calculated according to the above described method, to be lower than the predicted self-employment earnings. Indeed, this is what is found. However, the predicted wage/salary earnings do not decrease equally for self-employed immigrants and natives. The predicted drop for natives is around 11 percent, while the decline for immigrants is more than twice that (approximately 25 percent). This indicates that high-skilled immigrants earn higher returns to self-employment than natives. This is somewhat surprising given that we observe lower self-employment rates for high-skilled immigrants than for natives. If immigrants earn greater returns to self-employment than natives, we would have expected that they would also be more likely than natives to select self-employment.

One possible explanation for this finding is that there may be constraints—for example, capital constraints—that are more binding for immigrants than for natives, and that this prevents some high-skilled immigrants from becoming entrepreneurs. A finding that is consistent with the constraint conjecture is that for immigrants, the predicted self-employment earnings for wage/salary workers are *higher* than the predicted wage/salary earnings, by 6 percent, while it is *lower* for natives, by 6 percent. On average, high-skilled wage/salary immigrants would earn *more* if they had chosen self-employment.

To address the issue of the rate at which high-skilled immigrants assimilate into the U.S. labor market, and whether they are likely to reach earnings parity with high-skilled natives, we want to compare predicted earnings over the work life for immigrants and natives. A convenient way to analyze immigrant labor market assimilation is to compare predicted age-earnings profiles for natives and immigrants. Figures 7.1, 7.2, and 7.3 show the predicted age-earnings profiles derived from Model 4 in tables 7.7 and 7.8. It traces out the average predicted log weekly earnings over age by using the estimated coefficients.

The notes in the figures show the assumptions made and the reference groups used.

High-skilled immigrant entrepreneurs are likely to have higher earnings than statistically similar natives throughout their work life (see figure 7.1). Wage/salary immigrants are expected to have slightly higher earnings than natives at young ages, but they are predicted to lose this advantage later in their work life.

It is quite possible that the relative labor market performance varies across country of origin groups. To address this possibility, I derived separate age-earnings profiles for four large country of origin groups. Figures 7.2 and 7.3 present the predicted earnings for natives and these national origin groups: North East Asia, Mexico, India/Pakistan, and Europe/Canada/Australia/New Zealand.

The figures indicate that the variation in earnings across country of origin is less among self-employed immigrants. The results also suggest that within a country of origin group, there are differences in the relative success in the labor market. For example, high-skilled self-employed immigrants from Mexico show higher lifetime earnings than their self-employed native counterparts. Mexican immigrants who are working in the wage/salary sector are not even predicted to reach earnings parity with wage/salary natives. It is also worthwhile to point out that there appears to be no significant difference in the predicted earnings between whites, blacks, Hispanics, and Asians. The estimated coefficients in both the wage/salary and the self-employment equations are all within ±2 standard errors of each other.

Summary and Conclusions

Using data from the 1980 and 1990 U.S. censuses, this chapter has shown that a very high proportion of high-skilled workers are self-employed. Approximately one-fifth of both high-skilled natives and immigrants are entrepreneurs. The chapter also tested for enclave effects on the self-employment probability. Higher proportions of co-nationals and co-ethnics are found to increase the probability that an individual selects self-employment. The relative success of co-nationals and co-ethnics in the self-employment sector is also found to positively affect the self-employment probability.

Immigrants in high-skill occupations report higher annual earnings than natives. Self-employed natives in high-skill occupations reported 12 percent lower earnings than self-employed immigrants in 1989. The earnings advantage for wage/salary immigrants in that year was about 2 percent. Although both self-employed and wage/salary immigrants are predicted to at least reach earnings parity with natives over their

Figure 7.1. Predicted Age-Earnings Profile for Self-Employed and Wage/Salary Immigrants and Natives

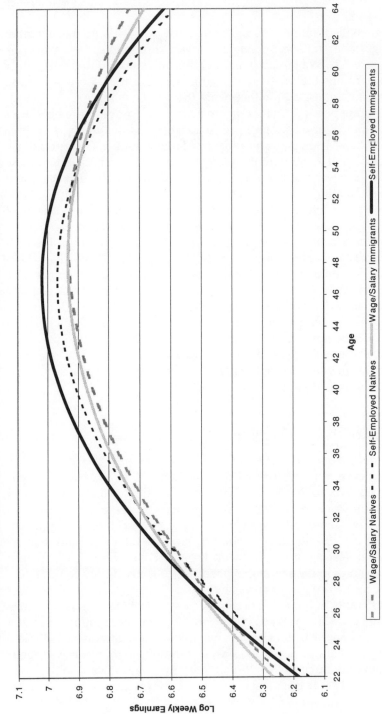

Wage/Salary Natives ▬ ▪ ▪ Self-Employed Natives ▬ ▬ Wage/Salary Immigrants ▬▬ Self-Employed Immigrants

Note: The age-earnings profiles are derived from the estimated Models 4 in tables 7.7 and 7.8. Individuals are assumed to be married, have 18 years of schooling and are residing in a SMSA. Furthermore, the estimates for North East Asian immigrants who arrived between 1975 and 1979 are used. Baseline is 1990.

Figure 7.2. Predicted Age-Earnings Profile for Self-Employed Immigrants and Natives by Country of Origin Group

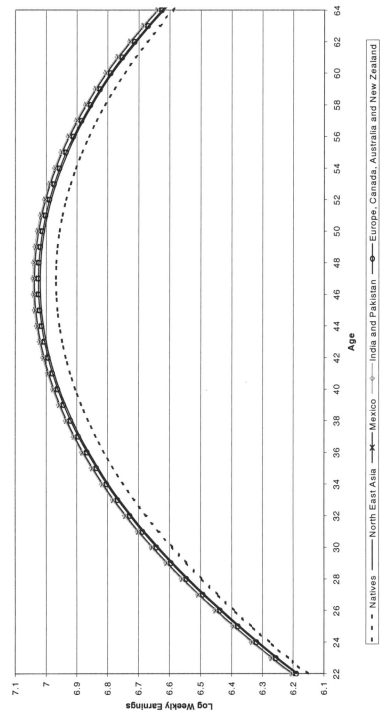

Note: The age-earnings profiles are derived from the estimated Model 4 in table 7.7. Individuals are assumed to be married, have 18 years of schooling and are residing in a SMSA. Furthermore, the estimates for who arrived between 1975 and 1979 are used. Baseline is 1990.

Figure 7.3. Predicted Age-Earnings Profile for Wage/Salary Immigrants and Natives by Country of Orgin Group

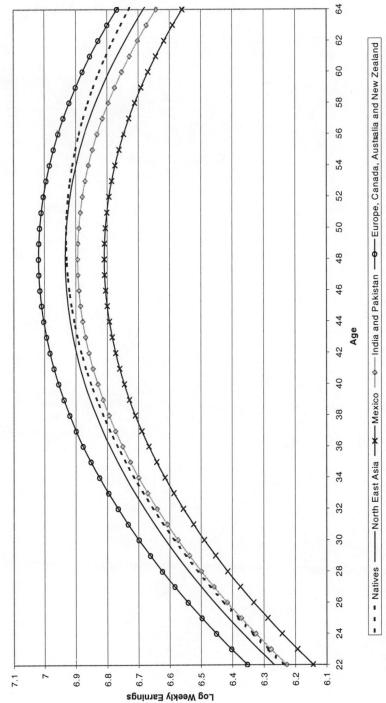

Note: The age-earnings profiles are derived from the estimated Model 4 in table 7.8. Individuals are assumed to be married, have 18 years of schooling and are residing in a SMSA. Furthermore, the estimates for who arrived between 1975 and 1979 are used. Baseline is 1990.

work life, self-employed immigrants are predicted to have higher earnings than self-employed natives throughout most of their work life.

I also found some indication that constraints to enter self-employment—such as capital constraints—may be more binding for high-skilled immigrants than for high-skilled natives.

The variation in earnings across country of origin is less among self-employed immigrants than among wage/salary immigrants. As has been found among the immigrant population overall, this chapter confirms that when compared to natives, high-skilled immigrant entrepreneurs do relatively better in the U.S. labor market than high-skilled immigrants working in the wage/salary sector. However, immigrants in both sectors generally do well in the labor market.

Given the findings in this chapter, it seems likely that high-skilled immigrants will contribute positively to the U.S. economy. This assumes, however, that immigrants do not have a negative impact on wages and employment opportunities. Although researchers studying these potential negative effects of immigration generally find no significant effects or only small negative effects (see, for example, Altonji and Card 1990; Borjas 1994), we do not know if this is also the case for high-skilled workers. Further research into the possible impact of high-skilled immigration on high-skilled natives' labor market outcomes appears to be warranted.

References

Aldrich, Howard E., and Roger Waldinger. 1990. "Ethnicity and Entrepreneurship," *Annual Review of Sociology* 16: 111–35.

Altonji, Joseph G., and David Card. 1991. "The Effects of Immigration on the Labor Market Outcomes of Less-Skilled Natives." In *Immigration, Trade, and the Labor Market*, edited by John Abowd and Richard Freeman. Chicago: University of Chicago Press.

Betts, Julian R., and Magnus Lofstrom. 2000. "The Educational Attainment of Immigrants: Trends and Implications." In *Issues in the Economics of Immigration*, edited by George Borjas. Chicago: University of Chicago Press.

Borjas, George J. 1985. "Assimilation Changes in Cohort Quality and the Earnings of Immigrants," *Journal of Labor Economics* 4: 463–89.

———. 1986. "The Self-Employment Experience of Immigrants," *Journal of Human Resources* 21: 485–506.

———. 1987. "Self-Selection and the Earnings of Immigrants," *The American Economic Review* 4: 531–53.

———. 1994. "The Economics of Immigration," *Journal of Economic Literature* 32: 1667–1717.

———. 1995. "Assimilation Changes in Cohort Quality Revisited: What Happened to Immigrant Earnings in the 1980's?" *Journal of Labor Economics* 2: 201–45.

Bregger, John E. 1996. "Measuring Self-employment in the United States," *Monthly Labor Review* 3–9.

Camarota, Steven A. 2000. "Reconsidering Immigrant Entrepreneurship: An Examination of Self-Employment among Natives and the Foreign Born." Washington, D.C.: Center for Immigration Studies.

Carliner, Geoffrey. 1980. "Wages, Earnings and Hours of First, Second, and Third Generation American Males," *Economic Inquiry* 1: 87–102.

Chiswick, Barry R. 1978. "The Effect of Americanization on the Earnings of Foreign-born Men," *Journal of Political Economy* 5: 897–921.

Cummings, Scott. 1980. *Self-Help in Urban America: Patterns of Minority Business Enterprise*. New York: Kenikart.

Dustmann, C. 1996. "Return Migration: The European Experience," *Economic Policy* 22: 213–50.

Fairlie, Robert W., and Bruce D. Meyer. 1996. "Ethnic and Racial Self-Employment Differences and Possible Explanations," *Journal of Human Resources* 31: 757–93.

Light, Ivan. 1984. "Immigrant and Ethnic Enterprise in North America," *Ethnic and Racial Studies* 7: 195–216.

Lofstrom, Magnus. 1999. "Labor Market Assimilation and the Self-Employment Decision of Immigrant Entrepreneurs." IZA Discussion Paper No. 54.

Yuengert, Andrew M. 1995. "Testing Hypotheses of Immigrant Self-Employment," *Journal of Human Resources* 30: 194–204.

Table 7.A1. Definition of National Origin Groups

Mexico: Mexico
South and Central America: Argentina, Bolivia, Brazil, Chile, Colombia, Ecuador, Falkland Islands, French Guyana, Guyana, Paraguay, Peru, Suriname, Uruguay, Venezuela, Belize, Costa Rica, El Salvador, Guatemala, Honduras, Nicaragua, Panama.
South East Asia: Bangladesh, Brunei, Burma, Cambodia, Indonesia, Laos, Macau, Malaysia, Philippines, Thailand, Vietnam.
North East Asia: China, Hong Kong, Japan, North Korea, Singapore, South Korea, Taiwan.
India/Pakistan: Bangladesh, Bhutan, India, Nepal, Pakistan, Sri Lanka.
Middle East/Egypt: Bahrain, Cyprus, Iran, Iraq, Israel, Jordan, Kuwait, Lebanon, Oman, Qatar, Saudi Arabia, Syria, Turkey, United Arab Emirates, Yemen, Egypt.
Europe, Canada, Australia, New Zealand: Albania, Andorra, Austria, Belgium, Bulgaria, Czechoslovakia, Denmark, Faeroe Islands, Finland, France, Germany, Gibraltar, Greece, Hungary, Iceland, Ireland, Italy, Liechtenstein, Luxembourg, Malta, Monaco, Netherlands, Norway, Poland, Portugal, Romania, San Marino, Spain, Sweden, Switzerland, United Kingdom, Vatican, Yugoslavia, Soviet Union, Canada, Australia, New Zealand.
Caribbean: Anguilla, Antigua and Barbuda, Aruba, Bahamas, Barbados, British Virgin Islands, Cayman Islands, Dominica, Dominican Republic, Grenada, Guadeloupe, Haiti, Jamaica, Martinique, Montserrat, Netherlands Antilles, St. Barthelemy, St. Kitts-Nevis, St. Lucia, St. Vincent and the Grenadines, Trinidad and Tobago, Turks and Caicos Islands.
Cuba: Cuba
Africa: Algeria, Angola, Benin, Botswana, British Indian Ocean Territory, Burkina Faso, Burundi, Cameroon, Cape Verde, Central African Republic, Chad, Comoros, Congo, Djibouti, Equatorial Guinea, Ethiopia, Gabon, Gambia, Ghana, Glorioso Islands, Guinea, Guinea-Bissau, Ivory Coast, Juan de Nova Island, Kenya, Lesotho, Liberia, Libya, Madagascar, Malawi, Mali, Mauritania, Mayotte, Morocco, Mozambique, Namibia, Niger, Nigeria, Reunion, Rwanda, Sao Tome and Principe, Senegal, Mauritius, Seychelles, Sierra Leone, Somalia, South Africa, St. Helena, Sudan, Swaziland, Tanzania, Togo, Tromelin Island, Tunisia, Uganda, Western Sahara, Zaire, Zambia, Zimbabwe.

8

Silicon Valley's New Immigrant Entrepreneurs

AnnaLee Saxenian

Debates over the immigration of scientists and engineers to the United States focus primarily on the extent to which foreign-born professionals displace native workers, or on the existence of invisible barriers to mobility—"glass ceilings"—experienced by non-native professionals. Both approaches assume that the primary economic contribution of immigrants is as a source of relatively low cost labor, even in the most technologically advanced sectors of the economy (McCarthy and Vernez 1997). The view from sending countries, by contrast, has historically been that the emigration of highly skilled personnel to the United States represents a significant economic loss, or "brain drain," which deprives their economies of their best and brightest.

Neither of these views is adequate in today's increasingly global economy. Debates over the extent to which immigrants displace native workers overlook evidence that foreign-born scientists and engineers are starting new businesses and generating jobs and wealth for the state economy at least as fast as their native counterparts (Borjas 1994, 1995; Smith and Edmonston 1997). Similarly, the dynamism of emerging regions in Asia and elsewhere means that it is no longer valid to assume that skilled immigrants will stay permanently in the United States. Recent research suggests that the "brain drain" may be giving way to a process of "brain circulation," as talented immigrants who study and work in the United States return to their home countries to take advantage of promising opportunities there (Johnson and Regets 1998). And advances in transportation and communications technologies mean that even when these skilled immigrants choose not to return home, they still play a critical role as middlemen linking businesses in the United States to those in geographically distant regions.

There is widespread recognition of the significance of immigrant entrepreneurship in traditional industries ranging from small-scale retail to garment manufacturing (Waldinger et al. 1990). Yet we have only anecdotal evidence of a parallel process in the newer, knowledge-based sectors of the economy (Hing and Lee 1996). It is in these dynamic new industries that immigrants with technical skills and strong connections to fast-growing overseas markets have the potential to make significant economic contributions. Not only are skilled immigrants highly mobile, but the technology industries in which they are concentrated are the largest and fastest-growing exporters and leading contributors to the nation's economic growth.

This study examines the entrepreneurial contribution of highly skilled immigrants—in this case, immigrant scientists and engineers—to the Silicon Valley economy. It has four goals. First, it quantifies immigrant engineers' and entrepreneurs' presence in and contribution to the Silicon Valley economy. Second, the study examines the extent to which foreign-born engineers are organizing ethnic networks in the region, like those found in traditional immigrant enterprises, to support the often risky process of starting new technology businesses. Third, it analyzes how these skilled immigrants build long-distance social and economic networks back to their home countries that further enhance entrepreneurial opportunities within Silicon Valley. Finally, it explores the implications of this new model of immigrant-led globalization for public policy.

This is a descriptive and exploratory study that employs a mix of research methods and strategies. It relies on three primary sources. Data on immigrants' education, occupations, and earnings are drawn from the Public Use Microdata Samples (PUMS) of the 1990 census. The decennial census provides the only comprehensive data on immigrants by industry and occupation in the United States. Ample evidence suggests that the Asian presence in Silicon Valley increased significantly during the 1990s, but industrial and occupational detail is not available. As a result, the data on the quantitative significance of immigrant engineers presented here almost certainly represent a significant undercount, which can only be corrected with data from the 2000 census.

This study relies on immigrant-run businesses as a proxy for immigrant-founded businesses. Data on immigrant-run businesses were drawn from a customized Dun and Bradstreet database of 11,443 high-technology firms founded in Silicon Valley between 1980 and 1998. Immigrant-run businesses are defined as companies with chief executive officers (CEOs) with Chinese and Indian surnames. This sample may understate the scale of immigrant entrepreneurship in the region because firms that were started by Chinese or Indians but have hired non-Asian outsiders as CEOs are not counted. While the sample also includes Chinese and Indians born in the United States, it appears unlikely that this is a large source of bias because the great majority of

Asian engineers in the region are foreign-born. There were a total of 59 public technology firms in Silicon Valley that were either founded or run by Chinese or Indians at the end of 1998.

The findings reported in the balance of this study are based on original data from more than 100 in-depth interviews with engineers, entrepreneurs, venture capitalists, policymakers, and other key actors in Silicon Valley. These interviews typically lasted at least one hour and were conducted between January 1997 and January 1998. An additional 67 interviews were conducted in the Taipei and Hsinchu regions of Taiwan (25) during May 1997, and the Bangalore, Bombay, and Delhi regions of India (42) during December 1997. The interviews in Asia included national and local policymakers as well as representatives of technology businesses. Although all the interviews were conducted in English, a Mandarin- or Hindi-speaking research assistant participated in the Chinese and Indian interviews, respectively, to assist with language and cultural clarification or translation.

Immigration and Entrepreneurship in Silicon Valley

Skilled immigrants are a growing presence in Silicon Valley, accounting for one-third of the engineering workforce in most technology firms and emerging as visible entrepreneurs in the 1980s and 1990s. This study documents the growing contribution of skilled Chinese and Indians to the Silicon Valley economy as entrepreneurs as well as engineers. The data presented here suggest that well-known technology companies like Yahoo! and Hotmail, which have immigrant founders, represent the tip of a significantly larger iceberg.

The New Asian Immigrants

Asian immigration to California began in the eighteenth century, but its modern history can be dated to the Immigration Act of 1965, often referred to as the Hart-Celler Act. Before 1965, the U.S. immigration system limited foreign entry by mandating extremely small quotas according to nation of origin. Hart-Celler, by contrast, allowed immigration based on both the possession of scarce skills and family ties to citizens or permanent residents. It also significantly increased the total number of immigrants allowed into the United States. For example, Taiwan, like most other Asian countries, was historically limited to a maximum of 100 immigrant visas per year. As a result, only 47 scientists and engineers emigrated to the United States from Taiwan in 1965. Two years later, the number had increased to 1,321 (Chang 1992).

The Hart-Celler Act thus created significant new opportunities for foreign-born engineers and other highly educated professionals whose skills were in short supply, as well as for their families and relatives. The great majority of these new skilled immigrants were of Asian origin, and they settled disproportionately on the West Coast of the United States. By 1990, one-quarter of the engineers and scientists employed in California's technology industries were foreign-born—more than twice the level in other highly industrialized states such as Massachusetts and Texas (Alarcón 1999). The Immigration and Nationality Act of 1990 further favored the immigration of engineers by almost tripling the number of visas granted on the basis of occupational skills, from 54,000 to 140,000 annually.

These changes in the immigration system coincided with the growth of a new generation of high-technology industries in Silicon Valley and, in turn, transformed the regional workforce. As the demand for skilled labor in the region's emerging electronics industry exploded during the 1970s and 1980s, so too did immigration to the region. Between 1975 and 1990, Silicon Valley's technology companies created more than 150,000 jobs—and the foreign-born population in the region more than doubled to almost 350,000 (Saxenian 1994). By 1990, 23 percent of the population of Santa Clara County (at the heart of Silicon Valley) was foreign-born, surpassing San Francisco County as the largest absolute concentration of immigrants in the Bay Area

Census data confirm the presence of a large technically skilled, foreign-born workforce in Silicon Valley. Although one-quarter of the total Silicon Valley workforce in 1990 was foreign-born, 30 percent of the high-technology workforce was foreign-born. These immigrants were concentrated in professional occupations. One-third of all scientists and engineers in Silicon Valley's technology industries in 1990 were foreign-born. Of those, almost two-thirds were Asians—and the majority were of Chinese and Indian descent. In fact, according to the 1990 census 5 percent PUMS, more than half of the Asian-born engineers in the region were of Chinese (51 percent) or Indian (23 percent) origin, and the balance included relatively small numbers of Vietnamese (13 percent), Filipinos (6 percent), Japanese (4 percent), and Koreans (3 percent).

The disproportionate representation of Chinese and Indian engineers in Silicon Valley's technology workforce explains the focus on these two groups in the balance of this study. This reflects broader national trends. Foreign-born engineers and computer scientists in the United States are significantly more likely to come from India, Taiwan, or China than from other Asian nations. The presence of large numbers of Chinese and Indians in Silicon Valley is a recent phenomenon, mirroring the timing of the changes in U.S. immigration legislation: 71 percent of the Chinese and 87 percent of the Indians working in Silicon Valley high-technology industries in 1990 arrived in the United States after 1970, and 41 percent of the Chinese and 60 percent of the Indians arrived after 1980. Although we must await the 2000 census data for confirmation, Asian immigration to the region almost certainly accelerated during the 1990s—particularly among highly educated professionals—as a result of the higher limits established by the Immigration Act of 1990.

There were very few Chinese technology workers in Silicon Valley prior to 1970. In the two subsequent decades, more than one-third of the region's Chinese immigrant engineers were from Taiwan. Immigrants from Mainland China have now become an important presence in the regional workforce. Between 1980 and 1997, for example, the University of California at Berkeley granted graduate degrees in science and engineering to a fast-growing proportion of students from Mainland China, whereas the proportion granted to students from Taiwan declined correspondingly during the same period. By the mid–1990s, over half of the degrees (53 percent) were granted to students from China, compared to 35 percent in the late 1980s and only 10 percent in the early 1980s. The number of graduate degrees granted can be seen as a leading indicator of labor supply in Silicon Valley, given that most graduates find jobs in the region's technology companies.

National patterns in graduate science and engineering education mirror these trends closely and provide insights into the changing composition of the Silicon Valley workforce. Between 1990 and 1996, the number of doctorates in science and engineering granted annually by U.S. universities to immigrants from China more than tripled (from 477 to 1,680), and those to Indian immigrants doubled (to 692), whereas those to Taiwanese students remained stable (at about 300). These three immigrant groups alone accounted for 81 percent of the doctorates granted to Asians and 62 percent of all foreign doctorates in science and engineering granted in the United States between 1985 and 1996 (Johnson 1998). Moreover, California's universities grant engineering degrees to Asian students at more than twice the rate of universities in the rest of the United States (American Association of Engineering Societies 1995). In short, we can expect the 2000 census to show a dramatic increase in the number of Mainland Chinese and Indian engineers in the Silicon Valley workforce.

Not surprisingly, Silicon Valley's Indian and Chinese workforce is highly educated. In 1990, they earned graduate degrees at significantly higher rates than their white counterparts: 32 percent of the Indians and 23 percent of the Chinese employed in Silicon Valley in 1990 had advanced degrees, compared to only 11 percent for the white population. Their superior educational attainment is even more pronounced in technology industries: 55 percent of Indian and 40 percent of Chinese technology workers held graduate degrees, compared to 18 percent of whites.

This educational attainment is only partially reflected in occupational status. Indians and Chinese working in the region's technology sector were better represented in professional and managerial occupations than their white counterparts, with 60 percent of Indians and 57 percent of Chinese employed as professionals and managers, compared to 53 percent of whites. However, these groups were significantly more concentrated in professional than managerial occupations: 45 percent of the Indians, 41 percent of the Chinese, and 27 percent of the whites were in professional occupations, but only 15 percent of the Indians and 16 percent of the Chinese were managers, compared to 26 percent of the whites. In other words, although Indians and Chinese accounted for 2 percent and 6 percent of Silicon Valley's technology professionals, respectively, they represented less than 1 percent and 4 percent of the managers.[1]

The relatively lower representation of Chinese and Indians in managerial positions could be due to several factors: biases favoring technical (as opposed to business) education, or to the linguistic and cultural difficulties of many new immigrants. It could also be a reflection of more subtle forms of discrimination or institutional barriers to mobility based on race—or the glass ceiling. However, income data provide little support for the glass ceiling hypothesis. Our analysis documents that there is no statistically significant difference between the earnings of Chinese and Indians in managerial, professional, and technical occupations and their white counterparts (Saxenian 1999). This is consistent with the findings of researchers who document greater disparities in managerial representation and upward mobility than in wage levels between Asian and white engineers with comparable skills and education (Fernandez 1998; Tang 1993).

Whatever the data show, many Chinese and Indians in Silicon Valley believe that there is a glass ceiling inhibiting their professional advancement. A 1991 survey of Asian professionals in the region found that two-thirds of those working in the private sector believed that advancement to managerial positions was limited by race. Moreover, these concerns increased significantly with respondents' age and experience. This perception is consistent with the finding that, in the technology industry at least, Chinese and Indians remain concentrated in

---

[1] The CorpTech Directory lists the names and titles of all the executives in public technology firms in the region. These data show Chinese and Indians in significantly greater numbers in research and development than in executive, marketing, or sales positions.

professional rather than managerial positions, despite superior levels of educational attainment. It is notable, however, that those surveyed attributed these limitations less to "racial prejudice and stereotypes" than to the perception of an "old boys' network that excludes Asians" and the "lack of role models" (AACI 1993).

Lester Lee, a native of Szechuan, China, who moved to Silicon Valley in 1958, describes the feeling of being an outsider that was common for Asian immigrants in that period. "When I first came to Silicon Valley," he remembers, "there were so few of us that if I saw another Chinese on the street I'd go over and shake his hand." This sense of being an outsider was reinforced in many ways. Lee notes, for example, that "nobody wanted to sell us houses in the 1960s." Although immigrants like Lee typically held graduate degrees in engineering from U.S. universities and worked for mainstream technology companies, they often felt personally and professionally isolated in a world dominated by white men.

Immigrant engineers like Lester Lee responded to the sense of exclusion from established business and social structures in two ways. Many responded individually by starting their own businesses. Lee became the region's first Chinese entrepreneur when he left Ampex in 1970 to start a company called Recortec. Other early Chinese engineers report that they felt as if they were seen as "good work horses, and not race horses" or "good technicians, rather than managers." David Lee, for example, left Xerox in 1973 to start Qume after a less experienced outsider was hired as his boss. Lee was able to raise start-up capital from the mainstream venture capital community, but only on the condition that he hire a non-Asian president for his company. David Lam similarly left Hewlett-Packard in 1979 after being passed over for a promotion and started a semiconductor equipment manufacturing business called Lam Research, now a publicly traded company with $1.3 billion in sales. Not surprisingly, these three individuals have become community leaders and role models for subsequent generations of Chinese entrepreneurs.

The New Immigrant Entrepreneurs

During the 1980s and 1990s, Silicon Valley's immigrant engineers increasingly followed the career trajectories of native engineers by starting technology businesses. In contrast to traditional immigrant entrepreneurs, who are concentrated in low-technology services and manufacturing sectors, these new immigrant entrepreneurs are a growing presence in the most technologically dynamic and globally competitive sectors of the Silicon Valley economy. At least 37 public technology companies in the region were started by Chinese immigrants; another 22 were started by Indians. The existence of so many immigrant-run publicly traded companies suggests a significant population of private, immigrant-founded companies. Unfortunately, it is difficult to get accurate estimates of ethnic or immigrant entrepreneurship in technology industries. The standard way to measure immigrant entrepreneurship is by examining the "self-employed" category in the U.S. census. Although this may be a good approximation for owner-run businesses in traditional industries, it almost certainly leads to a significant undercount in technology sectors because so many companies are funded with outside funds or venture capital—and hence are not owned by the founding entrepreneur.

A higher and probably more accurate estimate of ethnic entrepreneurship in Silicon Valley was obtained by identifying all businesses with CEOs having Chinese and Indian surnames in a Dun and Bradstreet database of technology firms started since 1980. According to this count, close to one-quarter (24 percent) of Silicon Valley's technology firms in 1998 had Chinese or Indian executives, and they created both jobs and wealth in the region. Of the 11,443 high-technology firms started during this period, 2,001 (17 percent) were run by Chinese and 774 (7 percent) by Indians. In 1998, these companies collectively accounted for over $16.8 billion in sales and 58,282 jobs (see table 8.1). These numbers may still understate the scale of immigrant entrepreneurship in the region because firms started by Chinese or Indians with non-Asian CEOs are not counted. Our interviews suggest that this has frequently been the case in Silicon Valley, where venture capital financing has often been tied to the requirement that non-Asian senior executives be hired. This seems a more likely source of bias than the opposite scenario—that is, firms started by non-Asians that hire a Chinese or Indian CEO. These data also indicate that the rate of Chinese and Indian entrepreneurship in Silicon Valley increased significantly over time. Chinese and Indians were at the helm of 13 percent of Silicon Valley's technology companies between 1980 and 1984, but they were running 29 percent of the region's high-technology companies started between 1995 and 1998 (see table 8.2). The following sections suggest that this growth has been fueled both by the emergence of role models and by supportive networks within ethnic communities in the region, as well as by growing ties to Asian markets and sources of capital and manufacturing capabilities.

Chinese and Indian firms remain small relative to the technology sector as a whole—with an average of 21 employees per firm, compared to 37 employees per firm for all firms. Although these immigrant-run firms employ fewer people, they appear to be at least as productive: Chinese-run firms have sales of $317,555 per employee, and

Indian-run firms have sales of $216,110 per employee (compared to $242,105 sales per employee for all technology firms in the Dun and Bradstreet database). It is impossible to identify and precisely track the progress of the technology companies started by immigrants, in part because so many have passed managerial responsibility to their native counterparts. However, most of the technology companies that were either founded by or are currently run by Chinese or Indian individuals and are publicly traded have average sales and employment that are much closer to the regional average.

Table 8.1
Sales and Employment of Silicon Valley High-Technology Firms Led by a Chinese or Indian CEO, 1998

	No. of Firms	Total Sales ($M)	Total Employment
Indian	774	3,588	16,598
Chinese	2,001	13,237	41,684
Total	**2,775**	**16,825**	**58,282**
Share of Silicon Valley high-tech firms	24%	17%	14%

Source: Dun and Bradstreet database, 1998.
Note: Statistics are for firms started by Chinese or Indians from 1980 to 1988.

There is an interesting sectoral division among these businesses. Chinese-run firms are more concentrated than Indian-run firms in computer and electronic hardware manufacturing and trade, whereas Indian-run companies are disproportionately found in software and business services. This difference is likely due to the differences in language skills between the two groups. Indian immigrants tend to be proficient in English, but most first-generation Chinese immigrants are not. This means that Indians can move more easily into software development, while Chinese immigrants gravitate toward sectors where language skills are less important. It is worth noting, however, that this appears to be changing. Two well-known public technology companies started by Taiwanese immigrants—Broadvision and AboveNet—are in the software and Internet sectors, respectively. Moreover, in absolute terms, there are more Chinese-run than Indian-run software and service companies.

Table 8.2
Chinese- and Indian-Run Companies as a Share of Total Silicon Valley
High-Technology Start-ups, 1980–1998

	1980–1984		1985–1989		1990–1994		1995–1998	
	N	%	N	%	N	%	N	%
Indian	47	3	90	4	252	7	385	9
Chinese	121	9	347	15	724	19	809	20
Other	1,181	88	1,827	81	2,787	74	2,869	71
Total	1,349	100	2,264	100	3,763	100	4,063	100

Source: Dun and Bradstreet database, 1988.

There is also a large number of Chinese firms in the wholesale sector, reflecting a distinctive, lower-skill segment of the Taiwanese technology community. These firms, which are on average quite small, specialize in selling computers and computer components manufactured in Taiwan. They appear to have some ties to the more technically sophisticated sector of the Chinese community through their association, the Chinese American Computer Corporation, as well as through personal and alumni networks. These ties allow the wholesale and retail communities to learn quickly about technology trends, as well as to provide market feedback.

The Origins of Silicon Valley's Ethnic Networks

The previous section portrays Chinese and Indian entrepreneurs as individuals or as collections of unrelated individuals. This conforms to the popular image of the entrepreneur as a lone pioneer. In reality, however, Silicon Valley's immigrant entrepreneurs—like their mainstream counterparts—rely on a diverse range of informal social structures and institutions to support their entrepreneurial activities.

Unlike traditional ethnic entrepreneurs who remain isolated in low-wage, low-skill industries (Waldinger et al. 1990), Silicon Valley's new immigrant entrepreneurs are professionals who are active in dynamic and technologically sophisticated industries. Yet like their less educated predecessors, the region's Chinese and Indian engineering communities rely on ethnic strategies to enhance their own entrepreneurial opportunities. Seeing themselves as outsiders to the mainstream technology community, Silicon Valley's immigrant engineers created local social and professional networks to mobilize the information, know-how, skill, and capital needed to start technology firms. This is reflected in a proliferation of ethnic professional associations.

Table 8.3 lists the professional and technical associations organized by Silicon Valley's Chinese and Indian immigrant engineers.[2] These organizations are among the most vibrant and active professional associations in the region, with memberships ranging from several hundred in the newer associations to over one thousand in the established organizations. The organizations combine elements of traditional immigrant culture with distinctly high technology practices. They simultaneously create ethnic identities within the region and facilitate the professional networking and information exchange that aid success in the highly mobile Silicon Valley economy. They are not traditional political or lobbying organizations. With the exception of the Asian American Manufacturers Association (AAMA), the activities of these groups are oriented exclusively to fostering the professional and technical advancement of their members.

Despite the distinct ethnic subcultures and the greater number and specialization of the Chinese associations, these associations share important functions as well. All mix socializing—over Chinese banquets, Indian dinners, or family-centered social events—with support for professional and technical advancement. Each organization, either explicitly or informally, provides first-generation immigrants with a source of professional contacts and networks within the local technology community. They serve as important sources of labor market information and recruitment channels, and they provide role models of successful immigrant entrepreneurs and managers. In addition, the associations sponsor regular speakers and conferences that provide forums for sharing specialized technical and market information, as well as basic information about the nuts and bolts of entrepreneurship and management for engineers with limited business experience. In addition to providing sessions on how to write a business plan or manage a business, some of the Chinese associations give seminars on English communication, negotiation skills, and stress management.

---

[2] This list includes only professional associations whose focus is technology industry and whose primary membership base is in Silicon Valley. It does not include the numerous Chinese and Indian political, social, and cultural organizations in the region; nor does it include ethnic business or trade associations for traditional, non-technology industries.

Table 8.3.

Indian and Chinese Professional Associations in Silicon Valley

Name	Year Founded	Membership	Brief Description
Indian			
Silicon Valley Indian Professionals Association (SIPA)	1991	1,000	Forum for expatriate Indians to contribute to cooperation between United States and India. Web site: www.sipa.org
The Indus Entrepreneur (TiE)	1992	560	Fosters entrepreneurship by providing mentorship and resources. Web site: www.tie.org
Chinese			
Chinese Institute of Engineers (CIE/USA)	1979	1,000	Promotes communication and interchange of information among Chinese engineers and scientists. Web site: www.cie-sf.org
Asian American Manufacturers Association (AAMA)	1980	> 700	Promotes the growth and success of U.S. technology enterprises throughout the Pacific Rim. Web site: www.aamasv.com
Chinese Software Professionals Association (CSPA)	1988	1,400	Promotes technology collaboration and facilitates information exchange in the software profession. Web site: www.cspa.com
Chinese American Computer Corporation (NBI)	1988	270 corporations	Mid-technology cluster of PC clone system sellers, majority from Taiwan. Web site: www.killerapp.com/nbi

Monte Jade Science and Technology Association (MJSTA)	1989	150 corp; 300 ind. (West Coast).	Promotes the cooperation and mutual flow of technology and investment between Taiwan and the United States. Web site: www.montejade.org
Silicon Valley Chinese Engineers Association (SCEA)	1989	400	Network of Mainland Chinese engineers to promote entrepreneurship and professionalism among members and establish ties to China. Web site: www.scea.org
Chinese American Semiconductor Professionals Association (CASPA)	1991	40 corporations; 1,600 individuals	Promotes technical, communication, information exchange, and collaboration among semiconductor professionals. Web site: www.caspa.com
North America Taiwanese Engineers Association (NATEA)	1991	400	Promotes exchange of scientific and technical information. Web site: http://natea.org
Chinese Information and Networking Association (CINA)	1992	700	Chinese professionals who advocate technologies and business opportunities in information industries. Web site: www.cina.org
Chinese Internet Technology Association (CITA)	1996	600	Forum and network for Chinese Internet professionals and entrepreneurs to incubate ideas, learn from each other, and form potential partnerships. Web site: www.cita.net
North America Chinese Semiconductor Association (NACSA)	1996	600	Professional advancement in semiconductor sector, interaction between the United States and China. Web site: www.nacsa.com

Source: Author interviews.

Many of these associations have become important forums for cross-generational investment and mentoring as well. An older generation of successful immigrant engineers and entrepreneurs in both the Chinese and the Indian communities now plays an active role in financing and mentoring younger generations of co-ethnic entrepreneurs. Individuals within these networks often invest individually or jointly in promising new ventures, acting as "angel" investors who are more accessible to immigrants than the mainstream venture capital community and who are also willing to invest smaller amounts of money. The goal of the Indus Entrepreneur (TiE), for example, is to "foster entrepreneurship by providing mentorship and resources" within the South Asian technology community. Similarly, both the AAMA and the Monte Jade Science and Technology Association sponsor annual investment conferences aimed at matching potential investors (often from Asia as well as Silicon Valley) with promising Chinese entrepreneurs.

This is not to suggest that these associations create self-contained ethnic businesses or communities. Many Chinese and Indian immigrants socialize primarily within the ethnic networks, but they routinely work with native engineers and native-run businesses. In fact, there is growing recognition within these communities that, although a start-up might be spawned with the support of the ethnic networks, it needs to become part of the mainstream to grow. It appears that the most successful immigrant entrepreneurs in Silicon Valley today are those who have drawn on ethnic resources while simultaneously integrating into mainstream technology and business networks.[3]

The remainder of this section traces the evolution of some of the region's leading Chinese and Indian professional associations to illuminate their origins and activities in more detail. Although this study focuses on Chinese and Indians, the phenomenon of ethnic networking and mutual support among skilled immigrants in Silicon Valley now extends to the region's Iranian, Korean, Japanese, Israeli, French, Filipino, and Singaporean immigrant engineers.

The Chinese Institute of Engineers: The "Grandfather" of the Chinese Associations

A handful of Chinese engineers—including Lester Lee, David Lee, and David Lam—started a local branch of the Chinese Institute of Engineers (CIE) in 1979 to promote better communication and organization among the region's Chinese engineers. The Bay Area chapter of CIE

---

[3] This parallels Granovetter's (1995) notion of balancing coupling and decoupling in the case of overseas Chinese entrepreneurs.

quickly became the largest in the country. Today CIE has some 1,000 members in the Bay Area, and it is regarded by old-timers as the "grandfather" of Silicon Valley's Chinese organizations.

The organization was dominated initially by Taiwanese immigrants, reflecting the composition of the Chinese technology community in Silicon Valley at the time. Its early dynamism built on preexisting professional and social ties among these engineers, a majority of whom were graduates of Taiwan's elite engineering universities. Most Taiwanese engineers report that by the mid–1980s they had dozens of classmates in Silicon Valley. The National Taiwan University Alumni Association, for example, has 1,500 members in the Bay Area alone. These alumni relations—which seemed more important to many Taiwanese immigrants when living abroad than they had at home—have become an important basis for the solidarity within the Chinese engineering community in Silicon Valley.

The CIE is primarily a technical organization. However, the initial meetings of the Bay Area chapter focused heavily on teaching members the mechanics of starting a business, getting legal and financial help, and providing basic management training to engineers who had only technical education. Over time, CIE became an important source of role models and mentors for recently arrived immigrants. Gerry Liu, who co-founded Knights Technology in 1987 with four Chinese friends, reports:

> When I was thinking of starting my own business, I went around to call on a few senior, established Chinese businessmen to seek their advice. I called David Lee.... I contacted David Lam and Winston Chen. I called up Ta-ling Hsu. They did not know me, but they took my calls. I went to their offices or their homes; they spent time with me telling me what I should or shouldn't be doing.

Not surprisingly, immigrants like Liu began starting businesses at an increasing rate in the late 1980s and 1990s.

The CIE remains the most technical of the region's ethnic associations. Its goal is "to foster friendship, provide a forum for technical exchange and promote cooperation among Chinese-American engineers to enhance their image and influence." It also plays a central role in promoting collaboration between Chinese American engineers and their counterparts in Asia. In 1989, CIE initiated an annual week-long technical seminar with the parallel organization in Taiwan, and this was extended to include engineers from Mainland China over the course of the 1990s. In addition, when the Taiwanese government initiates major engineering projects—from a transit system to a power station—they consult the Silicon Valley chapter of CIE. These forums not only transfer technical know-how but also create professional and social ties among Chinese engineers living on both sides of the Pacific.

Although CIE was the first organization of Chinese engineers in the Bay Area, there was already a well-developed infrastructure of Chinese associations in the region. San Francisco's Chinatown—historically the center of Chinese immigration to the area—was the home of hundreds of traditional Chinese ethnic associations, including regional and district hometown associations, kinship (clan, family, or multi-family), and dialect associations. There were also business and trade associations that supported the thousands of traditional ethnic businesses located in the city, including apparel contractors, jewelry and gift shops, neighborhood grocers, Chinese laundries, and restaurants (Wong 1998).

The CIE was distinguished from these established ethnic associations by both the social and economic background of its members and by geography. CIE members were highly educated professionals who had immigrated in recent decades from Taiwan or China and who lived and worked in the South Bay. They had little in common with the older generations of less skilled farmers and manual workers who had immigrated from Hong Kong and southern China (Guangdong and Fujian provinces) and who lived and worked in San Francisco. The early gatherings of Silicon Valley's Chinese engineers centered in the city because of its concentration of Chinese restaurants. By the mid–1980s, as the area's Chinese population increased significantly (and with it the number of Chinese restaurants suitable for holding meetings!), the center of gravity for socializing had shifted decisively to the Peninsula. Our interviews confirm that these two communities of Chinese immigrants coexist today in the Bay Area with limited social or professional interaction.

Into the Mainstream: The Asian American Manufacturers Association

The Asian American Manufacturers Association (AAMA) was founded in 1980 by a group of eight Chinese engineers at Lester Lee's company, Recortec. Motivated by the desire to be seen as professionals, rather than simply as good engineers, and to participate more directly in the political process, the founding members envisioned an institution that would help Asians join mainstream American society. There were only 21 members at the founding meeting, but they quickly achieved their vision of positioning the AAMA as a high-profile, high-caliber association with broad appeal to Asian professionals in the area.

The goals of the AAMA were broader and more political than those of the CIE. The original objectives were: "(1) To obtain resources from federal, state, and local governments, and private sectors to assist in the development, growth, and success of the organization; (2) To benefit individual members of the association through mutual support and sharing of resources, information and individual talents; and (3) To address issues that affect the welfare of the members of the association and the Asian Pacific American business community" (Gong 1996).

Despite a significantly broader agenda, the early AAMA meetings, like those of the CIE, focused primarily on teaching first-time entrepreneurs the nuts and bolts of starting and managing a technology business. These meetings also showcased role models of successful Asian Americans in the industry and provided a mutual support and networking forum for members. Such forums were intended to help their members advance professionally, but they also helped promote the adoption of American management models—rather than traditional Chinese business models based on family ties and obligations—in immigrant-run technology companies.

The AAMA currently has more than 700 members and is the most visible voice of the Asian community in Silicon Valley. Its goal now is more global—to "promote the growth and success of U.S. technology enterprises throughout the Pacific Rim." But the organization's objectives still include fostering business growth and networking, facilitating management and leadership development (including providing "management development training, opportunities, and managerial/executive role models and contacts that will help members break through the glass ceiling"), recognizing and publicizing the achievements of Asian Americans, and supporting equal opportunity.

The AAMA has the broadest potential membership base and agenda of the ethnic associations in Silicon Valley. All of its meetings are conducted in English, and its membership, which is open to all professionals, includes large numbers of investment bankers, consultants, lawyers, and accountants as well as engineers. Despite this umbrella-like character, three-quarters of AAMA members are Chinese.

These early professional associations had overlapping memberships and boards, reflecting in part the small scale of the Chinese technology community in Silicon Valley. Members describe both CIE and AAMA—and the social networks they support—as providing helpful job search networks and as sources of reliable information, advice and mentoring, seed capital, and trusted business partners. A former president of the AAMA describes these advantages: "Doing business is about building relationships; it's people betting on people, so you still want to trust the people you're dealing with. A lot of trust is developed through friendship and professional networks like school alumni relations, business associations, and industry ties." David Lam similarly describes the advantages of the ethnic networks:

> If there is someone that I know ... if we have some mutual business interest, then the deal can come together rather fast. And if we have known each other for some years and a certain level of mutual trust has already been established, it is much easier to go forward from there. In other situations I may not have known the person directly, but through some introduction I talked to them, and things also went along very well. So I think the connections play a very important role.

The Proliferation of Chinese Professional and Technical Associations

The growing scale and diversity of the Chinese engineering community in Silicon Valley during the 1980s and early 1990s generated a proliferation of professional and technical associations. As table 8.3 shows, at least nine more Chinese technology-related associations—or more than one per year—were started in Silicon Valley between 1988 and 1996. The new generation of Mainland Chinese have, in turn, created still more associations since that time, often parallel to comparable Taiwanese organizations. All of these associations bring together the Chinese members of a given industry, and all are dedicated broadly to promoting the professional advancement of individuals and member firms. Collectively, the Chinese associations represent nearly 6,000 members in Silicon Valley—although this number undoubtedly double counts individuals who belong to multiple associations.

Breaking the Glass Ceiling: The Indian Professionals Association

A young Intel engineer and his three Indian roommates started the Silicon Valley Indian Professionals Association (SIPA) in 1987 to provide a meeting place for Indian professionals to share their common concerns. Despite their superior mastery of the English language, which distinguished them from most of their Chinese counterparts, they, too, were concerned about limits on the opportunities for professional advancement in the technology industry. According to SIPA founder Prakash Chandra, "many Indians didn't see a career path beyond what they were doing." Many of the early SIPA meetings were thus focused on individual career strategies, as well as on the nuts and bolts of the technology industry.

Silicon Valley's Indian immigrants did not mobilize collectively until a decade later than their Chinese counterparts, in part because they were later in achieving a critical mass in the region. Many Indian engineers complained about a glass ceiling in the region's established companies, and they responded by starting their own businesses. "Why do you think there are so many Indian entrepreneurs in Silicon Valley? Because they know that sooner or later they will be held back." When they organized collectively, however, they created new associations such as SIPA, rather than joining existing groups such as the AAMA. This no doubt reflects the greater comfort they felt in being with other Indians, despite the fact that they were often from different regions of their home country and spoke different dialects. In fact, a sizable subset of these engineers grew up in Africa and had never lived in India. But like their Chinese counterparts, their backgrounds were often similar. Many were graduates of the prestigious Indian Institutes of Technology (IITs) or Indian Institutes of Science (IISs), and hence were unified by common professional identities along with the pull of shared ethnic ties.

Like its Chinese counterparts, SIPA's vision gradually expanded beyond the focus on individual professional advancement. In this case, largely in response to visits by Indian government delegations in the early 1990s seeking to build business ties in the United States, SIPA redefined its role to include attempting to "fill the information gap" between the United States and India. The association began sponsoring regular seminars and workshops that would allow U.S.–based Indian professionals to help their employers gain a better understanding of the recently opened Indian market and business environment, and simultaneously to explore professional opportunities for themselves in India. Today, SIPA has about 1,000 members (virtually all Indians) and holds regular seminars to disseminate information of interest and to strengthen ties with business and government officials in India.

Cross-Generational Mentoring: The Indus Entrepreneur

SIPA lost some of its momentum when its founder returned to India in 1992, but in the same year an older generation of Indian immigrants started the Indus Entrepreneur. TiE's goal was to nurture entrepreneurs from South Asia. Its founding members included three of the region's most successful Indian entrepreneurs: Suhas Patil (former MIT professor and founder of Cirrus Logic), Prabhu Goel (founder of Gateway Design Automation), and Kanwal Rekhi (who started and ran Excelan until it merged with Novell). This core group came together in response to a visit by India's secretary of electronics to Silicon Valley in 1992. When the minister's flight was delayed, they began to share complaints about the difficulties of running a business. In the words of another local entrepreneur who subsequently organized the first meeting of TiE: "I realized that we all had the same problems, but that we don't work together. That as individuals we are brilliant, but collectively we amounted to nothing." TiE began its monthly meetings with the intent of creating a forum for networking and for helping younger South Asians start their own businesses.

Like the first generation of Chinese immigrant entrepreneurs, Indians like Patil and Goel had succeeded despite their lack of contacts or community support. In the words of another early TiE member, Satish Gupta:

> When some of us started our businesses, we had nobody we could turn to for help. We literally had to scrounge and do it on our own. What we see in Silicon Valley, especially with the new start-up businesses, is that contacts are everything. All of us have struggled through developing contacts, so our business is to give the new person a little bit of a better start than we had.

This goal of mentoring and assisting entrepreneurs remains central to TiE's agenda, and it is achieved through monthly meetings and presentations, the annual conference, and extensive informal networking and mentoring. Even TiE founders were amazed by the popularity of the first annual conference in 1994, which attracted over 500 people. Today it draws close to 1,000.

TiE founders call themselves Indus (rather than Indian) entrepreneurs to include other South Asians such as Pakistanis, Bangladeshis, and Nepalese. However, the organization's Bay Area members are almost all Indian. Forty charter members form the core of the organization. Charter membership is by invitation only and includes successful entrepreneurs, corporate executives, and senior professionals with roots in or an interest in the Indus region. They support the organization with annual dues of $1,000. TiE has U.S. chapters in Southern California, Boston, and Austin as well, but the center of gravity remains in Silicon Valley. In 1999, TiE chapters were established in Bangalore, Bombay, and Delhi.

TiE's most distinctive contribution is its model of cross-generational investing and mentoring. Because of their earlier business successes, TiE's founders are able to provide start-up capital, business and financial advice, and professional contacts to a younger generation of Indian entrepreneurs. These engineers claim that one of the biggest obstacles to their own advancement has been the bias on the part of mainstream financial organizations and, in particular, the difficulties faced by nonnative applicants in raising venture capital. Like their Chinese counterparts, they felt like outsiders to the mainstream (primarily white and native) venture capital community.

TiE members often take on the roles of mentors, advisers, board members, and angel investors in new Indian companies. One early recipient of TiE funding, Naren Bakshi, presented the business plan for a company called Vision Software in 1995. Within months, TiE members had raised $1.7 million for Bakshi's company. Today, Vision Software has 60 employees and has raised additional funding. In fact, Bakshi was approached by more venture capitalists than he could use. This fits the vision of TiE founders of supporting "diamonds in the rough" and encouraging them to expand by diversifying their funding and integrating into the mainstream technology community.

Chandra Shekar, founder of Exodus Corporation, reports that the help from TiE members extends beyond providing capital and sitting on the board of directors to serving as a "trusted friend" or even the "brain behind moving the company where it is today." One of the most important contributions these experienced entrepreneurs and executives provide is access to "entry points" with potential customers or business alliances. According to Shekar,

> The Indian network works well, especially because the larger companies like Sun, Oracle, and HP have a large number of Indians.... You gain credibility through your association with a TiE member.... For example, if HP wants to do business with you, they see that you are a credible party to do business with. This is very important.

Vinod Khosla a co-founder of Sun Microsystems and now a partner at venture capital firm Kleiner, Perkins, summarizes:

> The ethnic networks clearly play a role here: people talk to each other, they test their ideas, they suggest other people they know, who are likely to be of the same ethnicity. There is more trust because the language and cultural approach are so similar.

Of course, once successful Indian entrepreneurs invest in a company, they provide the legitimacy that allows the entrepreneur to get a hearing from the region's more established venture capital funds. Satish Gupta of Cirrus Logic notes that:

> Networks work primarily with trust.... Elements of trust are not something that people develop in any kind of formal manner.... Trust has to do with the believability of the person, body language, mannerisms, behavior, cultural back-

> ground—all these things become important for building
> trust.... Caste may play a role; financial status may play a
> role.

But he adds that although organizations like TiE are instrumental in
creating trust in the community, they also create a set of duties and
sanctions:

> If you don't fulfill your obligations, you could be an outcast
> ... the pressure of, hey, you better not do this because I'm
> going to see you at the temple or sitting around the same cof-
> fee table at the TiE meeting.... I know another five guys that
> you have to work with, so you better not do anything wrong.

Groups like SIPA and TiE create common identities among an
otherwise fragmented nationality. Indians historically are deeply divided and typically segregate themselves by regional and linguistic
differences: the Bengalis, Punjabis, Tamil, and Gujaratis tend to stick
together. But in Silicon Valley it seems that the Indian identity has
become more powerful than these regional distinctions. As the author
V. S. Naipaul wrote of his own upbringing in Trinidad: "In these
special circumstances overseas Indians developed something they
would have never known in India: a sense of belonging to an Indian
community. This feeling of community could override religion and
caste." As with the overseas Chinese community, there are subgroups
with varied amounts of familiarity and trust, but the shared experience of immigration appears to strengthen, rather than undermine,
ethnic identities.

There is always a danger of insularity in these ethnic communities.
Some suggest that the TiE network remains so closed that it prevents
outsiders from participating. According to a charter member of TiE,
there is little desire in the organization to connect to the outside:

> This network just does not connect to the mainstream. If you
> look at the social gatherings that the TiE members go to, it's
> all Indians. There's nothing wrong with it.... But I think if
> you don't integrate as much, you don't leverage the benefit
> that much.

The challenge for Silicon Valley's immigrant entrepreneurs will continue to be to balance reliance on ethnic networks with integration into
the mainstream technology community.

The Benefits of Local Ethnic Networks

We cannot definitively demonstrate the economic benefits of these immigrant networks. However, the proliferation of ethnic professional associations in Silicon Valley during the 1980s and 1990s corresponded with the growing visibility and success of Chinese- and Indian-run businesses. The entrepreneurs themselves give the networks much credit. According to Mohan Trika, a CEO of an internal Xerox venture called inXight:

> Organizations like TiE create self-confidence in the community. This confidence is very important.... It provides a safety net around you, the feeling that you can approach somebody to get some help. It's all about managing risk. Your ability to manage risk is improved by these networks. If there are no role models, confidence builders to look to, then the chances of taking risk are not there. That's what we are saying: "come on with me, I'll help you." This quickly becomes a self-reinforcing process: you create five or ten entrepreneurs, and those ten create another ten.... I can approach literally any big company, or any company in the Bay Area, and find two or three contacts.... Through the TiE network I know so-and-so in Oracle, and so on.

This networking creates value, he says,

> Because we are a technology-selling company for the next generation of user interface, every major software company or any software company must have at least two or three Indians or Chinese in there.... And because they are there, it is very easy for me, or my technical officer, to create that bond, to pick up the phone and say: "Swaminathan, can you help me, can you tell me what's going on?"... He'll say, "Don't quote me, but the decision is because of this, this, and this." Based on this you can reformulate your strategy, your pricing, or your offer.... Such contacts are critical for start-ups.

The increased visibility of successful Chinese and Indian entrepreneurs and executives in Silicon Valley in the 1990s has transformed their image in the mainstream community as well. Some Asians today suggest that although the glass ceiling may remain a problem in traditional industries or in old-line technology companies, it is diminishing as a problem in Silicon Valley.

Sources of capital for Asian entrepreneurs are proliferating in part because of growing flows of capital from Taiwan, Hong Kong, and Singapore in the 1990s. Several new venture capital firms dedicated primarily to funding Asian immigrants were also started in the region during the 1990s. Alpine Technology Ventures, for example, has focused on Chinese companies, and the Draper International Fund specializes in financing Indian technology ventures. Other firms, such as Walden International Investment Group and Advent International, explicitly link Silicon Valley–based entrepreneurs to Asian sources of funding. Some of the major venture capital firms are even said to be hiring Asian American partners to avoid losing out on deals going to foreign-born entrepreneurs. In addition, Silicon Valley's immigrant entrepreneurs may now be advantaged relative to their mainstream counterparts by their privileged ties to Asian sources of capital, markets, and manufacturing capabilities.

Globalization of Silicon Valley's Ethnic Networks: Two Cases

At the same time that Silicon Valley's immigrant entrepreneurs organized local professional networks, they were also building ties back to their home countries. The region's Chinese engineers constructed a vibrant two-way bridge connecting the technology communities in Silicon Valley and Taiwan. Their Indian counterparts became key middlemen linking U.S. businesses to low-cost software expertise in India. These cross-Pacific networks represent more than an additional "ethnic resource" that supports entrepreneurial success; they provide the region's skilled immigrants with an important advantage over their mainstream competitors, who often lack the language skills, cultural know-how, and contacts to build business relationships in Asia.

The traditional image of the immigrant economy is the isolated Chinatown or "ethnic enclave" with limited ties to the outside economy. Silicon Valley's new immigrant entrepreneurs, by contrast, are increasingly building professional and social networks that span national boundaries and facilitate flows of capital, skill, and technology. In so doing, they are creating transnational communities that provide the shared information, contacts, and trust that allow local producers to participate in an increasingly global economy (Portes 1995).

As recently as the 1970s, only very large corporations had the resources and capabilities to grow internationally, and they did so primarily by establishing marketing offices or manufacturing plants overseas. Today, by contrast, new transportation and communications technologies allow even the smallest firms to build partnerships with foreign producers to tap overseas expertise, cost-savings, and markets. Start-ups in Silicon Valley today are often global actors from the day they begin operations. Many raise capital from Asian sources, others subcontract manufacturing to Taiwan or rely on software development in India, and virtually all sell their products in Asian markets.

The scarce resource in this new environment is the ability to locate foreign partners quickly and to manage complex business relationships across cultural and linguistic boundaries. This is a challenge particularly in high-technology industries in which products, markets, and technologies are continually being redefined—and where product cycles are routinely shorter than nine months. First-generation immigrants—like the Chinese and Indian engineers of Silicon Valley—who have the language, cultural, and technical skills to function well in both the United States and foreign markets are distinctly positioned to play a central role in this environment. They are creating social structures that enable even the smallest producers to locate and maintain mutually beneficial collaborations across long distances and that facilitate access to Asian sources of capital, manufacturing capabilities, skills, and markets.

These ties have measurable economic benefits. Research at the University of California at Berkeley has documented a significant correlation between the presence of first-generation immigrants from a given country and exports from California. For example, for every 1 percent increase in the number of first-generation immigrants from a given country, exports from California go up nearly 0.5 percent. Moreover, this effect is especially pronounced in the Asia-Pacific region where, all else being equal, California exports nearly four times more than it exports to comparable countries in other parts of the world (Bardhan and Howe 1998).

This section presents cases of immigrant entrepreneurs in Silicon Valley who have helped to construct the new transnational (and typically trans-local) networks. The region's Taiwanese engineers have forged close social and economic ties to their counterparts in the Hsinchu region of Taiwan (an area comparable in size to Silicon Valley), which extends from Taipei to the Hsinchu Science-Based Industrial Park. They have created a rich fabric of professional and business relationships that supports a two-way process of reciprocal industrial upgrading. Silicon Valley's Indian engineers, by contrast, play a more arm's-length role as middlemen linking U.S.–based companies with low-cost software expertise in localities like Bangalore and Hyderabad. In both cases, the immigrant engineers provide the critical contacts, information, and cultural know-how that link dynamic—but distant—regions in the global economy.

The Hsinchu Region and Silicon Valley

In the 1960s and 1970s, the relationship between Taiwan and the United States was a textbook First World–to–Third World relationship. American businesses invested in Taiwan primarily to take advantage of its low-wage manufacturing labor. Meanwhile, Taiwan's best and the brightest engineering students came to the United States for graduate education and created a classic "brain drain" when they remained in the United States for professional opportunities. Many ended up in Silicon Valley.

This relationship changed significantly during the past decade. By the late 1980s, engineers began returning to Taiwan in large numbers, drawn by active government recruitment and the opportunities created by rapid economic development (Lin 1998). At the same time, a growing cohort of highly mobile engineers began to work in both the United States and Taiwan, commuting across the Pacific regularly. Typically Taiwan-born, U.S.–educated engineers, they have the professional contacts and language skills to function fluently in both the Silicon Valley and Taiwanese business cultures and to draw on the complementary strengths of the two regional economies.

K. Y. Han is typical. After graduating from National Taiwan University in the 1970s, Han completed a master's program in solid state physics at the University of California, Santa Barbara. Like many Taiwanese engineers, Han was drawn to Silicon Valley in the early 1980s and worked for nearly a decade at a series of semiconductor companies before joining his college classmate and friend, Jimmy Lee, to start Integrated Silicon Solutions, Inc. (ISSI). After bootstrapping the initial start-up with their own funds and those of other Taiwanese colleagues, they raised more than $9 million in venture capital. Their lack of managerial experience meant that Lee and Han were unable to raise funds from Silicon Valley's mainstream venture capital community. The early rounds of funding were thus exclusively from Asian sources, including the Walden International Investment Group, a San Francisco–based venture fund that specializes in Asian investments, as well as from large industrial conglomerates based in Singapore and Taiwan.

Han and Lee mobilized their professional and personal networks in both Taiwan and the United States to expand ISSI. They recruited engineers (many of whom were Chinese) in their Silicon Valley headquarters to focus on research and development, product design, development, and sales of their high-speed static random access memory chips (SRAMs). They targeted their products at the personal computer market, and many of their initial customers were Taiwanese motherboard producers, which allowed them to grow very rapidly in the first several years. And, with the assistance of the Taiwanese government, they established manufacturing partnerships with Taiwan's state-of-the-art semiconductor foundries and incorporated in the Hsinchu Science-Based Industrial Park to oversee assembly, packaging, and testing.

By 1995, when ISSI was listed on the NASDAQ, Han was visiting Taiwan at least monthly to monitor the firm's manufacturing operations and to work with newly formed subsidiaries in Hong Kong and Mainland China. He finally joined thousands of other Silicon Valley "returnees" and moved his family back to Taiwan. This allowed Han to strengthen the already close relationship with their main foundry, the Taiwan Semiconductor Manufacturing Corporation, as well as to coordinate the logistics and production control process on a daily basis. The presence of a senior manager like Han also turned out to be an advantage for developing local customers. Han still spends an hour each day on the phone with Jimmy Lee, and he returns to Silicon Valley as often as ten times a year. Today ISSI has $110 million in sales and 500 employees worldwide, including 350 in Silicon Valley.

A closely knit community of Taiwanese returnees and U.S.–based engineers and entrepreneurs like Jimmy Lee and K. Y. Han has become the bridge between Silicon Valley and Hsinchu. These social ties, which often build on preexisting alumni relationships among graduates of Taiwan's elite engineering universities, were institutionalized in 1989 with the formation of the Monte Jade Science and Technology Association. Monte Jade's goal is the promotion of business cooperation, investment, and technology transfer between Chinese engineers in the Bay Area and Taiwan. Although the organization remains private, it works closely with local representatives of the Taiwanese government to encourage mutually beneficial investments and business collaborations. Like Silicon Valley's other ethnic associations, Monte Jade's social activities are often as important as its professional activities. Despite the fact that the organization's official language is Mandarin (Chinese), the annual conference typically draws over 1,000 attendees for a day of technical and business analysis, as well as a gala banquet.

This transnational community has accelerated the upgrading of Taiwan's technological infrastructure by transferring technical know-how and organizational models, as well as by forging closer ties with Silicon Valley. Observers note, for example, that management practices in Hsinchu companies are more like those of Silicon Valley than those of the traditional family-firm model that dominates older industries in Taiwan. As a result, according to the Institute for Information Industry's Market Intelligence Center, Taiwan is now the world's largest producer of notebook computers and a range of related PC components, including motherboards, monitors, scanners, power supplies, and keyboards. In addition, Taiwan's semiconductor and integrated circuit manufacturing capabilities are said to be on a par with the leading Japanese and U.S. producers; and its flexible and efficient networks of specialized small and midsize enterprises coordinate the diverse components of this sophisticated infrastructure (Hsu 1997; Mathews 1997).

Taiwan has also become an important source of capital for Silicon Valley start-ups—particularly those begun by immigrant entrepreneurs. It is impossible to estimate accurately the total flow of capital from Taiwan to Silicon Valley because so much of it is invested informally by individual angel investors, but there is no doubt that it increased dramatically in the 1990s. Formal investments from Asia (not including Japan) were more than $500 million in 1997 (Miller 1997). This includes investments by funds based in Taiwan, Hong Kong, and Singapore, as well as U.S.–based venture groups (such as Walden International and Advent International) that raise capital primarily from Asian sources. These investors often provide more than capital. According to Ken Tai, a founder of Acer and now head of venture fund InveStar Capital:

> When we invest, we are also helping bring entrepreneurs back to Taiwan. It is relationship building.... We help them get high-level introductions to foundries (for manufacturing), and we help establish strategic opportunities and relationships with customers.

The growing integration of the technological communities of Silicon Valley and Hsinchu offers substantial benefits to both economies. Silicon Valley remains the center of new product definition and design and of the development of leading-edge technologies, whereas Taiwan offers world-class manufacturing, flexible development and integration, and access to key customers and markets in China and Southeast Asia (Naughton 1997). This appears to be a classic case of the economic benefits of comparative advantage. However, these economic gains from specialization and trade would not be possible without the underlying social structures and institutions provided by the community of Taiwanese engineers, which ensures continuous flows of information between the two regions. Some say that Taiwan is like an extension of Silicon Valley, or that there is a "very small world" between Silicon Valley and Taiwan.

The reciprocal and decentralized nature of these relationships is distinctive. The ties between Japan and the United States in the 1980s were typically arm's-length, and technology transfers between large firms were managed from the top down. The Silicon Valley–Hsinchu relationship, by contrast, consists of formal and informal collaborations between individual investors and entrepreneurs, small and midsize firms, and divisions of larger companies located on both sides of the Pacific. In this complex mix, the rich social and professional ties among Taiwanese engineers and their U.S. counterparts are as important as the more formal corporate alliances and partnerships.

The Bangalore Region and Silicon Valley

Radha Basu left her conservative South Indian family to pursue graduate studies in computer science at the University of Southern California in the early 1970s. Like many other skilled immigrants, she was subsequently drawn into the fast-growing Silicon Valley labor market, where she began a long career at Hewlett-Packard. When Basu returned to India to participate in an electronics industry task force in the mid–1980s, the government invited her to set up one of the country's first foreign subsidiaries. She spent four years establishing HP's software center in Bangalore—pioneering the trend among foreign companies of tapping India's highly skilled but relatively low cost software talent. When Basu returned to Silicon Valley in 1989, the HP office in India employed 400 people, and it has since grown to become one of HP's most successful foreign subsidiaries.

Radha Basu was uniquely positioned to negotiate the complex and often bewildering bureaucracy and backward infrastructure of her home country. She explains that it takes both patience and cultural understanding to do business in India: "You can't just fly in and out and stay in a five-star hotel and expect to get things done like you can elsewhere. You have to understand India and its development needs and adapt to them." Many Indian engineers followed Basu's lead in the early 1990s. They exploited their cultural and linguistic capabilities and their contacts to help build software operations in their home country. Indians educated in the United States have been pivotal in setting up the Indian software facilities for Oracle, Novell, Bay Networks, and other Silicon Valley companies.

However, few Indian engineers choose to live and work permanently in India. Unlike the Taiwanese immigrants who have increasingly returned home to start businesses or to work in established companies, Indian engineers—if they return at all—typically do so on a temporary basis. This is due in part to the difference in standards of living, but most observers agree that the frustrations associated with doing business in India are equally important. Radha Basu explains that the first HP office in India consisted of a telex machine on her dining room table, and that for many years she had to produce physical evidence of software exports for customs officials who did not understand how the satellite datalink worked. She adds that when the Indian government talked about a "single window of clearance" to facilitate foreign trade, she would jokingly ask, "where is the window?"

Business conditions have improved dramatically in India since Basu arrived. The establishment of the Software Technology Parks (STPs) scheme in the late 1980s gave export-oriented software firms in designated zones tax exemptions for five years and guaranteed access to high-speed satellite links and reliable electricity. The national economic liberalization that began in 1991 greatly improved the climate for the software industry as well. Yet even today, expatriates complain bitterly about complex bureaucratic restrictions, corrupt and unresponsive officials, and an infrastructure that causes massive daily frustrations—from unreliable power supplies, water shortages, and backward and extremely costly telecommunications facilities to dangerous and congested highways.

Moreover, many overseas Indians, often referred to as non-resident Indians (NRIs), feel out of place in India. NRIs often face resentment when they return to India—a resentment that is not unrelated to India's long-standing hostility to foreign corporations. In contrast to the close collaboration between Taiwan's policymakers and U.S.–based engineers, there has been almost no communication between the Silicon Valley engineering community and India's policymakers—even those concerned directly with technology policy. Moreover, young engineers in India prefer to work for U.S. multinationals because they are seen as a ticket to Silicon Valley. Software companies in Bangalore report turnovers of 20 to 30 percent per year, primarily because so many workers jump at the first opportunity to emigrate. Of course, some U.S.–educated Indians return home and stay, but on balance the "brain drain" of skilled Indian workers to the United States continued unabated throughout the 1990s.

Silicon Valley's Indian engineers thus play an important but largely arm's-length role connecting U.S. firms with India's low-cost, high-quality skilled labor force. Although some, like Basu, have returned to establish subsidiaries, most do little more than promote India as a viable location for software development. As they became more visible in U.S. companies during the 1990s, NRIs were increasingly instrumental in convincing senior management in their firms to source software or establish operations in India. The cost differential remains a motivating factor for such moves. Wages in India for software programmers and systems analysts are one-tenth the U.S. wage, and the cost of an engineer is 35 to 40 percent lower than the cost in the United States. The availability of skill is, of course, the essential precondition for considering India, and it is of growing importance for Silicon Valley firms facing shortages of skilled labor. The low wages provide a viable trade-off to working in an environment plagued by chronic infrastructure problems.

The Indian software industry has boomed in recent years, but most of the growth is still driven by low-value-added services (Parthasarathy 1999; Arora et al. 2000; Heeks 1996). Throughout the 1980s and early 1990s, India was confined almost exclusively to low-value segments of software production such as coding, testing, and maintenance. A majority of this activity was in the form of on-site services overseas—or "body-shopping"—which proved to be extremely lucrative, given the size of the wage gap.[4] Although more of the work is now being done offshore (in India) and a handful of large Indian firms and American multinationals have started to provide higher-value-added design services, much of the software development in India today differs little from body-shopping. The time difference makes it possible to work around the clock, with programmers in India logging on to a customer's computers to perform relatively routine testing, coding, or programming tasks once a U.S.-based team has left for the day.

The climate for entrepreneurship in India is not hospitable, and it remained one of the main constraints on the upgrading of the Indian software industry in the 1990s. India lacks a venture capital industry, and the domestic market for information technology is very small. As a result, the software industry is dominated by a small number of large export-oriented domestic and foreign corporations that have minimal ties with each other, local entrepreneurs, or the Indian engineering community in Silicon Valley. These companies have been so profitable exploiting the wage gap that they have had few incentives to address higher-value-added segments of the market—or to nurture entrepreneurial companies that might do so.

As a result, most economic relations between Silicon Valley and regions like Bangalore are still conducted primarily by individuals within the large U.S. or Indian corporations. There are few U.S.-educated engineers who have their feet sufficiently in both worlds to transfer the information and know-how about new markets and technologies or to build the long-term relationships that would contribute to the upgrading of India's technological infrastructure. And there are no institutionalized mechanisms—public or private—that would both facilitate and reinforce the creation of more broad based interactions between the two regions.

---

[4] Body-shopping is defined narrowly: it refers to offering on-site programming services (in the United States, for example) on the basis of "time and material" contracts. On-site services accounted for approximately 90 percent of the value of Indian software exports in 1990 and for 61 percent in 1995.

However, communications between the engineering communities in India and the United States are growing fast, especially among the younger generation. Alumni associations from the elite Indian Institutes of Technology (who have many graduates in Silicon Valley) are starting to play a bridging role by organizing seminars and social events. A new journal, *siliconindia* (www.siliconindia.com), provides up-to-date information on technology businesses in the United States and India and has recruited several of Silicon Valley's most successful engineers onto its editorial board. And a growing number of U.S.-educated Indians report a desire to return home, whereas others have left the large Indian companies to try their hand at entrepreneurship in Silicon Valley. In short, there is a small but growing technical community linking Silicon Valley and Bangalore—one that could play an important role in the upgrading of the Indian software industry in the future.

Taiwan and India Meet in Silicon Valley

Silicon Valley–based firms are now well positioned to exploit both India's software talent and Taiwan's manufacturing capabilities. Mahesh Veerina started Ramp Networks (initially named Trancell Systems) in 1993 with several Indian friends, relatives, and colleagues. Their vision was to develop low-cost devices that speed Internet access for small businesses. By 1994 they were short on money and decided to hire programmers in India for one-quarter of the Silicon Valley rate. One founder spent two years setting up and managing their software development center in the southern city of Hyderabad, which was seen as "a big sacrifice." They followed the current trend of choosing Hyderabad over increasingly congested Bangalore because business costs and labor turnover were lower. Ramp obtained funding to expand the Indian operation from Draper International—a San Francisco–based venture fund dedicated to financing technology activity in India.

Veerina did not discover Taiwan until 1997 when he was introduced to the principals at the Taiwanese investment fund InveStar Capital. After investing in Ramp, InveStar partners Ken Tai and Herbert Chang convinced Veerina to visit Taiwan. They set up two days of appointments with high-level executives in Taiwanese technology companies. Veerina, who travels regularly to India but had never visited East Asia, was amazed: "the Taiwanese are a tight community and very receptive to and knowledgeable about new technologies and companies over here. They also do deals very quickly.... It is incredible the way they operate, the speed with which they move, and the dynamism of the place." He told Tai and Chang that he wanted to return to Taiwan immediately.

In less than three months, Veerina established Original Equipment Manufacturing (OEM) relationships for high-volume manufacture of Ramp's routers with three Taiwanese manufacturers (compared to the nine months it took for them to establish a similar partnership with a U.S. manufacturer). The unit price quoted by the Taiwanese was almost half what Ramp was paying for manufacturing in the United States, and the company was able to increase its output one-hundred-fold because of the relationships that Veerina subsequently built with key customers in the Taiwanese PC industry. Ramp also decided to use the worldwide distribution channels of its Taiwanese partners. Moreover, when Ramp designed a new model, the Taiwanese manufacturer was prepared to ship product in two weeks, compared to the six months it would have taken in the United States.

Veerina says he could never have built these business relationships without the help of InveStar's partners and their network of high-level contacts in Taiwan. In a business where product cycles are often shorter than nine months, the speed and the cost savings provided by these relationships provide critical competitive advantages to a firm like Ramp. InveStar's Tai and Chang see this as one of their key assets: intimate knowledge of the ins and outs of the business infrastructure in Taiwan's decentralized industrial system. By helping outsiders (Chinese as well as non-Chinese) negotiate these complicated social and business networks to tap into Taiwan's cost-effective and high-quality infrastructure and capability for speedy and flexible integration, they provide their clients with far more than access to capital. In 1999, when Ramp went public on the NASDAQ, its software development was in India, its manufacturing in Taiwan, and its new product definition and headquarters in Silicon Valley.

As Silicon Valley's skilled Chinese and Indian immigrants create social and economic links to their home countries, they simultaneously open foreign markets, identify manufacturing options, and link technical skills in growing regions of Asia to the broader business community in California. Firms in both traditional and technology sectors, for example, now increasingly turn to India for software programming talent. Meanwhile, California's complex of technology-related sectors increasingly relies on Taiwan's fast and flexible infrastructure for manufacturing semiconductors and PCs, as well as their growing markets for advanced technology components (Dedrick and Kraemer 1998). It is particularly striking that these advantages are now equally accessible to entrepreneurs like Ramp's Veerina and to more established corporations. In short, although these new international linkages are being forged by a relatively small community of highly skilled immigrants, they are strengthening the economic infrastructure of Silicon Valley as well.

Conclusion

This research underscores important changes in the relationship between immigration, trade, and economic development in the 1990s. In the past, the primary economic linkages created by immigrants to their countries of origin were remittances sent to family members left behind. Today, however, a growing number of skilled immigrants return to their home countries after studying and working abroad. Those who stay often become part of transnational communities that link the United States to the economies of distant regions. The new immigrant entrepreneurs thus foster economic development directly, by creating new jobs and wealth, as well as indirectly, by coordinating the information flows and providing the linguistic and cultural know-how that promote trade and investment flows with their home countries.

Scholars and policymakers need to recognize the growing interrelationships between immigration, trade, and economic development policy. The economic impact of skilled immigrants, in particular, is not limited to labor supply and wage effects. Some of their economic contributions, such as enhanced trade and investment flows, are difficult to quantify, but they must figure into our debates. The national debate over the increase in H1–B visas for high-skilled immigrants, for example, focused primarily on the extent to which immigrants displace native workers. Yet we have seen here that these immigrants also create new jobs and economic linkages in their role as entrepreneurs. Economic openness has its costs, to be sure, but the strength of the California economy has historically derived from its openness and diversity, and this will be increasingly true as the economy becomes more global. The experience of Silicon Valley's new immigrant entrepreneurs suggests that California should resist the view that immigration and trade are zero-sum processes. We need to encourage the immigration of skilled workers, while simultaneously devoting resources to improving the education of native workers.

The fastest-growing groups of immigrant engineers in Silicon Valley today are from Mainland China and India. Chinese, in particular, are increasingly visible in the computer science and engineering departments of local universities, as well as in the workforces of the region's established companies. Although still relative newcomers to Silicon Valley, they appear poised to follow the trajectory of their Taiwanese predecessors. Several have started their own companies. And they are already building ties back home, encouraged by the active efforts of

Chinese bureaucrats and universities—and by the powerful incentive provided by the promise of the China market. Ties between Silicon Valley and India will almost certainly continue to expand as well. Whether the emerging connections between Silicon Valley and regions in China and India generate broader ties that contribute to industrial upgrading in these nations—as well as creating new markets and partners for Silicon Valley producers—will depend largely on political and economic developments within these nations. Whatever the outcome, the task for policymakers remains to maintain open boundaries so that regions like Silicon Valley continue to both build and benefit from their growing ties to the Asian economy.

References

AACI (Asian Americans for Community Involvement). 1993. *Qualified, But.... A Report on Glass Ceiling Issues Facing Asian Americans in Silicon Valley.* San Jose, Calif.: AACI.

Alarcón, Rafael. 1999. "Recruitment Processes among Foreign-Born Engineers and Scientists in Silicon Valley," *American Behavioral Scientist* 42 (9): 1381–97.

American Association of Engineering Societies. 1995. "Engineering and Technology Degrees." New York: AAES.

Arora, Ashish, V. S. Arunchalam, Jai Asundi, and Ronald Fernandez. 2000. "The Indian Software Services Industry." Working Paper. Pittsburgh, Penn.: Heinz School of Public Policy and Management, Carnegie-Mellon University.

Bardhan, Ashok Deo, and David K. Howe. 1998. "Transnational Social Networks and Globalization: The Geography of California's Exports." Working Paper No. 98-262. Berkeley: Fisher Center for Real Estate and Urban Economics, University of California, Berkeley.

Borjas, George J. 1994. "The Economics of Immigration," *Journal of Economic Literature* 32 (4).

———. 1995. "The Economic Benefits from Immigration," *Journal of Economic Perspectives* 9 (2).

Chang, Shirley L. 1992. "Causes of Brain Drain and Solutions: The Taiwan Experience," *Studies in Comparative International Development* 27 (1): 27–43.

Dedrick, Jason, and Kenneth L. Kraemer. 1998. *Asia's Computer Challenge: Threat or Opportunity for the United States and the World.* New York: Oxford University Press.

Fernandez, Marilyn. 1998. "Asian Indian Americans in the Bay Area and the Glass Ceiling," *Sociological Perspectives* 42 (1): 119–49.

Gong, Margie. 1996. "A Forward Look Towards the Origin of AAMA-Part 1," *AAMA News*, October, p.1.

Granovetter, Mark. 1995. "The Economic Sociology of Firms and Entrepreneurs." In *The Economic Sociology of Immigration: Essays on Networks, Ethnic-*

ity and Entrepreneurship, edited by Alejandro Portes. New York: Russell Sage.

Hamilton, Gary. 1997. "Organization and Market Processes in Taiwan's Capitalist Economy." In *The Economic Organization of East Asian Capitalism*, edited by Marco Orru, Nicole Biggart, and Gary Hamilton. Thousand Oaks, Calif.: Russell Sage.

Heeks, Richard. 1996. *India's Software Industry: State Policy, Liberalisation and Industrial Development*. New Delhi: Sage.

Hing, Bill Ong, and Ronald Lee, eds. 1996. *The State of Asian Pacific America: Reframing the Immigration Debate*. Los Angeles: Leadership Education for Asian Pacifics and the Asian American Studies Center, University of California, Los Angeles.

Hsu, Jinn-yuh. 1997. "A Late Industrial District? Learning Networks in the Hsinchu Science-Based Industrial Park." Ph.D. dissertation, University of California, Berkeley.

Johnson, Jean M. 1998. "Statistical Profiles of Foreign Doctoral Recipients in Science and Engineering: Plans to Stay in the United States." NSF 99-304. Arlington, Va.: Division of Science Resources Studies, National Science Foundation, November.

Johnson, Jean M., and Mark C. Regets. 1998. "International Mobility of Scientists and Engineers to the United States—Brain Drain or Brain Circulation?" NSF Issue Brief 98–316. Arlington, Va.: National Science Foundation, June 22.

Kanjanapan, Wilawan. 1995. "The Immigration of Asian Professionals to the United States: 1988–1990," *International Migration Review* 29 (1) : 7–32.

Levy, Brian, and Wen-Jeng Kuo. 1991. "The Strategic Orientation of Firms and the Performance of Korea and Taiwan in Frontier Industries: Lessons from Comparative Case Studies of the Keyboard and Personal Computer Assembly," *World Development* 19 (4).

Lin, Otto. 1998. "Science and Technology Policy and Its Influence on Economic Development in Taiwan." In *Behind East Asian Growth: The Political and Social Foundations of Prosperity*, edited by Henry S. Rowen. London: Routledge.

Mathews, John. 1997. "A Silicon Valley of the East: Creating Taiwan's Semiconductor Industry," *California Management Review* 39 (4).

McCarthy, Kevin F., and Georges Vernez. 1997. *Immigration in a Changing Economy: California's Experience*. Santa Monica, Calif. Rand Corporation.

Miller, Matt. 1997. "Venture Forth," *Far Eastern Economic Review*, November 6, pp. 62–63.

Naughton, Barry, ed. 1997. *The China Circle: Economics and Technology in the PRC, Taiwan, and Hong Kong*. Washington, D.C.: Brookings Institution Press.

Parthasarathy, Balaji. 1999. "The Indian Software Industry in Bangalore," Ph.D. dissertation, University of California, Berkeley.

Portes, Alejandro, ed. 1995. *The Economic Sociology of Immigration: Essays on Networks, Ethnicity, and Entrepreneurship*. New York: Russell Sage.

Saxenian, AnnaLee. 1994. *Regional Advantage: Culture and Competition in Silicon Valley and Route 128*. Cambridge, Mass.: Harvard University Press.

————. 1999. *Silicon Valley's New Immigrant Entrepreneurs.* San Francisco: Public Policy Institute of California.

Smith, James P., and Barry Edmonston, eds. 1997. *The New Americans: Economic, Demographic, and Fiscal Effects of Immigration.* Washington, D.C.: National Academy Press.

Tang, Joyce. 1993. "The Career Attainment of Caucasian and Asian Engineers," *Sociological Quarterly* 34 (3): 467–96.

Waldinger, Roger, Howard Aldrich, Robin Ward, et al., eds. 1990. *Ethnic Entrepreneurs: Immigrant Business in Industrial Societies.* Newbury Park, Calif.: Sage.

Wong, Bernard. 1998. *Ethnicity and Entrepreneurship: The New Chinese Immigrants in the San Francisco Bay Area.* Needham Heights, Mass.: Allyn and Bacon.

9

Immigrant Niches in the U.S. High-Technology Industry

Rafael Alarcón

There is currently a heated debate about the impact of skilled immigrants on the employment and wages of U.S. workers who work or aspire to find employment in the information technology industry.[1] This controversy has intensified with recent discussions regarding the expansion of the H–1B non-immigrant visa program. Under the 1990 Immigration and Nationality Act (INA), the H–1B program is designed for temporary workers employed in "specialty occupations" that require highly specialized knowledge and at least a bachelor's degree or its equivalent. High-tech companies are the main beneficiaries of this program because they hire the largest number of "high tech" *braceros* or *cerebreros*.[2]

An unlikely coalition has emerged to support the increase of the permanent and temporary immigration of the highly skilled. This coa-

I was able to write this chapter thanks to grants from the Social Science Research Council through its International Migration Program, and from the Center for U.S.–Mexican Studies at the University of California, San Diego (see Alarcón 1998). I am grateful for comments from Wayne Cornelius, Idean Salehyan, and Christian Zlolniski.

[1] The information technology (IT) or high-technology industry encompasses the following manufacturing sectors: computing and office equipment, communications equipment, electronic components, guided missiles, and space vehicles and instruments. From the service industry, it also includes the software and data-processing sector (Saxenian 1994: 209).

[2] I call migrants who hold H–IB visas "high-tech *braceros*" or "*cerebreros*" because, like the Mexican braceros of the past (1942–1964), these migrants work in the United States temporarily. I also use the term cerebreros because, unlike Mexican braceros who worked with their arms (*brazos* in Spanish), cerebreros work with their brains (*cerebros*) (Alarcón 2000).

lition ranges from the Clinton administration to the Democratic Party, high-tech companies, church groups, ethnic lobbies, and the "growth wing" of the Republican Party. CEOs and managers in the information technology industry maintain that, because their companies are competing in a global economy, they need access to the best and brightest workers of the world. For instance, recognizing that 50 percent of Ph.D. graduate students in electrical engineering at U.S. universities are foreign-born, Michael Maibach, government affairs director at Intel Corporation, wants the U.S. Congress to allow high-tech companies continued access to these individuals. "If America's universities educate the world's best and brightest," he writes, "America's industry should have the ability to hire them. Let's staple a green card to engineering Ph.D.s" (Maibach 1995).

However, the U.S. Immigration and Naturalization Service (INS) notes that most visas granted to immigrants on employment grounds go to technicians with two years of training, not to persons with "extraordinary ability" or to "outstanding professors and researchers" (*Migration News*, March–April 1996). Critics of the H–1B program contend that most H–1B workers are hired by temporary staffing agencies that lease them to U.S. employers. In fact, among the ten top firms that brought H–1B workers between October 1, 1997, and March 31, 1998, were Indian "body shopping" companies such as Tata Consultancy Services and Tata Infotech (*Migration News*, December 1998). Others argue that the presence of a large number of foreign-born engineers and scientists has reduced pressure to make major reforms in K–12 science and engineering education and has eased, if not eliminated, the pressure to recruit women and minorities in science and engineering careers (North 1995).

Immigration policy regulates the entry of foreign-born professionals who obtain visas as permanent residents or temporary workers. There are four main avenues through which foreign-born engineers and scientists find employment in high-technology companies. First, some enter the United States as children of immigrant families. They resemble the native population because of their exposure to the U.S. educational system and their integration into the economic, political, social, and cultural institutions of the United States. Second, some are former employees of subsidiaries of U.S. high-tech companies located abroad. These professionals obtain specific training, work under the discipline of the U.S. labor system, and learn about employment opportunities in the parent company in the United States through daily contact with U.S. workers and managers. A third group is composed of former foreign students at U.S. universities who originally came to the United States to pursue studies in science and engineering fields. High-tech companies may recruit these professionals when they graduate thanks to immigration law provisions that favor the permanent and temporary migration of skilled persons. Finally, the cerebreros work in the United States with temporary visas such as the H–1B, which allows a maximum stay of six years (Alarcón 2000).

This chapter examines the role that U.S. immigration policy has played in the formation of immigrant labor market niches in the high-technology industry of the United States. To this end, I compare and contrast the experiences of two immigrant groups—Indians and Mexicans—in regard to their employment incorporation into the high-technology industry.

According to Waldinger (1994), immigrants from the same country often cluster in a limited number of occupations or industries, forming niches. Social networks are crucial in the formation of labor market niches because they organize information flows between new immigrants and settlers, on the one hand, and between workers and employers, on the other. Niches generate two important effects; they increase immigrants' ability to access employment, and at the same time they reduce employers' costs and risks associated with hiring and training. Furthermore, the existence of a niche dominated by an immigrant group in a particular sector of the labor market arguably prevents the native-born and other immigrants from getting jobs in this sector. Waldinger and Bozorgmehr (1996) contend that poor African Americans in Los Angeles have been displaced from lower-level jobs as domestics, janitors, and sewing machine operators by the expansion of Mexican and Central American immigrant niches that have captured these jobs, as they have also done in the furniture manufacturing and apparel industries. These immigrants have taken over these jobs for two reasons. First, the immigrants enjoy good connections with employers; hiring is conducted through networks, diminishing opportunities for African Americas in the process. Second, employers may consider Latino immigrants more productive and more docile than African Americans.

Immigration policy can play an important role in the formation of immigrant niches by selecting immigrants according to certain demographic and economic characteristics that can give them a comparative advantage over native-born workers and other immigrants. In the particular case of the information technology industry, research has consistently shown that educational attainment among immigrant engineers and scientists is much higher than among their native-born counterparts (Alarcón 1999; Bouvier and Martin 1995).

Portes and Borocs (1989) emphasize the importance of immigration policy in determining successful labor market integration. They contend that there are a number of modes of incorporation of contemporary immigrants in developed countries that result from the combination of three factors: conditions of exit, class origins, and contexts of reception. The context of reception—in addition to the immigration policy of the host country—includes the attitudes of employers and the native population toward the immigrant group and the characteristics of the preexisting ethnic community. These authors use the case of British, Canadian, and other white foreign-born professionals, who enjoy a neutral context of reception, to demonstrate situations in which individual merit and skills are the most important determinants of a successful adaptation to the United States. On the other hand, they assert that Mexican and Dominican immigrants, who are generally manual laborers, face an adverse context upon arrival because they are seen as unwelcome foreigners. The question, then, is: what is the context of reception for foreign-born professionals from developing countries in Asia and Latin America?

I use INS and census data to analyze the existence of niches in the high-technology industry. The census data are the Public Use Microdata Samples (PUMS) of the 1980 and 1990 Census of Population and Housing that contain records representing 5 percent of housing units and their occupants. In the first part of this chapter, I present a general overview of the presence of immigrant engineers and scientists in the most important high-tech regions in the United States. In the second, I review the impact of the Immigration and Nationality Act of 1990 in facilitating the immigration of the highly skilled. In the third section, I compare the immigration histories of India and Mexico with respect to the formation of "niches" in the high-tech industry. I end with a presentation of the main conclusions of the study.

Immigrant Engineers and Scientists in High-Tech Regions of the United States

Since the 1980s, the United States has experienced a profound transformation as a result of increased immigration. Labor markets in the most important metropolitan areas have become more diversified with the rapid growth of immigrant niches. New immigrants have also ventured into new destinations and industries that were once dominated by the native-born. The information technology industry has not escaped the impact of immigration.

The professional fields that comprise the high-tech industry have changed substantially. According to census data, the number of engineers, mathematicians/computer scientists, and natural scientists in the United States rose from 2,150,707 in 1980 to 3,064,705 in 1990 (a 42.5

percent increase).[3] The demographic composition of these professions changed significantly during the 1980s, with a dramatic gain for women and a significant increase in the number of Asian immigrants and Americans of Asian ancestry.[4] Figure 9.1 shows the distribution of the three groups of engineers and scientists by nativity in 1990.

Figure 9.1. Nativity of Engineers and Scientists in the United States, 1990

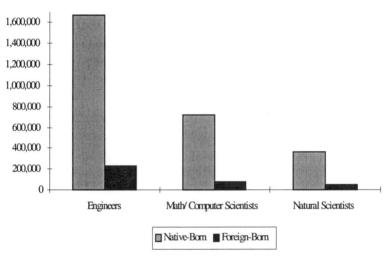

Source: Figure constructed from data from Bouvier and Martin 1995: 16.

Considering that the foreign-born constituted 7.9 percent of the total population in 1990, their participation in these three professional fields was significant, averaging 11.7 percent. While most of these immigrants were born in Asia (especially China and India) and some European

---

[3] There were far more engineers: (1,876,523 in 1990) than the other two groups of scientists. Their number had increased by 23.7 percent since 1980. However, the most rapid growth occurred among mathematicians and computer scientists, whose numbers increased 138.8 percent during the decade, from 326,495 to 779,507. Natural scientists grew at a more modest rate, from 307,295 in 1980 to 408,675 in 1990 (a 33 percent increase) (Bouvier and Martin 1995).

[4] Despite an increase in the number of women, they accounted for only 10 percent of the engineers, 36 percent of mathematicians and computer scientists, and 26.5 percent of natural scientists. In most cases, the share of female scientists is a bit larger among the native-born than the foreign-born population (Bouvier and Martin 1995: 17).

countries, there were very few engineers and scientists from Latin America, Africa, or the Caribbean.

With regard to native-born engineers and scientists, non-Hispanic whites were overrepresented, making up an overwhelming 92 percent in 1990. African Americans comprised only 4.3 percent of these professional groups, followed by 2.3 percent Hispanics and 1.4 percent Asians. Although in real terms there is a disproportionate number of non–Hispanic whites among engineers and scientists, as a proportion of their overall population, U.S. citizens of Indian and Chinese ancestry are more likely than members of the other ethnic groups to be professionals in these three fields. At the other end of the spectrum, U.S. citizens of Hispanic ancestry and Native Americans have the lowest rates of participation in professional occupations.

The presence of burgeoning immigrant communities in many high-technology regions has been largely ignored in the industrial location literature. Clearly, immigrant communities provide low-skilled workers for assembly plants and labor-intensive services. However, the role of these communities and their countries of origin in providing highly educated engineers and scientists has not been explored.

In order to estimate the importance of these immigrant workers in the development of the high-tech industry, it is useful to examine the concentration of foreign-born professionals in "high-tech" states. Table 9.1 focuses on the 1980–1990 period; it shows the distribution of foreign-born engineers and scientists employed in high-technology industries in the states that contain the most important high-tech regions in the United States: Silicon Valley and Southern California (both in California); Route 128 in Massachusetts; the "Research Triangle" in North Carolina; and Austin, Texas.

In 1980, California not only had the largest number of engineers and scientists employed in high-technology occupations (nearly 100,000), but also the highest proportion of the foreign-born. This is not surprising given that California is the most important high-tech state, and it also has the largest share of the U.S. immigrant population. On the other hand, North Carolina had the smallest number of professionals employed in the high-technology industry and the lowest percentage of the foreign-born. The importance of foreign-born engineers and scientists is underscored by the fact that in 1980, with the exception of California, the share of foreign-born engineers and scientists was higher than the share of the foreign-born employed in the civilian labor force. This is particularly significant in North Carolina.

Between 1980 and 1990, these four states experienced a rapid growth in the number of engineers and scientists employed in high technology and in their share of the foreign-born. These two processes are the result of the growth of the high-technology industry and of the participation of immigrants in this industry. In Texas and North Carolina, the number of professionals employed in high technology doubled during the 1980s. The immigrant engineers and scientists also significantly increased their participation in both states. Again, this process was particularly notable in North Carolina.

As a result of these changes, in 1990 one of every five high-tech professionals in California was a long-term or recent immigrant. California continued not only to have the largest number of engineers and scientists employed in high technology (nearly 150,000), but also the highest proportion of those who were born outside the United States. On the other hand, despite the rapid growth of its immigrant professional population during the 1980s, North Carolina continued to have the smallest number of these professionals and the lowest percentage of the foreign-born. As in 1980, in all of the states (with the exception of California), the share of the foreign-born working in high-tech occupations was higher than the share of the foreign-born in the rest of the civilian labor force.

Data in table 9.1 suggest that during the 1980s most of the "high-tech" states experienced rapid growth in their high-tech sectors, judging by the fast increase in the number of engineers and scientists. The number of these professionals increased by 53 percent in California and by almost 100 percent in Texas and North Carolina. Massachusetts had the slowest growth of the four states (45 percent). In the four states, the share of foreign-born engineers and scientists grew significantly during the decade. This is the result of the relocation of immigrant professionals who had been living in the United States earlier and the emergence of high-tech regions as destinations for new skilled immigrants.

The Immigration Act of 1990: Employment versus Family Reunification

In 1990 the U.S. Congress addressed the question of the human capital of immigrants and its consequences for the global competitiveness of the United States by more strongly promoting the immigration of skilled persons and by emphasizing the employment skills of new immigrants (Papademetriou 1996). In this sense, the Immigration Act of 1990 followed the trend visible in countries like Canada and Australia, which have adopted a visa allocation system geared toward skilled immigrants rather than family reunification (Kanajapan 1995; Borjas 1996).

Table 9.1

Foreign-born Engineers and Scientists Employed in the High-Technology Industry in States with High-Technology Regions, 1980 and 1990

	California Total	% FB	Massachusetts Total	% FB	Texas Total	% FB	North Carolina Total	% FB
1980								
Engineers	77,580	16.8	17,040	9.2	15,620	7.2	3,680	2.7
Mathematicians and computer scientists	17,200	10.9	5,560	6.1	5,780	6.6	1,060	7.5
Natural scientists	2,260	19.5	500	36.0	320	6.3	80	0.0
Total	97,040	15.8	23,100	9.0	21,720	7.0	4,820	3.7
Employed civilians	10,596,040	16.5	2,661,040	8.3	6,293,220	6.5	2,607,960	1.4
1990								
Engineers	98,972	23.7	18,123	14.2	26,932	11.5	5,622	7.5
Mathematicians and computer scientists	47,055	21.5	15,238	15.2	15,581	9.8	3,594	6.7
Natural scientists	2,233	23.2	238	0	445	11.5	75	0
Total	148,260	23.0	33,599	14.5	42,958	10.9	9,291	7.1
Employed civilians	13,970,000	25.0	3,031,859	10.0	7,629,518	10.5	3,228,309	2.0

Source: Bureau of the Census, 1992.

FB = Foreign-born.

Note: Weighting of data was different for 1990 and 1980. For 1990 data, the explicit weights added to the PUMS files by the Bureau of the Census were used. For 1980, the data were weighted by 20, applying the inverse of the sampling fraction (see Myers 1992: 88).

Immigration Legislation before 1990

Before the Immigration Act of 1990, there had been two major shifts in immigration policy—in the 1920s and the 1960s (Borjas 1996). During the 1920s, economic conditions and a growing anti-immigrant sentiment led to severe restrictions on immigration that came to be known as the "national origins quota system." This immigration regime would shape immigration flows until the mid–1960s. A 1921 immigration act limited the annual number of legal immigrants to 3 percent of the foreign-born population of each nationality as enumerated in the 1910 census. This provision favored immigration from Northern and Western Europe, and it drastically reduced immigration from Asia, Africa, and Eastern Europe. Restrictions on immigration from Asia had been initiated in 1882 with the Chinese Exclusion Act and the "Gentlemen's Agreement" of 1910, which halted labor immigration from Japan (Heer 1996).

The Immigration Act of 1924 had two quota provisions. The U.S. Congress set the annual quota of any restricted nationality at 2 percent of the number of foreign-born persons of that nationality residing in the continental United States in 1890. The total quota was established at 164,667 per year and was in effect between May 1924 and June 1927. The second provision established that the annual quota from any country or nationality was some fraction of 150,000 that corresponded to the number of immigrants of that country who were residing in the continental United States in 1920. This quota system was in effect from July 1927 through December 1952 (INS 1992: A.1–6). The Immigration Act of 1924 also granted preference under the quota to immediate relatives of U.S. citizens and quota immigrants and their families who were skilled in agriculture. Wives and unmarried children of U.S. citizens and natives of Western Hemisphere countries were not included in the quota. These Acts made it especially difficult for Asians, Africans, and Eastern Europeans to immigrate to the United States from the 1920s to the mid–1960s. For the most part, only the highly educated from these countries were able to immigrate during this period.

In 1952 when Congress passed the Immigration and Nationality Act, legal immigration to the United States was based on two cornerstones: family reunification and occupational qualifications. The INA basically continued the national origins quota system, but it also made major reforms to immigration policy. It made all races eligible for naturalization and established a preference system (which continues today) that favored family reunification. It granted first preference to the immediate relatives of U.S. citizens and legal residents. Skilled and unskilled workers in certain occupational categories were also eligible to enter the United States (INS 1992: A.1–6; Calavita 1994).

In the mid–1960s there was a major revolution in U.S. immigration policy. In 1965, the INA was substantially amended under pressure from the civil rights movement. The new act abolished the national origins quota system, eliminating national origin, race, or ancestry as a basis for immigration to the United States. This led to a more diverse pool of immigrants from regions other than Europe. However, the 1965 Immigration and Nationality Act (also known as the Hart-Celler Act) maintained the principle of numerical restriction, limiting Eastern Hemisphere immigration to 170,000 and placing, for the first time, a ceiling on Western Hemisphere immigration of 120,000. This legislation also set a per-country limit of 20,000 persons. The act further established a seven-category preference system for relatives of U.S. citizens and permanent residents and for persons with special occupational skills to meet labor market needs in the United States. In the end, neither the preference system nor the per-country limit was applied to the Western Hemisphere (INS 1992).[5]

Current immigration flows have also been shaped by the Refugee Act of 1980 and the Immigration Reform and Control Act of 1986 (IRCA), which granted amnesty to undocumented workers already residing in the United States, established sanctions against employers who knowingly hire undocumented workers, and increased enforcement at U.S. borders.

The Immigration Act of 1990 and Beyond

Even though the Immigration Act of 1990 gave family reunification a resounding affirmation, it significantly expanded the proportion of employment-based visas, from 54,000 under previous immigration law to 140,000 per year (Papademetriou 1996). Before 1990, less than 10 percent of immigrants could enter the United States each year based on their job skills. Thanks to the Immigration Act of 1990, approximately 21 percent of the new immigrants each year are admitted because of their occupational skills. As shown in table 9.2, the 140,000 employment-based visas granted to the principal immigrants and their families

---

[5] The third preference granted 27,000 visas per year to attract foreign-born professionals of exceptional ability, along with their spouses and children. The sixth preference provided another 27,000 visas per year for skilled and unskilled immigrants and their spouses and children in occupations in which workers were in short supply in the United States. The immediate relatives of U.S. citizens and some special immigrants (such as certain religious ministers and former employees of the U.S. government abroad) were not subject to numerical restrictions.

Table 9.2
Immigrant Categories of the Immigration Act of 1990

Family-Sponsored Immigrants		480,000
1. Adult unmarried children of U.S. citizens	23,400	
2.		
2A Spouses and minor children of permanent residents	114,200	
2B Adult children of permanent residents		
3. Married children of U.S. citizens	23,400	
4. Brothers and sisters of adult U.S. citizens	65,000	
Total (family preference floor)	226,000	
Employment-Based Immigrants		140,000
1. Priority workers	40,000	
2. Immigrants with advanced degrees	40,000	
3. Skilled and unskilled workers	40,000	
4. Special immigrants	10,000	
5. Investors	10,000	
Diversity Immigrants		55,000
Total (overall immigration cap)		675,000

Source: Table constructed from Yale-Loehr 1991.

were allocated under a system of five preferences that encourages the immigration of university professors, artists, athletes, religious workers, investors, engineers, and scientists.

The Immigration Act of 1990 also continued the long-standing tradition of not restricting the number of immediate relatives of U.S. citizens who can enter the United States each year (spouses, children, and parents of U.S. citizens). In this sense, the act allocated 480,000 visas for family reunification purposes, giving unlimited access to the immediate relatives of U.S. citizens and then granting the remaining visas under a four-preference system benefiting the adult children of U.S. citizens and the direct relatives of permanent residents (see table 9.2).

In response to the fact that the Immigration Act of 1965 favored immigration from countries in Asia and Latin America, the U.S. Congress wanted to promote diversity among other immigrant groups. For this reason, Congress allocated 55,000 visas to natives of low-admission countries. Although Irish immigrants were the main beneficiaries of this measure, natives of twelve high-admission countries—including Canada, Mexico, El Salvador, India, China, and the United Kingdom—were ineligible for this program.

According to the Immigration and Nationality Act of 1990, priority workers are immigrants with extraordinary ability in the sciences, arts, education, business, or athletics, as well as outstanding professors and researchers and certain executives and managers of multinational corporations. These individuals are not required to obtain labor certification to obtain these visas. Papademetriou (1996) considers that there is a minimum of regulatory interference because these talented individuals are de facto global citizens. The second category includes immigrants with advanced degrees or with exceptional ability in the sciences, arts, or business. In order to obtain visas, they need to show a concrete offer of employment and labor certification. The third category is designed for skilled and unskilled workers and requires a job offer and labor certification.[6] Only 10,000 visas are available to unskilled workers. The Special Immigrants are certain religious ministers and workers and overseas employees of the U.S. government. Finally, the fifth category allocates 10,000 visas for entrepreneurs who establish a new commercial enterprise and invest between $500,000 and $3,000,000 in the United States. The investment must create at least ten full-time jobs for U.S. workers (Calavita 1994; Papademetriou 1996; Yale-Loehr 1991). Interestingly, Louie and Ong's (1995) study of the early use of the investor visa by East Asian immigrants found a lack of interest on the part of potential investors.

Table 9.3 illustrates the impact of the Immigration Act of 1990. Column 1 presents the total number of visas granted to each country in 1994. Column 2 contains the number of persons admitted under one of the five employment preferences the same year, and column 3 shows the percentage of persons holding such visas. The table reveals that immigration from European countries and Canada is mainly composed of persons with employment visas. On the other hand, India and Mexico have a small percentage of persons with employment-based visas, showing that family reunification has more importance in the migration streams of these two developing countries.

---

[6] To confer the labor certification, the Department of Labor requires information about wages and the availability of U.S. workers. The union representative of the company that is applying for an employment-based visa must be notified, and a notice about the labor certification application must be posted "in conspicuous locations" in the company (Yale-Loehr 1991).

Table 9.3

Permanent Residents Admitted on Employment-based Preferences, 1994

	Total Number of Visas	Employment-Based Visas	% Employment-Based Visas
China	23,074	13,107	56.8
The Philippines	23,628	9,620	40.7
India	21,879	8,431	38.5
Canada	8,481	7,070	83.4
United Kingdom	6,400	5,189	81.1
Korea	8,379	4,607	55.0
El Salvador	8,871	3,810	42.9
Mexico	15,064	3,663	24.3
Taiwan	6,685	3,627	54.3
Soviet Union	2,706	2,524	93.3
Total	335,252	123,291	36.8

Source: *Migration News*, December 1998.

The Immigration and Nationality Act of 1990 also revised the non-immigrant visas, especially the H–1B non-immigrant visa that has been at the center of controversy because of alleged displacement of U.S. high-tech professionals by migrant engineers and scientists. There was originally an annual cap of 65,000 workers, and H–1B visa holders were allowed to stay in the United States for a maximum of six years.[7] However, responding to business pressures, Congress passed the American Competitiveness Act in October 1998, increasing the number of H–1B visas over the 1999–2001 period. The annual ceiling on the number of H–1B visas issued was set at 115,000 in 1999 and 2000, and 107,500 in 2001. In 2002, the number of visas was to return to the original quota of 65,000 per year (*Migration News* 1998). In October 2000, however, Congress approved another increase in the number of H–1B visas, setting the cap at 195,000 for a three-year period.

Table 9.4 shows the countries of origin of the H–1B visa holders who entered the United States in 1994. India is by far the most important contributor of H–1B workers. This underscores the importance of the temporary migration of software engineers and programmers from this

---

[7] The law requires employers wishing to hire H–1B workers to file a labor attestation with the Department of Labor, documenting wages, working conditions, and the absence of a strike or lockout (Yale-Loehr 1991).

country. The Philippines and Mexico are two other developing countries that send a large number of temporary skilled workers.

Other non-immigrant visas included in the Immigration and Nationality Act of 1990 were for treaty traders (E–1), treaty investors (E–2), intra-company transferees (L–1), business trainees (Q), professional nurses (H–1A), agricultural workers (H–2A), exchange visitors (J–1), and aliens with extraordinary ability such as athletes and entertainers (O and P).

Table 9.4
Temporary Migrants with Specialty Occupations
(H-1B Visa Holders), 1994

	N	%
India	16,948	16.0
United Kingdom	13,696	12.9
Japan	7,317	6.9
The Philippines	5,098	4.8
France	4,548	4.3
Germany	4,042	3.8
Canada	3,527	3.3
Mexico	3,256	3.1
China	2,721	2.6
Australia	2,676	2.5
Brazil	2,354	2.2
Italy	2,107	2.0
Soviet Union	2,104	2.0
Netherlands	2,068	2.0
Israel	1,897	1.8
Other countries	31,540	29.8
Total	105,899	100.00

Source: Immigration and Naturalization Service 1996.

Evidently, the Immigration and Nationality Act of 1990 has shaped labor markets in the information technology industry by encouraging the temporary and permanent migration of highly educated persons from certain countries. Engineers and scientists from Asia are coming in large numbers, both as temporary migrants and as permanent residents. Is this purely the effect of demographics? Are there more engineers and scientists from India and China in the United States because these two countries have extremely large populations? I address these issues by examining the experience of migrants from Mexico and India.

U.S. Immigration Policy toward India and Mexico and the Formation of Immigrant Niches

Immigrants in the United States from India and Mexico are quite different. They concentrate in different places in the United States, bring different levels of human capital, and seem to cluster in distinct labor market niches.

According to the 1990 census, 65 percent of Indian immigrants in the United States had a college degree, in contrast to only 3.5 percent of Mexican immigrants. In terms of occupations, Indian immigrants were highly concentrated in specialty occupations; one-third of Indians but only 3 percent of Mexican immigrants 16 years or older had such jobs.[8] As a result of these differences, the annual median household income in 1989 was $48,320 for Indian immigrants and $21,926 for Mexican immigrants (Portes and Rumbaut 1996). These differences are the result in part of specific immigration policies implemented by the United States since the turn of the last century.

Indian and Mexican Migration: A Comparative History

Unlike Mexicans, whose main destination is the United States, Indians have formed strong immigrant communities in many countries. According to Madhavan (1985), emigration from India has been a persistent phenomenon since the eighteenth century, when small numbers of Indians migrated to nearby countries such as Ceylon (now Sri Lanka), Malaysia, and Burma. Most emigration took place after the abolition of slavery in the British territories in 1834. Colonial planters used Indians to replace slaves in the production of sugar, coffee, tea, and other raw materials in Fiji, the West Indies, and Mauritius, and in the construction of the Ugandan railway.

Indian migrants began to work in agriculture in the United States around 1900. The first sizable influx of Indian immigrants occurred around 1907, when 1,072 migrants entered the United States. These early migrants came from the rural areas of Punjab and, to a lesser extent, from Bengal, Gurat, and Uttar Pradesh. The vast majority of immigrants from Punjab were Sikhs (Rogers 1994). Most of these immi-

---

[8] Some of these occupations are: engineers, mathematicians and computer scientists, natural scientists, health professionals, teachers, social scientists, lawyers, artists, entertainers, and athletes.

grants settled on the West Coast (primarily in California) and worked in agriculture.[9]

Indian immigrants encountered extreme hostility and became victims of the widely prevalent anti-Asian sentiment in California. Responding to pressure from the Asiatic Exclusion League of San Francisco, U.S. immigration officials began to deny admission to Indians in 1908 (Minocha 1987). In 1917, immigration laws completely prohibited Indians from entering the United States, leaving small, male Indian communities extant in Sacramento and Imperial Valley until the mid–1940s.

In 1946, amendments to U.S. immigration law relaxed restrictions on the immigration of Asians in general, and granted Indians an annual quota of 100 people. The same year, Congress dropped all legal discrimination against "natives of India." In part, these changes were the result of the work of Indian American lobbyists. Between 1946 and 1965, nearly 6,000 Indian immigrants were admitted into the United States; and of those who were employed, an overwhelming majority worked as professional and technical workers (Minocha 1987).

According to Madhavan (1985), since 1945 there have been important changes in the patterns of immigration from India. Nepal became the most important destination, and in 1981 there were 3.2 million Indians living in that country. Between 1945 and 1980, nearly 750,000 Indians moved permanently to developed countries, with the United Kingdom accounting for 44 percent of that outflow, the United States 26 percent, Canada 14 percent, Western Europe (excluding the United Kingdom) 11 percent, and Australia 5 percent. Madhavan (1985) believes that Indian migration to these developed countries was mainly due to changes in immigration policies that emphasize skills as the major determinant of admission.

Beginning in 1965, thanks to reforms of the Immigration and Nationality Act, the number of Indian immigrants to the United States increased dramatically, and highly educated professionals began to dominate the flow. During this period, the number of Indian immigrants increased rapidly—from 582 admitted in 1965 to 21,562 becoming permanent residents in 1981. After 1965, most Indian applicants used employment visas to enter the United States. According to Minocha (1987), professional, technical, and kindred workers comprised al-

---

[9] Due to the absence of Indian women in California, some Indian males began courting Mexican immigrant women, angering the Mexican men in the process. Despite this opposition, there were some "Punjabi-Mexican" families in the Imperial Valley of California during the 1910s, such as those formed by Mola Singh and Carmen Barrientos, Rulia Singh and Valentina Alvarez, and Albert Joe and Alejandrina Cárdenas (Leonard 1992).

most 91 percent of all Indians admitted in 1971. But by the mid–1980s, a great majority (over 80 percent) of Indians were admitted under family preferences. Nevertheless, India has remained a very important source of immigrants with professional expertise or technical qualifications. Of the total number of professional or highly skilled immigrants admitted to the United States from throughout the world, India contributed as much as 19.5 percent between 1971 and 1980, and 13.4 percent between 1981 and 1990. These disproportionately high rates are striking because India's share in total immigration to the United States was much lower than this, at 3.8 percent in the 1970s and 3.6 percent in the 1980s.

During the 1970s, many Indians migrated to Middle Eastern countries on a temporary basis. Malaysia, Singapore, and the East African countries became progressively less important as major destinations, due in part to these countries' restrictive immigration policies. For instance, only professionals who were under contract, and entrepreneurs with their dependents were admitted into Malaysia and Singapore (Madhavan 1985).

Today most Indian immigrants in the United States are young and highly educated. Many are engineers and scientists employed by information technology companies. Thus they differ from their earlier counterparts, who were mainly comprised of middle-aged, illiterate male farmers from rural areas. There are also many Indian immigrants who have become entrepreneurs. In most large cities Indian restaurants are the most visible sign of this, but Indians also own a number of gas stations and hotels. According to Rogers (1994), the fact that there are many Indians surnamed Patel in the motel business has led to the community joke of "hotel, motel, Patel." Saxenian and Edulbehram (1998) have also found that Indian immigrants own important high-technology companies in Silicon Valley in California.

In the case of Mexico, from 1800 until the Great Depression, Mexican and U.S. government policies were at odds. While the U.S. government promoted immigration, its Mexican counterpart tried to discourage it. During this period, an informal "open border" policy toward Mexico was implemented, as was an active process of recruitment. Mexico began to provide employers with a growing pool of both legal and illegal workers for farmwork, mining, and railroad maintenance in the United States. The construction of railways in the United States provided another incentive to recruit labor from Mexico. Labor recruiters, or *enganchadores*, were sent to Mexico's central plateau states to hire workers for railroad construction (Cardoso 1980). The process of recruitment was so effective in promoting migration that several rural localities in central western Mexico, where recruitment was especially intense, remain the most important sending localities today.[10]

As a result of the exclusion of Asian immigration, the U.S. government implemented several immigration policies to further attract Mexican workers. The history of intentional lenience began with the exemption of Mexicans from the literacy requirements of the 1917 Immigration Act (Bilateral Commission 1989). Furthermore, between 1917 and 1922, the U.S. government unilaterally launched a guest-worker program to compensate for the labor shortages created by World War I. Finally, Mexicans were also exempted from the National Origins Acts of 1921 and 1924.

During the Great Depression, approximately half a million Mexicans were deported from the United States, including many U.S. citizens of Mexican descent. Jobs that remained were given to U.S. citizens, and economic relief was denied to Mexicans, who were repatriated voluntarily or by coercion. In response to this, the Lázaro Cárdenas administration (1934–1940) launched a powerful drive to attract Mexicans in the United States back to their home country through agrarian reform and expropriation of foreign investments.

However, the United States' entry into World War II revitalized the massive recruitment of Mexican labor. In 1942, the governments of Mexico and the United States established a temporary worker arrangement known as the "bracero program," which lasted until 1964. According to Ernesto Galarza, a scholar and farmworker leader, "the Bracero system was a cover-up of the government as the junior partner of agribusiness" (1977: 374). Despite these efforts to attract Mexican braceros, the U.S. government conducted another round of deportations in the 1950s known as "Operation Wetback," which returned many undocumented workers to Mexico.

The bracero program was dismantled unilaterally by the United States in 1964. Some 4.5 million contracts had been issued by the end of the program. During this period, people in Mexican rural communities, besides gaining experience in migrating to the United States and establishing contacts with employers, began to depend on income earned in this country. In 1965 the Mexican government implemented the Border Industrialization Program (commonly known as the *maquiladora* program) to promote local economic development in border cities and to provide jobs for those Mexicans who could no longer expect to work in the United States (Wilson 1992). However, maquiladoras (in-bond processing plants) have not played an important role in deterring illegal immigration.

---

[10] Central western Mexico comprises the states of Aguascalientes, Colima, Guanajuato, Jalisco, Michoacán, and Nayarit.

The occupational distribution of Mexican immigrants following the end of the bracero program suggests the existence of solid niches in a few industries. In 1980, a very small proportion of Mexican immigrant males held a professional occupation (2.5 percent). The rest were mainly concentrated in five low-skilled occupations: operatives (30 percent), crafts (18 percent), laborers (14 percent), service workers (13 percent), and farm laborers (12 percent). Mexican immigrant females had similar occupational profiles. Only 3.5 percent of them held professional occupations, while the majority clustered in four occupations: operatives (37 percent), service workers (22 percent), clerical workers (16 percent), and farm laborers (9 percent) (Bean and Tienda 1987).

The legal migration of families began to rise in the mid–1960s, when former "braceros" took advantage of the family reunification provisions of the 1965 Immigration and Nationality Act. Between 1961 and 1980, 1.1 million Mexicans immigrated legally to the United States, and another 1.6 million entered in the period from 1981 to 1990. In 1991, in large part due to the legalization process, nearly one million more Mexican migrants were admitted as legal residents (INS 1992).

Undocumented migration had begun to grow rapidly during the 1950s, as the demand for bracero visas exceeded the supply. The best estimates suggest that 2.1 million undocumented immigrants were included in the 1980 U.S. population census. Eight years later, after amnesty was granted to undocumented immigrants under the Immigration Reform and Control Act, Woodrow and Passel (1990) found that 1.9 million undocumented immigrants (1.1 million from Mexico) were included in the June 1988 Current Population Survey.[11] Overall, IRCA legalized nearly three million Mexicans. Many of them began to bring their families, leading to the rapid growth of Mexican communities in California and elsewhere.

Mexico's proximity to the United States has allowed the development of a temporary pattern of migration in which unskilled, usually young males work for a fixed period or seasonally and then return to Mexico. But between the early 1980s and the mid–1990s, thanks to the legalization process brought about by IRCA, migration from Mexico became more permanent and heterogeneous in terms of settlement patterns, gender, legal status, and employment experience (Cornelius 1992). Mexico's long-running economic crisis that began in the early 1980s has also encouraged the migration of educated professionals who had formerly been reluctant to look for employment in the United

---

[11] According to Woodrow and Passel (1990: 65), an analysis of the 1980 census suggests that 20 to 40 percent of the undocumented immigrants residing permanently in the United States were not included in the census that year. Therefore, a similar range may be reasonable for the Current Population Survey.

States. Furthermore, since 1994, due to tightened border restrictions, there have been important changes in the pattern of Mexican migration. There is increased family separation as males crossing alone risk their lives to enter the United States without proper documentation. However, the North American Free Trade Agreement (NAFTA) has facilitated the temporary movement of businesspeople, investors, and professionals between Mexico, the United States, and Canada, thanks to the "NAFTA visas."

U.S. Immigration Policy and the Formation of Immigrant Niches

This review of U.S. immigration policy explains in part why Indian and Mexican immigrants have access to different labor markets and therefore create niches in different industries. Table 9.5 illustrates these trends by showing the occupations declared by Indian and Mexican immigrants who became permanent residents in 1994. While nearly one-fourth of Indian immigrants reported employment in the "professional and technical" or "executive, administrative, and managerial" categories, only 1 percent of Mexican immigrants held such occupations. On the other hand, while almost one-fourth of Mexican immigrants worked in the categories marked "operator, fabricator, and laborer" and "farming, forestry, and fishing," only 3 percent of Indian immigrants did so.

The fact that Indian immigrants are highly educated and concentrated in professional occupations, while Mexican immigrants have low levels of education and congregate in low-skilled occupations, suggests the existence of an Indian niche in the high-technology industry. To explore this issue further, in the next section I focus on the case of Silicon Valley, identifying the industries and occupations where immigrants from India and Mexico concentrate in this high-tech region.

Since the 1970s, Silicon Valley, located in the San Francisco Bay area, has attracted worldwide attention as the most important high-technology region and the leading center of technological innovation in the world. Table 9.6 describes how three different ethnic groups—non–Hispanic whites, Indian immigrants, and Mexican immigrants—access employment in the high-technology industry in Santa Clara County, the core of the region. High-technology refers here to the industry that encompasses the following manufacturing sectors: computing and office equipment, communications equipment, electronic components, guided missiles, and space vehicles and instruments. From the service industry, it also includes the software and data-processing sector (Saxenian 1994: 209).

The first portion of table 9.6 shows the percentages of each of the three ethnic groups working in the high-technology industry. It is apparent that although Indian males and females are overwhelmingly represented in this industry, their Mexican counterparts have very little participation in this sector. The second part of table 9.6 describes employment in all industries. Here high technology is included in durable goods manufacturing and in the software and data-processing sector that is part of business and repair services. Employment in durable goods manufacturing is composed mainly of workers in the high-technology industry (89 percent). Employment in the software and data-processing sector is a small portion of total employment in business and repair services.

Table 9.6 reveals that Indian immigrants and non–Hispanic white males have similar employment patterns, clustering in the most dynamic industries of the region. Nearly three-quarters (73 percent) of the Indian males and more than half (51 percent) of the non–Hispanic white males concentrate in three areas: durable goods manufacturing, professional services, and retail trade. Similarly, most non–Hispanic white females (52 percent) and Indian females (57 percent) also converge in these three industries.

On the other hand, Mexican immigrants are heavily concentrated in traditional low-skill industries. Most males work in retail trade, durable goods, construction, and agriculture (58 percent). Nearly one-third of Mexican women are not in the labor force, surpassing the comparable figures for white and Indian females. Working Mexican women are employed in durable goods, professional and related services, retail trade, and nondurable goods (46 percent). Given the high participation of Mexican immigrants in the informal economy, a large number of women may work as housecleaners and baby-sitters, and in other labor-intensive services (Zlolniski 1994).

Table 9.7 describes participation of the three ethnic groups in "high-tech" occupations (engineers, math and computer scientists, and natural scientists). Persons holding these jobs are likely to be employed by the region's high-tech companies. This table clearly shows that Indian immigrants are heavily overrepresented in these fields. The proportion of Indians working in the high-tech industry, relative to their overall population, by far surpasses the participation of non–Hispanic whites of both sexes in such occupations. While 32.5 percent of Indian males and 7.9 percent of Indian females are high-tech professionals, only 11.3 percent of non–Hispanic white men and 2.4 percent of non–Hispanic white women hold such jobs. On the other hand, the percentage of Mexican men and women in these occupations is very low, not even reaching 1 percent.

Table 9.5
Immigrants Admitted by Major Occupation Group and Country of Birth, 1994

	All Immigrants	%	Mexican	%	Indian	%
Professional & technical	67,286	8.4	843	0.8	6,202	17.8
Executive, administrative, and managerial	26,931	3.3	428	0.4	1,786	5.1
Sales	13,024	1.6	1,590	1.4	386	1.1
Administrative support	21,590	2.7	1,438	1.3	747	2.1
Precision production, craft & repair	24,518	3.0	3,409	3.1	192	0.5
Operator, fabricator & laborer	67,486	8.4	22,069	19.8	155	0.4
Farming, forestry & fishing	15,606	1.9	4,738	4.3	914	2.6
Service	50,646	6.3	7,167	6.4	846	2.4
No occupation[a]	517,329	64.3	69,716	62.6	23,693	67.8
Total	804,416	100.0	111,398	100.0	34,921	100.0

Source: Immigration and Naturalization Service 1996: table 31.
[a] Includes homemakers, students, unemployed , retired persons, and others no reporting an occupation.

Table 9.6

Employment in High Technology and other industries in Santa Clara County by Ethnicity and Gender, Persons 16 years and over, 1990 (percents)

	White		Mexican		Indian	
	Males		Males		Males	
		Females		Females		Females
High Technology	20.5	11.6	5.3	6.0	46.9	22.5
Industry						
Agriculture, forestry, and fisheries	1.2	0.6	10.7	3.2	0	0.5
Mining	0	0	0.	0	0	0
Construction	8.2	1.0	13.8	0.5	4.2	0.9
Manufacturing						
Nondurable goods	3.2	2.6	5.7	8.1	1.5	0.7
Durable goods	26.2	13.7	15.7	13.8	52.3	30.9
Transportation and public utilities	5.6	2.8	3.1	1.0	3.2	1.4
Wholesale trade	5.0	2.8	4.0	2.9	2.7	1.7
Retail trade	11.9	12.9	18.2	11.6	10.8	5.5
Finance, insurance, real estate services	4.2	6.2	0.8	1.3	0.6	4.7
Business and repair services	6.6	4.8	10.3	5.1	9.0	3.5
Personal services	1.0	2.4	2.1	6.3	1.0	0.4
Entertainment and recreational services	1.3	1.3	0.9	0.6	0.4	0
Professional and related services	13.2	25.3	3.7	12.9	10.5	20.7
Government	2.7	1.9	0.7	1.0	0.4	0.9
Military	1.0	0.2	0	0	0	0
Unemployed	0.1	0.1	0.1	0.2	0	0.9
Not in the labor force	8.6	21.3	10.1	31.6	3.3	27.3
Total	100.0	100.0	100.0	100.0	100.0	100.0
Weighted Number	320,669	324,582	37,817	28,093	6,715	4,535

Source: Bureau of the Census 1992.

Table 9.7

Engineers and Scientists by Ethnicity and Gender, Santa Clara County, 1990

	White		Mexican		Indian	
	Male	Female	Male	Female	Male	Female
Engineers	25,156	3,175	204	23	1,258	127
Mathematicians and computer scientists	8,624	3,662	49	47	870	199
Natural scientists	2,423	1,044	29	31	54	34
Total	36,203	7,881	282	101	2,182	360
Other occupations	284,466	316,701	37,535	27,992	4,533	4,175
Engineers and scientists (% of total occupied population)	11.3	2.4	0.7	0.4	32.5	7.9
Weighted Number	320,669	324,582	37,817	28,093	6,715	4,535

Source: Bureau of the Census 1992.

Conclusion

This chapter has shown that immigration policy has been a powerful instrument in promoting the concentration of immigrants from certain nations in specific industries and occupations in the United States by selecting them according to their skills. Indians have clustered in professional and technical occupations, and Mexican immigrants are found in low-skill manufacturing industries, construction, and agriculture.

The review of the history of immigration policy reveals that the profound transformation of immigration policy in the mid–1960s instituted a selection process that facilitated the immigration of Indians and other Asians with high education levels. This is the main factor that explains why these immigrants are so highly educated and why they concentrate in the high-technology industry. Portes and Rumbaut (1996) contend that, unlike Europeans and some Latin Americans (such as Mexicans), after the 1965 immigration reform Asians and Africans generally could not obtain immigrant visas to enter the United States through family reunification provisions. There were few immigrants from these regions living in the United States due to the long-term effects of immigration restrictions such as the Chinese Exclusion Act of 1882 and the national origins quota system instituted in the 1920s. Consequently, the only path open to them to get immigrant visas was the use of occupational skills. For this reason, at least in the immediate period after the 1965 immigration reforms, most Indians who entered the United States using employment-based visas were highly educated. This initial movement created a strong network of highly educated Indian immigrants that has reproduced itself since that time. The educational attainment of Indian immigrants began to decline as family reunification and other provisions allowed the immigration of less skilled persons. Nevertheless, Indian immigrants remain one of the most educated immigrant groups today.

On the other hand, Mexican immigrants constitute the largest group of unskilled workers because geographical proximity has lessened the selection process by lowering the economic and social costs of immigration. In addition, specific U.S. immigration policies, direct recruitment, and the development of strong social networks have encouraged the immigration of unskilled workers.

Clearly, immigrants from India and Mexico who reside in the United States do not represent a cross-section of their societies of origin. Professionals among the Indian population and unskilled workers among Mexicans are overrepresented. Interestingly, although Mexicans have a higher per capita income and higher literacy rates than Indians in their native country, it is only the highly skilled Indians and the relatively low skilled Mexicans who are more likely to migrate to the United States (Alarcón 1999; Portes and Rumbaut 1996).

Immigration policy—and to a lesser extent sending countries' specific domestic industrial policies—have contributed to the specialization of immigrants in certain occupations. In fact, there are some immigration programs that are largely identified as "belonging" to certain nationalities. For instance, the H–1B program is widely identified as an "Indian program." The H–1A program, designed to provide professional nurses for the United States on a temporary basis, is considered a program for Filipino nurses. Finally, the H–2A program for temporary agricultural workers is a "Mexican program."

Skilled migrants face fewer restrictions than unskilled migrants in U.S. labor markets. Immigration policy, corporate power, and their own class resources allow them to cross borders with greater ease than low-skilled migrants. This privileged position stems from the fact that these professionals seem to be vital to corporations that are involved in global production processes and markets (Alarcón 2000). The recent changes in immigration policy, with their emphasis on skills rather than family reunification, have placed the United States in line with other countries like Canada, Australia, and New Zealand, which favor the entry of professionals and high-skilled workers. These countries use "point systems" that consider educational attainment, occupation, English-language proficiency, and age, as well as family connections (Borjas 1996).

The recent emphasis on skills and a more open immigration system have enabled employers in U.S. high-tech industries to gain a comparative advantage over competing nations with more restrictive immigration policies. High-tech companies in the United States with access to a global pool of workers can, in theory, reach out to the best and brightest workers of the world.

References

Alarcón, Rafael. 1998. "The Migrants of the Information Age. Foreign-Born Engineers and Scientists and Regional Development in Silicon Valley." Ph.D. dissertation, University of California, Berkeley.

———. 1999. "Recruitment Processes among Foreign-Born Engineers and Scientists in Silicon Valley," *American Behavioral Scientist* 42 (9): 1380–99.

———. 2000. "Skilled Immigrants and Cerebreros: Foreign Born Engineers and Scientists in the High Technology Industry of Silicon Valley." In *Immigration and Immigration Research for a New Century: Multidisciplinary Perspectives*, edited by Nancy Foner, Rubén Rumbaut, and Steve Gold. New York: Russell Sage Foundation.

Bean, Frank, and Marta Tienda. 1987 *The Hispanic Population of the United States.* New York: Russell Sage Foundation.

Bilateral Commission on the Future of United States–Mexican Relations. 1989. *The Challenge of Interdependence: Mexico and the United States.* Lanham, Md.: University Press of America.

Borjas, George. 1996. "The New Economics of Immigration: Affluent Americans Gain; Poor Americans Lose," *Atlantic Monthly* 278 (5).

Bouvier, Leon, and John Martin. 1995. *Foreign-Born Scientists, Engineers and Mathematicians in the United States.* Washington, D.C.: Center for Immigration Studies.

Bureau of the Census. 1990–1992. Census of Population and Housing: Public Use Microdata Samples (5 %) U.S. Machine-Readable Data Files. Washington, D.C.: U.S. Government Printing Office.

Calavita, Kitty. 1994. "U.S. Immigration and Policy Responses: The Limits of Legislation." In *Controlling Immigration. A Global Perspective*, edited by Wayne Cornelius, Philip Martin, and James Hollifield. Stanford: Stanford University Press.

Cardoso, Lawrence. 1980. *Mexican Emigration to the United States. 1897–1931: Socio-economic Patterns.* Tucson: University of Arizona Press.

Cornelius, Wayne. 1992. "From Sojourners to Settlers: The Changing Profile of Mexican Migration to the United States." In *U.S.–Mexico Relations: Labor Market Interdependence*, edited by Jorge Bustamante, Raúl Hinojosa, and Clark Reynolds. Stanford, Calif.: Stanford University Press.

Galarza, Ernesto. 1977 *Merchants of Labor. The Mexican Bracero Story.* McNally and Lofti.

García y Griego, Manuel. 1994. "Canada: Flexibility and Control in Immigration and Refugee Policy." In *Controlling Immigration. A Global Perspective*, edited by Wayne Cornelius, Philip Martin, and James Hollifield. Stanford, Calif.: Stanford University Press.

Heer, David. 1996. *Immigration in America's Future.* Boulder, Colo.: Westview.

INS (U.S. Immigration and Naturalization Service). 1992. *1991 Statistical Yearbook of the Immigration and Naturalization Service.* Washington, D.C.: U.S. Government Printing Office.

———. 1996. *1994 Statistical Yearbook of the Immigration and Naturalization Service.* Washington, D.C.: U.S. Government Printing Office.

Kanjanapan, Wilawan. 1995. "The Immigration of Asian Professionals to the United States," *International Migration Review* 29 (1).

Lakha, Salim. 1992. "The Internationalization of Indian Computer Professionals," *South Asia* 15 (2): 93–113.

Leonard, Karen. 1992. *Making Ethnic Choices: California's Punjabi Mexican Americans.* Philadelphia, Penn.: Temple University Press.

Louie, Winnie, and Paul Ong. 1995. "*Asian Immigrant Investors and the Immigration Act of 1990.*" CPS Brief. California Policy Seminar 7 (13).

Madhavan, M. C. 1985. "Indian Emigrants: Numbers, Characteristics, and Economic Impact," *Population and Development Review* 11 (3).

Maibach, Michael. 1995. "High Tech's Agenda for 1996," *Upside* 7 (12).

Migration News. 1996a. "Congress Moves to Curb Illegal Immigration," April. At http://migration.ucdavis.edu.

———. 1996b. "Congress Moves on Immigration Reform," March. At http://migration.ucdavis.edu.

———. 1998. "INS: Congress: H–1Bs Approved; Farm Workers Rejected. Naturalization, Deportations," December. At http://migration.ucdavis.edu.

Minocha, Urmil. 1987. "South Asian Immigrants: Trends and Impacts on the Sending and Receiving Societies." In *Pacific Bridges. The New Immigration from Asia and the Pacific Islands,* edited by James Fawcett and Benjamin Cariño. New York: Center for Migration Studies.

Myers, Dowell. 1992. *Analysis with Local Census Data. Portraits of Change.* Boston: Academic Press.

North, David. 1995. *Soothing the Establishment. The Impact of Foreign-Born Scientists and Engineers on America.* Lanham, Md.: University Press of America.

Papademetriou, Demetrios. 1996. "U.S. Immigration Policy after the Cold War." In *The American Impasse. U.S. Domestic and Foreign Policy after the Cold War,* edited by Michael Minkenberg and Herbert Dittgen. Pittsburgh, Penn.: University of Pittsburgh Press.

Parthasarathy, Balaji. 2000. "Globalization and Agglomeration in Newly Industrializing Countries: The State and the Information Technology Industry in Bangalore, India." Ph.D. dissertation, University of California, Berkeley.

Portes, Alejandro, and Jozsef Borocs. 1989. "Contemporary Immigration: Theoretical Perspectives on Its Determinants and Modes of Incorporation," *International Migration Review* 23 (3).

Portes, Alejandro, and Rubén Rumbaut. 1996. *Immigrant America. A Portrait.* Berkeley: University of California Press.

Rogers, Daniel. 1994. "The Indian Diaspora in the United States." In *Migration: The Asian Experience,* edited by Judith Brown and Rosemary Foot. New York: St. Martin's.

Saxenian, AnnaLee. 1994. *Regional Advantage. Culture and Competition in Silicon Valley and Route 128.* Cambridge, Mass.: Harvard University Press.

Saxenian, AnnaLee, and Jumbi Edulbehram. 1998. "Immigrant Entrepreneurs in Silicon Valley," *Berkeley Planning Journal* 12.

Stremlau, John. 1996. "Dateline Bangalore: Third World Technopolis (India)," *Foreign Policy* 102.

Valbrun, Marjorie. 2000. "Immigration Foe's Reversal Bodes Well for Silicon Valley," *Wall Street Journal,* May 2.

Waldinger, Roger. 1994. "The Making of an Immigrant Niche," *International Migration Review* 28 (105).

Waldinger Roger, and Medhi Bozorgmehr. 1996. "The Making of a Multicultural Metropolis." In *Ethnic Los Angeles,* edited by Roger Waldinger and Medhi Bozorgmehr. New York: Russell Sage Foundation.

Wilson, Patricia. 1992. "*Exports and Local Development. Mexico's New Maquiladoras.*" Austin: University of Texas Press.

Woodrow, Karen, and Jeffrey Passel. 1990. "Post–IRCA Undocumented Immigration to the United States: An Assessment Based on the June 1980 CPS." In *Undocumented Migration to the United States: IRCA and the Experience of the 1980s,* edited by Frank Bean, Barry Edmonston, and Jeffrey Passel. Washington, D.C.: Rand Corporation and the Urban Institute.

Yale-Loehr, Stephen. 1991. *Understanding the Immigration Act of 1990*. Washington, D.C.: Federal Publications.

Zlolniski, Christian. 1994. "The Informal Economy in an Advanced Industrialized Society: Mexican Immigrant Labor in Silicon Valley," *The Yale Law Journal* 103 (8).

10

Unskilled Immigrants in High-Tech Companies: The Case of Mexican Janitors in Silicon Valley

Christian Zlolniski

Silicon Valley is internationally known as the heart of the high-technology industry and a paradigmatic example of the new economy that many other regions in the United States seek to emulate. The region is also well known for its high concentration of foreign-born computer engineers, programmers, scientists, and other highly educated technical workers whose labor critically contributes to the vitality and success of the high-tech industry (Alarcón 1999). Less known is the large concentration of low-skilled Mexican immigrants who work and live in the region and are employed in many types of service occupations directly connected to the maintenance of the high-technology industry complex. A case in point is the thousands of Mexican immigrants who work as janitors in Silicon Valley's building-cleaning industry. Mostly employed by independent firms and contractors, this army of night-shift workers is in charge of cleaning the offices, administrative buildings, and "clean rooms" of the hundreds of high-tech companies concentrated in this region. Mexicans, and to a lesser extent Central American workers, represent the bulk of the workforce employed in this industry, providing an abundant and reliable source of cheap and flexible labor for the high-tech client corporations that subcontract their services. Yet Silicon Valley's glamorous public image and the celebration of its spectacular economic success and wealth shadow the existence of these and many other immigrants employed in low-skill industries, whose working and labor conditions are intrinsically linked to the "hourglass" employment structure generated by the region's high-tech economy.

In this chapter I examine the case of Mexican immigrants employed as janitorial workers in the buildings of large high-tech corporations in the region. The chapter seeks to address three major and interrelated questions. What explains the almost complete dependence of Silicon Valley's building-cleaning industry on Mexican immigrant labor? What are the labor and working conditions of the thousands of Mexican immigrants who clean the office buildings of high-tech corporations in this region? And how have Mexican workers responded to the working and labor conditions of their jobs? In order to address these questions, I use a combination of quantitative methods based on the analysis of aggregate census data, and ethnographic qualitative methods based on fieldwork I conducted with Mexican immigrant janitors employed by large high-tech companies in Silicon Valley. Most of the information about the experiences of these workers was gathered by formal and informal interviews conducted in their homes and in public spaces where they gather to socialize. This information was complemented with interviews of managers in these high-tech companies and one of its largest janitorial contractors. Quantitative data about the building-cleaning industry and janitorial workers in Silicon Valley come from the Public Use Microdata Samples of the 1990 census, official surveys of the Employment Development Department (EDD) in California, and other secondary sources.[1]

The chapter is divided in four parts. First, I analyze the structural factors that led the building-cleaning industry in Silicon Valley to depend on Mexican immigrant workers starting in the early 1980s. Then I examine the major sociodemographic characteristics of contract janitors employed in the private sector, where most immigrants are concentrated, and compare them to those of janitorial workers employed in the public sector. In the third section, I use the case study of Sonix[2]—a major high-tech corporation in Silicon Valley which has employed Mexican immigrants to clean its office buildings through independent contractors since the mid–1980s—to illustrate how subcontracting has affected the labor and working conditions of immigrant janitors employed in the private sector of this industry. The fourth part examines the response of Mexican workers to the poor wages and labor conditions of their jobs, and the reasons that led them to unionize as part of the "Justice for Janitors" campaign developed in Silicon Valley during the early 1990s.

---

[1] I want to thank Rafael Alarcón for his generosity in sharing the Public Use Microdata Samples (PUMS) for Silicon Valley. I also thank Jimena Méndez, of El Colegio de la Frontera Norte, for her help with the PUMS.

[2] This and other companies' names have been changed to preserve the anonymity of my informants.

The Restructuring of the Building-Cleaning Industry and the Influx of Mexican Workers in the 1980s

Up until the 1950s, Santa Clara Valley, at the core of Silicon Valley, was an important agricultural and canning center. The region began a rapid transformation when the microelectronics industry developed in the late 1950s for military purposes, and it experienced even faster growth with the development of the market for personal computers in the 1970s (Saxenian 1985). The success of the new industry fueled a period of intense economic and demographic growth in the region. Between 1977 and 1985, for example, the number of high-tech firms in the Santa Clara Valley jumped from 905 to 2,660 (Flores 1987: 94). By the mid–1990s, nearly 1,500 of the largest 2,500 electronics companies in the United States were located in the region (Rosaldo and Flores 1997: 64). Not surprisingly, high-tech employment alone accounted for 150,000 new jobs between 1975 and 1990 (Saxenian 1994). This explosive economic development was the major factor behind an equally impressive demographic growth: between 1960 and 1980, the population of Santa Clara County almost doubled (from 658,700 to 1,265,200 people). And by the early 1990s, there were 1,497,577 people living in this former agricultural region (U.S. Department of Commerce 1991).

The expansion of the high-tech industry brought enormous wealth to the region, which soon became the epicenter of the new, postindustrial U.S. economy. As the high-tech industry evolved, Silicon Valley became more ethnically diverse, as a large number of skilled immigrants from India, Taiwan, China, and other countries joined the ranks of the scientists, engineers, programmers, and other highly educated workers already living in the region. At the same time, the development of the high-tech industry also attracted thousands of low-skilled immigrants to fill the manual and service jobs that were being created at a rapid pace. In the 1960s and 1970s, the robust growth of the electronics industry created a large number of unskilled, low-wage manufacturing assembly occupations that were filled mostly by immigrant women from Mexico, China, Vietnam, Korea, the Philippines, and other Third World countries (Hossfeld 1988; Green 1983). Later, in the 1980s and 1990s, as the pace of manufacturing employment declined while employment in the service sector expanded, a new wave of Latino—especially Mexican—immigrants arrived in the region and became the bulk of the labor force in the low-wage segment of the service sector (Blakely and Sullivan 1989; Martínez Saldaña 1993).[3]

---

[3] According to a study conducted by Blakely and Sullivan, for example, by the mid–1980s Latinos (many of them Mexican immigrants) held almost 80 percent of the clerical and operating jobs in the low-wage service sector (1989: 4).

Few cases better illustrate the relationship between the development of the high-tech industry, economic restructuring, and the influx of low-skilled Latino immigrants to Silicon Valley than the building-cleaning industry. Employment in this industry experienced rapid growth as a result of the development of the high-tech economy. The massive construction of corporate buildings, high-tech labs, banks, hotels, restaurants, and other commercial infrastructure produced a vast demand for janitorial workers. Between 1965 and 1990, for example, the demand for janitors in the Santa Clara Valley grew fivefold (Mines and Avina 1992: 441). By 1995, employment occupation statistics of the California Employment Development Department estimated that there were 12,110 janitorial workers in this county, almost as many as the 12,690 computer engineers working in the region (EDD 1998a). When we consider San Mateo and Santa Cruz counties, where Silicon Valley has expanded, the number of janitors is even higher than the population of computer engineers (see table 10.1). While it is difficult to arrive at an accurate number of Latino immigrants employed in the private janitorial sector, it is estimated that about 90 percent of contract janitorial workers come from Mexico and Central America, especially El Salvador (Alvarado et al. 1991).

Table 10.1.
Employment of Computer Engineers and Janitorial Workers by County in Silicon Valley, 1990

Occupation	Santa Clara	Santa Cruz	San Mateo	Total
Computer Engineers	12,690	520	2,100	15,310
Janitors	12,110	1,350	4,450	17,910

Source: Employment Development Department, occupational employment projections for Santa Clara, Santa Cruz, and San Mateo counties.

The dependence of Silicon Valley's building-cleaning industry on Mexican immigrant workers is the result of a major restructuring process initiated in the early 1980s through which former "in-house" custodial and union contract workers were replaced by non-union contract janitors employed by independent cleaning firms. In effect, until the late 1970s, workers employed as janitors in Silicon Valley's private sector (the bulk of which is made up of workers cleaning high-tech office buildings) fell under two main categories: in-house custodial workers directly employed by the high-tech companies where they performed their services, and contract janitors employed by independent janitorial firms. In-house janitors usually earned between $7 and $10 an hour, with benefits (such as health insurance and sick leave) similar to other low-skilled and semi-skilled employees in high-tech companies. For many of them, janitorial employment was an entry-level job that could lead to better-paid semi-skilled occupations if they gained the necessary experience and skills. In turn, labor conditions for contract janitors were not as good as those of their in-house counterparts. But given that the industry was highly unionized, they were comparable to other unskilled or semi-skilled occupations in the region. Wages for unionized janitors ranged between $5 and $7.50, and these workers received ample benefits, including health care, sick leave, paid holidays, and pension benefits. At the time, Chicano, Filipino, Portuguese, and old-time Mexican immigrants made up the bulk of the workers employed in the industry (Mines and Avina 1992: 441).

During the 1980s, high-tech companies and building owners sought to reduce cleaning costs by contracting non-union independent firms that relied on cheap, mostly undocumented, immigrant labor. In the midst of an economic recession, the building owners and managers of high-tech companies opted for contracting non-union janitorial firms to cut operating and maintenance costs. This process involved two stages. The first changes occurred when non-union, midsize janitorial firms took over a significant share of the cleaning market previously in the hands of large, union cleaning firms. Later, in the mid–1980s, many high-tech corporations that still employed their own in-house custodial workers also started to contract out their cleaning services to independent janitorial firms. Former in-house janitors were given early retirement packages, moved to other maintenance positions, or simply laid off. Both midsize companies and small contractors seized on the opportunity, displacing both in-house and union contract janitorial workers. This restructuring process was facilitated by two factors—namely, the ability of non-union firms to capitalize on immigrant social networks as a major mechanism to recruit newly arrived immigrant workers, and the lack of skill barriers that could have prevented the replacement of experienced custodial workers by recent immigrants without previous experience in this occupation (Mines and Avina 1992: 431–35).

The restructuring of janitorial work led to a sharp decline in wages and labor benefits for janitors employed in the private sector. By 1985, non-union contractors were paying between minimum wage and $5 an hour, while wages mandated by the union contract ranged between $5.12 and $7.96, with ample benefits (Mines and Avina 1992: 442). Such differences were an incentive for many high-tech companies to shift from in-house to contract janitors because this shift represented a significant reduction in cleaning and labor costs. As a result, by the late

1980s the building-cleaning industry in Silicon Valley had been transformed into a labor niche for recent Mexican and Central American
immigrants. The group of settled immigrant workers who were the
backbone of union janitorial firms experienced wage depression and
labor displacement by recent immigrants employed by midsize non-
union firms. Some of these janitors eventually became self-employed
independent contractors, often at the request of the client companies
where they were formerly employed; some were hired as supervisors
by non-union firms because of their experience; and others were left
unemployed and/or retired early. As a result, janitorial work devolved
from a stable, well-paid, entry-level occupation for minority and established immigrants, to an unstable, low-wage, dead-end job for recent,
mostly undocumented, immigrants who arrived in the region in the
1980s.

Characteristics of Contract and Public-Sector Janitors in Silicon Valley in 1990

While the restructuring of janitorial work affected workers employed in
both the private and public sectors, the extent of this process and its
consequences for labor were most acutely felt among janitors employed
by private firms. Moreover, as in other regions in California (Cranford
1998), restructuring most rapidly affected janitorial work in the business services sector, where janitors (who were formerly either in-house
employees or union contract workers) were now employed by independent, non-union cleaning firms. In this section, I examine the ethnic
and sociodemographic profile of janitors employed in the building
service industry in Silicon Valley, and then compare it to that of janitors
employed in the public sector. These groups of workers stand at opposite ends of a continuum: at one end are the janitors most affected by
restructuring (private contract janitors), and at the other end are the
janitors least affected by this process (public janitorial employees).
Public-sector janitors can be considered to be the most privileged group
within this occupation, and this sector is one of the last arenas in which
janitorial work is still considered a stable, well-paying job with ample
labor benefits for semi-skilled, minority, and old-time immigrant workers.[4] In order to best capture the janitors employed by independent
contractors who clean the buildings of Silicon Valley's high-tech com-

---

[4] By the early 1990s, the use of contract janitors in the public sector was already
under way. For example, a public university and some public buildings in San
Jose had shifted from in-house to contract janitors.

panies, I define my sample of "private contract janitors" as those employed by private firms in the building-cleaning industry.[5]

According to census figures (see table 10.2), by the early 1990s the ratio of Hispanic to non-Hispanic workers among janitors in the private and the public sectors, respectively, was almost reversed: more than 70 percent of the janitors working for private contractors were Hispanic, while non-Hispanic janitors made up about 70 percent of the workforce in the public sector. This important difference is mirrored in a similarly sharp contrast between the citizenship status of janitors in the two sectors: about 60 percent of contract janitors were foreign, non–U.S. citizens, while 63 percent of public-sector janitors were U.S. citizens. The replacement of old-time, in-house janitors by young immigrant contract workers in the private sector is also reflected in the younger average age of these workers—35 years—as compared to that of public-sector janitors—43 years. In addition, restructuring led to a feminization of janitorial work in the private sector, although probably to a lesser extent than in cities like Los Angeles (Cranford 1998). By 1990, more than 25 percent of the janitorial workforce in the building-cleaning industry was made up of women workers, while women represented only 15 percent of the workforce in the public sector.[6]

The influx of young immigrant workers in the industry also explains differences in the marital status of workers in the two groups. Close to 40 percent of contract janitors were single, as compared to about 22 percent of janitors working in the public sector. Nevertheless, more than 50 percent of contract janitors are married. Although there are no data on whether married immigrant janitors have their families in the United States, I learned through my fieldwork experience that this was

---

[5] The analysis is based on the Public Use Microdata Samples of the 1990 census. Silicon Valley is defined as the region that encompasses the counties of Santa Clara, San Mateo, Santa Cruz, and the southern section of Alameda County, including the cities of Fremont, Union City, and Newark. The coding for janitors in the 1990 census is 453. The building-cleaning industry is operationalized as "Services to dwellings and other buildings," which in the 1990 census corresponds to code 722. I have limited the samples to those janitors who at the time were holding a paid job. Private contract janitors are defined as those wage workers employed by a private firm in this industry (class 1 in the 1990 PUMS), while public-sector janitors are defined as cleaning workers employed by the local, state, or federal governments (class 3, 4, and 5).

[6] The proportion of women working as janitors in the private sector might be underestimated in this sample because (among other reasons) the sample only includes janitors holding a paid job, which might have excluded women who were temporarily out of the labor force for maternity-related reasons. If we include all workers in this sector, regardless of whether they have a paid job, the proportion of women rises to 32.1 percent.

the case for many janitors. The high proportion of immigrant janitors who are married and have their families in the United States provides further support for the hypothesis that a considerable share of Mexican immigrants working in California are settled workers employed in year-round, unskilled urban jobs such as janitorial occupations (Cornelius 1992).

Finally, the average income earned by contract janitors supports the characterization of these workers as the "working poor." Their annual incomes from wage work are just above $12,000—often with no benefits—compared to almost $20,000 for their public-sector counterparts, a figure that does not include the ample benefits they receive.[7]

By 1990, as a result of restructuring and the growth of subcontracting, about 46 percent of contract janitors were Mexican immigrants, and about 12 percent were Central American workers (see figure 10.1). By contrast, 63 percent of the janitors working in the public sector were born in the United States, and only 8 percent were Mexican and 5.2 percent were Central American immigrants. Meanwhile, Filipino workers (who were one of the largest groups formerly employed as in-house janitors in the private sector) still accounted for almost 11 percent of the janitorial employees in the public sector. Moreover, about 44 percent of immigrant contract janitors employed in Silicon Valley had arrived in the United States during in the 1980s, as compared to only 14 percent of janitors working in the public sector (see figure 10.2), which provides further evidence of the close relationship between industrial restructuring and the "Mexicanization" of the janitorial workforce in the private sector. Another 24 percent of immigrant janitors had arrived between 1965 and 1980; some of them probably worked either as union contract or in-house janitors before industrial restructuring began in the early 1980s.

Finally, the educational status of contract janitors working in the building-cleaning industry shows that even a region like Silicon Valley, generally known for its knowledge-based high-tech economy, generates a large demand for low-skilled maintenance workers. As shown in figure 10.3, about 11 percent of janitors employed as contract workers have no formal education, and some 33 percent have completed only primary school, as compared to 4 and 13 percent, respectively, for

---

[7] Earnings of contract janitors reflect what I observed during fieldwork regarding the workers who clean the buildings of high-tech firms. Many of them were making between $5 and $5.50 an hour in 1993, notably less than former in-house janitors, whose wage and working conditions were similar to those of custodial workers in the public sector.

Table 10.2.
Selected Characteristics of Private Contract and Public-Sector Janitors in Silicon Valley, 1990

	Private Contract Janitors	Public-Sector Janitors
Hispanic	72.5%	29.2%
Non-Hispanic	27.5%	70.8%
Citizenship		
U.S. native[a]	28.7%	63%
Naturalized	10.7%	15.6%
Not U.S. citizen	60.7%	21.4%
Age (mean)	35.1	43.4
Sex		
Male	73.6%	84.4%
Female	26.4%	15.6%
Marital Status		
Married	51.1%	57.8%
Single	39.6%	22.4%
Other	9.3%	19.8%
Annual Wage Income	$ 12,237	$19,978

Source: U.S. Department of Commerce 1992.
[a] Includes persons born in the United States and abroad of American parents, as well as those born in Puerto Rico, Guam, and outlying areas.

janitors employed in the public sector. Notwithstanding this figure, about 20 percent of contract janitors have a high school diploma or its equivalent in their countries of origin, and 12 percent have even more schooling. Such heterogeneity might reflect an ironic trend noticed by some scholars—namely, while the new U.S. economy generates a large supply of unskilled jobs that attract thousands of new Mexican and Latino immigrants, the educational status of Mexican immigrants employed in these jobs has risen with respect to previous immigrant cohorts. This trend is due to both a general increase in formal schooling in Mexico and the economic crises of the early 1980s and 1995, which prompted many college-educated and professional workers to emigrate to the United States in search of better job opportunities (Cornelius 1992).

Figure 10.1.
Country/Region of Birth of Private Contract and Public-Sector
Janitors in Silicon Valley, 1990

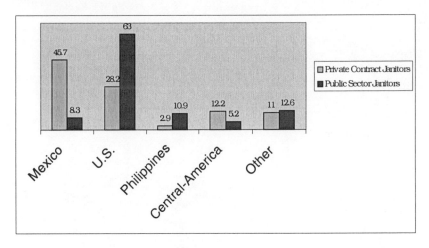

Source: U.S. Department of Commerce 1992.

Figure 10.2.
Proportion of U.S.-born Immigrants, by Year of Arrival, among Building Services and Public-sector Janitors in Silicon Valley, 1990

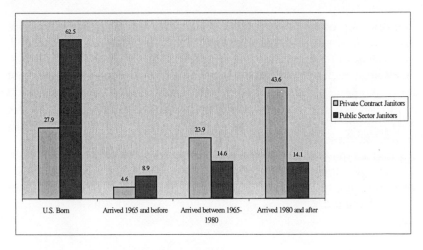

Source: U.S. Department of Commerce 1992.

In sum, the shift from in-house and union contract janitors to non-union workers employed by independent firms in Silicon Valley led to a sharp increase in the number of recent Mexican immigrants in this industry in the 1980s, a process that was consolidated throughout the early 1990s. While a similar trend was well under way by then in the public sector, it was in the private segment of the building-cleaning industry that this trend, and the consequent deterioration in wages and labor conditions, was most acutely felt. The form in which such restructuring worked itself out in particular cases, how it affected the labor and working conditions of recent immigrant janitors, and the ways in which janitors responded to such conditions are the subject of the following two sections.

Figure 10.3.
Comparative Educational Attainment of Building Services and Public-Sector Janitors in Silicon Valley, 1990 (percents)

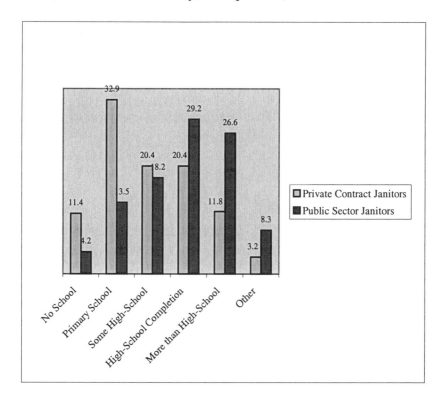

Source: U.S. Department of Commerce 1992.

From In-House Employees to Subcontracted Janitors: The Case of Sonix

The labor conditions and predicaments of Mexican janitors who are employed by independent private contractors to clean the office buildings of high-tech corporations in Silicon Valley are illustrated by the case of Sonix. One of the largest high-tech companies in Silicon Valley, Sonix owns numerous buildings in the region and uses about 250 contract janitors. Formerly employing its own "in-house" custodial workers, in 1983 the company started a "non-replacement of personnel policy" to reduce costs associated with its Custodial Department. In-house cleaning workers were gradually replaced by janitors employed by independent contractors, following a trend started by other large high-tech companies in the early 1980s.

According to one of Sonix's maintenance managers interviewed during fieldwork, this change was part of a larger decentralizing plan the company used to reduce labor and operating costs related to all service operations not considered central to its core businesses. In the case of janitorial work, this manager explained, former custodial workers were given the option of being trained and moved to other semi-skilled positions (such as shipping and receiving, and maintenance), receiving a compensation package with an early-retirement plan, or simply being laid off.

The economic incentives for subcontracting were clear. According to Sonix's managers, former in-house custodial workers were paid an average of $10 an hour, plus insurance and a generous "full package" of benefits. Subcontracted janitors were paid an average of $5.50 an hour by their employers, and because they were with non-union companies, they received no health insurance or any other benefits. This translated into considerable savings for Sonix as a client company. In addition to labor costs, Sonix's manager estimated that outsourcing cleaning operations had also contributed to the reduction of administrative costs, as well as expenses related to the management of the company's former cleaning warehouse. According to the manager, the maintenance cost of their former in-house cleaning operation was $1.15 per square foot; independent contractors offered to do the job for as little as 6 cents per square foot.

In addition to reducing labor and operating costs, shifting to subcontracted workers was seen by Sonix's maintenance management as a strategy to make cleaning a more efficient and flexible service. Sonix wanted to avoid a rigid, vertical organizational structure typical of large cleaning firms, preferring a decentralized scheme more in tune with the company's philosophy. Small, non-union cleaning firms without complex organizational structures were considered the ideal vehicles to accomplish this goal. In addition, subcontracting offered two advantages. First, it allowed the manager of each of Sonix's numerous buildings to select a janitorial contractor for that building, rather than all having to work with a single cleaning company through a thick bureaucratic structure. The second advantage was that the owners of the small cleaning companies had direct control over their workers, which made it easier for Sonix's maintenance managers to maintain direct contact with the companies and have their orders followed. As a result, by the early 1990s, Sonix had contracts with more than a dozen independent non-union cleaning firms, mostly midsize and small companies that relied almost exclusively on Mexican immigrant workers. In the words of Sonix's manager,

> We prefer working with small janitorial companies because they allow for more flexibility and better service, as, for example, when we request a non-scheduled service and have janitors respond promptly.... They are managed by their own boss who normally is on the site, which makes communication between us and these companies very easy, and which leads to a very good service.... The better the relationship between Sonix and these companies' owners, the better the quality of the service and the lower the cost.... [With them] we've had instant service.

The fact that the new janitorial workers were young Mexican immigrants was positively valued by Sonix's maintenance management. Mexican workers were considered ideal for the flexible organizational structure of janitorial work the company wanted to implement, not only because they were cheaper than their in-house counterparts, but also because they worked hard, were highly motivated, and offered little resistance to the on-site demands of Sonix managers. According to three maintenance managers at Sonix whom I interviewed, the advantages of working with Mexican janitors include their willingness to change their work routines when asked to do so, their availability to work overtime on short notice, and their ability to send relatives or friends to substitute for them whenever they are sick or quit their jobs. To overcome the language barriers that separated Sonix managers— mostly middle-aged Anglo men—from Mexican janitors, few of whom were fluent in English, Sonix promoted a few of its former in-house custodial workers to supervisory positions so that they could serve as intermediaries in the daily operations of janitorial work. One of them, a Mexican immigrant who had lived in the United States since he was a child and who was fluent in both English and Spanish, was considered by Sonix's managers to be a valuable asset for the company because of his knowledge and familiarity with Mexican workers' "culture and

habits." His role was to serve as a cultural broker for Sonix's maintenance management, bridging "language and cultural barriers" that
separated them from janitorial workers, and helping them to develop
training and organizational methods for Mexican workers.

Although the shift to subcontracted janitors started well before the
passage of the Immigration Reform and Control Act (IRCA) in 1986 (a
law that for the first time threatened to penalize employers who
knowingly hired undocumented workers), the use of independent contractors also allowed Sonix to delegate responsibility over the legal
status and labor conditions of janitorial workers to its contractors.
Sonix's maintenance managers acknowledged that, according to their
information, around 80 percent of the janitors employed by the cleaning firms they contracted were undocumented immigrants. In their
opinion, this was a matter for concern because undocumented immigrants were not integrated into the "official system as taxpayers."
Moreover, in their opinion, a real or "effective" minimum wage for
janitors such as those employed by Sonix's subcontractors should be
$7.75 plus benefits to make ends meet in Silicon Valley, a place charac-
terized by high housing and living costs (the minimum wage then was
$4.25). This, however, was considered to be the sole responsibility of
the janitorial contractors. According to Sonix managers, the solution
was either to legalize undocumented workers or to enforce IRCA and
thus have a legal, more stable workforce that would diminish the high
turnover rate of janitorial workers—one of the most significant problems identified by Sonix's management regarding the company's janitorial services.[8] In sum, subcontracting allowed Sonix to have access to
an abundant, cheap, and reliable immigrant workforce without the legal risks involved in directly employing them and, at the same time,
still maintain a high degree of control over the subcontracted janitors
and the organization of janitorial work within the company.

Workers Join the Union: The Justice for Janitors Campaign in Sonix

Subcontracting's effects on the working conditions of janitors who
cleaned Sonix buildings, as well as the response that such conditions
elicited from workers, are illustrated by the case of Bay-Clean, Sonix's
largest janitorial contractor in the early 1990s. Owned by a Korean en-

---

[8] This approach did not consider that a major factor accounting for turnover differences among janitorial companies, particularly between union and non-union
firms, is wages and labor benefits, given that most companies in this industry
have largely relied on undocumented workers since the early 1980s.

trepreneur, Bay-Clean was a midsize company of about 275 workers with a simple internal structure consisting of a thin layer of managers, most of them Koreans, and a large base of workers, most of them Mexicans and Central Americans, and a small group of Korean janitors. In each of Sonix's buildings, Bay-Clean maintained one manager and, depending on building size, one or two floor supervisors who worked in close contact with Sonix's maintenance managers, serving as intermediaries between them and the janitors. This allowed Sonix's managers to maintain a great deal of control over the organization of janitorial work and the daily activities of the subcontracted workers. Average wages for most Bay-Clean janitors (excluding those in charge of waxing floors and cleaning windows) was $5.50 an hour, and workers did not have any benefits, a considerable difference with wages and labor conditions formerly enjoyed by Sonix's in-house custodial workers.

With time, however, janitorial workers at Bay-Clean started to demand better wages and labor conditions. Workers complained about low and stagnant wages; many had been with the company for several years without receiving any pay increase. They also resented not receiving fringe benefits, particularly health insurance, which made them feel unprotected and vulnerable. This was especially true for workers who had settled in the region with their families. Janitors were also angered by the poor material conditions in which they had to carry out their daily tasks, as well as by the lack of a clear policy regarding job promotions and the distribution of workloads. A central complaint of many workers was that they were discriminated against by their employer because of their race and immigration status. Bay-Clean workers deeply resented what they considered "blatant racial discrimination" by their Korean employers, including unfair treatment, arbitrary decisions, and the general contempt with which supervisors treated them in the workplace. Many workers accused Bay-Clean of using a double standard, assigning the hardest cleaning jobs to Mexican workers, while giving the few Korean workers in the company the lightest and easiest tasks and quickly promoting them to supervisory positions. This feeling was captured by the comments of a Mexican janitor in Bay-Clean:

> After all, they [the Koreans] are also immigrants like us, but they want to step on us.... One thing is that you are exploited by the country's own people; another is to be exploited by other immigrants.... That is too much.

Tired, frustrated, and with little hope that their situation would improve, a group of Bay-Clean workers decided to contact Local 1877, the union representing custodial workers in the region. The Bay-Clean workers' petition come at a good time for Local 1877, which had recently launched the "Justice for Janitors" campaign (hereinafter JfJ) to organize immigrant janitorial workers who cleaned major high-tech office buildings in Silicon Valley.[9] JfJ's strategy was to target prestigious high-tech companies that were using non-union contractors and press them to switch to union firms by employing innovative tactics such as grassroots organizing, coalition building, consumer boycotts, hunger strikes, public relations campaigns, rallies, and demonstrations in front of high-tech companies that were sensitive to negative publicity. Union representatives told Bay-Clean workers that the best strategy to solve their problems was to organize and join the union. A group of about twelve workers then started to promote the union's cause among their peers.

The response of Bay-Clean janitors was initially timid. Many were recent undocumented immigrants who had never heard about the union and were afraid of getting involved with any kind of political activity that could jeopardize their jobs. Others were skeptical and suspicious about the union's motives, including many Mexican workers who were familiar with and critical of corrupt official unions in Mexico. Still others believed this was a good opportunity to air their grievances with Bay-Clean outside of the company. With the strategic advice of the local union, the janitors who cleaned Sonix's facilities started to organize in each of the company's buildings, gathering the support of an increasing number of their peers.

The principal demands of Bay-Clean's employees included better wages and a plan for wage increases based on seniority, the establishment of a clear and fair policy about the distribution of workloads, the promotion of Mexican janitors to supervisory positions, medical insurance for the company's employees, and adequate supplies to do their jobs. To press for such demands, they organized a rally in front of Bay-Clean offices, with the support of Local 1877. The turning point in this campaign, however, took place only a few weeks later, when Bay-Clean's janitors held another rally, this time in front of one of Sonix's main administrative offices, to press the company to use union contractors. This tactic produced immediate results. Afraid of negative publicity that could affect its image, Sonix soon announced that it was going

---

[9] "Justice for Janitors" is a nationwide campaign originally launched by the Service Employees International Union in 1987 in large cities such as Washington, D.C., Denver, Los Angeles, Chicago, San Diego, Detroit, and San Jose, to press owners of big buildings to employ union janitorial contractors rather than non-union cleaning firms. The goals of this campaign are to regain control of the cleaning market lost to non-union contractors in the 1980s, improve the wages and general working conditions of the janitors who clean large buildings and commercial facilities in these cities, and incorporate immigrant workers as union members.

to "consolidate" its janitorial services and hire only one cleaning contractor. The contract was awarded to CLS, a large multinational union firm with a good reputation in the industry. This was good news for Bay-Clean janitors who, under an agreement reached between the union and CLS, were hired by this company to continue cleaning Sonix's buildings, now as union workers.

The unionization of the janitors who cleaned Sonix's offices brought a significant improvement in their wages and labor conditions. Wages for most janitors rose from $5.50 to $6.10 (the entry-level wage established by the union master contract at the time), and that of specialized workers such as window cleaners and floor waxers increased proportionately. While modest, the raise was welcomed by most workers, who saw it as the beginning of a wage system based on job seniority. Janitors also gained important benefits, including health care (after three months working for CLS), sick leave, and one-week paid vacation after one year of employment. And as union workers, they were now protected from unfair labor practices by their employer, which many considered important in light of the numerous abuses they had endured at Bay-Clean.

Not all the changes, however, were positive. When CLS replaced Bay-Clean and the rest of the non-union contractors, it reduced the number of janitors employed to clean Sonix's facilities from 285 to 240, a strategy commonly used by cleaning companies to offer the most competitive bids. This led to greater workloads, and janitors had to clean larger areas to make up for the difference. Janitors complained about the additional workload and about orders from their supervisors who, on the one hand, asked them to work faster and, on the other, expected them to maintain the quality of their work. Summarizing the feeling of many of his co-workers, one janitor complained, "What do they [supervisors] want, quantity or quality?"

In 1995, the janitors who cleaned Sonix buildings suffered a major setback when the U.S. Immigration and Naturalization Service (INS) audited CLS. As a result, about 400 workers who did not have valid work authorization papers (most of whom were assigned to Sonix) lost their jobs. All of a sudden janitors lost not only their jobs, but also all of the benefits for which they had struggled so hard during the JfJ campaign. The workers' reaction was a mixture of disappointment, anger, and resignation. Many believed that everything was a CLS plot to replace them with new workers at entry-level wages. Others believed in the authenticity of the INS investigation, but felt that CLS had taken advantage of the situation.

Pressed by economic need, most affected workers looked for work in other janitorial companies, often with the assistance of the local union. Most of the replacement janitors hired to clean Sonix buildings were Mexican immigrants like themselves (many of them undocumented), and some were their own relatives or acquaintances. Since then, many other janitors in Sonix buildings have lost their jobs when their employer requested verification of their social security numbers. According to a Local 1877 official, this has become a common strategy that large janitorial firms, including union contractors, began using in the late 1990s to maintain a high turnover rate and keep the wages and working benefits of their employees depressed. This tactic has prevented many workers from reaching the top seniority wages established by the union contract, generating a "revolving-door" effect in the industry in which janitors shift companies whenever they are laid off by their employers because of their undocumented immigration status.

Conclusion

Few places better symbolize the essence of the new, high-tech economy of the late twentieth century than Silicon Valley. One of the most dynamic economic regions in the United States, Silicon Valley has become one of the main growth engines of the so-called new economy and the center of wealth and affluence associated with the high-tech industry. At the same time, the very success of the high-tech industry has generated a large supply of low-skill manufacturing and service jobs at the bottom of Silicon Valley's occupational structure.

This hourglass occupational structure, and the specific labor demands of the high-tech industry, account for yet another important characteristic of Silicon Valley—namely, a high demand for both high- and low-skilled immigrant workers from diverse ethnic backgrounds to fill jobs generated at both ends of the labor market. The strong labor demand for both kinds of occupations will not recede in the near future. Projections by the California Employment Development Department for Santa Clara County show that the twenty occupations with the greatest absolute growth in the region between 1995 and 2002 include both high-skill jobs for computer and electronic engineers, computer programmers, and electronic engineering technicians, *and* low-skill jobs for janitors, cleaners, waiters and waitresses, and electronic assemblers (EDD 1998b).[10] If we compare current and projected employment numbers for two representative occupations—computer engineers and

---

[10] This finding adds support to the position maintained by authors like Sassen and Smith (1992), Cornelius (1992, 1998), and others, who emphasize that the supply of low-skill jobs, especially in the service sector, represents a central feature of the postindustrial U.S. economy, which is structurally linked with the demand for immigrant workers from Mexico and other Central American countries.

janitors—we discover that there will be a significant demand for both types of workers in the near future (see table 10.3).[11]

Table 10.3.
Projected Employment Growth for Computer Engineers and Janitors in Santa Clara and San Mateo Counties, 1995–2002

County	Occupation	1995	2002	Absolute Change	Percent Change
Santa	Computer engineer	12,690	20,220	7,530	59.3
Clara	Janitor	12,110	14,880	2,770	22.9
San	Computer engineer.	2,100	3,980	1,880	89.5
Mateo	Janitor	4,550	5,470	920	20.2

Source: Employment Development Department, occupational employment projections.

The case study examined here also reveals the link that often exists between high-tech companies and low-skilled immigrant workers through labor contractors. Thus, even cutting-edge, high-tech companies like Sonix use large numbers of such immigrant workers by contracting out to cleaning companies like CLS as a strategy to reduce labor costs and develop flexible forms of work organization. As a result, new immigrants have become an integral part of the proletarian working class in the region—the "proletarian servants in the paragon of 'post-industrial' society," to borrow anthropologist Roger Rouse's expression (cited in Cornelius 1992: 170). Unlike former cohorts of Mexican immigrants in this region, today's low-skilled immigrants have fewer prospects for occupational and economic mobility. This seems to be the case for thousands of Mexican immigrants employed as subcontracted janitors in Silicon Valley who, despite contributing to the maintenance of the high-tech industrial complex, struggle hard to make ends

---

[11] This figure does not reflect the total growth of janitorial employment in counties like Santa Cruz and Alameda, where new urbanization from the expansion of the high-tech industry is taking place.

meet in a region characterized by high housing and living costs. In other words, as a result of restructuring and the rise of labor subcontracting, the wages, working conditions, and career prospects of janitors who currently clean the office buildings of Silicon Valley's high-tech companies have declined considerably with respect to the in-house custodial workers who used to do the job.

Beyond the structural conditions that generate a demand for low-skilled immigrant labor in places like Silicon Valley, we also have to consider the responses that immigrants, as political actors, develop to resist such conditions. The successful unionization of thousands of Mexican and Central American immigrants who work as janitors in Los Angeles, San Diego, and Silicon Valley shows that low-income immigrants, including the undocumented, are not passive actors unable or unwilling to organize to improve their labor and working conditions. More specifically, the Justice for Janitors campaign in Silicon Valley has critically contributed to improve the wages and fringe benefits of janitors employed as subcontracted workers by large high-tech firms.

Ironically, the high visibility of high-tech companies like Sonix, and their desire to avoid negative publicity, has been a critical factor facilitating the unionization of thousands of immigrant janitorial workers in the region, reversing to a certain extent the general decline of wages and benefits that contract janitors experienced during the 1980s. By early 2000, the union had about 5,500 members in the region, a significant increase over the 1,500 members it had in the early 1990s, when the JfJ was newly launched. In the meantime, the union has been less successful in organizing the thousands of immigrants who work as contract janitors in the facilities of other than high-tech companies or large buildings in downtown San Jose (restaurants, commercial centers, and so on). These individuals are often employed by midsize and small, non-union contractors, many of which operate in the informal sector.

In sum, the organization of large numbers of immigrant workers in this and other industries further contributes to debunking the myth that immigrants employed in low-wage occupations cannot—or will not—be organized. Today, the organization of immigrants in low-skilled industries in this and other regions of California is often considered by the labor movement as a model for the revitalization of U.S. unions, which have been in decline for several decades (Milkman 2000).[12]

In the policy realm, an effective approach to the problems of the immigrant working poor should start with an acknowledgment that the immigration of low-skilled workers is driven by structural demands in

---

[12] For the union organization of Mexican and other Latino immigrants, see also Delgado 1993; Waldinger et al. 1996; Milkman 2000.

the U.S. economy. Hence the issue of low-skilled workers cannot be thought of as the result of an "immigration problem," but rather as a labor issue. Effective policies should seek to raise wages and labor standards in low-skill industries where these workers are concentrated. This means enforcing wage, labor, and health safety standards in industries (such as building cleaning) that mostly employ immigrant workers, targeting midsize and small labor firms and contractors that often violate minimum wage and other labor and safety standards.[13]

An effective policy approach should also protect the right of immigrants to unionize, regardless of their immigrant status, preventing employers from using immigration legislation as a labor weapon and/or a strategy to maintain high worker turnover. These labor policies should be complemented with a reform of the current immigration legislation to also acknowledge the structural demand for low-skilled workers in the economy, instead of penalizing immigrants who are employed in these jobs.

Currently, immigration policies, and the way in which employers use them, tend to reinforce the vulnerability of undocumented immigrants, as in the case of CLS janitors who lost their jobs at the hands of the INS, only to be replaced by a cadre of cheaper undocumented workers. Just as the demand for highly skilled foreign-born workers in the high-tech industry is used to reform current immigration legislation, so too, the demand for low-skilled immigrant workers by the same structural forces should be used as a realistic premise to reform immigration laws concerning undocumented immigrants who work and live in this country.

References

Alarcón, Rafael. 1999. "Recruitment Processes among Foreign-Born Engineers and Scientists in Silicon Valley," *American Behavioral Scientist* 42 (9): 1381–97.

Alvarado, Jaime, et al. 1991. *The Rich, the Poor, and the Forgotten ... in the Silicon Valley.* San Jose, Calif.: Cleaning Up Silicon Valley Coalition.

Blakely, E., and S. Sullivan. 1989. "The Latino Workforce in Santa Clara County: The Dilemmas of High Technology Change on a Minority Popula-

---

[13] According to the underground economy task force of the California Economic Development Department, in addition to garments and agriculture, janitorial services is an industry in which labor and tax law violations are common (*Migration News* 2000). As a result, janitorial services were added to the Targeted Industries Partnership Program in 1999, a joint federal and California state program originally developed for overseeing compliance with wage, safety, and other labor standards in the garment industry and agriculture.

tion." Study commissioned by the Latino Issues Forum of Santa Clara County, California.

Cornelius, Wayne A.. 1992. "From Sojourners to Settlers: The Changing Profile of Mexican Immigration to the United States." In *U.S.–Mexico Relations: Labor Market Interdependence*, edited by Jorge Bustamante, Clark Reynolds, and Raúl Hinojosa-Ojeda. Stanford, Calif.: Stanford University Press.

———. 1998. "The Structural Embeddedness of Demand for Mexican Immigrant Labor: New Evidence from California." In *Crossings: Mexican Immigration in Interdisciplinary Perspectives*, edited by Marcelo M. Suárez-Orozco. Cambridge, Mass.: Harvard University Press.

Cranford, Cynthia. 1998. "Gender and Citizenship in the Restructuring of Janitorial Work in Los Angeles," *Gender Issues* 16 (4): 25–51.

Delgado, Héctor L. 1993. *New Immigrants, Old Unions: Organizing Undocumented Workers in Los Angeles*. Philadelphia, Penn.: Temple University Press.

EDD (Employment Development Department). 1998a. "Santa Clara County: Occupations with Greatest Growth, 1995–2000." Projections and Planning Information.

———. 1998b. "Industry Trends and Outlook, 1995–2000. Santa Clara County."

Flores, William Vincent. 1987. "The Dilemma of Survival: Organizational Dependence, Conflict and Change in a Chicano Community." Ph.D. dissertation, Stanford University.

Green, Susan S. 1983. "Silicon Valley's Women Workers: A Theoretical Analysis of Sex-segregation in the Electronics Industry Labor." In *Women, Men, and the International Division of Labor*, edited by June Nash and María Patricia Fernández-Kelly. Albany: State University of New York Press.

Hossfeld, Karen. 1988. "Divisions of Labor, Divisions of Lives: Immigrant Women Workers in Silicon Valley." Ph.D. dissertation, University of California, Santa Cruz.

Martínez Saldaña, Jesús. 1993. "At the Periphery of Democracy: The Binational Politics of Mexican Immigrants in Silicon Valley." Ph.D. dissertation, University of California, Berkeley.

Migration News. 2000. "Labor: H–1Bs, Janitors, Vanguard," vol 7, no. 8.

Milkman, Ruth. 2000. *Organizing Immigrants : The Challenge for Unions in Contemporary California.* Ithaca, N.Y.: Cornell University Press.

Mines, Richard, and Jeffrey Avina. 1992. "Immigrants and Labor Standards: The Case of California Janitors." In *U.S.–Mexico Relations: Labor Market Interdependence*, edited by Jorge Bustamante, Clark Reynolds, and Raúl Hinojosa-Ojeda. Stanford, Calif.: Stanford University Press.

Rosaldo, Renato, and William V. Flores. 1997. "Identity, Conflict, and Evolving Latino Communities: Cultural Citizenship in San Jose, California." In *Latino Cultural Citizenship: Claiming Identity, Space, and Rights*, edited by William V. Flores and Rina Benmayor. Boston, Mass.: Beacon.

Sassen, Saskia, and Robert C. Smith. 1992. "Post-Industrial Growth and Economic Reorganization: Their Impact on Immigration Employment." In *U.S.–Mexico Relations: Labor Market Interdependence*, edited by Jorge Bustamante, Clark Reynolds, and Raúl Hinojosa-Ojeda. Stanford, Calif.: Stanford University Press.

Saxenian, AnnaLee. 1985. "Silicon Valley and Route 128: Regional Prototypes or Historic Exceptions?" In *High Technology, Space, and Society,* edited by Manuel Castells. Beverly Hills, Calif.: Sage.

———. 1994. *Regional Advantage: Culture and Competition in Silicon Valley and Route 128.* Cambridge, Mass.: Harvard University Press.

U.S. Department of Commerce. Bureau of the Census. 1991. Economics and Statistics Administration. *1990 Census of Population and Housing, Summary Population and Housing Characteristics, California.* Washington, D.C.: U.S. Government Printing Office, August.

———. 1992. 1990 Census of Population and Housing: Public Use Microdata Samples (5%). U.S. Machine Readable Data Files. Washington, D.C.: U.S. Government Printing Office.

Waldinger, Roger, et al. 1996. "Helots No More: A Case Study of the Justice for Janitors Campaign in Los Angeles." Working Paper No. 15. Los Angeles: Lewis Center for Regional Policy Studies, School of Public Policy and Social Research, University of California, Los Angeles.

11

The Migration of High-Skilled Workers from Canada to the United States: The Economic Basis of the Brain Drain

Mahmood Iqbal

There is a growing perception that although Canada is attracting skilled personnel from around the world, it is also losing many of its best and brightest to the United States (a phenomenon commonly known as the "brain drain"). This emigration has become more prominent since the Free Trade Agreement (FTA) in 1989, and especially after the implementation of the North American Free Trade Agreement (NAFTA) in 1994. However, there is great controversy as to the extent of the brain drain.

Citizenship and Immigration Canada, the national agency responsible for collecting and disseminating migration data, only keeps track of immigrants entering Canada. Statistics Canada, on the other hand, estimates Canadian high-skilled workers leaving for the United States through secondary sources: the U.S. Current Population Survey, the Canadian Census, and personal tax filer data. Unfortunately, these approaches primarily focus on those Canadians who emigrate to the United States on a "permanent" basis. They fail to include emigration of Canadian professionals to the United States on a "non-permanent" basis, and they result, therefore, in incomplete counting (Zhao, Drew, and Murray 2000).[1] In fact, in recent years, most emigration to the United States has been taking place under NAFTA temporary work visas.

---

[1] See a series of presentations by Statistics Canada staff under various titles, made in October 1997 in Quebec City, September 1999 in Toronto, and October 1999 in Ottawa (in Zhao, Drew, and Murray 2000).

This chapter is a comprehensive examination of the brain drain.[2] First, it demonstrates the significance of the issue from the Canadian perspective. It then provides a historical view of overall migration between Canada and the United States; it also provides data on immigrants in Canada from other parts of the world. Next, it looks at recent trends in emigration (both permanent and non-permanent) of highly educated and skilled Canadians to the United States and examines its significance in a broader economic context. Using national data, the chapter also provides empirical evidence of factors responsible for the brain drain and establishes a quantitative link between the trend and its determinants. Since the tax wedge between Canada and the United States is often identified as the main cause of the brain drain, details on differences in personal taxes between the two countries also are provided.

The main, historically consistent data source on the emigration of Canadian professionals to the United States is the *Statistical Yearbook*, published by the U.S. Immigration and Naturalization Service (INS). According to this source (INS 1999), there are two principal categories of Canadian professionals moving to the United States: "permanent" and "non-permanent." Permanent immigrants are those who move with the intention of holding permanent employment.[3] Non-permanent immigrants are those who receive temporary visas to work in specific fields. In this study, they mainly include workers under NAFTA (for whom visas are issued for a year or more), intracompany transferees (for whom visas are issued for up to seven years), and persons in specialty occupations (for whom visas are issued for up to six years). Key features of these temporary visas are provided in table 11.1.

Although business visitors, traders, and investors may receive visas for one year, they are *not* included in the study because their visits are intermittent and each of their trips cannot exceed six months. Nor does this study include spouses and dependents.

Why Is the Brain Drain an Important Issue for Canada?

The lion's share of public spending in Canada is allocated to education, health, and social services. They account for 57 percent of total consolidated expenditure at all levels of government (Treff and Perry 1999: table A.4). These expenditures are essential for producing a well-educated, healthy, and productive citizenry. Every graduate produced

---

[2] The chapter draws primarily on Iqbal 1999 and Iqbal 2000.

[3] But many Canadians who emigrate to the United States do not know beforehand whether they intend to stay there or not, given the ease of return.

in Canada, therefore, is highly subsidized by public money or tax expenditures. When these graduates leave for other countries, most notably to the United States, they create a significant negative balance in Canada's public account.

Table 11.1
Main Categories of Temporary Visas

Criteria	H-1B Visa (Outside NAFTA)	TN Visa (NAFTA)
Proof that U.S. workers will not be adversely affected	Required	Not required
Application	Apply to Depts. of Labor and Immigration	Apply at border
Time to process	6-10 weeks	Instant approval
Initial duration	3 years renewable	1 year renewable
Maximum time limit	6 years	Unlimited
Limit on level	World immigration capped at 115,000[a]	Unlimited

[a] Legislation passed in October 2000 will raise the cap to 195,000.

Note: H–1B specialty workers are professionals and highly skilled individuals in specialty occupations. Similarly, to qualify for a TN visa, the individual must work in a professional occupation listed in Schedule 2 of NAFTA and provide documentation of credentials. Also, TN applicants need a letter from the intended U.S. employer which includes remuneration arrangements.

Source: U.S. Immigration and Naturalization Service, as cited in Williamson 2000.

Though there is much controversy in Canada about the actual extent of high-skilled workers emigrating to the United States, there is complete agreement that they are the best and brightest of Canada's human resource pool (Schwanen 2000).[4] Their departure negatively affects the country's economic growth, productivity, and ultimately the living standards of ordinary Canadians.

Furthermore, most of the Canadian highly skilled workers who emigrate to the United States fall in the high-income category. Their departure leads to an erosion of the tax base and government revenues. These revenues are essential to finance the social programs that Canadians are so proud of.

---

[4] This aspect of the brain drain is best analyzed by Daniel Schwanen (2000).

In recent years, the Canadian economy has been booming like that of the United States, although not to the same extent. For example, the national unemployment rate in Canada decreased to 6.8 percent in 2000, from more than 10 percent a few years back (the national unemployment rate in the United States at the time of writing is 3.9 percent) (Egan 2000). The Canadian business community, especially in high-tech areas, has been complaining about shortages of skilled workers for the last several years. The emigration of scarce Canadian high-skilled workers to the United States in the presence of existing shortages would have further negative implications for the Canadian economy.

Although there has been an increasing demand for knowledge workers in the United States with the exponential growth of high-tech industries, the supply of U.S. graduates is lagging. Consequently, the United States will increasingly rely on other countries to meet its needs. Canada is well-known for its high-quality, well-educated workforce. Being close to the United States, where economic opportunities abound, and with NAFTA visas easily available, Canada is afraid of losing its valuable human resources.

There is severe competition among various developed countries—notably the United States, Canada, and Western Europe—to attract well-educated and highly skilled workers from developing countries such as India and China. Many developing countries have also started progressing in areas where the demand for knowledge workers in technology-related industries is growing significantly. Therefore, it will be increasingly difficult for the West to convince workers from these countries to leave their homes and migrate to alien territories.

Migration between Canada and the United States

Total "permanent" migration (high-skilled and all other categories of people) between Canada and the United States is presented in figure 11.1.

Historically, more Canadians have moved to the United States than Americans have immigrated to Canada. In recent years, for every American who moved to Canada, about three Canadians emigrated south of the border. A similar picture (in a more dramatic way) appears for "temporary" migration between the two countries, presented in a later section of the chapter.

Furthermore, in high-skill areas, significantly more Canadians are emigrating to the United States on a permanent basis than the other way around (see figure 11.2a). For example, for every American coming to Canada in managerial occupations, there are 59 Canadians moving to the United States (figure 11.2b). Canadian engineers, nurses, and physicians have similarly high rates of emigration to the United States. However, in global perspective, Canada receives four university graduates from other parts of the world for every Canadian graduate departing to the United States, as estimated by Statistics Canada.[5]

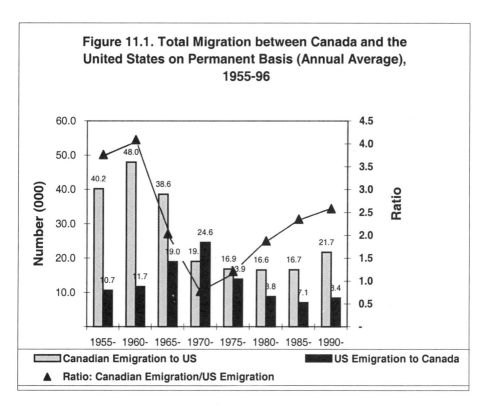

Figure 11.1. Total Migration between Canada and the United States on Permanent Basis (Annual Average), 1955-96

Source: Statistics Canada and *Education Quarterly Review*, May 2000, vol. 6, no. 3; The Conference Board of Canada.

---

[5] The ratio of four to one (four entries in Canada against one departure to the United States) estimated by Statistics Canada is very questionable because it grossly underestimates outflow from Canada. First, it does not include Canadian outflow to other countries beside the United States. Outflow to the United States accounts for only half of Canada's total outflow. Second, the ratio does not include Canadian professionals emigrating to the United States on a temporary basis. All immigrants from the rest of the world enter Canada on a permanent basis, whereas a significant majority of Canadians move to the United States on a temporary basis. When these facts are included in the calculation, the ratio of outflow to inflow could turn against Canada's advantage.

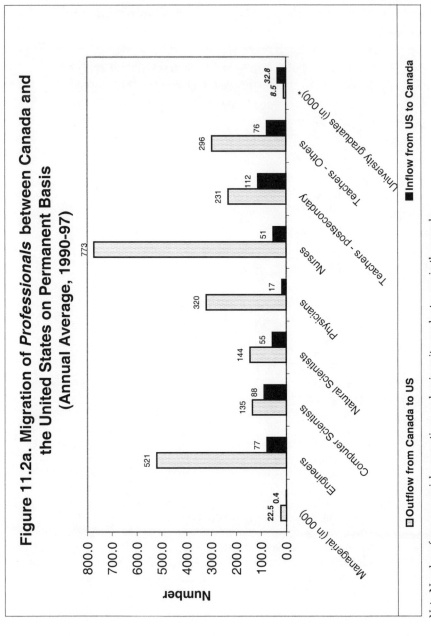

Figure 11.2a. Migration of *Professionals* between Canada and the United States on Permanent Basis (Annual Average, 1990-97)

☐ Outflow from Canada to US   ■ Inflow from US to Canada

Note: Numbers for managerial occupations and university graduates are in thousands.
* For university graduates, outflow is from Canada to the United States and inflow is from all over the world in Canada.
Source: Statistics Canada, *Education Quarterly Review*, May 2000, vol. 6, no. 3; The Conference Board of Canada.

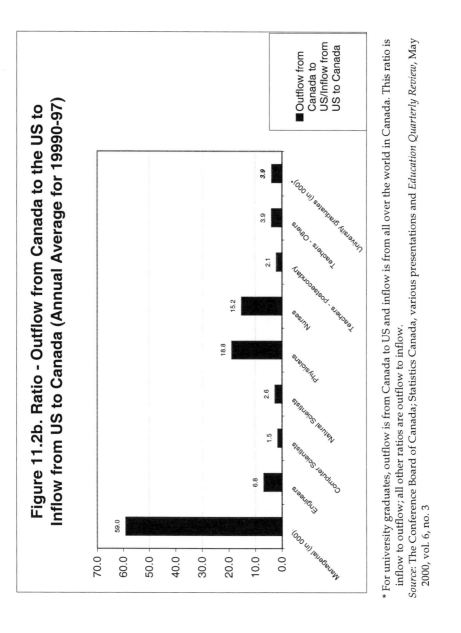

Figure 11.2b. Ratio – Outflow from Canada to the US to Inflow from US to Canada (Annual Average for 19990-97)

Legend: ■ Outflow from Canada to US/Inflow from US to Canada

Values by category:
- Managerial (in 000): 59.0
- Engineers: 6.8
- Computer Scientists: 1.5
- Natural Scientists: 2.6
- Physicians: 18.8
- Nurses: 15.2
- Teachers - postsecondary: 2.1
- Teachers - Others: 3.9
- University graduates (in 000)*: 3.9

* For university graduates, outflow is from Canada to US and inflow is from all over the world in Canada. This ratio is inflow to outflow; all other ratios are outflow to inflow.

Source: The Conference Board of Canada; Statistics Canada, various presentations and *Education Quarterly Review*, May 2000, vol. 6, no. 3

Overall, the level of migration between Canada, the United States, and the rest of the world is presented in figure 11.3. The number of Canadians migrating to the United States during the 1990s is small in a historical sense as well as relative to the inflow of immigrants from all over the world. In the 1990s (1990–1996), for every Canadian who moved to the United States, Canada received more than ten immigrants from the rest of the world.

But one needs to be extremely careful while analyzing these data. They completely exclude temporary migration. Since the implementation of NAFTA, more than 90 percent of emigration (based on numbers of visas issued) from Canada to the United States in the high-skill area has been taking place in the "temporary" category (TN and H–1B, and so on). Hence figure 11.3 grossly underestimates total emigration of Canadian professionals to the United States.

For example, figure 11.4(a) clearly shows significant growth in the emigration of Canadians—especially workers under TN categories—to the United States. (This is explained in a later part of the chapter.) As is the case with permanent migration, U.S. emigration to Canada under temporary work visas is very small (see figure 11.4(b)). For example, under the TN category, only one American came to Canada for every seven Canadians who moved to the United States in 1997.

The Controversy over Numbers

The Statistics Canada data discount the migration data collected by the INS due to the possibility of multiple counting and other administrative anomalies (Zhao, Drew, and Murray 2000: 15). Further, the agency believes that emigration from Canada to the United States is more than offset by immigration to Canada from other countries. This is not surprising given that the agency focuses on "permanent" migration, whereas it is the "non-permanent" workers who account for a large and rising share of current emigration of highly educated and highly skilled Canadians to the United States. Even the temporary absence of these workers could have significant negative consequences for the Canadian economy, especially if there is a shortage of these professionals, as is often suggested by the business community.

NAFTA workers account for the bulk of temporary visas. Workers generally receive visas (TN–1) for one year, with the option of renewing them for an indefinite period or, after meeting certain legal requirements, converting to permanent status. The NAFTA visa has generated a lot of confusion regarding the actual number of Canadian professionals leaving for the United States. Many people get confused between employment visas and regular border crossings. They believe

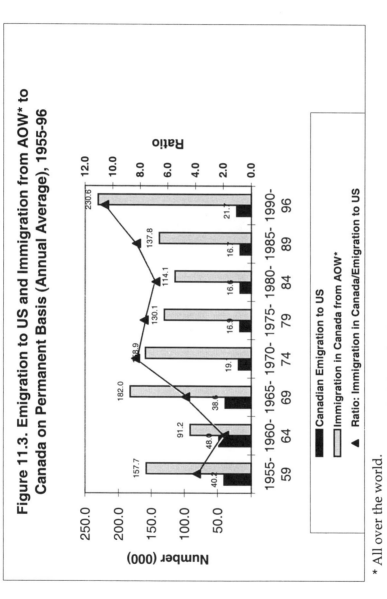

Figure 11.3. Emigration to US and Immigration from AOW* to Canada on Permanent Basis (Annual Average), 1955-96

■ Canadian Emigration to US
□ Immigration in Canada from AOW*
▲ Ratio: Immigration in Canada/Emigration to US

* All over the world.
Source: The Conference Board of Canada; Statistics Canada, various presentations and *Education Quarterly Review*, May 2000, vol. 6, no. 3.

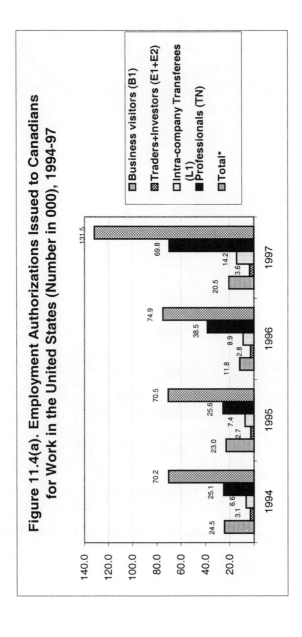

Figure 11.4(a). Employment Authorizations Issued to Canadians for Work in the United States (Number in 000), 1994-97

Business visitors (B1)
Traders+Investors (E1+E2)
Intra-company Transferees (L1)
Professionals (TN)
Total*

* Total includes dependents like those in visa categories of L2 and TD.

Source: US Immigration and Naturalization Service (obtained by Department of Foreign Affairs and International Trade, Canada); The Conference Board of Canada.

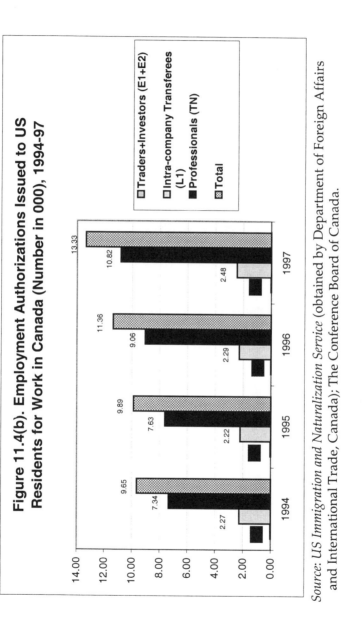

Figure 11.4(b). Employment Authorizations Issued to US Residents for Work in Canada (Number in 000), 1994-97

Legend:
- Traders+Investors (E1+E2)
- Intra-company Transferees (L1)
- Professionals (TN)
- Total

Source: US Immigration and Naturalization Service (obtained by Department of Foreign Affairs and International Trade, Canada); The Conference Board of Canada.

that the high number of TN–1 visas is attributable to the problem of multiple countings of the same emigrant.

There are sound reasons for including temporary and NAFTA workers in this study. NAFTA visas offer advantages over the traditional method of emigrating to the United States on a permanent basis. They are convenient, quickly obtained, and more flexible. As a result, they account for more than 90 percent of the total number of visas issued to Canadians working in the United States, which makes their inclusion crucial to understanding the brain drain issue.

If the movement of professionals were analyzed purely on the traditional criterion of "permanent" emigration, the result would be inaccurate and misleading. Indeed, adopting such an approach would be like adding a new lane to a major highway, and then not counting the cars and trucks that use the new lane in the statistics on highway use. For example, permanent emigration in 1997 (the latest year for which data are available) was about 30 percent less than in 1996. This drop is likely the result of the new, more easily accessible visas. Indeed, given the convenience of NAFTA visas, advancements in communications, and better economic opportunities in the United States, it is not difficult to find compelling economic arguments to support the notion that the brain drain is increasing.

From the perspective of a company or a national economy, what is important here is the output and tax revenue contributed by a worker in a given period. The economic cost to the country, in terms of persons lost per year, is the same whether one Canadian moves to the United States for two consecutive years or two Canadians move for one year each. Therefore, in a given time period, the absence of these professionals from the Canadian economy has the same implications whether the move is temporary or permanent.

It has often been claimed that Canada is a "net brain gainer." For each professional that Canada loses to the United States, it receives four from the rest of the world (see figure 11.2). These numbers are valid only for permanent emigration. Once temporary numbers (which account for the bulk of Canadian professionals emigrating to the United States) are included in the calculation, the ratio is reversed. Moreover, the suggestion that a Canadian professional leaving for the United States is easily and perfectly replaced by a newly arriving professional immigrant is misleading. A large body of research shows that it takes years for new immigrants to assimilate into North American culture, learn the language, and integrate into the labor market structure. There is a significant lapse of time before new immigrants find jobs closely related to their specialized disciplines, and secure salaries and responsibilities commensurate with their education and experience. Indeed, some estimates suggest that it may cost more than $200,000 (Canadian dollars) to replace a Canadian-born trained professional with a newly landed foreign professional (DeVoretz and Laryea 1998: 21).

It is interesting to note that according to the October 1996 INS estimate (INS 1997: 199–200), there are 120,000 Canadians (Canadian-born and immigrant Canadians) living in the United States illegally, or as "undocumented immigrants." About half of them entered legally on a temporary basis and failed to depart. All published studies have failed to recognize their existence. These individuals are supposedly young, energetic, hardworking Canadians who are contributing to the U.S. economy.

Trends in Canadian Emigration to the United States

The emigration numbers for skilled workers presented in figure 11.5 are based on numbers of employment visas granted. They include engineers, computer scientists, physicians, nurses, professors, teachers, managerial personnel, and social scientists. There has not been much growth in "permanent" skilled emigration to the United States. However, when non-permanent emigration is included in the analysis, the picture changes dramatically, especially after the implementation of NAFTA. In 1997, non-permanent emigrants accounted for 94 percent of the total outflow of Canadian professionals to the United States, as compared to 77 percent in 1986. The number of permanent and non-permanent emigrants (based on visas issued) jumped from 17,000 in 1989 to 98,000 in 1997. Again, this growth is largely attributable to the non-permanent category.

In order to eliminate the problem of multiple counting, particularly for those individuals who renew their non-permanent visas before they expire, this study attempts to convert the number of emigration visas into the actual number of Canadians who moved to the United States (see figure 11.6). Based on a series of conservative assumptions (given in the appendix), the estimate shows that in 1997, about 35,000 Canadian professionals moved to the United States. This overall trend is the same as presented in figure 11.5 (based on the number of visas issued).

Figure 11.7 examines the impact of FTA/NAFTA on emigration in key occupational categories. For each occupational group, data are divided into three periods: 1986–1988 (pre–FTA, emigration based on number of employment visas issued); 1989–1993 (during FTA, emigration based on actual number of professionals moved); and 1994–1997 (post–NAFTA, emigration based on actual number of professionals moved). Within each category, growth in emigration accelerated after the trade agreements were implemented. In fact, during the pre–FTA period, there was either negligible growth or even a decline in emigra-

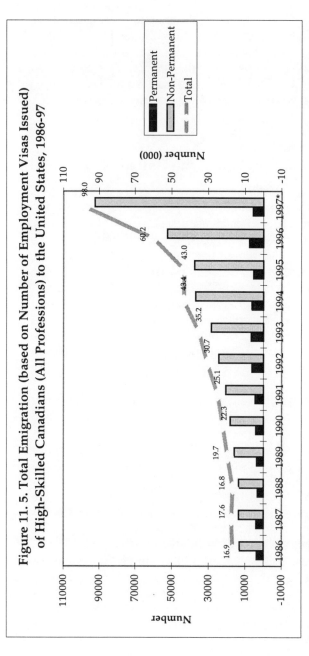

Figure 11.5. Total Emigration (based on Number of Employment Visas Issued) of High-Skilled Canadians (All Professions) to the United States, 1986–97

Note: Admissions under FTA (TC visa) began January 1989 and ended December 31, 1993. Admissions under NAFTA (TN visa) began January 1, 1994.

* The TN-visa number for 1997, which is 75 percent of total high-skilled Canadian emigrants to the United States is from US INS (supplied by the Department of Foreign Affairs and International Trade, Ottawa). Numbers for permanent emigrants are also from US INS. Other numbers are estimates. Of those Canadians who go to the United States as students, some 5 percent change their status to permanent immigrants. They are included in these charts according to their proportions in different occupational categories.

Sources: Estimates by the author using the following: Various presentations by Statistics Canada; John Zhao, Doug Drew and Scott Murray of Statistics Canada, "Brain Drain and Brain Gain: The Migration of Knowledge Workers from and to Canada," *Education Quarterly Review,* May 2000, vol. 6, no. 3, Statistics Canada, catalogue no. 81-003; US INS, INS Tapes and *Statistical Yearbook of the Immigration and Naturalization Service* (various years); Don DeVoretz and Samuel A. Laryea, *Canadian Human Capital Transfers: The United States and Beyond,* Commentary no. 115 (Toronto: C.D. Howe Institute, October 1998); Industry Canada, *Perspective on the "Brain Drain,"* (Draft), December 1998.

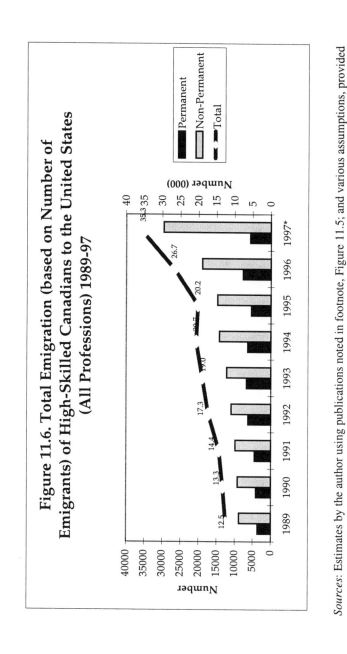

Figure 11.6. Total Emigration (based on Number of Emigrants) of High-Skilled Canadians to the United States (All Professions) 1989-97

Sources: Estimates by the author using publications noted in footnote, Figure 11.5; and various assumptions, provided in the Appendix.

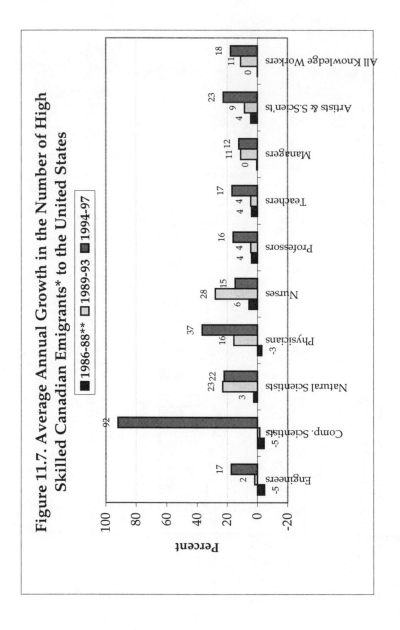

Figure 11.7. Average Annual Growth in the Number of High Skilled Canadian Emigrants* to the United States

■ 1986-88** ▢ 1989-93 ▨ 1994-97

Percent

* Includes both permanent and non-permanent.

** Based on number of employment visas issued. For other periods, actual number of Canadian emigrants to U.S.

Sources: see footnote, Figures 11.5 and 11.6.

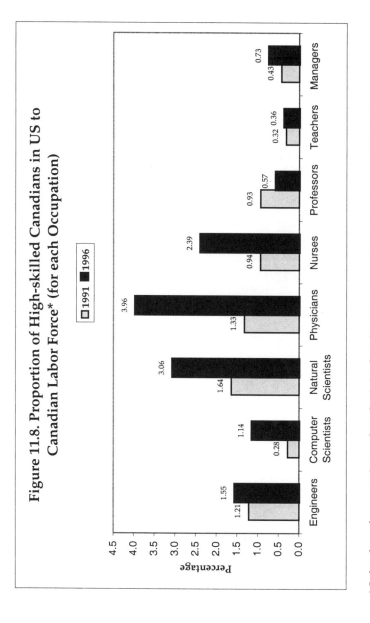

Figure 11.8. Proportion of High-skilled Canadians in US to Canadian Labor Force* (for each Occupation)

* Labor force data are estimates from Statistics Canada, cat. no. 93-327. Number of emigrants includes both permanent and non-permanent.

Sources: See footnote, Figures 11.5 and 11.6.

tion. The FTA resulted in a significant overall increase in emigration, especially for physicians and nurses. NAFTA resulted in a sharp increase for all groups of emigrants in knowledge areas, especially for computer scientists.

When this rapid growth in the emigration of highly skilled Canadians to the United States is viewed in the context of the overall Canadian labor force, the potential for significant negative economic repercussions becomes evident (see figure 11.8). In 1991, for example, only 1.3 percent of Canada's physicians emigrated to the United States. By 1996, the proportion had increased to 4 percent, a jump of nearly 300 percent.

The proportion of natural scientists, nurses, and engineers pursuing careers south of the border also recorded significant growth. Because these professionals are leaving Canada at a rate higher than their rate of entry into the Canadian labor force, the country's reservoir of human capital is diminishing.

Causes for Emigration

Despite the attraction of better economic opportunities, migration in general is "costly" in both monetary and psychological terms. Relocation to a distant country with alien traditions, language, and culture presents the newcomer with the risk of being excluded from the mainstream. This difficulty is greatly diminished for migrants between Canada and the United States. Similarities between the two countries open an easier path to relocation.

In addition, with the advent of the Internet, people who are considering emigration can collect valuable information on the key factors associated with the decision to move—salary range, tax rates, cost of living, housing, education facilities, and quality of life. Information supplied by relatives and friends provides further support to the decision to move.

Most emigrants are young (*Inside* 1999). They are at a stage in their lives when they can move without the burden of many family responsibilities. Also, there has been an important attitude shift across generations. In this era of globalization and economic opportunism, many younger people are willing—even eager—to relocate to another country.

Surveys by various research and business organizations invariably identify the same reasons for emigrating to the United States (though not necessarily in the same order): higher salary, paid in U.S. dollars; more growth opportunities; exposure to leading-edge technology; lower taxes; better management; and even a warmer climate. But surveys have limitations—namely, questionnaire bias, restricted sample size, limited time frames, and questionable statistical validity. A more comprehensive study requires historically consistent national data on differences in earnings, employment opportunities, and taxes between the two countries, which are often considered to be the main economic factors for the brain drain. These data are presented in figures 11.9, 11.10, and 11.11.

Until the mid–1980s, earnings in Canada were close to those in the United States. In some cases (for example, for nurses and teachers), they were even higher (Iqbal 1999: 18). From 1990 onward, Canada has lagged in growth in earnings, and the gap between the two countries has been widening (see figure 11.9). In recent years, the discrepancy has been particularly apparent in the computer sciences, engineering, medicine, and university teaching professions.

The differences in job opportunities between the two countries are best reflected by the gap in the unemployment rate (see figure 11.10(a)). After 1988, the gap in the unemployment rate narrowed, but then it widened. In recent years, the gap has been stable, but still there is a significant difference in the unemployment rates in the two countries, especially in knowledge areas, as shown in figure 11.10(b).

The tax wedge—the difference in the level of tax burden—is often mentioned as the key reason for the brain drain. The ratio of taxes to gross domestic product (GDP) has been consistently higher in Canada than in the United States since the 1960s, but the gap widened in the 1990s (see figure 11.11).

Growth Opportunity

Compared to Canada, the United States has a GDP that is 11 times higher and a population that is 9 times larger. It accounts for 27 percent of world output, 16 percent of world trade, and 25 percent of world foreign direct investment (OECD 1999). It is the hub of international financial activities and world technological breakthroughs. Therefore, by inference, the United States also offers a higher level of learning and growth opportunities. This superiority is particularly evident in the knowledge areas, as demonstrated by the level of research and development (the ratio of R&D expenditure to GDP is 1.66 in Canada, against 2.62 in the United States) and the concentration of researchers (5.4 per thousand workers in Canada, against 7.4 in the United States) (OECD 1998).

Therefore, the United States has become a major destination for skilled high-tech professionals. It provides all the necessary ingredients—venture capital, learning opportunities, and growth prospects—to business people and talented individuals who are willing to take on

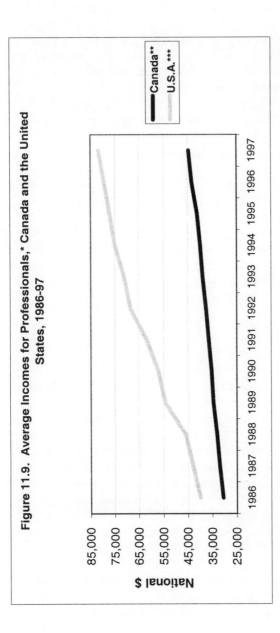

Figure 11.9. Average Incomes for Professionals,* Canada and the United States, 1986-97

Canada**
U.S.A.***

National $

85,000
75,000
65,000
55,000
45,000
35,000
25,000

1986 1987 1988 1989 1990 1991 1992 1993 1994 1995 1996 1997

Note: Canadian earnings are converted into U.S.$ using purchasing power parity rate.

*Average of average incomes of engineers, computer scientists, professors, teachers, physicians, nurses, and managerial occupation.

** Canada: an average of average income of Alberta, Quebec, Ontario and Nova Scotia. Average income for cities were not available.

*** USA: an average of average income of Chicago, Houston, Los Angeles, Miami, New York and San Jose. For San Jose, it is only for the period from 1991 onward.

Sources: Estimates by the author using following: Statistics Canada, 1996 Census, 93F0029XDB96004; Census, *Employment Income by Occupation(The Nation),* cat. no. 93-332; *Education Quarterly Review,* 1997, cat. no. 81-003-XPB, vol. 4, no. 1;*Labour Force Update,* 1998, cat. no. 71-005-XPB; Marie Lavoie and Ross Finnie, "Science and Technology Careers in Canada: Analysis of Recent University Graduates," *Education Quarterly Review,* 1997, cat. no. 81-003-XPB, vol.4, no. 3; US Department of Commerce, *1998 Statistical Abstract;* U.S. Bureau of Labor Statistics, *Employment and Wages;* and US Bureau of the Census, *Current Population Reports.*

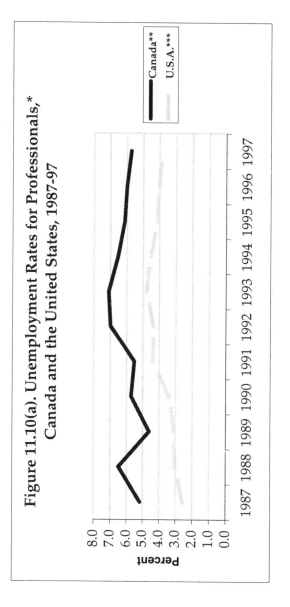

Figure 11.10(a). Unemployment Rates for Professionals,*
Canada and the United States, 1987-97

Canada**
U.S.A.***

*Average of unemployment rates of engineers, computer and natural scientists, professors, teachers, physicians,
nurses, managerial occupations, and social scientists.
** Canada: an average of unemployment rate in Vancouver, Calgary, Toronto, Ottawa-Hull, Montreal and Halifax.
*** United States: an average of unemployment rate in New York, Los Angeles, Chicago, Houston and Miami.
Sources: Estimates by the author using following:

For Canada: Statistics Canada, *Historical Labour Force Statistics, 1997*, catalogue no. 71-201-XPB; and Marie
Lavoie and Ross Finnie, "Science and Technology Careers in Canada: Analysis of Recent University Graduates,"
Education Quarterly Review, 1997, cat. no. 81-003-XPB, vol. 4, no. 3.
For the United States: U.S. Bureau of Labor Statistics, *Employment and Wages*; US Department of Commerce, *1998
Statistical Abstract*.

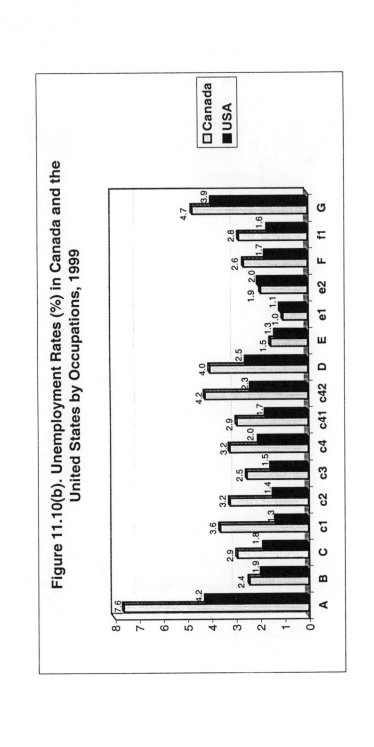

Figure 11.10(b). Unemployment Rates (%) in Canada and the United States by Occupations, 1999

Note: A=All Occupations

B=Executive & Managerial Occupations

C=Professional Occupations in Natural & Applied Sciences

c1=Phyisical scientists

c2=Life scientists

c3=Engineers

c4=Math.,system analysts & computer programmers

c41compter systems analysts

c42=computer programmers

D=Technical Occupations in Natural & Applied Sciences

E=Health Occupations

e1=Professional occupations in health & nursing

e2=Technical, assisting & related occupations

F=Social Science, Education, Govt. & Religion

f1=Teachers and professors

G=Occupations in Art, culture, recreation & sport

Source: Unpublished data, Statistics Canada, the Bureau of Labor Statistics and the Conference Board of Canada. Cited in Shane Williamson presentation, *A Perspective on the International Migration of Skilled Workers* (IRRP and CERF Conference, Ottawa, Canada, June 3-4, 2000).

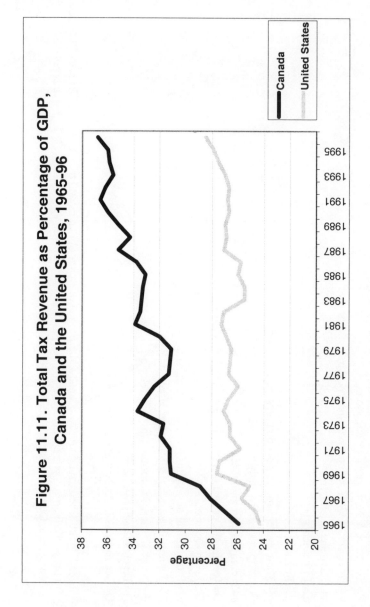

Figure 11.11. Total Tax Revenue as Percentage of GDP, Canada and the United States, 1965-96

Canada

United States

Source: Organization for Economic Co-operation and Development, *Revenue Statistics, 1965-97* (Paris: OECD, 1998).

new risks and challenges. These people are hungry to prove their abilities and conduct innovative research in the United States, where they are greeted by a more competitive environment.

The Gap in Personal Taxes

Because the gap in personal taxes between the two countries could be one of the main motivations for emigration, an in-depth examination is presented here. It focuses on the differences in all types of personal taxes: federal income tax, provincial/state tax, income tax, social security–related taxes (such as pension plans, employment insurance, Medicare), sales tax, property tax, and private health care cost in Canada and the United States. It examines the tax burden of households with three levels of income—$50,000, $100,000, and $250,000—in six Canadian cities (Calgary, Halifax, Montreal, Ottawa, Toronto, and Vancouver) and six U.S. cities (Charlotte, NC, Chicago, IL, Jacksonville, FL, Houston, TX, Los Angeles, and New York City) where many skilled emigrants reside. All income and tax calculations are based on national currencies (Canadian dollars for Canada, U.S. dollars for the United States).

It is clear that, overall, taxes are higher in Canada than in the United States (see figure 11.12). For example, a person who earns $50,000 pays 36.8 percent of their gross income in various taxes in Canada, compared to 31.7 percent in the United States (a gap of 5.1 percentage points). This suggests that, from the taxation viewpoint, even lower income earners can benefit from moving to the United States. As income increases, the gap widens. At the $250,000 level, the total tax payment rises to 41.2 percent of gross income in Canada, but only 29.7 percent in the United States (a gap of 11.5 percentage points). The major reason for this gap is the high income tax and surtax in Canada, especially at the provincial level. Although taxes related to social security are significantly higher in the United States, their weight in the overall tax burden is low. Property tax is also relatively higher in the United States. Sales tax, on the other hand, is high in Canada, largely because there is no U.S. federal tax equivalent to the goods and service tax.

Econometric Analysis

The purpose of econometric analysis is to establish a link between the emigration of Canadian high-skilled workers to the United States and the factors responsible for it. The analysis conducted in this study indicates that economic factors like earnings, taxes, and job opportunities influence decisions of Canadian professionals emigrating to the United States.

According to regression estimates (based on annual observations of cross-section data, 1986–1997), a $2 increase in the gap between incomes in Canada and the United States, with the effects of all other variables held constant, will result in the emigration of one more highly skilled Canadian to the United States. Also, a 1 percent increase in the existing tax gap (measured by the ratio of total tax revenue to GDP) can push 2 percent more Canadians toward the United States.

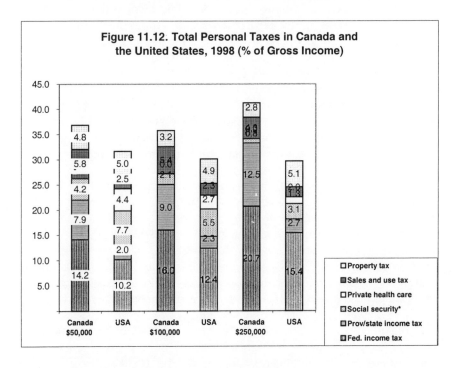

Figure 11.12. Total Personal Taxes in Canada and the United States, 1998 (% of Gross Income)

* Includes Canada/Quebec Pension Plan and Employment Insurance in Canada; FICA, OSADI, medicare and private health care in the United States.

Note: - A household of a spouse and two children, tax filed jointly for 1998 tax year.

    - Canada is an average of six cities: Calgary, Halifax, Montreal, Ottawa, Toronto, and Vancouver.

    - USA is an average of six cities: Charlotte NC, Chicago IL, Jacksonville FL, Houston TX, New York City (Queens), and Los Angeles CA.

Sources: Estimates by the author using the following: Karin Treff and David Perry, *Finances of the Nation*, 1998 (Toronto: Canadian Tax Foundation, 1999); *Canadian Master Tax Guide* (North York, Ontario: CCH Canadian, 1998); *US Master Tax Guide* (Chicago: CCH Inc., 1998); and U.S. Department of Commerce, *Statistical Abstract of the United States*, 1998.

Better employment opportunities, reflected in lower unemployment rates in the United States, would also result in a higher level of brain drain. Even warmer weather in the United States factors into the decision to move, and this is supported by statistical results (see table 11.2).[6]

Methodology

Dependent and Independent Variables

Dependent variable
Number of highly skilled Canadian emigrants to the United States.

Independent variables[7]
- difference in earnings, measured by the earnings gap between Canada and the United States in the occupational categories in knowledge areas;[8]
- difference in employment opportunity, measured by the rate of unemployment gap;
- difference in tax burden, measured by the ratio of tax to GDP gap; and
- difference in climate, measured by the temperature gap.[9]

Expected signs (based on a priori economic theory)
- The higher the earnings in the United States compared to Canada, the greater would be the outflow of Canadians to the United States. Therefore, the expected sign is positive.
- The better the employment opportunities in the United States (i.e., lower unemployment rate) compared to Canada, the greater would be the outflow of Canadians to the United States. Therefore, the expected sign is positive.

---

[6] These results are meant to provide a guideline to the relationship between brain drain and the various economic factors that influence it. They should be interpreted with caution and not be taken literally.

[7] Independent variables are gaps or differences between Canadian and U.S. determinants and are expressed as positive values. Regressions fit better with logarithms, which can only be estimated for positive values.

[8] Canadian earnings are converted into U.S. dollars using purchasing power parity rates.

[9] Warm weather, measured by the annual average temperature of the selected Canadian and U.S. cities, is a proxy for capturing climate difference. Climate is a composite index of factors beyond temperature. It includes weather severity, such as amount and frequency of precipitation, chill factor, and so on. It also includes the intensity of natural calamities, such as tornadoes, floods, earthquakes, snowstorms, and so on. Data for these factors were not available.

Table 11.2. Impact on Emigration of Income, Taxes and Unemployment

Dependent Variable: LOG(EMIGRATION)
Method: Least Squares
Sample (adjusted): 1986–97
Included observations: 46 after adjusting endpoints
Convergence achieved after 6 iterations

Variable	Coefficient	Std. Error	t-Statistic	Prob.
LOG(INCOMEGAP)	0.4549	0.0887	5.1249	0.0000
LOG(TAXGAP)	2.0967	0.4675	4.4842	0.0001
LOG(UNEMPGAP)	0.1648	0.1169	1.4096	0.1662
AR(1)	0.9169	0.1664	5.5091	0.0000
AR(2)	-0.0552	0.1645	-0.3358	0.7387

R-squared	0.7158	Mean dependent var	8.6831
Adjusted R-squared	0.6881	S.D. dependent var	0.7939
S.E. of regression	0.4434	Akaike info criterion	1.3137
Sum squared resid	8.0615	Schwarz criterion	1.5124
Log likelihood	-25.2157	F-statistic	25.8210
Durbin-Watson stat	1.949	Prob(F-statistic)	0.0000

Inverted AR Roots	.85	.06

Source: The Conference Board of Canada.

- The lower the tax burden in the United States compared to Canada, the greater would be the outflow of Canadians to the United States. Therefore, the expected sign is positive.
- The warmer the climate in the United States (i.e., higher temperature) compared to Canada, the greater would be the outflow of Canadians to the United States. Therefore, the expected sign is positive.

Results

Regression was performed for two sets of equations. In the first set, due to the limited size of observations (12–year data), the dependent variable (number of highly skilled Canadians moving to the United States) was regressed individually for each independent variable. Results for each equation produced the expected signs for the coefficients and met criteria for statistical significance, especially for the income gap and the tax gap. However, values for R–square were low, and Durbin-Watson (DW) statistics indicated the presence of serial correlation.

In the second set of regressions, the objective was to capture the effect of key independent variables on emigration simultaneously. The time series data for emigrants, income, and unemployment rate are available for the cross-section of each occupational category. Also, historical data on the ratio of total tax revenue to GDP provide good summary statistics of the tax burden. Therefore, regression was performed with pooled data using these variables.

Coefficient values for all variables, especially tax, were meaningful in economic terms and significant in terms of t-statistics and R–square (not shown here). However, DW statistics indicated the presence of serial correlation in the estimated residual. Re-estimating the equation with second-order serial correlation corrected the problem while it maintained the economic and statistical characteristics.

Conclusion

We can debate the actual numbers associated with the brain drain and the methods used for their estimation. However, we cannot minimize the significance of the emerging trend: the brain drain is rising and perhaps at an increasing rate. The conclusion is the same whether analyzed using temporary employment authorization visas issued to Canadians, or Canadian professionals moving to the United States permanently. In a post–NAFTA environment, it would be shortsighted to exclude temporary emigration numbers. Given the convenience, flexibility, and opportunity, an increasing number of Canadian professionals have been taking the temporary emigration route, rather than relying on costly and time-consuming traditional methods of migrating on a permanent basis.

A significant increase in the number of Canadian professionals emigrating to the United States is not surprising. All economic factors—such as higher income, better employment opportunities, and lower taxes—have consistently been weighted in favor of the United States. The regression analysis performed in this study suggests that Canadian professionals respond to these economic factors in a strong way.

In addition, the emotional and psychological barriers that used to keep Canadians at home are now much less relevant. The health care and welfare systems, a hallmark of Canadian distinctiveness, similarly do not carry much weight. Indeed, the professionals who are moving to the United States can afford to buy the services they need with the new wealth they are acquiring. For many professionals working in the United States, the cost of health care is covered by their employer, and the quality of the service is superior to that provided in Canada.

References

DeVoretz, Don, and Samuel Laryea. 1998. *Canadian Human Capital Transfers: The United States and Beyond.* Commentary No. 115. Toronto: C.D. Howe Institute, October.

Egan, Mark. 2000. "US Jobless Rate Hits 30 Year Low," *Globe and Mail*, May 6.

INS (U.S. Immigration and Naturalization Service). 1999. *Statistical Yearbook of the Immigration and Naturalization Service, 1997.* Washington, D.C.: U.S. Government Printing Office.

Inside. 1999. "The Lure of the US Hi-tech Jobs." No. 1. Prepared by Personal Systems, Ottawa, April.

Iqbal, Mahmood. 1999. *Are We Losing Our Minds? Trends, Determinants and the Role of Taxation in Brain Drain to the United States.* Detailed Findings no. 265-99. Ottawa: Conference Board of Canada, August.

———. 2000. "Brain Drain: Empirical Evidence of Emigration of Canadian Professionals to the United States," *Canadian Tax Journal* 48 (3).

OECD (Organisation for Economic Co-operation and Development). 1998. *Science and Technology, Main Indicators.* Paris, OECD.

———. 1999. *Main Economic Indicators.* Paris: OECD, April.

Schwanen, Daniel. 2000. *Putting the Brain Drain in Context: Canada and the Global Competition for Scientists and Engineers.* Commentary 140. Toronto: C.D. Howe Institute, April.

Treff, Karin, and David Perry. 1999. *Finances of the Nation, 1998.* Toronto: Canadian Tax Foundation.

Williamson, Shane. 2000. "A Perspective on the International Migration of Skilled Workers." Paper presented at the IRPP/CERF conference, Ottawa, June 3–4.

Zhao, John, Doug Drew, and Scott Murray. 2000. "Brain Drain and Brain Gain: The Migration of Knowledge Workers from and to Canada," *Education Quarterly Review* 6 (3).

Appendix to Chapter 11

Assumptions Used for Converting Temporary Employment Authorization Visas into Permanent Emigration Numbers

Assumptions used for NAFTA TN–1 Workers

- 70 percent have new I–94 form each year, while 30 percent have NO new I–94 form. Of the 30 percent, half stay permanently, the rest come back to Canada.
- 30 percent held two visas in one year.
- After the 1st year, 70 percent stay in the United States (renewal); 30 percent come back to Canada.
- After the 2nd year, 70 percent of the balance stay in the United States (renewal); 30 percent come back to Canada.
- After the 3rd year, 70 percent of the balance stay in the United States (renewal); 30 percent come back to Canada.
- After the 4th year, 10 percent of the balance convert into permanent; 60 percent stay as temporary in the United States (renewal); 30 percent come back to Canada.
- After the 5th year, 20 percent of the balance convert into permanent; 60 percent stay as temporary in the United States (renewal); 20 percent come back to Canada.
- After the 6th year, 30 percent of the balance convert into permanent; 40 percent stay as temporary in the United States (renewal); 30 percent come back to Canada.
- After the 7th year, 50 percent of the balance convert into permanent; 40 percent stay as temporary in the United States (renewal); 10 percent come back to Canada.
- After the 8th year, 90 percent of the balance convert into permanent status in the United States; the rest come back to Canada.

Assumptions for Other Temporary Visa Holders: (L–1, O–1, H–1A, H–1B, H–3 and P types): Visas for 3+ Years

- All staying first 3 years.
- After the 3rd year, 40 percent convert into permanent; 40 percent stay in the United States (renewal); 20 percent come back to Canada.
- After the 4th year, 60 percent of the balance convert into permanent; 20 percent stay in the United States (renewal); 20 percent come back to Canada.

- After the 5th year, 80 percent of the balance convert into permanent status in the United States; 20 percent come back to Canada.

12

The Emigration of High-Skilled Indian Workers to the United States: Flexible Citizenship and India's Information Economy

Paula Chakravartty

A visitor to samachar.com, one of the most popular Indian-content Web sites from and about India, is greeted with an enticing ad-banner for Citibank ATM cards that can be used in India. The text of the advertisement reads: "NRIs [non-resident Indians], want to send money to your folks in India? Just give them an ATM card." If the visitor clicks on a picture of a distinguished elderly man reading a newspaper, the following text appears:

> While you're overseas and away from home, you still have to manage your financial commitments in India. It may be purchase of property, paying college fees, sister's marriage, renovation of your house in India, insurance premiums.... The list goes on. So how can you manage all these commitments conveniently? The answer is simple—with a Citibank Rupee Checking Account (from an on-line ad placed at samachar.com, April 30, 2000: http://www.citibank.com/india/nri/banlead/index.htmlRCS004).

This advertisement makes apparent the close link between India and the West based on familial ties that speak to assumptions about "mobile masculinity and localized femininity" in a global information

Research for this chapter was made possible through support from the Canadian Social Science and Humanities Research Council and the American Institute of Indian Studies. The author wishes to thank Gianpaolo Baiocchi and Yehzhi Zhao for their comments.

economy (Ong 1999: 22). Today, emigration from India to the United States is not understood as a permanent departure to another nation-state. Ong argues that "new strategies of flexible accumulation have promoted a flexible attitude toward citizenship." By flexible citizenship, Ong is referring to "flexible practices, strategies, and disciplines associated with transnational capitalism" that create new capitalist heroes of Asian modernity (1999: 17–19). Ong is one of several scholars who have written about how successful Asian entrepreneurs are valorized as national heroes, despite their transnational identity based on corporate success in the West (Pinches 1999). While Ong provides an insightful analysis of the complex relationship between these new flexible citizens and the mostly authoritarian political cultures of East and Southeast Asia, this chapter examines similar processes of the practice of flexible citizenship in relation to India's democratic political culture. I argue that new strategies of flexible accumulation linking India to the United States promote new meanings of cultural and economic citizenship in relation to India's attempts to position itself as an information superpower.

Like several other large emerging economies such as Brazil, China, and South Korea, India has since the 1980s targeted the information technology (IT) sector as a priority in its larger development agenda. Today, the export of software is the fastest-growing sector in the Indian economy, expanding by nearly 60 percent per year and accounting for approximately US$2.65 billion in 1999. The National Association of Software and Services Companies (NASSCOM) claims that the industry will reach the $50 billion mark by 2008, making up 10 percent of the global software market and employing some 2.2 million workers.[1] A significant portion of India's software exports takes the form of Indian workers employed on short-term contracts for foreign firms, a practice referred to as "body shopping." In the United States, this would include workers in the H–1B visa category of high-skilled temporary workers. This chapter does not directly address the role of the Indian government in enabling the practice of body shopping, precisely because the process is more complex and dynamic than such a causal approach would assume. Instead, I examine the social context within which Indian flexible citizens—the financiers and brokers of the practices of body shopping, long-term emigration, and return migration—influence domestic economic policy. In other words, I examine the changing symbolic and institutional role of the flexible citizen in rela-

---

[1] According to NASSCOM, the industry has grown by 57 percent since 1992 and in 1999 employed somewhere between 160,000 and 250,000 people in India (Taylor 1999).

tion to the Indian postcolonial state as India enters an era of free trade in goods, capital, and labor.

In the past twenty years, Indian national and regional governments have embraced, enticed, and tried to formalize networks with non-resident Indians in high-tech sectors, particularly in the United States (McDowell 1997). These sectors include telecommunications, information technology, and electronic commerce. Education for and employment in the transnational information technology sector most graphically symbolize a new relationship between the state, science, and the market in India. As the fastest-growing and most prominent industry in India's new economy, the export of software and the development of e-commerce promise to erase structural barriers between India and the First World. Since the mid–1980s, the Indian state has rapidly expanded its technological infrastructure and promoted the nation's vast pool of highly trained low-wage labor, alongside the unmet market potential of its growing middle class, in order to attract foreign investment. Domestic and transnational firms have responded with unprecedented levels of investment, while the state has formalized networks of labor and capital between regional high-tech growth areas like Bangalore, Chennai, Hyderabad, and Mumbai and their global counterparts in Hong Kong, Tokyo, New Jersey, and Silicon Valley.

While it might be obvious that the Indian state is interested in promoting economic and technological linkages through investment, expertise, and job creation, I argue that the high-tech non-resident Indian in the United States also plays a pivotal role in legitimizing a relatively new technocratic development agenda in India. This development agenda, initiated in the 1980s and codified in the 1990s, appeals to the symbolic power of postcolonial technological nationalism with a new emphasis on the meritocratic logic of the global marketplace.

The research for this chapter is based on popular media accounts, trade publications, and interviews conducted in New Delhi in 1997. In order to make sense of this complex political landscape, the first section of the chapter briefly outlines the history of high-tech emigration to the United States. The second examines the role of these powerful flexible citizens in the context of political reforms, which have fundamentally changed the relationship between science, the state, and the market in the past two decades. The third section examines how the new discourse on technology and development shaped policy in the 1990s, provoking new tensions in the relationship between science, the state, and the market. The concluding section ties together the previous discussions by examining the legitimizing role played by U.S.–based Indian flexible citizens in relation to the terms of high-tech development at home.

The History of High-Tech Emigration to the United States

From Brain Drain to the Non-Resident Indian (1950–1990)

Economic historians have separated the postcolonial history of emigration from India into two phases. People with professional expertise and technical skills characterized most of the first period of emigration, from independence in the 1950s until the mid–1970s. The majority of these skilled populations were destined for the United Kingdom, the United States, and Canada, with fewer going to Western Europe and Australia. A second phase of emigration, beginning in the mid–1970s, saw a significant expansion in the flow of less skilled laborers on temporary contracts to the Gulf oil economies of the Middle East. This change in the profile of emigrants in the mid–1970s is evident if we note the fact that 57 percent of emigrants in 1975 were from the professional or technical category, whereas between 1971 and 1975, 88 percent of emigrants fell into these categories.

While these numbers are significant for gauging the changing overall profile of emigrants from India during this period, emigration to the United States remained concentrated in the high-skilled "professional expertise or technical qualifications" category. Deepak Nayyar found that of the professional, highly skilled immigrants admitted to the United States from all countries, India made up 19.5 percent of the total between 1971 and 1980 and 13.4 percent between 1981 and 1990 (Nayyar 1994: 21–22). These numbers are disproportionate in relation to overall immigration given that India's share in total immigration was much lower—3.8 and 3.6 percent for the two periods, respectively (see table 12.1).

The economic impact of the emigration of Indian high-skilled labor was examined at length by development economists of the 1970s in the literature on brain drain (Sen 1973; Bhagwati 1976). As Nayyar (1994) pointed out, the brain drain approach assumes that the emigration of workers is permanent, which has not been the case since the mid–1970s.[2] Nayyar's work considers the dynamic economic relationships between immigrants from India in terms of the state's balance of payments through remittances and capital flows, as well as through exports, imports, and tourism. Most importantly, recognizing the trend in greater communication and travel between India and the West, the Indian government created the category of non-resident Indian in 1975 to introduce a financial facility to allow persons of Indian origin in the

---

[2] The "brain drain" literature examined the costs of emigration from the home country versus the benefits of immigration for the host countries. See Nayyar 1994.

United States and the United Kingdom to open and maintain foreign-currency non-resident accounts in U.S. dollars or British pounds sterling. For India, the incentive was hard currency in a period of economic transition, while for the NRIs, their balances and interest were securely repatriable in a financial period that saw the beginning of the flexible exchange rate.[3] There was a spurt in remittances from the Middle East during the second half of the 1970s until the mid–1980s. They accounted for 57 percent of total remittances, compared to 32 percent from industrialized countries. However, the latter half of the 1980s saw remittances from the Middle East fall to 47 percent, while remittances from industrialized countries rose to 43 percent (Nayyar 1994: 50).

Table 12.1. U.S. Immigration by Country of Birth, 1981–1997 (1000s)

Country of Birth	1981-90 (total)	1991-95 (total)	1996	1997
Ireland	32.8	53.2	1.7	NA
Soviet Union, former	84.0	277.1	62.8	NA
China	388.8*	227.0	41.7	41.1
India	**261.9**	**191.6**	**44.9**	**38.1**
Brazil	23.7	26.5	5.9	NA
Mexico	1,653.3	1,487.9	163.6	146.9
Canada	119.2	74.2	15.8	11.6

*Data for Taiwan included with China.

Sources: U.S. Immigration and Naturalization Service, Annual Statistical Year-book, and releases.

Emigration under a Liberalized Economy (1990–2000)

Between 1983 and 1990, interest rates were higher in India than in international markets, and there was little perceived risk. As a result, the net inflow of foreign currency to NRI accounts grew substantially, especially to U.S. dollar–denominated accounts. In 1990, electoral instability, coupled with rising debt, drove India's credit ratings in international capital markets down, and access to international lines of credit from private and commercial sources was closed in February 1991. The balance of payments situation became acute in this period because of

---

[3] This policy originated to encourage NRIs to open and maintain rupee accounts in the early 1970s, but it was more successful when the facility was enhanced to allow foreign currency denomination. It was extended in 1988 to allow accounts to be denominated in Deutsche marks or Japanese yen.

an oil crisis resulting from Iraq's invasion of Kuwait (Bhaduri and Nayyar 1996). The vulnerability of the balance of payments was exacerbated by the fact that some 60 percent of India's foreign reserves were in the form of NRI deposits.[4] India's foreign reserves faced a liquidity crisis with virtually no access to international credit, coupled with a "near avalanche" in capital flight from NRI investments leaving the country.[5]

Facing a severe balance of payments crisis, India was forced to accept stringent conditions as part of a World Bank structural adjustment program. Along with the International Monetary Fund and World Bank's orthodox restructuring strategies of stabilizing fiscal policy through tight monetary controls and a major currency devaluation, India's eighth Five-Year Plan would promote an export-led development strategy to replace the failed import-substitution industrialization [ISI] approach. Chatterjee (1998: 36) has argued that 1991 was significant in terms of both actual economic changes and the symbolic importance of the state's successful effort to bring this new economic model of development "to the forefront of the political debate." This was particularly relevant for U.S. entrepreneurial NRIs, who almost uniformly agree that 1991 marked the beginning of advancement in India's development strategy.

Since the state initiated liberalization policies in 1991, direct remittances and NRI savings bonds have increased once again. NRI deposits in Indian banks surpassed US$21 billion in 1999. Despite India's overall move toward economic liberalization, NRI deposits continue to be vulnerable to political uncertainty. For example, in May 1998, NRIs withdrew nearly US$750 million, "fearing international economic sanctions" following India's nuclear tests. Similarly, NRI direct investments,

---

[4] The late 1970s and early 1980s had seen a boom in foreign exchange remittances, mostly from Indian workers in the oil and gas industry in the Middle East. The majority of NRI investments in India are "portfolio investments," interest-bearing bank deposits on financial assets, as opposed to direct foreign investment in physical assets. Although India's capital markets are not liberalized as in East Asian and Latin American countries, NRI investment has received special consideration by the state since the late 1970s, and it is subject to the same kind of volatility as portfolio investment in other emerging countries.

[5] Nayyar argues that the degree of sensitivity to exchange rates suggests that repatriable deposits originated from relatively high-skilled, high-income, permanent migrants, largely based in industrialized countries, as opposed to the Middle East, because such migrants are more likely to assess investment opportunities and redeploy investments (Nayyar 1994: 62–63).

which had peaked at US$715 million in 1995–1996, had fallen below US$62 million in 1998–1999.[6]

As discussed in more detail below, the Indian state recognizes the importance of NRIs in shaping the nation's economic future. Most significantly, the geography of the capital flows has brought state attention to the importance of U.S. NRIs and their special relationship to the Hindu right-wing Bharatiya Janata Party (BJP) government. One example of this special relationship takes the form of the U.S. NRI lobby that has pressed the Indian government to grant dual citizenship to overseas Indians. In December 1998, the Indian Merchants Chamber organized a conference (entitled "India Calling") for overseas entrepreneurs, at which discussion focused on the terms and timing of the proposed "Orange Card." Interestingly, the BJP government argued that it was only willing to grant "dual citizenship ... when they come and swear unconditional loyalty to this country."

In a similar venue—the "Global Indian Entrepreneurs Conference" in New Delhi in 1998—Prime Minister Atul Vajpayee stated that although India continues to próvide low-skilled labor to the Gulf states, "a more important segment comprises professionals, teachers, scientists, computer engineers and programmers, doctors, managers, bankers, and even gurus, who are being acclaimed in areas of top management and creative thought." Vajpayee's message encouraged NRIs to continue to invest in India. While avoiding the politically volatile issue of dual citizenship, the Prime Minister proposed establishing suitable mechanisms for a "forum in the government for effective ongoing consultation with NRIs."[7]

State v. Market: Debates about Technology and Development

State-Sponsored Scientific Development (1950–1980)

This section examines the relationship between non-resident Indians and the state in terms of the debates about the role of technology and the market in relation to economic development. In postcolonial India, science has played an important role in legitimizing the terms of India's state-led market economy. The state created a highly skewed educational system where public resources subsidized higher education at

---

[6] See http://206.20.14.67/achal/archive/aug99/Gleaning%20&%20Spot%20Checks.html.

[7] The speech, delivered on November 11, 1998, can be found at http://www. indianembassy.org/inews/December98/11.html.

the expense of the spread of literacy and elementary education.[8] In addition to public-sector investment in large dam projects, steel mills, and other temples of the future, concerns about national security led to a disproportionate amount of resources spent on high-technology research and development in capital-intensive areas like aerospace, nuclear power, and electronics.

The objective of state-sponsored scientific development and self-reliance took various forms, including investment in research in the electronics sector beginning in the mid–1960s. Geopolitical concerns about India's nuclear capability in the late 1960s led to autarkic pressure among Indian scientific and political elites, who saw an urgent need to develop indigenous technological capabilities in electronics.[9] In 1967, the Electronics Corporation of India Limited (ECIL) was formed under the high-profile Department of Atomic Energy (DAE) to produce nuclear electronic instruments. Nationally renowned scientists carrying out the Nehruvian mission of self-reliance and modernization worked closely with the Bhabha Atomic Research Center (BARC) and ECIL to design the indigenous TDC microcomputer series that would become the national champion in computers in the 1970s and 1980s. The Department of Electronics (DoE) was created as the body to regulate the industry in order to produce indigenously designed electronics through the public-sector operations of ECIL, CMC Limited, and others. The DoE coordinated activities among various public-sector research institutions, functioning under the assumption that the domestic private sector did not hold these same national priorities of technological self-reliance. The DoE thus encouraged indigenous technology, but it dis-

---

[8] The neglect of primary compulsory education is contrasted with the highly organized pressure groups in Indian society that historically made higher education a priority for public policy: "The sections of the population that are most affected by the absence of literacy are typically much worse off than the groups that benefit from higher education. In terms of consequences, the bias in educational priorities has tended to reinforce existing inequalities, and has been least kind to the most deprived" (Drèze and Sen 1996: 91).

[9] In 1968, the United States, the Soviet Union, the United Kingdom, and other states signed the Nonproliferation Treaty. India refused to sign because it wanted to keep its options for future nuclear device–testing programs open. Improved Sino–U.S. relations in the 1970s only reinforced strategic concerns in India's national security establishment. Sridharan (1996) has argued persuasively that the need to design and manufacture a "broad range of industrial electronic instrumentation, computers, telecom equipment, as well as critical components" reflected an understanding in important policy circles that the nuclear option would warrant technological and economic sanctions as a result of the Nonproliferation Treaty.

couraged domestic demand for consumer goods through indirect taxes (Evans 1995).

Although the 1970s are often characterized as India's "socialist" era, populist politics promising the "removal of poverty" went hand in hand with significant increases in spending on electronics research. In this period, public funding for scientific research institutions like the Indian Institute of Technology (IIT), modeled after MIT, increased substantially. The result was the training of thousands of highly qualified engineers and scientists. Many members of this vast pool of hi-tech labor left the country to find more lucrative employment possibilities. The techno-nationalism of the 1970s inspired various successful experiments in "conspicuous technology" (Nandy 1996). The development of indigenized computer technology, advances in nuclear technology, the launching of a national television satellite broadcast, and the development of the nation's first computer-mediated network were all part of this push. Furthermore, the legitimacy of science was used to mobilize a specific public: the urban Indian middle classes. In political discourse, the benefits of these kinds of technological innovations were extended to include the general public in terms of national defense and national integration. For example, the National Informatics Centre's computer network (NICNET), established in the late 1970s, linked the country's 440 district headquarters in order to coordinate information, but it was "exclusively for government use" (Evans 1995: 152). However, the rationale for prioritizing investment in science and technology was explicitly outside the realm of public political discussions.

It was in this same period of political turmoil that public sentiment against the abuse of state power merged with the rise of a vocal middle class that benefited from India's mixed economic model but demanded new consumer goods and services. As the Nehruvian era drew to a close in the late 1970s, the state faced a new set of challenges. People resented the modernizing state's arrogance and its presence in everyday life; the inaccessibility and inscrutably of the state became a central concern in political discourse. Included in these discussions were colonial vestiges such as the Official Secrets Act of 1923, which continued to prohibit public access to official government documents on national security grounds. It is important to keep in mind that the object of public political resentment against the state had to do with its "manner rather than its policies" (Kaviraj 1991). Beginning in the 1980s, advocates of pro-market reform appealed to this public sentiment against the state's colonial culture of secrecy to promote a new direction in economic policy. Although the vast majority of poor Indian citizens were the real victims of the state's failed development strategy, reform advocates used the Nehruvian state's empty promises of redistribution to brush aside concerns of the poor and to emphasize instead the new possibilities of a market society.

The Market Replaces the State: Techno-Culture in the 1980s

It is in this political landscape that the bureaucratic and political elites were making new connections between science and the market. By the end of the 1970s, several domestic private-sector companies using IN-TEL and Motorola microprocessors had entered the Indian personal computer market and were outselling ECIL's indigenous products.[10] In addition to these changes in the computer hardware market, top bureaucrats in the DoE began to recognize that both public-sector and private-sector firms in India had a global comparative advantage in software production. IBM's departure in 1978 pushed various banks and businesses to consider alternatives to IBM software environments. In the private sector, computer engineers began to focus on developing commercial UNIX applications, and in the public sector, former staff from IBM and other firms worked in ECIL and CMC, writing software and working on large infrastructure projects (Evans 1995).

The DoE recognized that not only was this type of software expertise uncommon in the Third World, it was innovative even in comparison to developments in the First World. At this time, key figures within the DoE bureaucracy and the public sector began to reassess the rules of economic governance. By 1980, several top engineers in key bureaucratic positions within the DoE and ECIL were advocating a liberalization of rules in the IT sector based on "watching world trends and the industry's poor performance" (Sridharan 1996: 180). The new pro-market turn in the electronics bureaucracy coincided with the globalization of the economic bureaucracies in the form of new lateral appointments of World Bank–experienced economists eager to reform India's centrally planned economy. In the 1980s these economists entered top advisory positions in the Ministry of Finance, the Department of Economic Affairs, and within the Prime Minister's Office, promoting an alternative agenda of economic development to replace India's import-substitution-industrialization strategy (Chakravartty 1999).

---

[10] The most successful company in the late 1970s and early 1980s was Hindustan Computers Ltd. (HCL), which launched a microcomputer in 1977 when these were first entering the global market. HCL's "Busybee" became the leading seller in the PC market. Despite HCL's early success in computer hardware, its expertise in software engineering would be the company's main line of business in the future (see Evans 1995).

The assassination of Indira Gandhi in 1984 unexpectedly brought a politically inexperienced Rajiv Gandhi to power. Rajiv quickly surrounded himself with experts in new technologies and neoliberal economics, promising a clean break from the old, corrupt forms of economic governance. Rajiv's "Mr. Clean" image—based on his relative inexperience in Indian politics and his outsider status—reinforced his campaign to end corruption by eliminating "power-brokers from the political arena" (Vithal 1997: 205). The Indian and Western media initially embraced the new prime minister, seeing in him the embodiment of the new trend in populist neoliberalism. Some saw him as the "Ronald Reagan of India."[11]

Rajiv Gandhi came to power promising a "new era of Indian politics" based on a freer economy and an emphasis on rapid technological modernization. Although other sectors of the economy received attention behind the scenes, Rajiv's most public priority was expanding and modernizing the nation's communications industries. Within a month in office, he passed a new computer policy deregulating the industry and expanding access to imported computer equipment. The influence of economic strategies employed by the successful East Asian Tigers played an important role in this transformation. The DoE's reconceptualization of the Indian IT sector in global terms is summarized in the following statement.

> India was not to try to reinvent the wheel, but to use imported hardware, systems software and software tools to develop custom application software for export to foreign clients for their specific needs (Sridharan 1996: 184).

As the DoE redefined its relationship to the private sector and to the global market, industry associations became more organized in the policy arena and had greater access to policymakers in Rajiv Gandhi's administration. Older business associations like the Federation of Indian Chambers of Commerce and Industry (FICCI) and the Associated Chambers of Commerce (ASSOCHAM), along with newer associations like the Confederation of Indian Industries (CII) and the National Association of Software and Services Companies (NASSCOM), pushed for the deregulation of domestic industry. The CII, formed in 1974 as an engineering industry association, took an especially aggressive ap-

---

[11] Jagdish Bhagwati, one of the foremost advocates of neoliberal reforms, argues that American newspapers like the *Wall Street Journal* "mistakenly saw a Reagan in Rajiv Gandhi and applauded India's turn from defunct socialist doctrines. The applause turned out to be premature" (Bhagwati 1993: 79).

proach to proactive lobbying efforts in high-tech sectors. The CII's practice of submitting proposals for policy reform to various levels of the bureaucracy, organizing closed-door seminars and workshops around specific sectoral interests, and organizing missions abroad to promote Indian industry represented a new and more powerful role for corporate actors in shaping economic policy.

The new partnership between public and private actors in the electronics and IT sector came to fruition in 1985 with the passing of the Integrated Policy Measures on Electronics, which exempted the electronics sector from various taxes and import duties paid by other industrial activities. A favorite phrase used by pro-market economists, policymakers, and journalists was the need to "unleash entrepreneurial instincts" after decades of unnecessary bureaucratic intervention in economic production (Ghosh 1998). Allowing "entrepreneurship among the professional classes to blossom" (Subrahmanyam 1998) would enable the nation to return to its roots. As one observer put it, "British colonial rule and Nehru's Russian socialism suppressed our entrepreneurial history."[12]

India's unusual combination of a large pool of skilled labor along with a relatively small market for computer services translated into a policy environment that encouraged firms to develop software primarily for export. The New Software Policy of 1984 officially recognized India's comparative advantage in low-wage, English-speaking skilled labor in data-processing and software services. The new policy liberalized software imports, terminated restrictions on foreign equity, and liberalized rules regarding foreign subsidiaries entering the Indian market to set up 100 percent export-oriented software companies. Transnational firms like Texas Instruments (TI) and Hewlett Packard (HP) entered the Indian market in the mid–1980s. TI was the first of several transnational corporations to invest in a much publicized, multimillion-dollar offshore software operation in Bangalore in 1986, officially inaugurating the global recognition of India's Silicon Valley.

Thus a growing consensus emerged in the mid–1980s among policymakers, business elites, and high-level bureaucrats over the failure of politics to deliver the nation from economic stagnation. What is important to keep in mind when we examine the populist appeal of the anti-state discourse is that it was the style, rather than the policies, of the

---

[12] Author interview with M. R. Athreya, New Delhi, September 1997. Athreya is a management consultant who has worked for both the state and the private sector. In 1991 he chaired the committee that developed the "Report of the High Level Committee on Reorganization of Telecom Department" which recommended corporatization of the Department of Telecommunications (DoT).

interventionist state that became the target of social movements in the 1970s and 1980s (Kaviraj 1998). Pro-market reformers appealed to public resentment of the state's colonial culture of secrecy and arrogance to promote a new direction in economic policy. Sections of the political and business elite, beginning in the Rajiv Gandhi era, were able to co-opt liberal and leftist criticisms of state-led development in order to promote the idea of efficient—and accountable—market governance (Kothari 1995).

Throughout this period, new economic, political, and cultural networks were being cultivated between the Indian state, domestic corporate actors, and non-resident Indians living in the West, especially the United States. Links to India through family, travel, remittances, and investments bound non-resident Indians to their homeland, while many features of home changed because of these new economic and cultural networks. The growing demand for Western-quality consumer goods and services among the urban Indian middle class in the 1980s is generally seen as one of the greatest impacts of these new NRI networks (Pendakur 1989).

One of the most interesting examples of the impact of these new transnational networks is the role of Sam Pitroda, an NRI businessman and close personal friend of Prime Minister Rajiv Gandhi who became a top policymaker and bureaucrat in the telecommunications and electronics bureaucracies. Pitroda's peculiar combination of transnational nationalism and technological populism symbolized a radical break from the techno-nationalist discourse of the past (see Chakravartty 1999). As one astute social commentator wrote at the time:

> The son of a carpenter, he is now a millionaire. But his is not the genteel mobility of the older types of scientists.... It is the spectacular leap-frogging of a self-confessed entrepreneur, committed to Schumpeterian breakthroughs into the system. He is the rarest of Indian breeds, the scientist as entrepreneur.... He carries his new Indian passport like a flag. There is a technological machismo here and none of the namby-pamby debates about pilot plans or the dithering caution of the CSIR (Vishvanathan 1985).

The new connection between scientist and entrepreneur marked a break from the older model of nationalist scientific research that had characterized the Nehruvian development model. Pitroda encouraged a supposedly egalitarian work culture, invoking a distinctly American management ethos. India's ability to develop technologically in the field of electronics was "an exercise in national self-assurance":

> Part of our mission was to inspire a whole generation of young talent and thumb our noses at the nay-sayers, the political reactionaries, and the vested interests whose prosperity rested entirely on imports.... I cheered people on, knowing as I did that young Indians did well in the United States.... I was almost brutal in my determination to root out hierarchy and bureaucracy.... I opened our doors to the media, which responded with excitement, optimism, and the kind of hero worship that we hoped would attract more young people to technology careers (Pitroda 1993: 73).

The linkage between the success of NRIs in the United States and untapped potential would become the dominant theme for the Americanization of India's technology culture, which needed to shed its state-centered logic. Thus, beginning with the Rajiv Gandhi administration in 1984 and accelerating after the fiscal crisis and subsequent turn to liberalization in 1991, this new discourse of India's entrepreneurial capabilities and the relationship between science and the market challenged the older model of state-led development. In 1991, when the Indian state underwent its most acute foreign exchange crisis, the break from its socialist past was symbolically complete.

The next section considers how the new discourse on technology and development shaped national policy in the 1990s.

India in a Global Information Economy (1991–2000)

Locating a New Populist Pro-Market Discourse of Development

Since 1991, the discourse of the new, confident India has moved from introducing market reforms in the electronics and IT sectors to focusing on India's role in the global economy. In India, the new populist discourse on technology has a clearly nationalist agenda based on overturning four decades of "Brahminized socialism," when businessmen with relatively limited clout had to approach the "dispensers of permits and licenses essentially as supplicants" (Bardhan 1984: 58). As in other parts of the developing world where the state's heavy hand and inscrutable power have become the object of public political resentment, Indian policymakers and new corporate elites have co-opted the criticisms of the social movements to promote an indigenized version of the American ideal of the "democratic market place" (Pinches 1999).

In practice, despite beginning at the high end of computer software development (the design and implementation of complex information systems), in the late 1970s the Indian IT industry emerged as a significant global player in the lower end of the software business (routine code writing). Most of the export revenue that the IT sector generates in

India comes from services performed by "information workers," not product development. For example, between 1985 and 1995, the Indian IT industry grew from US$10 million to $800 million, with 60 percent of this revenue coming from outsourced labor. Indian workers were either employed by transnational corporations that set up parts of their operations in India, or they went abroad for short-term contracts in foreign firms, a practice that is commonly referred to as body shopping.[13] As one NRI management expert explained, "other countries sell cheap labor, India sells cheap intellect" (Flanigan 2000: C1).

American NRIs have played a prominent role in the development of India's high-tech economy, functioning as economic and cultural brokers in terms of body-shopping contracts and establishing offshore software facilities in India. NRI companies in the United States, such as Syntel, have come under investigation by the U.S. Department of Labor for paying H–1B workers less than the legal salary. Although Syntel has responded to political pressures to hire local talent, in 1997, 60 percent of its U.S. workforce worked under H–1B visas (see Pandya 1998). The NRI high-tech entrepreneurs also play an important role in the new flexible arrangements between Indian and U.S. software firms, adopting a "cross-border model." They facilitate new institutional arrangements across borders, including maintaining local subsidiaries of Indian companies in the United States and establishing "software factories" for the American parent company in India.[14] The NRI entrepreneur is perfectly positioned to maneuver between the two geographic locations of the transnational software firm. With a cross-border model of operation, the NRI entrepreneur can facilitate access to clients who want consultation at the design stage in the U.S. location and low labor costs at the production end in the software factory in India (Guha 1999: 16).

---

[13] In 1996, 82 percent of the companies that outsourced information workers were U.S.–based corporations (see McDowell 1997). The issue of how H–1B visa holders affect the wages of U.S. workers in the IT sector is exacerbated by anti-immigrant sentiment (see Mir and Yajnik 1995).

[14] This model was inspired by the success of Origins, a Dutch consulting firm that has a "front-office/back office" model. The front office team in developed markets in Europe and North America works with clients to design software solutions. Once the specific software is designed, it is developed in a dedicated production line in an Indian software factory. In the case of Origins, the factory was located in Bombay. Clients deal with the "front office" in the West, while production line "team leaders" are flown from India to the West to meet clients at the first stage of the software design process. This cross-border model is more expensive than the traditional offshore model, but it is significantly cheaper than an entirely on-shore operation. See Guha 1999.

Today, companies like IBM and Microsoft are investing in "the transfer of skills and intellectual assets" of India's scientific labor by subsidizing several high-profile academic training programs through established national universities and technical colleges (Anantha-Nageswaran 1997). Despite slick publicity campaigns, the motives of these transnational corporations are not taken for granted in India. Responding to Microsoft mogul Bill Gates's highly publicized visit to India in 1997, one newspaper editorial referred to Gates's "headhunting mission" as follows: "Much like the East India Company's journey eastward in search of spices, Gates is now scoring the world for computer programmers" (*Indian Express*, March 10, 1997). Equating corporate bottom lines and a favorable balance of payments with national interests, Gates responded by assuring that India will be the "largest source of trained manpower for the global IT industry" (*Disycom*, April 1997). It is not surprising that the economic strategy based on low-wage, high-skilled workers has spurred debates about whether or not "manpower" export should become India's official state policy. Proponents argue that exploiting this comparative advantage for "foreign earnings, enriched skills and experience" will benefit national development (Vittal 1997: 7). Critics maintain that this strategy is a new form of colonial trade on unequal terms, where India's software talent is wasted on low-end work for transnational firms. As one Indian executive states: "It's the old story.... We are exporting cotton and buying back the finished cloth" (Evans 1995: 196).

The Lure and Limits of High-Tech Development in India

Today, intense competition persists between different Indian states to draw IT and telecom transnationals to specific cities and regions that are being designated as "techno-parks" and "high-tech cities." Transnationals that have set up shop either directly or though joint ventures with Indian companies in the outskirts of New Delhi and in cities like Bangalore and Hyderabad include AT&T, Citicorp, 3M, General Electric, IBM, Hewlett Packard, Oracle, Microsoft, Texas Instruments, and Sun Microsystems. Differences in labor costs for these firms are remarkable. A basic programmer in New York made $80,000 in 1995; the same job in India paid $4,000 (Mir and Yajnik 1995). Still, at the higher end of the information economy, wages of Indian software executives in Bangalore, New Delhi, and the mushrooming high-tech centers spreading across the country are impressive by Indian standards, and even occasionally by global standards. Indian H–1B visa holders working in places such as Silicon Valley are also often well paid for their services. And it is hard to find an Indian-content Web site that does not celebrate the "Desi [Indian] Dot-Com" mania by focusing on how well South Asians are doing in the IT sector, both in the United States and at home in India. These Web sites boast that some 160 Fortune 500 companies outsource software projects to India, and they highlight the fact that Silicon Valley–based NRI executives are increasingly turning to India to help fledgling Indian startups.[15]

Despite this enthusiasm, the majority of new jobs in the information economy remain in basic programming and data processing, which increasingly rely on virtual work performed through satellite links and fiber-optic lines, collapsing the distinctions between work in the IT versus the telecom sectors. The Indian government's decision to allow competition in Internet provision and its plans to open its international long-distance market to private players mean that the major growth area for jobs in the information economy will be in customer teleservices. NRI economic strategists argue that workers in India—from the fields of airline reservations, medical transcription, telephone operations, and mail-order services to computer service and customer-support personnel—"would be happy to work" for five to ten times less than their counterparts in the United States (Subrahmanyam 1998). In 1999, software industry representatives stated that India already had 14,000 tele-work jobs, accounting for $140 million in wages (Anklesaria Aiyer 1999).

Heated discussions over the economic pitfalls of a low-wage strategy are taking place in corporate, bureaucratic, and political circles, but they are almost entirely confined to debates about India's ability to attract foreign investment, generate export revenue, and improve the competence of Indian capital in global markets. The machismo of bottom-line, techno-corporate discourse repeatedly asserts that Indian workers will be "happy" to hold a job at any cost and that national interests will be realized if India can "produce its own Bill Gates" (Subrahmanyam 1998). As one prominent management consultant noted,

> India has two major advantages. We have a potentially huge market, and if someone comes in and invests $10 million and creates 100,000 jobs, he may remit 75 percent of the revenue. Second, India is a great source market for the world. We need to make India the workshop of the world. So we want

---

[15] See, for example, "The Dotcom Bug," June 24, 2000, at http://www.rediff.com/us/2000/jun/24us1.htm.

the world's capital, technology, and greed to work for this country.[16]

Unfortunately for these reformers, not all Indian citizens have accepted the changing terms of economic development with the new emphasis on high-tech expansion. In the past decade, India's history as a "democracy without prosperity" (Khilnani 1998) has seen the advent of unprecedented democratic political activity by those segments of the population once thought to be politically inert. Since 1991 the consensus among policymakers to open up the economy has galvanized mass demonstrations and strikes, created consistent electoral uncertainty, and unleashed an unprecedented identity-based politics of caste and region, with voters demanding a share of the fruits of the new economy. At issue in these increasingly intense political debates are questions about access to the state and "to whom it ultimately belongs"— questions of public interest that fundamentally politicize what appear to be mundane technical areas of economic policy (Khilnani 1998; Kothari 1995). Throughout this politically messy process, which has included numerous national elections and a series of fragile coalition governments since 1996, one of the strongest pressures to accelerate the pace of liberalization has come from American NRIs as policy experts and business leaders.[17]

The next section attempts to tie together the previous discussion in order to argue that India's successful flexible citizens abroad, particularly NRIs in the United States, play a crucial role in legitimating this new discourse of technology- and market-led development.

The New Global Nabobs of Networking

New Transnational Networks

The Indian postcolonial state currently encourages the emigration of students pursuing high-tech degrees on the assumption that when graduates return from countries like the United States, "they bring money, they bring a tested education, and above all, they come back bitten by the entrepreneurship bug" (Gardner 2000: 19). These entrepreneurial efforts are seen as important in improving Indo–U.S. relations as well as increasing American investor confidence and trade with

---

[16] Author interview with M. B. Athreya, September 1997.

[17] Some of the most vocal and convincing arguments for liberalization came from abroad, from "the ranks of dispersed intellectuals and economists lodged in the international economic agencies and universities" (Khilnani 1998: 98).

India. Similar to visible disporan-Chinese who use "orientalist codes to (re)frame overseas Chinese as enlightened cosmopolitans who possess both economic capital and humanistic values" (Ong 1999: 131), we see new advocates of Indian (specifically Hindu) capitalist values. Perhaps the most recognizable for Western audiences is Deepak Chopra, the ubiquitous Indian New Age leader and alternative medicine pioneer. Chopra's creative reinterpretation of Hindu texts in such best-sellers as *Creating Affluence: Wealth Consciousness in the Field of All Possibilities* (1993) is required reading for The Indus Entrepreneurs (TIE) (Fan 2000). Organizations like TIE, founded in Silicon Valley in 1992, foster "entrepreneurship, networking and guidance among aspiring professionals" in both the United States and South Asia. TIE, which is funded by NRI corporate sponsorship, organizes annual conferences in Silicon Valley and holds monthly meetings and interactive sessions both in the United States and in regional chapters in Chennai, Bangalore, Hyderabad, and Mumbai (*The Hindu*, January 15, 2000).

These corporate networks between India and the United States promote a cyber-capitalist rereading of Hindu values, locating the success of high-tech Indian entrepreneurs in essential characteristics associated with ethno-religious identity. For example, Indian competence in the Internet economy is associated with the "web of interrelations" that tie together Indian families across national borders. More common is the argument that "Indians have a long history of excelling in abstract thinking useful in writing computer code." This line of reasoning is almost always followed by the assertion that "the concept of zero was developed by Indians ... and therefore Indians are naturals for software development" (Frauenheim 1999). The success of Indian IT entrepreneurs is invoked repeatedly in articles about India's rosy high-tech future. The new (trans)national heroes include Vinod Dham, CEO of Silicon Spice and former group leader of the team that designed the Pentium chip for Intel; Saheer Bhatia, founder of Hotmail.com, who sold his company to Microsoft in 1997 for US$400 million; and N. R. Murthy, co-founder of Infosys Technologies based in Bangalore, which was the first Indian software firm to list on NASDAQ, commanding a market capitalization of US$15 billion. When Mumbai-based Rajesh Jain sold indiaworld.com to Satyam Infoway for $116 million, the business press claimed that he had wiped out the differences between Mumbai and San Jose, California. Enthusiasm for the Internet economy accounts for NASSCOM'S estimates that two or three new Indian Web sites appear on the net each day, and that in April 2000 there were 23,000 India-specific sites and more than 100,000 domain names registered by Indians (Lundstrom 1999).

Transnational Nationalism and the "Don't Look Down" Economy

Indian entrepreneurial success is explained through the Hindu work ethic based on industriousness, discipline, and frugality. In contrast to Western capitalist culture, this Indianized version appeals to a distinctly flexible notion of family and community. As one successful NRI entrepreneur noted, Indians have been successful in the information age because "Indian parents ... stress science or technological careers" (Frauenheim 1999). This argument emphasizes qualities associated with Indian family values, speaking directly to U.S. racial politics of the supposed "model minority," as distinct from the minorities that fail. However, this line of reasoning also addresses the thorny issue of meritocracy in India, where illiteracy remains at 52 percent and a skewed education system is a politically charged topic. To resolve this tension within the discursive parameters of the transnational Hindu work ethic, advocates argue that the "weeding out process teaches an important lesson to Indian students.... Because college positions are limited, students have to battle mightily in secondary school for a spot." It is this experience that helps Indians "develop a better work ethic."[18]

TIE currently plans to raise US$1 billion in contributions for the Indian Institutes of Technology (IIT), provided that the IITs become less beholden to national caste-based affirmative action policies. In other words, associations like TIE see the privatization of higher education as the solution to India's deeply stratified education system. Interest in the booming IT economy spurred 729,000 applicants for engineering courses across India in 1999, with 200,000 to the six IITs—the "jewels in India's science crown." The success of India's IITs, which offer a total of 2,200 coveted seats, is measured by the fact that U.S.–based transnationals recruit directly from these institutes (Rajghatta 1999). IT industry leaders concur with NRI alumni that the solution to the increased national and global demand for skilled techno-workers rests on the privatization of higher education based on corporate and alumni donations and market-priced tuition.[19]

The issue of the "cream leaving India" can be "positively used in the interest of the institutes by nurturing ongoing communication with them, by getting their feedback in running the institutes, and finally by leveraging their reach and influence in the world market" (Ridi 1999).

---

[18] This quote is from an H–1B visa holder working for IBM in Santa Clara, California. See Frauenheim 1999.

[19] For more on the TIE perspective on reformulating the IIT system, see Deshpande 2000.

Leading the way, IIT Mumbai has established a nonprofit corporation in the United States (the Heritage Fund) which raised US$3 million in three years. According to some NRI donors, they are more likely than India-based entrepreneurs to give to IITs due as much to cultural ties as to tax laws. As one observer put it, it is the "American culture of non-profit institutions and the tax structure that makes it easier." While NRIs righteously argue that the "notion of paying back to society is not well established in India," locally based entrepreneurs argue that they are repaying the taxpayer that made their IIT education possible by "generating employment, paying taxes, and earning foreign exchange for [India]."[20] Thus flexible citizens help liberate their less flexible counterparts from the grip of the postcolonial state. They do so by highlighting the success of Indian-origin entrepreneurs in the global IT industry while ignoring the difficult realities associated with inequality and redistribution of socioeconomic resources both at home and across national boundaries.

Conclusion

The new discourse of high-tech development that has emerged in India since the 1980s is based on new configurations of public and private, national and transnational, and science and industry. Central to these new logics is the institutional and symbolic role played by the new he-roes of Indian digital capitalism: the technologically savvy and entre-preneurial non-resident Indians living in the developed world, espe-cially the United States.

Despite the impressive growth figures associated with the Indian IT sector, Indian policymakers have to contend with the fact that software-related services account for little more than 1 percent of the overall GDP. Despite the hype associated with high-tech development in India, the vast majority of Indian citizens—70 percent—live in rural areas, and almost 40 percent of the population lives in abject poverty. The celebration of the economic success of hundreds, perhaps thousands, of NRI high-tech entrepreneurs must be recognized in this political-economic context. Both the print and electronic media that speak to a transnational Indian public repeatedly reaffirm indigenized capitalism based on a Hindu work ethic and Indian family values. Much of this

---

[20] Interestingly, one India-based entrepreneur argued that the Bangalore-based In-dian Institute of Science was apparently started by "a huge gift of the Mysore Ma-haraja and an endowment of Rs. 120 million by Jamshedi Tata," two prominent political and economic brokers of colonial rule in India. See Ridi 1999.

discourse challenges the "hegemonic link between whiteness and global capitalism" (Ong 1999: 181).

This new form of flexible economic and cultural citizenship leads to two types of political practice. It allows a specific segment of NRIs to address inter-community racial politics in the United States, and it simultaneously justifies intra-community class and caste politics across national boundaries. My objective in this chapter was not to show how flexible citizenship allows for the strategic deployment of identity as an extension of cosmopolitanism working in favor of wealthy South Asians in the United States—in relation to other "less-model" minority groups.[21] Rather, I concentrated on the political practice associated with flexible citizenship as it relates to the terms of economic governance in the context of India's democratic political culture.

The first section provided a brief outline of the history of Indian emigration to the United States and located the different arenas of influence in India's political economy since the 1970s. The remaining sections identified three separate but interrelated features of NRI high-tech flexible citizenship in relation to India's national policy goals of becoming an information superpower.

First, these strategically placed flexible citizens reconfigure the role of science and its relationship to the state versus the market. Although postcolonial India has had a long history of state sponsorship of science for national self-reliance (Prakash 1999), these NRI flexible citizens advocate an entrepreneurial approach to scientific knowledge production that marks a conspicuous departure from Nehruvian investments in science.

Second, the nationalism of the NRI is based upon a nationalist, Americanized business culture that is pro-nation but anti-state. This version of nationalism resonates with a powerful cosmopolitan, urban, upper-caste elite that is increasingly anxious about its place in a largely low-income democracy. This has particular ramifications in justifying the nature of state versus market interventions in setting the terms of economic governance.

Finally, these NRI flexible citizens have a conflicted relationship with their larger national family regarding their obligations and responsibilities. While state intervention is ruled out, new forms of corporate citizenship and voluntary charity are encouraged. Interestingly, the predominant object of this kind of corporate charity has been the privatization of higher education, which directly addresses the social relations that made non-resident Indians' success possible in the first place.

---

[21] Visweswaran (1997) addresses the absence of class in recent academic writing about the Indian diaspora, as distinct from African Americans and Latinos.

References

Anantha-Nageswaran, V. 1997. "IT Corporate Education," *Economic Times*, November 23.

Anklesaria Aiyar, Swaminath S. 1999. "India's Economic Prospects, the Promise of Services." Center for Advanced Study of India Occasional Paper 9. At http://www.sas.upenn.edu/casi/reports/Aiyerpaper042299. html#_Toc450115777.

Bardhan, Pranab. 1984. *The Political Economy of Development in India.* New Delhi: Oxford University Press.

Bhaduri, Amit, and Deepak Nayyar. 1996. *The Intelligent Person's Guide to Liberalization.* New Delhi: Penguin.

Bhagwati, Jagdish. 1976. *Protection, Industrialization, Export Performance and Economic Development.* New York: United Nations Conference on Trade and Development.

———. 1993. *India in Transition: Freeing the Economy.* New York: Oxford University Press.

Chakravartty, Paula. 1999. "The Democratic Politics of Telecommunications Reform: 1947–1997." Ph.D. dissertation, University of Wisconsin, Madison.

Chatterjee, Partha. 1998. "Introduction: The Wages of Freedom." In *Wages of Freedom: Fifty Years of the Indian Nation State*, edited by Partha Chatterjee. New Delhi: Oxford University Press.

Chopra, Deepak. 1993. *Creating Affluence: Wealth Consciousness in the Field of All Possibilities.* New York: New World Library and Amber Allen.

Deshpande, Shubada. 2000. "Old IIT Boys Network," June, at http://www.littleindia.com/India/bizdir/oldiit.htm.

Drèze, Jean, and Amartya Sen. 1996. *India: Economic Development and Social Opportunity.* New Delhi: Oxford University Press.

Evans, Peter. 1995. *Embedded Autonomy-States and Industrial Transformation.* Princeton, N.J.: Princeton University Press.

Fan, Maureen. 2000. "New Age Leader, Medical Pioneer Addresses 700," *San Jose Mercury News*, February 17, at http://www.tie.org/02-00-chopra.html.

Flanigan, James. 2000. "India's Tech Economy Shows Promise as It Opens to US," *Los Angeles Times*, March 5.

Frauenheim, Ed. 1999. "Networking Innovator Kanwal Rekhi Has Been a Model for Many," *TechWeek India Inc.*, September 20, at http://www.tie.org/TechWeek%20India%20Inc%205B9-20-99%5D.htm.

Gardner, David. 2000. "Comment and Analysis, India's Plans to Plug the Brain Drain," *Financial Times* [United Kingdom], April 24.

Ghosh, Jayant. 1998. "Liberalization Debates." In *The Indian Economy: Major Debates since Independence*, edited by John Byeres. New Delhi: Oxford University Press.

Guha, Krishna. 1999. "High-end Skills at a Price," *Financial Times* [United Kingdom], May 17.

Kaviraj, Sudipta. 1991. "On State, Society and Discourse in India." In *Rethinking Third World Politics*, edited by John Manor. New York: Longman.

————. 1998. "The Culture of Representative Democracy." In *Wages of Freedom: Fifty Years of the Indian Nation State*, edited by Partha Chatterjee. New Delhi: Oxford University Press.

Khilnani, Sunil. 1998. *The Idea of India*. New Delhi: Farrar, Straus, and Giroux.

Kothari, Rajni. 1995. "Interpreting Indian Politics: A Personal Statement." In *Crisis and Change in Contemporary India*, edited by Upendra Baxi and Bikhu Parekh. New Delhi: Sage.

Lundstrom, Meg. 1999. *Businessweek.com*, September 27, http://www.business-leaders.com/200feb/cover2.htm.

McDowell, Stephen. 1997. *Globalization, Liberalization and Policy Change: A Political Economy of India's Communications Sector*. New York: St. Martin's.

Mir, Ali, and Michael Yajnik. 1995. "The Uneven Development of Places: From Bodyshopping to Global Assembly Lines," *Samar*, December 7–15.

Nandy, Ashish. 1996. "Introduction: Science as Reason of State." In *Science, Hegemony and Violence: A Requiem for Modernity*, edited by Ashish Nandy. 4th ed. New Delhi: Oxford University Press.

Nayyar, Deepak. 1994. *Migration, Remittances, and Capital Flows: The Indian Experience*. New Delhi: Oxford University Press.

Ong, Aiwa. 1999. *Flexible Citizenship: The Cultural Logics of Transnationality*. Durham, N.C.: Duke University Press.

Pandya, Mukul. 1998. "Counting All Their Chips," *Littleindia.com*, August, at http://206.20.14.67/achal/archive/Aug98/chips.htm.

Pendakur, Manjunath. 1990. "A Political Economy of Television: State, Class and Corporate Influence in India." In *Electronic Dependency: Third World Communications and Information in an Age of Transnationalism*, edited by Gerald Sussman and John Lent. Newbury Park, Calif.: Sage.

Pinches, Michael. 1999. "Cultural Relations and the New Rich." In *Culture and Privilege in Capitalist Asia*, edited by Michael Pinches. London: Routledge.

Pitroda, Sam. 1993. "Development, Democracy and the Village Telephone," *Harvard Business Review*, November–December, pp. 66–79.

Prakash, Gyan. 1999. *Another Reason: Science and the Imagination of Modern India*. Princeton, N.J. Princeton University Press.

Rajghatta, Chidanand. 1999. "Brain Curry: American Campuses Crave for IIT Glory," expressindia.com, December 7, at http://www.expressindia.com/ie/daily20000520/svsaga5.htm.

Ridi, M. D. 1999. "Are You Educated?" *Rediff.com*, April 20, at http://www.tie.org/Rediff0999.htm.

Sen, Amartya. 1973. *On Economic Inequality*. Delhi : Oxford University Press.

Sridharan, E. 1996. *The Political Economy of Industrial Promotion: Indian, Brazilian, and Korean Electronics in Comparative Perspective 1969–1994*. Westport, Conn.: Praeger.

Subrahmanyam, Marti, G. 1998. "The New Asian Tiger: India at the Crossroads," *Siliconindia*, May/June, at http://www.siliconindia.com/magazine/MayJune98crossroads.html.

Taylor, Paul. 1999. "A Growing Force and Going Places," *Financial Times* [United Kingdom], June 2.

Visvanathan, Shiv. 1985. *Organizing for Science: The Making of an Industrial Research Laboratory*. New Delhi: Oxford University Press.

Visweswaran, Kamala. 1997. "Diaspora by Design: Flexible Citizenship and South Asians in US Racial Formations," *Diaspora* 6: 1.

Vithal, B. P. R. 1997. "Evolving Trends in the Bureaucracy." In *State and Politics in India*, edited by Partha Chatterjee. New Delhi: Oxford University Press.

Vittal, N. 1997. " Manpower Export," *Economic Times*, June 1.

13

Rethinking Migration: On-Line Labor Flows from India to the United States

A. Aneesh

A qualitatively new organization of capital and labor is affecting migration practices in a way unimaginable a decade ago. In an increasingly global economy, information technologies are producing a form of migration that adds a new dimension to what is termed "the international division of labor." This study explores the rapidly growing—but little researched—practice of on-line labor flows from India to the United States. It then compares on-line labor flows to the corresponding physical migration of programmers. This practice, called "body shopping,"[1] involves bringing programmers from India to the United States and arranging work visas for them to work on site there.

While on-line programming implies migration of skills but not bodies, body shopping implies migration of both bodies and skills. By comparing the software engineering projects undertaken on-line with those carried out on site and examining whether information technologies can potentially render the migration of high-tech workers from India to the United States redundant, this study attempts to introduce a new perspective on prevailing immigration debates in the United States regarding high-tech workers. What it explores, in effect, is the changing channels of labor supply.

The majority of labor in the United States is increasingly being converted into information work—especially in service industries that oc-

I would like to thank the Social Science Research Council and the Population Council for funding for this project.

[1] The term "body shopping" is generally avoided in formal conversation. The more accepted term is "consultancy." I retain the former term because it captures the sense of bodily presence at the site of work.

cupy a large employment space in the economy. This research takes the on-line delivery of work across national borders as its object of analysis and integrates it with immigration issues. A study of this relatively less visible usage of on-line, offshore labor offers a new conceptual hinge to the immigration debates raging in the United States. The debate as to whether the United States as a nation stands to gain or lose from immigrant workers—in terms of economic, fiscal, demographic, or cultural consequences—has been intensifying for some time (Borjas and Freeman 1992; Espenshade and Hempstead 1996; Friedberg and Hunt 1995; Smith and Edmonston 1997). Lately, a large demand and influx of information technology (IT) workers has forced the debate to enter the high-skill domains of employment, as reflected in various media discussions. Although the corporate world has continuously pressed the federal government to relax quotas on labor immigration—arguing a shortage of IT labor, upward wage pressure, and competitive advantage (Gleckman 1998; Moschella 1998)—others fear that such immigration will take high-tech jobs away from native-born Americans and lower their wages (Archey and Matloff 1998; Matloff 1995, 1996).

To illustrate the practical consequences of such debates, the U.S. Congress imposed a quota in 1991 to allow only 65,000 temporary workers to enter the country annually on H–1B visas.[2] The cap was part of a larger scheme to stem the flow of immigrants. In 1997, when the limit of 65,000 was reached before the end of the year, there was heated debate about whether the limit should be raised. These discussions were intensified by employers' increased demand for high-skilled IT labor in a booming information economy. The intensity of the debate is reflected in various bills that were introduced, defeated, revived, passed, and rewritten in exchanges between the House of Representatives, the Senate, and the White House. The final bill that was enacted allowed 115,000 visas to be granted to foreign workers for fiscal years 1999 and 2000. The number of visas would drop slightly in 2001 and then revert to 65,000 in 2002. This American Competitiveness and Workforce Improvement Act of 1998 also required employers to pay a new H–1B worker fee of $500 in order to fund training and educational programs for U.S. workers.

The 115,000 visas allotted for fiscal year 2000 were exhausted in March 2000, however, forcing Congress to pass the American Competitiveness in the Twenty-First Century Act. This Act increased the number of H–1B visas to 195,000 a year for three years. Under this Act,

---

[2] The H–1B is a non-immigrant classification used for a foreign worker who is employed temporarily in a specialty occupation. A specialty occupation requires theoretical or practical application of a body of specialized knowledge, along with at least a bachelor's degree or its equivalent.

employers must pay a $1,000 fee for each H–1B application, with the monies used to generate a projected $150 million annually for scholarships for U.S. students. Most H–1B visas go to programmers.

These debates on the future of immigrant IT labor will clearly need to be reformulated. This study demonstrates the inefficacy of border enforcement against on-line IT labor flows even as it confirms enforcement's effectiveness against the flow of bodies (that is, physical migration). Using high-speed datacom links, programmers based in their national territories can work on-line and in real time on computers located anywhere in the world, thus obviating the need for either labor or corporations to undergo the tedious process of physical migration.

This on-line labor practice—after passing through the conventional frames of economics and national bureaucracies—is variously understood as "trade" and "subcontracting," but never as "labor migration," a term that is still reserved for the physical migration of human bodies.[3] Such conventional frames, I argue, constitute the "new" in terms of the "old." With the growth of information technologies and the resulting separation of work performance from the site, we need a different set of frames for understanding what is "labor" and how it "flows." In the context of programming labor, if projects completed on site—by physically bringing programmers from India to the United States—are similar in nature to offshore projects completed on-line, we need to rethink the framing, and thus the constitution, of these practices in terms of "migration" and "trade." Through an inquiry into the above practice, this study integrates the macro questions of transnational capitalism, migration, and the nation-state to the micro practices of software work conducted at the firm level.

This chapter compares practices of on-line and on-site labor (body shopping) in terms of their similarities and differences. It also identifies some core aspects of the relatively new phenomenon of on-line, offshore labor and clarifies how on-line programming works. Rather than limiting the inquiry to *what* is achieved through the new labor practice, *what* the content of work is, or *what* competitive advantages corporations gain by hiring on-line labor, I begin by asking *how* this form of labor functions. This question brings out the contours of a new regime of labor practice, which requires new analytical tools to understand current transformations in work organization and labor migration.

The chapter is organized as follows. I first outline an important dimension that this study may add to the literature on globalization and migration. I then explain the operation of body shopping and on-line labor, arguing that both are part of a single regime that seeks to harness global labor in more flexible ways. I next discuss how on-line labor acts

---

[3] The term "international telecommuting" could also be used.

as a mechanism for reducing tensions between nation-states and transnational capitalism regarding labor migration.

Globalization and Migration

In some ways, recent debates on globalization corroborate the assertions of Fordist, post-Fordist, and world-systems analyses about the ever-growing incorporation of scattered societies into the capitalist global system. Literature on globalization explains both the unprecedented expansion of transnational corporations (see, for example, Dicken 1992; Kamel 1990) and the increased flow of commodities across national borders (Knox 1995: 6). Transnational corporations, however, share an uneasy relationship with nation-states. As contemporary capitalism, with its transnational corporations, is increasingly able to penetrate the sacred boundaries of nations, the historical primacy of the nation-state as the regulator of the national economy is increasingly undermined (Johnston 1982). The world economy is not merely undergoing a process of internationalization (an intensified networking of *national* economies) but also a process of globalization by supranational powers (Dicken 1992).

Some scholars recognize, however, that the role of nation-states acquires more significance as nations try to enhance their strengths in order to compete globally with other national economies; they act as the source of the skills and technology that underpin competitive advantage (Chesnais 1986: 87; Porter 1990: 19). But most scholarship, in order to illuminate transnational practices, moves away from state-centric models (Keohane and Nye 1973; Sklair 1995) though privileging by default the global over the local.

Faced with fiercer competition and higher wages in the developed world, corporations tend to move their standardized production to capitalize on low-cost labor in less developed countries (Frobel, Heinrichs, and Kreye 1980; Harvey 1989; Lipietz 1986). While cheaper labor may be only one of the factors influencing a corporation's move overseas (Dunning 1980; Elson 1988; Schoenberger 1988), all factors seem eventually to bring corporations, workers, and national states into direct contact with one another.

Although this study views emerging on-line labor as part of the common move in contemporary capitalism to tap globally dispersed labor in a more flexible manner, it departs from the general literature in some important ways. First, on-line labor has very limited direct, face-to-face contact with corporations in the United States. Second, on-line work cannot be understood as truly transnational in character because it takes place within the bounds of nations. For instance, programmers in India, while indirectly working for U.S. corporations, still carry a single, unambiguous national identity, unlike immigrant programmers who are physically present in the United States. Indian on-line programmers do not go through the agonizing hurdles that immigrant workers face in terms of visa requirements, alien status, nativist reaction, and cultural opposition (Cornelius et al. 1994). Third, programmers based in India are also governed by local practices of employment, taxation, and labor regulations. Yet, like other immigrant workers, they do break national barriers by directly occupying some employment space in concerned sectors of the United States. In short, they migrate without migrating, a phenomenon I call "virtual migration." The concept of virtual migration recognizes that the programmer in India can access and implement changes on a computer in the United States. Such invisible and disembodied processes of labor supply may add a new dimension to the literature on labor migration.

The migration literature consists of macro perspectives that stress immigrant labor's structural causes and functions for developed nations (Boyd 1989; Burawoy 1976; Castells 1975; Pedraza-Bailey 1990; Portes 1978) through the articulation of the international system (Portes and Böröcz 1989), as well as micro perspectives, such as Everette Lee's seminal "push" and "pull" theory of migration (Grasmuck and Pessar 1991; Lee 1966). Yet, with the growth of information technologies, there are new empirical and theoretical challenges facing immigration research.

Recent technological advances have generated a curious phenomenon—the textualization of work (Zuboff 1988). In other words, work is mostly symbolic manipulation on the screen through software systems. The resulting dematerialization of work, which can now be textually controlled through software, reduces the need for the on-site presence of the body to perform the work. This research stresses the need to acknowledge the invisible, disembodied migration of labor, comparing it with well-documented processes of physical migration. Economic migration can no longer be seen only in terms of physical human movement. Some recent suggestions for a sociology of borders and flows (Böröcz 1997) provide new theoretical axes for a unified analysis of social flows—including capital, labor, bodies, commodities, cultural patterns, and information. Developing such perspectives may offer important analytical tools to compare embodied and disembodied labor flows across national borders.

We may also draw upon Sassen's (1997) recent attempt to bring the issues of a global economic regime, the national state, and migration together. Sassen challenges two prevalent assumptions: first, that whatever the global economy gains, the national state loses, and vice-versa; and, second, if an event (such as a business transaction) takes place in a national territory, it is a national event. Thus the global economy is not a phenomenon divorced from national states, and the national event is not merely "national." Offshore, on-line labor practice is a case that fits perfectly into this hybridity of the national and the global.

It is necessary at this point to briefly describe the field research that informs this study.[4] To gain grounded, contextualized, and ethnographic information about on-line labor practice, I conducted formal and informal, semi-structured and open-ended in-depth interviews with programmers, as well as with high-level management executives, at many software firms in India and in the United States. In the first phase of research, the target group consisted of programmers and project managers in and around New Delhi. During the second phase, programmers and business executives were interviewed in New Jersey and surrounding areas. One of the important reasons for selecting New Jersey as a site of study relates to the presence there of many large high-tech corporations and smaller companies that employ large numbers of Indian programmers. Most of the programmers interviewed in the United States immigrated through the practice of body shopping. In the last phase of the research, I interviewed mostly high-level executives— chief executive officers, managing directors, and vice presidents—of small, midsize, and large software firms based in New Delhi, Gurgaon, and Noida (India). Software development sites, corporate centers, and work processes were observed during all phases of the research. In India, firms included Tata Consultancy Services (TCS), Netacross, HCL, LogicSoft, and Softek, as well as some U.S. subsidiaries like Microsoft, Adobe, Metamore, and iDLX, among others. Data collected include annual reports of the National Association of Software and Service Companies (henceforth, Nasscom), reports regarding the information technology task force of the Government of India, and the Information Technology Bill presented in India's Parliament.

The study included 50 formal interviews (35 in India and 15 in the United States) and a similar number of informal conversations with software professionals and executives in India and the United States. For extended interviews, programmers were selected through snowball sampling and higher-level executives were selected by contacting all the firms located in Delhi, Noida, and Gurgaon that are listed in Nasscom's directory of software firms. The response rate of higher-level executives was about 25 percent. I conducted interviews in both Hindi and English.

---

[4] Fieldwork was conducted over an eighteen-month period in 1999 and 2000.

Bringing the Body to the Work Site: Body Shopping and On-Site Labor

Our understanding of labor migration is generally situated within the framework of "body migration," a legacy of the times when labor could not move without the body. At the beginning of the twenty-first century, the continuous revolutionizing of the instruments of production has enabled the creation of a new labor regime whereby labor can move and migrate without the laborer's body. This is not to say that earlier ways of doing work are going to suddenly vanish without a trace. Just as the theater did not disappear with the appearance of the cinema, virtual labor will not *entirely* replace on-site labor. At the beginning of the year 2000, people hired through body shopping still outnumbered people providing their labor on-line from India. Their proportion, though, is gradually declining. Let us look at what body shopping is and how it functions. One of my informants in India explained body shopping as follows:

> Body shopping is essentially when people are sitting in some kind of recruitment shops in India.... They're really sending out our talented people.... They do not enter into any kind of service contract but only into contract for providing people on a temporary basis. So while those people continue to work for their local company, they're deploying their services for an overseas customer, for a foreign customer on site.

Another informant explained it as follows:

> You can say, these are like headhunters.... They can get you an interview for all these big companies. If they need a full-time employee, they can place you there. You work for them...[but] you do exactly the same thing.

Body shopping has a negative connotation, as reflected in the preceding statements. There are two modes in which business and software executives in India talk about body shopping. First, companies in India that do not engage in body shopping tend to deny having anything to do with it; they consider it an inferior, though lucrative, business practice. They emphasize the fact that they are into real services (like developing software systems for various clients) and carefully avoid this sham—that is, merely placing software professionals with corporations in the United States. Most of the large software firms in India developed initially through body shopping; the second reaction to the practice involves how companies that engage in body shopping couch their practices in euphemisms such as "consultancy." Body shopping is characterized by four key features:

- Just-in-time labor.
- High-earning but low-cost labor.
- Universal, as opposed to specific, labor.
- System-level labor.

Just-in-Time Labor

Body shopping demonstrates with extraordinary clarity what "flexible" forms of post-industrial labor entail. This form of labor is analogous to the application of the just-in-time (JIT) techniques developed by several Japanese firms in the 1970s for inventory management. This new system drastically reduced large inventories and associated overhead costs throughout the entire production system by relying on the careful scheduling of small, accurate delivery of parts and supplies to be made by vendors *just in time*. As with a large inventory, keeping a large permanent workforce without regard to the seasonal highs and lows of the business cycle is a costly practice, which body shopping attempts to address. By supplying software professionals on time and only for the length of time needed, body shopping firms help companies avoid the cost of keeping a large workforce on a permanent basis. One informant, who works for a U.S. investment and banking company through a body shopping firm, explains it in the following terms:

> This company doesn't have to hire an employee. They don't have to pay for my insurance. And they can fire me. I'm not a liability for them. But in return, they have to pay more money.... The other thing is, if they hired a full-time employee, they will have to train him [or her].

High-Earning but Low-Cost Labor

The preceding statement resolves the apparent paradox of better-paid low-cost labor. Although contractual workers placed with different companies by their parent body-shopping firms may be earning more in the short term, they are still low-cost labor from a long-term perspective. Although annual contracts fetch these temporary workers higher incomes than the annual salaries of regular employees in similar positions, they allow the receiving company to trim its workforce, take these temporary workers into service only in times of need, and economize on long-term benefits (such as retirement contributions and health insurance) that are required for permanent employees.

Universal, as Opposed to Specific, Labor

Another characteristic of just-in-time software labor is its universality. Unlike specific forms of labor, such as a surgeon's skill or a civil engineer's expertise, software professionals are not limited to any specific form of organization or industry. Software is fast becoming the medium and language of all work. Whether the task is to control heavy machines or track banking operations, software professionals lend their labor and expertise to an unprecedented diversity of businesses. This explains the phenomenal growth of body shopping in the software industry. In light of the more universal application of their work, programmers can be quickly deployed, transferred, and redeployed to different firms.

System-Level Labor

The universality of programming is not like the universality of secretarial work. Unlike secretaries, software professionals are system-level workers—that is, they can potentially transform how organizations function from within. As programmers, they not only help translate the previous work setup into a digital format (e.g., converting a face-to-face banking system into on-line banking), they also help transform—in their capacity as systems analysts—some fundamental aspects of how an organization functions. They reconfigure various departments and hierarchies through Enterprise Resource Planning (ERP) systems. Using ERP systems, software professionals can chalk out a new work flow, identify redundancies and duplication, and mechanize the whole work process from the design stage to the shop floor.

Surprisingly, body shopping is not flexible enough for the emerging labor paradigm because it still involves actual border crossing and authorization by the nation-state. On-line labor emerges as an even more flexible alternative for labor movement from India to the United States, bypassing immigration controls by confining the laboring body to the geographical jurisdiction of the home state. This virtual flow of labor provides a unique vantage point from which to explore relationships between transnational capitalism, the nation-state, and labor migration.

On-Line Labor: India and the United States

Although the Indian software industry is more than twenty years old, only in the last decade did the industry take off, and only in the last five to eight years has India become a global player. These were also the years of the emergence of on-line labor. There are three basic features of on-line, offshore software engineering: (1) programmers in India are connected to clients' machines in the United States through 64 Kbps and higher satellite links and Internet/e-mail; (2) when the situation demands, the client is able to continuously monitor progress, implement quality checks, and communicate with the programmers and analysts, as if they were on site; (3) because the United States and India have an average 12–hour time difference, the client enjoys—for certain software projects—virtual round-the-clock office hours. Although some Indian companies are moving up the value chain, these on-line projects specialize not in packaged products but in re-engineering projects and high-skilled services, chiefly providing high-skilled information labor to companies around the world.

There is an ever-growing number of companies in India that organize programmers to provide on-line software labor to corporations in the United States and other countries. By December 1998, more than 109 Indian software firms had acquired international quality certification (Nasscom 1999). Some well-known U.S. firms that are on the client lists of these Indian firms are Intel, Merrill Lynch, AT&T, and IBM. According to the *Economist* (1996: 32), "More than 100 of America's top 500 firms buy software services from firms in India, where programmers are typically paid less than a quarter of the American rate." By 1998, Indian software providers had already captured an 18.5 percent market share in global cross-country customized software work, and the Indian IT sector has consistently achieved more than a 50 percent compounded annual growth rate since 1991 (Nasscom 1999), as portrayed in figure 13.1.

The reason for discussing the Indian software industry in the context of on-line labor relates to the fact that the U.S. market for Indian industry is very small compared to its offshore market, which offers major on-line contracts for Indian firms. This offshore market is expected to assume even greater proportions. Earnings from software exports are projected to gross $9 billion by 2001–2002, and the National Task Force on Information Technology—a support arm of the Indian government—has set a target of $50 billion in exports by 2008 (Nasscom 1999). It must be noted that these U.S. dollar earnings assume even greater purchasing power when converted to Indian rupees.

Figure 13.1. India's Software Export Earnings: 1992-1998

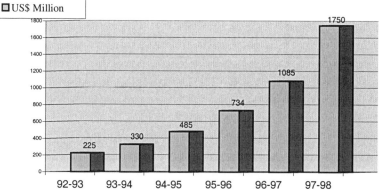

Annual Growth Rate: 50.72%
(based on figures from Nasscom 1999)

The software relationship between India and the United States is particularly significant. Just as India is becoming the largest supplier of software labor to the United States in terms of both body shopping and on-line labor, the United States has turned out to be the largest source of software earnings for India, as shown in figure 13.2.

Figure 13.2. Indian Software Earnings from Different Destinations 1997-98

Source: Nasscom 1999.

The mutually important U.S.–India relationship is reflected in the following statement by a spokesperson for the National Association of Software and Service Companies (NASSCOM):

> We can't deny the fact that the United States is a major mar-
> ket for our software industry. In fact ... nearly 64 percent of
> the total software exports for the year 1999 we expect will be
> derived from the U.S. market alone. So we can't deny the fact
> that it's the largest market in the world. It continues to be a
> major driver in terms of innovation and new technologies,
> and dictating, I would say, new standards for the global IT
> industry. Over a period of time the, Indian software talent
> pool has been really able to achieve a certain recognition in
> the U.S. IT industry. If Indian software engineers were to go
> back home, the U.S. IT industry would collapse the next
> morning.

This informant also acknowledged the lobbying efforts that Nasscom carries out in the United States to promote its transnational interests, highlighting a restive relationship between global capitalism and national states:

> We have been working rather actively ... in the United
> States. In fact, on the recent H–1B amendment that an-
> nounced an increase of 50,000 for the new quota for the H–
> 1B visas, starting on October 1 and lasting through Septem-
> ber 30, 1999, we feel we acted as a major catalyst in driving
> that.... Even before that [we had been] lobbying on Capitol
> Hill on various issues like Social Security, taxes, and so on,
> because we feel various kinds of taxes and various kinds of
> demands that are put forth by the revenue service depart-
> ment of the U.S. government are basically tantamount to
> double taxation on allowances given to the software engi-
> neers working in the United States.[5]

This lobbying exemplifies an increasingly uneasy relationship between transnational capitalism and national bureaucracies regarding
the status and flow of workers. This troubled relationship also ex-
presses itself in the constant tug of war between corporations and Congress. While U.S. corporations have been demanding an unhindered
inflow of foreign labor and fewer restrictions on their moving overseas,
Congress is always inclined to intensify border patrols, erect border

---

[5] The informant is referring to software professionals who come to the United
States to work on site.

fences, impose restrictions on immigration (for reasons that are both cultural and economic), and control the activities of U.S. corporations abroad. Similarly, in the case of the Indian state, emigration of skilled labor has been a constant source of debate, and the consequences of the "brain drain" for the domestic economy have always been a matter of concern. The feared hegemony of multinational corporations has been resisted continuously since independence, reflected, for example, in the expulsion of Coca-Cola in 1977 and in the temporary cancellation of contracts with Enron Corporation in 1996.

The Nation-State, Transnational Capitalism, and On-Line Labor Flows

Transnational capitalism and the nation-state seem, however, to have negotiated a truce in the electronic space of on-line labor flows, which both allows unhampered movement of labor and skills and prevents alien cultural bodies from crossing national spaces. Increased globalization seems at once to also be a process of increasing localization. The software firms are able to provide real labor at a global level, yet both workers in India and corporations in the United States remain on their national turf.

The question remains, why should we describe on-line practices in terms of labor flows and not as movements of goods and services? Although the classification of on-line labor flows as exports and imports—owing to national bureaucratic mechanisms—is understandable, I perceive three main reasons why on-line practices are basically a technique for supplying labor. First, unlike other regular imports, on-line labor flows do not come under any import regime, given that there are no taxes or tariffs imposed by the U.S. government on them and no mechanisms to monitor billions of software lines whizzing across national borders at tremendously fast speeds. Second, Indian software companies rarely specialize in tradable products and packages. They are mostly suppliers of high-skilled information labor, either through body shopping or through virtual migration. The labor supplied through body shopping and on-line practices makes up 91.2 percent of the total earnings of these firms from foreign sources, while software products and packages constitute only 8.8 percent (Nasscom 1999). Third, there is not much discernible difference between on-site and on-line labor engagements. In fact, the decline in on-site engagements is directly linked to the rise of offshore engagements, bringing these practices together as two alternate forms of labor supply. Many informants alluded to a gradual shift from body shopping to offshore project development, especially with the rise of fast and reliable communication links. The Nasscom annual review connects visa restrictions with the accelerated growth of on-line off-loading of work:

> With the proliferation of Software Technology Parks, service of high speed datacom provided by VSNL,[6] liberalized economic policy, unnatural visa restrictions by the U.S. and some Western European countries, the component of off-shore development is expected to increase further.
>
> The degree of on-site development is still very high ... but it is expected to decrease further in the coming years with improved data communication links. In 1988, the percentage of on-site development [through body shopping] was almost as high as 90% [it dropped to 59 percent in 1998] (Nasscom 1999: 18).

When asked why on-site services have not completely given way to on-line services, a vice president of a software company in New Delhi replied: "because the management [in U.S. corporations] is often lazy in providing complete systems specifications." However, upon further research, many other factors regarding the need for at least a limited on-site presence emerged, including the time-zone difference, which both facilitates and hampers the reach and access of on-line labor. A more detailed description of on-line, offshore labor practices will further clarify the argument. One major software company in Bombay, which also has a small unit in the United States, provides 24–hour information systems management for insurance-claims processing to the American International Group, Inc. (AIG). One of the informants—who moved briefly from Bombay to North Carolina while working for the company—described this software work as follows:

> The Bombay team can directly access the client's mainframe. Usually what we have is a maintenance project, and we support AIG's insurance business for 24 hours.... There are different groups in AIG, and [we] support most of them.... So suppose someone is claiming [insurance] money from AIG due to some accident. He would go to AIG agents, [who] would enter the data on CICS [Customer Information Control System] screens, [inputs] like where this accident happened, what's the cause, and other details of the accident. And when this information is entered on CICS screens and daytime is over in the USA, that information is captured and written to a file, which is the input for our nightly batch

---

[6] "VSNL" stands for Videsh Sanchar Nigam Limited, an autonomous governmental agency providing communications-related services at commercial rates.

processing. So at 10:00 [p.m.] here, which will be around 8:30 a.m. in Bombay, our daily batch cycles run. What it will do is, the claims that are entered in the day [in the United States by AIG staff], whatever information is changed—like claim name is changed, address is changed, and other stuff—all this information will be processed in the nightly batch cycle in Bombay. We actually have about 60 jobs running one after the other, which update the table information [in] VB2 [Visual Basic 2] tables.

Time-zone difference was both an asset and a problem in this case. It was an asset because by the time the work day is over in the United States, software workers in India can start working on the back-end tasks during their daytime. When the CICS system is not in use in the United States, Indian workers can provide solutions and complete them on-line. When the U.S.–based AIG office opens in the morning, a lot of back-end work has already been completed, allowing a virtual 24–hour office for the U.S. client. However, the time difference could also be a problem if the team in India fails to finish all the tasks during their work day:

> Some of the files, which we [the Bombay team and U.S. team] use, are common ... so unless and until these files are closed, we cannot start our cycles. So the CICS has to be down [before the Bombay team can start working]. Around 10:00 p.m. [U.S. eastern time] the CICS is down, no information can be entered after that, so our batch cycle [in Bombay] can run. And if the batch cycle is not successfully finished within a certain time, or if it gets delayed due to some reason, then there will be a problem because these people [in the United States] won't be able to enter the information [in the morning]. So it's very critical to resolve everything [before they open their office in the United States].

As another example of on-line labor support, one of the programmers cited an instance when they supported Citibank operations:

> Citibank had [changed] all their retail business; there were a lot of changes required in the programs already existing, like day-to-day maintenance.... There are always hundreds and hundreds of changes that are needed. One way is that they have their own people do it. The other way is how the work in their bank in Japan was done.... There was a team of 3 to 4 people working in India, and there was a project manager on site. I was the project manager. I would take work from the Japanese managers and I would send it offshore to India,

and the Indian people will be working on their machines in a different environment. So any changes, any production problems, anything will immediately come to the people who were in India.

Describing the advantages of a 24–hour time zone for software support to the companies in the United States, he said:

Basically it's night in the United States and early morning here. In the [daytime] here, there are a lot of things developed and given to them, and in the morning there, it's already there for them to test it, implement it. At the end of their day, they just have to [compile] their problems and the changes they want us to do, and we can fix them in our normal working hours, fix them just in time, and it will be there next morning when they come to their office.

However, when there are glitches, the time-zone difference hampers instant communication with the client to resolve some of the problems. This is the reason that some Indian software companies establish a small unit in the United States for physical and temporal proximity. At times, some companies open a branch in the same time zone but outside the United States, as in the Caribbean, to avoid higher wage costs. As one informant, who joined J. P. Morgan through body shopping to work on site, described:

J. P. Morgan had people work in India on projects. But … the time lag [was a problem]. They are sleeping and you are working, and you cannot really talk to them at the same time. [The work was done] through a [software] consulting company … [that] hired people in India and gave them some work; they worked there and sent back code. But it didn't work. So instead, what the consulting company came up with was that they moved them to Barbados.

In addition to the constant support for information systems, Indian software companies also work on independent software projects by cloning the client's systems environment—a unique feature of information technologies—and then redesigning and re-engineering the system. Such clients include banks, airline companies, and manufacturing companies. As one of the software professionals in Noida, India, mentioned:

We support your daily requirements for banking applications—like daily branch opening, your account handling, your money transfers, everything, the routine tasks for which there's a need to build the software. It's very routine because most rules are documented. You just have to implement those business rules into software programs.

Some of the projects involve a limited on-site presence of Indian software professionals who are flown to the United States for a brief period to develop an initial understanding of what exactly the client wants, given that it is not always possible for the client to come up with complete project specifications and communicate them on-line. Similarly, at the end of the project, despite the on-line delivery of completed software projects, senior software engineers fly to the United States to see to the successful implementation of their projects. One of the project managers in New Delhi described how they helped Gap develop a new information system to track their orders to vendors:

> All Gap clothes are produced in the Third World—Latin America, India, Bangladesh, and all these countries. They have vendors in all these places, so purchase orders are created between these vendors and Gap. You want to purchase so many goods of a certain style and cut, of a certain size, and this order is sent out to these vendors. So the process of automation is purchase-order creation, and then getting the goods back and things like that. We were involved in the development activity. The Gap had given us a complete project. We cloned their environment on our own mainframe. We developed the project, we developed the complete software, and then I was in the United States implementing it and making changes.

The option of environment cloning, constant on-line monitoring across continents, and on-line shipping of programming work makes possible a new global labor regime that increasingly competes with the practice of shipping people—body shopping—across national boundaries. Physical immigration is not likely to end, especially for manual laborers needed to work in agriculture, restaurants, and construction, but it does seem to have a limited future in the high-tech sector, considering the continuing growth in offshore software development thanks to faster communication links.

Conclusion

Since the 1980s, information technologies have triggered extensive transformations in production and work. These changes not only influence how work is organized within national boundaries, but they also have global ramifications. On-line virtual labor across national spaces provides a new angle to explore this global shift, and it informs debates that transcend the site and nature of this specific work practice. With no ready grasp of the practice, on-line labor is too easily inserted into old schema and modes of understanding. It is ascribed either to the trade schema of "export/import" or to the organizational schema of "subcontracting" and "out-sourcing," missing the complex interconnections of new practices with a multiplicity of processes, such as labor migration and mechanisms of national bureaucracies.

The metamorphosis of work into something that can be performed at a distance and delivered on-line is structurally dependent on distinctive features of information technologies. Using this understanding of the new technologies, this chapter has sought to free discussions of labor migration from the confines of the body. This enables us to see how globalizing forces can potentially produce localizing effects by helping to restrict laboring populations to their national territory.

With newly gained flexibility in labor supply, contemporary capitalism seems to have resolved two major problems. First, corporations can, to a degree, avoid confrontation with the nation-state on the issue of alien immigration because they can harness foreign labor on-line, bypassing the nationalist politics of culture. In contrast to physical migration—which requires tolerance of cultural differences, education for migrants' children, possible long-term settlement, and social services from the affluent society—virtual labor flows do not require alien humans to join the nation. Second, the invisibility of virtual labor helps U.S. corporations avoid somewhat the possible charge of preferring immigrants to citizens in terms of employment and job creation for the society in general.

Future research might examine how the constant revolution in the instruments of production may necessitate a reconfiguration of existing relationships among states, corporate management, and the global workforce.

References

Archey, William T., and Norman Matloff. 1998. "Should More Foreign High-Tech Workers Be Allowed into the United States? (Pro and Con)," *CQ Researcher* 8 (16): 377.

Borjas, George, and R. V. Freeman. 1992. *Immigration and the Work Force: Economic Consequences for the United States and Source Areas.* Chicago: University of Chicago Press.

Böröcz, József. 1997. "Doors on the Bridge: The Border as Contingent Closure." Paper presented at the American Sociological Association Annual Meetings, Toronto, August.

Boyd, Monica. 1989. "Family and Personal Networks in International Migration: Recent Developments and New Agendas," *International Migration Review.*

Burawoy, M. 1976. "The Function and Reproduction of Migrant Labor: Comparative Material from Southern Africa and the United States," *American Journal of Sociology.*

Castells, Manuel. 1975. "Immigrant Workers and Class Struggle in Advanced Capitalism: The Western Europe Experience," *Political Sociology* 533–66.

Chesnais, F. 1986. "Science, Technology and Competitiveness," *Science Technology Industry Review* 185–129.

Cornelius, Wayne, Philip Martin, and James Hollifield, eds. 1994. *Controlling Immigration: A Global Perspective.* Stanford, Calif.: Stanford University Press.

Dicken, Peter. 1992. *Global Shift: The Internationalization of Economic Activity.* London: Paul Chapman.

Dunning, J. H. 1980. "Towards an Eclectic Theory of International Production: Some Empirical Tests," *Journal of International Business Studies* 119–31.

Economist. 1996. "A Survey of the World Economy (supplement)," September 28.

Elson, D. 1988. "Transnational Corporations in the New International Division of Labor: A Critique of 'Cheap Labor' Hypothesis," *Manchester Papers on Development* IV 352–76.

Espenshade, Thomas, and K. Hempstead. 1996. "Contemporary American Attitudes toward U.S. Immigration," *International Migration Review* 30 (2): 535–70.

Espenshade, Thomas, and V .E. King. 1994. "State and Local Fiscal Impact of U.S. Immigrants: Evidence from New Jersey," *Population Research and Policy Review* 13: 225–56.

Friedberg, R., and J. Hunt. 1995. "The Impact of Immigrants on Host Country Wages, Employment and Growth," *Journal of Economic Perspectives* 9 (2): 23–44.

Frobel, F., J. Heinrichs, and O. Kreye. 1980. *The New International Division of Labor.* Cambridge: Cambridge University Press.

Gleckman, Howard. 1998. "High-Tech Talent: Don't Bolt the Golden Door," *Business Week*, March 16.

Grasmuck, S., and Patricia Pessar. 1991. *Between Two Islands: Dominican International Migration.* Berkeley: University of California Press.

Harvey, David. 1989. *The Condition of Postmodernity: An Enquiry into the Origins of Cultural Change.* Oxford: Blackwell.

Johnston, R. J. 1982. *Geography and the State.* London: Macmillan.

Kamel, Rachael. 1990. *The Global Factory: Analysis and Action for a New Economic Era.* Philadelphia, Penn.: American Friends Service Committee.

Keohane, Robert, and Joseph Nye. 1973. *Transnational Relations and World Politics.* Cambridge, Mass.: Harvard University Press.

Knox, Paul L. 1995. "World Cities in a World-System." In *World Cities in a World-System*, edited by Paul L. Knox and Peter J. Taylor. Cambridge: Cambridge University Press.

Lee, E. S. 1966. "A Theory of Migration," *Demography* 347–57.

Lipietz, A. 1986. "New Tendencies in the International Division of Labour: Regimes of Accumulation and Modes of Regulation." In *Production, Work, Territory: The Geographical Anatomy of Industrial Capitalism*, edited by A. Scott and M. Storper. Boston: Allen and Unwin.

Matloff, Norman. 1995. "Debugging Immigration: Immigrants with Computer Skills versus the Domestic Labor Pool," *National Review* 47 (19): 28–30.

———. 1996. "How Immigration Harms Minorities," *Public Interest*.

Moschella, David. 1998. "Foreign IT Workers? The More the Merrier," *Computer World* 32 (12): 38.

Nasscom (National Association of Software and Service Companies). 1999. "The Software Industry in India: A Strategic Review."

Pedraza-Bailey, S. 1990. "Immigration Research: A Conceptual Map," *Social Science History* 14: 43–67.

Porter, M. E. 1990. *The Competitive Advantage of Nations*. London: Macmillan.

Portes, Alejandro. 1978. "Migration and Underdevelopment," *Political Sociology* 81: 48.

Portes, Alejandro, and József Böröcz. 1989. "Contemporary Immigration: Theoretical Perspectives on Its Determinants and Modes of Incorporation," *International Migration Review* 23 (3): 606–31.

Sassen, Saskia. 1997. "Immigration Policy in the Global Economy," *SAIS Review* 17 (2): 1–19.

Schoenberger, E. 1988. "Multinational Corporations and the New International Division of Labor: A Critical Appraisal," *International Regional Science Review*.

Sklair, Leslie. 1995. *Sociology of the Global System*. 2d ed. Baltimore, Md.: Johns Hopkins University Press.

Smith, J. B., and B. Edmonston, eds. 1997. *The New Americans: Economic, Demographic, and Fiscal Effects of Immigration*. Washington, D.C.: National Academy Press.

Zuboff, Shoshana. 1988. *In the Age of the Smart Machine: The Future of Work and Power*. New York: Basil Books.

PART 6

CONCLUSION

14

High-Skilled Immigration and the U.S. National Interest

Marc Rosenblum

I begin this concluding chapter by summarizing the empirical findings of preceding chapters regarding the supply of and demand for high-skilled migrants. This issue cuts to the heart of the debate about high-skilled visa policy. Do employers demand high-skilled immigrants in a push to obtain the most qualified personnel in the world (the "best and brightest" hypothesis), or do employers seek to hold down labor costs by replacing natives with lower-cost immigrants (the "race to the bottom" hypothesis)? The evidence suggests that both practices occur.

Second, having said something about the causes of high-skilled immigration, the chapters in this volume suggest some tentative conclusions about its effects. What do we know about the size and character of high-skilled migrant flows? What are high-skilled migration's effects on U.S. workers and firms? And what are the effects of high-skilled *emigration* on migrant-sending states? I address these questions in the second section of this chapter.

Given what we know about the causes and effects of high-skilled immigration, what policy options exist, and what policies would advance U.S. interests? As I argue in the third section below, it is necessary to place current economic changes in the context of previous industrial revolutions before answering these questions. Whereas growth during previous transitional periods was limited by access to capital and industrial raw materials, the limiting factor of production in the present period is access to high-skilled labor. Thus, to promote wealth and national security, migrant-receiving states must emphasize the re-

I gratefully acknowledge the comments of Wayne Cornelius, Tom Espenshade, Michael Huelshoff, Chris Rudolph, and Idean Salehyan. Remaining errors—as well as policy recommendations—are my own.

cruitment and integration of the best and brightest high-skilled immigrants. The dilemma for policymakers, however, is that a focus on recruitment also implies a race to the bottom; and policymakers should balance these goals against distributive concerns. Nonetheless, labor-importing firms exert disproportionate influence over high-skilled immigration policy, and the 2000 H–1B reforms largely ignored distributive issues.

I conclude with a discussion of how the information revolution and the aspects of high-skilled immigration discussed in this volume fit within a broader context of globalization and changing notions of state sovereignty. In particular, I argue that technology-producing firms *and high-skilled immigrants* are becoming "players" in the international system. These changes also have distributive consequences at national and international levels.

The Supply and Demand of High-Skilled Immigration

The combination of falling transportation costs, dense global social networks, and the diffusion of new technologies to less developed countries has caused a sharp increase in the global supply of potential migrants with high levels of human capital.[1] As Alarcón shows, at least four types of high-skilled immigrants to the United States exist: those who migrated as children and received U.S. education (the so-called 1.5 generation), former employees of U.S. subsidiaries based abroad who enter the United States as employees of these firms, former foreign students who enter the United States on "J" student visas and then take U.S. jobs upon graduating, and the group that Alarcón refers to as "cerebreros": free lance professionals who sell their labor to the highest (global) bidder.[2]

These high-skilled immigrants come disproportionately from India, followed by China and other developing countries in Asia. This distri-

---

[1] Like most of the chapters in this volume, this conclusion focuses on workers in the information technology (IT) sector. Roughly two-thirds of high-skilled immigrants to the United States work directly in computer-related fields, with the remainder divided among biotechnology, higher education, architecture, and other professional fields. As Lowell's figures (this volume) show, 80 percent of the employers who brought in H–1B immigrants in 1999-2000 were in IT industries, up from just 11.4 percent in 1989. Although the focus on IT workers glosses over some differences among immigrants, so does the U.S. policy debate, which also focuses disproportionately on the IT industry. Moreover, many of the features that characterize migrant IT workers extend to high-skilled migrants in other fields.

[2] The term is a play on "braceros"—the short-term migrants to the United States who worked with their *brazos* (Spanish for arms) between 1942 and 1964. "Cerebreros" work with their *cerebros*, Spanish for brains.

bution reflects historical factors in the United States and abroad. On the U.S. side (discussed in this volume by Gurcak et al. and by Alarcón), the closure of the immigration system to most Asian migrants until the 1965 amendments to the Immigration and Nationality Act (INA) ensured that when the system was made more open in 1968, those Asians who wished to immigrate lacked family ties in the United States. Thus initial emigration patterns from Asian countries reflected the skills-based categories then in existence. A second reason high-skilled immigrants come disproportionately from a small number of sending states is that these countries pursued industrial policies, including the development of advanced weapons programs, that created native computer industries. As Alarcón shows, India's promotion of a software industry in the absence of a native hardware industry ensured that programmers would become fluent in numerous programming platforms, making them natural cerebreros.

A final point about the global supply of high-skilled immigrants deserves emphasis: while all of these individuals have a high level of human capital relative to other immigrants, "high-skilled labor" is far from a homogenous category. On the one hand, "elite" immigrants possess the skills and creativity to contribute to the most cutting edge firms in the world. But the majority of high-skilled immigrants—"low-end" immigrants—are simply average individuals with some technical training who find themselves in a tight global labor market.

This bifurcated supply of highly skilled labor is mirrored on the demand side of the equation. High-technology employers echo lobbyists' arguments that firms require expanded access to elite immigrants to remain competitive in the global economy. At its heart, the argument for elite recruitment rests on two relatively uncontroversial premises. First, there is the assertion that rapid changes in existing technology, and the premium that companies place on being the first to bring new products to market, requires firms to maximize their intellectual capital. Indeed, a firm that fails to take every possible step to innovate—including global recruitment—can expect its competitors to drive it out of business.

The second premise behind the claim that high-tech firms require international talent is that there is a shortage of qualified workers in the United States. The chapter by Gurcak et al. confirms that, in fact, math and science programs in U.S. schools *have* fallen behind those of many developing countries. In part, problems in schools reflect long-term trends in which the best U.S. students favor law, business, medicine, and other high-wage careers over the pure and applied sciences.[3] But

---

[3] Thus this is a long-term problem, and firms are not in a position to simply raise wages to recruit more talented U.S. employees. At best, high salaries will lure

even if U.S. schools were the best in the world and the best students consistently obtained high-tech training, the fact that 95 percent of the world lives outside of the United States implies that a large number of foreign workers will always be better and brighter than their U.S. counterparts.

As noted above, however, demand is not limited to these elite immigrants, and most employers of high-skilled immigrants recruit globally in order to hold down labor costs. These high-tech firms are not centers of innovation, but factories that produce lower-cost versions of existing designs. For this reason, despite the fact that the information technology (IT) sector was responsible for half of the growth in the U.S. economy during the 1990s, wages throughout this sector have not come close to keeping up with profits (Espenshade et al. 2000). It should be emphasized that these employers do not necessarily "choose" a race-to-the-bottom business plan, but they are forced by the logic of collective action to accept one. That is, an individual firm that chooses (perhaps for moral reasons) to pay higher wages to a well-qualified native rather than to shop the globe for the cheapest labor available is sure to be undercut by the majority of firms that do not make this choice.[4] Thus at both ends of the production spectrum, producers must recruit immigrant labor; and demand for elite *and* low-end high-skilled immigrants exists.

A cross-national comparison of high-tech immigration and industrial policies confirms that competition for high-skilled immigrants is not limited to the United States. Other settler countries like Australia and Canada have replaced family-based immigration regimes with point systems that favor high-skilled workers. The chapters here by Boyd and Chakravartty describe aggressive efforts by Canada and India to recruit new high-skilled immigrants (in the Canadian case), and to encourage return migration (in the Indian case). Barry Naughton (2000) argues that China joins India in seeing skilled emigrants as a latent resource, and China supports its IT industry through appeals to nationalism and investment opportunities to attract migrant remittances and migrants themselves.

---

higher-quality students into science programs and eventually result in more funding for science in U.S. schools and universities, but the demand for talented employees is immediate.

[4] The same logic of collective action makes it difficult for high-minded employers of undocumented immigrants to choose to pay higher salaries or improve working conditions to attract legal immigrants or natives; weak enforcement ensures that their competition will then undercut them.

The Effects of High-Skilled Immigration

In addition to addressing the supply and demand—or causes—of high-skilled migration, this volume suggests tentative conclusions about its effects, including demographic and economic characteristics of high-skilled migrants, and the effects of high-skilled immigration on U.S. workers, U.S. firms, and migrant-sending states.

Characteristics of High-Skilled Immigrants

Ironically, there is no firm consensus on the basic issue of how many high-skilled immigrants actually live in the United States. Although the U.S. Immigration and Naturalization Service keeps official statistics on how many high-skilled migrants enter and how many adjust their status, no effort has been made to monitor the number who depart or who illegally overstay their visas. Lowell's chapter in this volume represents an important first effort to estimate these numbers in the case of H–1B visa holders. Taking account of legislative changes completed as this book was going to press (and assuming no future legislative changes), Lowell would estimate that the 250,000 unadjusted H–1Bs residing in the United States in the year 2000 would climb to 800,000 during the first decade of the millennium, and that a roughly equal number would adjust to legal permanent resident (LPR) status.

There is also some confusion regarding the precise role played by high-skilled immigrants in the U.S. economy—partly due to the fact that most analyses are based on data from the 1990 census, data that predate the IT boom. But even at that point, immigrants played a significant role in the U.S. economy, making up 23 percent of the population of Santa Clara County (the heart of Silicon Valley) and 30 percent of its high-tech workers in 1990. More generally, immigrants in 1990 represented 6 percent of the scientists in the United States, 10 percent of the computer scientists, and 12 percent of the engineers. More research on these basic demographic questions, using more recent data, is clearly needed, however.

It has become commonplace to observe that immigrants in general have an "hourglass" demographic spread, with large numbers at the top and bottom of the human capital scale, but few in the middle. By definition, high-skilled immigrants represent the upper portion of this spread, especially in terms of their education level, which is higher than that of their native U.S. co-workers. Thus, according to Gurcak et al., while 18 percent of native-born engineers and 16 percent of native-born computer scientists have advanced degrees, the numbers are 41 percent in both categories for immigrants. And while immigrants constitute only 9.8 percent of the engineers in the United States with bachelor's degrees, they represent 23 percent of the engineers with doctorates and 28 percent of the engineering Ph.D.s in research positions (Saxenian, this volume). These numbers, too, have climbed and continue to do so as immigrants make up an increasingly large share of U.S. graduate students. On the other hand, among all H–1B visa holders, only 56 percent have bachelor's degrees or higher, and only 8 percent have the foreign equivalents of doctoral degrees (Bach, this volume).[5]

In three other ways, high-skilled immigrants resemble other migrants to the United States. First, as several volume contributors noted (Alarcón, Lofstrom, and Saxenian), high-skilled immigrants settle in geographic enclaves and appear to fill specific economic niches. This pattern is reinforced in the IT industry given its existing propensity toward geographic concentration in a handful of locations within the United States and around the globe.[6] As Saxenian documents, Indian and Chinese immigrant communities in the United States have formed a number of ethnic business associations which mirror those found among traditional immigrant groups in other industries. It is not surprising, given these ethnic enclaves, that Boyd identifies variation in wages and career paths as a function of migrants' countries of origin.

A second way in which high-skilled immigrants resemble other immigrants is that they face numerous disadvantages relative to native workers. As Boyd's quantitative analysis shows, high-skilled immigrants in Canada are more likely to be unemployed, more likely to be overqualified for their positions, and less likely to be in management positions. Although Gurcak et al. cite ambiguous evidence about a "glass ceiling" for high-skilled immigrants in the United States, Saxenian shows that immigrants to the United States face similar obstacles as those described by Boyd in the Canadian case. Migrants face barriers to advancement in part as a result of their shorter tenure and language barriers, but also because of hard-to-measure factors like racism, cultural differences, and so on. Second-class status at the workplace also reflects legislative biases that ensure that the majority of high-skilled immigrants enter as non-immigrant visa holders rather than as permanent residents (see below). As "non-immigrants," H–1Bs have limited legal rights (see Schuck 1998), and they are likely to suffer depressed

---

[5] While most (55 percent) H–1B visa holders work directly in computer-related fields (followed, at 15 percent, by engineering, architecture, and surveying), many H–1B visa holders work in less training intensive jobs, including as fashion models, administrators, and so on.

[6] In the U.S. case, Northern California's Silicon Valley is joined by Boston's Route 128, North Carolina's Research Triangle, Austin, Texas, and the San Diego area as centers of IT production.

wages as a result.[7] Although most H–1Bs eventually adjust to permanent resident status, it typically takes one or more years to initiate the process and up to three years to complete it. Moreover, prior to the year 2000 H–1B reforms, visa holders were prohibited from changing jobs while adjustment procedures were pending, severely compromising their wage bargaining position.

The Labor Market

The third way in which high-skilled immigrants resemble other migrants is that it is difficult to assess their precise impact on native wages. On the one hand, evidence in this volume supports previous studies reviewed by Gurcak et al. that found little evidence that immigration causes wages to fall significantly in any sector of the U.S. economy (also see Borjas 1994). There is no evidence than high-tech employees break H–1B wage rules (that is, by paying less than the prevailing wage) with any frequency, and Lofstrom actually finds that high-skilled immigrants to the United States earn roughly 5 percent *more* than natives. Moreover, some high-skilled immigrants—like their low-tech counterparts—raise native wages by creating new jobs. Lofstrom finds that one in five high-tech immigrants is self-employed, and he argues that most of these self-employed immigrants are entrepreneurs who create new jobs. Saxenian estimates that almost one in four Silicon Valley technology firms is owned by an individual with a Chinese or Indian surname; and prominent new economy firms—including Hotmail, Yahoo!, and Sun Microsystems—were founded by immigrants.

Nonetheless, there is some truth to the common-sense economics observation that more workers must drive down the price of labor. Wage-depressing effects are exacerbated if young workers from developing countries are willing to put in long hours for lower pay than their U.S. counterparts.[8] Thus, while immigrants earn more absolutely, Lofstrom finds that they earn 7 percent *less* than natives when controlling for education, geographic location, and other factors. Likewise, Boyd finds that high-skilled immigrants to Canada are much more likely to

---

[7] To my knowledge, neither Lofstrom (this volume) nor anyone else has used an econometric model to estimate the wage benefit to skilled migrants of obtaining LPR status, while controlling for tenure in the United States and other factors.

[8] Younger immigrants bring newer technological skills, a fact that makes it difficult for older U.S. programmers to prove allegations of age discrimination. Many companies see a double benefit in replacing high-salaried employees with out-of-date formal training, with low-salaried young immigrants who have cutting-edge training.

be in the "contingent sector," employed as low-wage subcontractors or temporary workers.[9] Moreover, these studies underestimate wage depression by ignoring the fact that immigrants—especially those with temporary visas—are much less likely to receive benefits packages. Even the contribution of immigrant entrepreneurs must be qualified: although high-tech immigrants are likely to be entrepreneurial, they are still less likely than native high-tech workers to start new businesses. Moreover, immigrant entrepreneurs are much more likely to employ other immigrants than they are to employ natives, limiting the positive effects of immigration on native wages.

In sum, the most definitive conclusion this volume offers on wages is that the overall effect of high-tech immigrants on the U.S. labor market is poorly understood. More research is needed. Much of the conflicting evidence appears to reflect the bifurcation of the high-tech labor market discussed above: while low-end, high-skilled immigrants depress wages, elite immigrants have been highly successful as entrepreneurs.[10] This trend toward a bifurcated labor market extends beyond the high-tech sector, and the availability of immigrants is only a small part of the broad problem.

High-Tech Firms

Turning to U.S. firms, there is evidence of both unmet demand for high-skilled immigrants and great frustration with existing programs. On a basic level, the inability of the H–1B program to keep up with employer demand is testimony to the popularity of the program. High-technology employers benefit from the availability of foreign labor whether firms are innovators who demand the best and brightest workers or low-end manufacturers seeking to depress wages. Foreign nationals also provide firms with insight into foreign markets. Finally, Aneesh (this volume) notes that, just as traditional manufacturers have turned to "just in time" inventory as a way to cut costs, the H–1B program offers firms flexibility in their labor supply. Temporary workers may be hired and fired quickly, without long-term commitments or benefit packages.

---

[9] In general, wages in the contingent sector have risen more slowly—or failed to rise at all—in comparison to the rest of the IT industry. As Aneesh (this volume) argues, however, there is also a subset of true cerebreros able to sell their services at the highest industry rates on a project-by-project basis.

[10] Similarly, low-end H–1B workers have facilitated the outsourcing of high-tech production to low-wage body shops; but the *shortage* of H–1B workers has contributed to the growth of offshore body shops, with an even greater depressing effect on U.S. wages.

On the other hand, even greater than employers' desire to expand the H–1B program is, perhaps, their desire to streamline it. Many high-tech firms have hired full-time in-house immigration specialists to help their employees navigate the maze of paperwork involved in an LPR application.[11] High-tech firms complain of 90–day waiting periods (lightening quick, in INS time) between the beginning of the application process for a specific individual and the delivery of the worker. Just as the ability to hire the best employee may make or break a project, firms argue, the ability to hire someone *immediately* is often essential. Along with the waiting period comes a great deal of uncertainty. What if needs change in 90 days? What if the cap is reached in the next 90 days? What if the worker received a better offer in that time? Thus, as popular as the H–1B program is, firms may feel compelled to hire a less-qualified but more readily available U.S. resident when an important project arises.[12]

Immigration into high-tech industry is mirrored at research universities; 40 percent of U.S. doctorates awarded in 1995 went to foreign-born students. Here, too, immigrants appear to have somewhat complex effects on U.S. markets. On the one hand, the abundance of foreign-born students may contribute to falling native enrollment rates, and to falling minority enrollment in particular. But at the same time, falling native enrollment is self-reinforcing; and many academic departments are now dependent on immigrants to maintain a critical mass of teachers and researchers. Thus immigration has closed doors to some native students, but cuts in immigration would likely contribute to further closure of academic positions overall.

Migrant-Sending States

Finally, high-skilled immigration is an issue for migrant-sending states. If actions by India, China, and other sending countries in support of their own educational systems and software industries have been partly responsible for the creation of a high-skilled migrant class, then the outflow of well-educated professionals represents lost resources to

---

[11] One San Diego employer provides foreign workers with a 20–page flowchart to describe the adjustment process.

[12] Indeed, the waiting period biases the H–1B program against best-and-brightest employers, and in favor of race-to-the-bottom employers because the latter's needs are more predictable: a medium-skilled programmer will always be in demand at a low-end body shop.

these countries. Chakravartty and Iqbal document growing skilled labor shortages in India and Canada, respectively.[13]

However, it is still early in the history of this particular migratory flow, and as Saxenian observes, it is unclear whether the outflow of high-tech workers from developing countries represents "brain drain" or "brain circulation." Chakravartty and Iqbal show that countries take seriously the project of encouraging their "latent resources" to come home as entrepreneur-heroes, and they have demonstrated some success in attracting back U.S.–trained talent. In many cases—most notably China—it appears that the return migration pattern is still developing, and it is not yet clear what the equilibrium emigration-immigration level will be.[14] Even migrants who do not return to their countries of origin may play an important role in sending-state development by investing in home-country companies and by providing business linkages.[15]

High-Skilled Immigration Policy: Issues and Answers

Up to now, I have reviewed the general causes and effects of high-skilled immigration. There is worldwide supply of and demand for high-skilled workers at the present time, and their movement has immediate effects in migrant-sending and migrant-receiving states. But an implicit goal of this volume is to evaluate the extent to which these patterns are desirable in some sense, and whether U.S. high-skilled immigration policy does or can improve outcomes.[16] In this section, I argue that the expansion of high-skilled immigration has occurred within the context of a "third industrial revolution," and that analysts and policymakers must take these economic changes into account when

---

[13] Even though Canada is a net "brain gainer" because it receives more high-tech immigrants than it loses to the United States (by a ratio of 4 to 1), it is a net *loser* by the same ratio if temporary emigrants are included.

[14] Net migration levels may never stabilize because rates of return are a function of relative economic development, as Gurcak et al. show.

[15] Microsoft and Adobe have recently established 24–hour shifts, with engineers in Bangalore, India, picking up where Seattle-ites leave off at the end of the day, and then passing the work back to Seattle twelve hours later, as Aneesh describes. Linkages between Indian programmers in India and in the United States undoubtedly facilitated this arrangement.

[16] Although economic and demographic pushes and pulls, as well as social networks, are the underlying causes of international migration, there is no question that immigration *policy* further affects the costs and benefits of migrating. As Alarcón and Lowell show (this volume), policy decisions have decisively influenced the previous distribution of high-skilled immigration to the United States, and current decisions will have a great impact on its future.

evaluating policy options. I then evaluate the U.S. national interest in immigration, consider policy options, and evaluate the actual reforms enacted in the year 2000.

The Third Industrial Revolution

As in previous periods of mass migration flows—most notably the 1890–1920 period—current demand for high-skilled immigration reflects a profound shift in the world economy, what Thurow (1999) and others have labeled a "third industrial revolution." In this context, policy decisions have important long-term implications.

The first and second industrial revolutions reshaped the balance of power in the international system and sparked the social and political processes that dominated the last two centuries. The first industrial revolution resulted from the development of the steam engine in the late 1700s, making possible large-scale factory production. Industrial production demanded plentiful unskilled labor, but labor supply was not a limiting factor thanks to a steady supply of rural-to-urban (in Europe) and international immigration. But growth was limited by other factors; factories' high fixed start-up costs and the difficulty of transporting coal meant that only states with access to coal and capital—especially England, Germany, and the United States—were in a position to reap the benefits of industrialization in the nineteenth century.

If the steam engine made possible the first industrial revolution, the development of electrical power created the second, allowing the creation of more factories with a wider range of sizes and across a wider geographic spread. Three factors defined the limits of industrial production in this era. First, capital remained a key factor that provided a continuing advantage to core states, with their sophisticated financial markets and high capital reserves. But at the same time, improved communications technology (the telegraph and then the telephone) made capital more mobile, and firms throughout the world had access to capital. A second key factor was the labor to staff new factories, an area in which Europe and Asia had advantages over the settler countries in the Western Hemisphere and Australia. However, because demand was for unskilled labor, large-scale rural-urban and international migration (often aided by official recruitment efforts, as Usdansky and Espenshade describe in this volume) ensured that labor—like capital—was not a limiting factor on industrial growth in most cases.

Thus, in this case, economic growth was mainly limited by a third factor: the ability to make the most of new technology—or intellectual capital. Labor and capital were widespread, but scientific training and support for entrepreneurship were not. For this reason, the United States, which emphasized entrepreneurship, and Germany, with its strong science programs, were the countries most able to practice what Schumpeter (1942) called "creative destruction," and they displaced England as global leaders at the turn of the twentieth century.[17]

How does the third industrial revolution—the information revolution sparked by widespread use of computers and high-technology—compare to the first two? In general, trends already identified have progressed farther during the current period. As in the first two industrial revolutions, access to capital is a limiting factor which provides an advantage to more developed countries. However, just as capital was less discriminatory at the turn of the twentieth century than during the nineteenth, unequal distribution of capital provides even fewer advantages in the twenty-first century because capital markets are more interconnected than ever and because cutting-edge production materials are simply not as costly (relatively) as they were in the past. In the Internet age, anyone with a laptop computer and access to a Web server is in a position to transform the global economy.

As in the previous industrial revolution, then, the limits of growth are determined by the two remaining factors—labor and intellectual capital. But in this case these factors are fused into one, a crucial change in how we conceptualize "land, labor, and capital." In the past, innovation occurred within elite research and development divisions of large firms otherwise staffed by unskilled labor. Now innovation *is* labor, and entire firms at the forefront of the information revolution exist for no purpose other than research and development. For this reason, in contrast to the previous periods, access to skilled labor is the primary limiting factor that will define the geography and long-term distributive effects of the information revolution. Thus, high-skilled immigration policy decisions made in the current period will have implications far beyond the short-range period that typically dominates immigration policy-making.

High-Technology, High-Skilled Immigration and the U.S. National Interest

What is the U.S. national interest in high-skilled immigration during this third industrial revolution?[18] For the purpose of this question, I

---

[17] As Thurow (1999) observes, it was only the outcomes of two world wars that ensured that the 1900s would become the American, not the German, century.

[18] I make two simplifying assumptions in my effort to describe a national interest in high-skilled immigration. First, I consider high-skilled immigration in isolation from low-skilled, family-based, and refugee issues. This arbitrary division is con-

adopt the minimalist assumption that the policies should aim to raise gross national product (GNP) and strengthen national security. Second, I also recognize that immigration has distributive consequences and that policies that maximize wealth may exacerbate inequality (Borjas 1999). Thus, like Borjas, I will assume that a third broad policy goal is to avoid increasing inequality.[19] But as Demetrios Papademetriou (2000) has observed, it is unclear that highly skilled native IT workers deserve the same level of protection as do, say, farmworkers. Does minimizing inequality in this context mean that IT wages should be brought down to the level of wages in other industries? I do not believe it does. Rather, a distributive *problem* occurs if immigrants flood the labor market and so depress wages, causing a socially undesirable transfer from labor to capital. Thus by "inequality" I refer mainly to the gap between owners of capital and labor. And the third broad immigration policy goal, consistent with the primary objectives of maximizing national wealth and security, is to maximize wages throughout the labor market, starting with those of immigrants themselves.

It follows from my discussion of the third industrial revolution that, in order to promote national wealth and security, the first principle of high-skilled immigration policy must be to ensure that U.S. employers have sufficient access to high-skilled labor. In short, all countries have a national interest in assuring access to labor when true shortages exist, a point recognized by U.S. policymakers during previous periods of industrial expansion (see Usdansky and Espenshade, this volume) and by European states in the immediate post–World War II period. Access to labor is the most important limit on current and future growth in the high-tech sector—the sector responsible for half of all U.S. growth during the booming 1990s—and the availability of high-skilled labor is highly responsive to policy manipulation.

---

sistent with Congress's approach to the issue, and not with that of the Clinton administration (as explained by Bach, this volume). I choose to adopt Congress's perspective as a way to speak directly to the existing policy debate. Second, I also limit my evaluation to economic and security issues, ignoring the far less objective normative and ideational issues which, nonetheless, also influence policy-making.

[19] I do not assume that states always, or even usually, pursue the national interest in this sense of the term. That is, I am *not* employing the term "national interest" in the sense that Krasner (1978) and other "statists" use it, which is the objectives pursued by central state actors. Rather, like Borjas (1999), I recognize that it is not possible to evaluate U.S. immigration (or other) policies without *assuming* a standard against which policies should be judged. As Borjas points out, the standard could just as easily be defined at a global level (i.e., maximizing global welfare and minimizing global inequality), or it could consider efficiency without regard to distributive effects. I have accepted Borjas's assumptions because they are a reasonable shorthand for the actual terms of the U.S. immigration policy debate.

From a security perspective, high-skilled immigrants make important contributions by increasing the U.S. advantage in sophisticated computer modeling and other cutting-edge technologies that are at the heart of modern weapons design and military equipment. Moreover, if I am correct that high-skilled immigrants promote immediate and long-term economic growth, then immigrants provide important relative gains for the United States over its rivals; and by assumption, these economic gains translate into military ones. To the extent that India and China are the two most likely future challengers to American hegemony, as many argue (see, for example, Kugler, Tammen, and Swaminathan 2000), then high-skilled immigrants from these states represent an even more significant security transfer.

As already noted, however, too much access to immigrant labor will eventually drive wages down in high-skilled sectors, with ripple effects throughout the labor market. Thus, in order to minimize negative distributive effects—and also to enhance the contribution immigrants make to national wealth and security—two additional principles should guide policy-making. First, immigration policy should take steps to promote high-skilled immigrant integration. By facilitating integration, policy would promote long-term relocation by high-skilled immigrants in the United States. Migrant integration engenders long-term relationships between high-skilled individuals and U.S. firms, and it increases the likelihood that high-skilled individuals' future jobs will also be in the United States. Long-term immigrants also generate positive economic externalities by purchasing houses and other durable goods, and they are more likely to become entrepreneurs who create new jobs. To the extent that high-technology production has spillover effects for national security, it is highly desirable to promote the long-term residence of high-skilled workers in the United States and to promote their adoption of U.S. citizenship and values.[20] Finally, studies by Lofstrom (this volume) and others have repeatedly shown that immigrants' wages approach parity with native wages only over the course of several years, so downward wage effects are minimized by promoting long-term immigration, rather than a pattern of cyclical immigra-

---

[20] One could argue the opposite, that U.S. security interests demand that high-skilled immigration be minimized, to avoid allowing infiltration by disloyal immigrants into sensitive industries. The history of U.S. policy toward Japanese and German immigrants during World War II, and toward Middle Eastern immigrants more recently, reflects this line of thought. The question is whether the risk of disloyalty outweighs the benefits that loyal immigrants offer (and taking account of the fact that excluding loyal immigrants is a double negative if it causes them to work for weapons programs in rival states instead). Nonetheless, if immigrants are to work in sensitive U.S. industries, promoting immigrant integration can only improve immigrant loyalty.

tion with a steady flow in and out. Thus, overall, the faster and more completely immigrants become integrated within the United States, the more they contribute to U.S. wealth and security and the less they bring down wages.

A final principle to guide high-skilled immigration policy-making is that policy should maximize the "quality" of immigrants admitted within the high-skilled category. While elite high-skilled immigrants bring skills that are otherwise difficult or impossible to find in the United States, low-end immigrants simply lower the price on high-tech skills that are *already* available in the United States. Thus elite immigrants make the greatest contribution to U.S. wealth and security, and their unique skills promote greater equality (by raising wage levels); but low-end immigrants contribute little to U.S. wealth and security, while transferring wealth to owners of capital and so exacerbating inequality. But maximizing migrant skill levels does not come without costs. In the absence of plentiful low-end, high-skilled labor, some portion of high-tech manufacturing currently done in the United States will be moved offshore, where wages and working conditions will almost certainly be below U.S. standards. In a globally connected market, therefore, the ability to protect wages by limiting low-end immigration is inherently limited. And the loss of these jobs not only depresses high-tech wages, but it also has ripple effects throughout the low-skilled service sector, which supports high-tech production, as Zlolniski's chapter shows. Thus assuring sufficient access to high-skilled immigrants and promoting their integration are more important principles than is maximizing immigrants' skill level.

One final point should be made in anticipation of a likely criticism: while it is desirable in the long run to meet skilled labor demands by improving the domestic "best and brightest industry" (that is, by improving science and technology training in U.S. schools) or by promoting on-line solutions ("virtual migration," discussed further below), high-skilled immigration per se has its own advantages. First, in an era in which product life cycles may be measured in months or weeks, improving U.S. schools and attracting smart students to computer science classes will not produce a large number of highly skilled workers quickly enough to maximize growth and competitiveness. Second, the job growth produced within immigrant enclaves is likely to increase as immigrant communities become better established. Third, the creative process is cooperative, and bringing together a diverse group of brilliant people creates synergistic effects. Finally, face-to-face time (as opposed to virtual migration) also minimizes communication and principal-agent problems within firms.

In sum, if the U.S. national interest in high-skilled immigration is to maximize wealth and security while minimizing negative wage effects, policies should be guided by three principles, in decreasing order of priority: the recruitment of high-technology labor, the promotion of immigrant integration, and maximization of the "quality" of the high-skilled immigrants admitted.

Policy Options

The United States' demand for high-skilled labor could be met in at least three (not mutually exclusive) ways: through temporary high-skilled immigration, through permanent high-skilled migration, and through virtual migration. Given the goals and principles identified above, permanent immigration would be the most desirable approach.

The H–1B Visa Program

The 1952 Immigration and Nationality Act (INA) established the H–1 visa to allow migrants "of distinguished merit and ability" to come to the United States for one to three years to perform specific temporary jobs.[21] In 1970 Congress passed legislation to allow temporary migrants to work in *permanent* positions, and concern grew in the following years that H–1 immigrants were being recruited for "ordinary" entry-level jobs (against the intent of the legislation). Between 1989 and 1990, the H–1 visa was broken up into H–1A visas for nurses, O and P visas for persons with extraordinary skills and internationally recognized athletes and entertainers, and H–1B visas for "temporary workers of distinguished merit and ability" performing services other than as a registered nurse. H–1B employers were required to establish the existence of a labor shortage and to provide prevailing wages and working conditions. The program was originally capped at 65,000 per year, but in 1998 the cap was raised to 115,000 for 1999 and 2000, and to 107,500 for 2001. In 2000, the cap was raised to 195,000 for each year between 2001 and 2003.

How well does the H–1B visa system perform in terms of meeting the demand for high-tech labor, encouraging migrant integration, and minimizing downward wage effects? First, as noted above, the H–1B program has been popular with employers because (relative to the permanent visa system, discussed below) it is a quick way to obtain workers. Although the program has not met the demand for labor in recent years, the shortage of H–1B visas will very likely be solved by the expansion of the program under the H–1B reforms of 2000.

On the other hand, the H–1B program includes several features— only some of which will be addressed when the 2000 reforms are im-

---

[21] See Lowell, this volume, for a more detailed history of H–1 visas.

plemented—that discourage recruitment of the highest quality workers, inhibit migrant integration, and exacerbate downward wage effects. First, the whole U.S. philosophy of guest-worker visas—privatizing the immigrant selection process—places the fox in charge of the hen house and so encourages low-end firms to recruit low-end individuals.[22] Second, by encouraging short-term immigration, the H–1B program discourages true wage parity (which, we have seen, occurs only after immigrants have spent several years in the United States), and it discourages long-term migrant investments, entrepreneurship, and other positive wealth and security externalities associated with immigrant integration. In theory, the H–1B program addresses these problems by allowing immigrants to adjust to LPR status; but in practice, the adjustment process typically lasts three years or more, and has been described as "Kafka-esque" in its bureaucratic complexity and apparent arbitrariness. When visas expire during this period of legal limbo, immigrants have been forced to choose between re-applying for entry a year later, or remaining in the United States as undocumented immigrants. Finally, during the *years* in which LPR adjustment is pending, immigrants have been barred from changing jobs, a prohibition that reduces national wealth by interfering with the market allocation of labor and sharply reduces immigrants' ability to bargain for fair wages, with negative effects throughout the high-tech labor market.

Skills-based Permanent Immigration

A second alternative is to issue more skills-based permanent visas.[23] Since the passage of the INA, a proportion of permanent visas to enter the United States ("green cards") has been reserved, within per-country limits, for "those with special skills or education deemed important to the U.S. economy."[24] The 1952 Act established that 50 percent of a total permanent immigration level of 154,000 would be skills-based, a figure lowered to less than 20 percent of 290,000 total permanent migrants in 1965. In 1990, the skills-based and family-based systems were separated, and an annual quota of 140,000 skills-based visa positions was established, with most of these visas designated for high-skilled and professional workers and their families.

---

[22] The policy presents the INS with a classic principal-agent problem: by delegating immigrant screening to employers, the INS theoretically takes advantage of firms' greater knowledge of their own needs and of workers' skills; but that very information asymmetry ensures that firms are also in a position to misrepresent their own needs and workers' skills.

[23] See Usdansky and Espenshade, this volume, for a thorough overview of the history of skills-based U.S. immigration policy.

[24] The remainder have been reserved for family members of U.S. citizens and permanent residents and, between 1965 and 1980, for refugees.

How does the skills-based permanent immigration system function in terms of the three goals identified above? Although the 1990 Immigration Act more than doubled the number of high-skilled permanent visas that may be allotted each year, the 140,000 visas theoretically available are inadequate. First, the actual number of skills-based green cards that go to high-tech workers is lower than that because high bureaucratic hurdles and 20,000–per-country caps mean that only half of the 140,000 permanent skills-based visas are used each year. Second, between a third and a half of these visas actually go to the *families* of high-skilled immigrants, and 20,000 go to low-skilled immigrants and their families, leaving only 50,000 or so permanent visas available. Third, the waiting period to obtain a skills-based green card can last anywhere from several months to several years, and many U.S. firms and foreign workers are unwilling to wait while the process runs its course.

On the other hand, the permanent visa system scores well in terms of minimizing negative distributive effects and promoting immigrant integration. By definition, these immigrants come to the United States with the intention of settling on a permanent basis, and they are, therefore, more likely to make major purchases, invest in businesses, and generate additional positive externalities, as discussed above. Legal permanent residents may also apply for citizenship after five years, and these individuals are more likely than "non-immigrants" to become national security assets. As permanent immigrants, green-card holders also enjoy the same labor rights as do U.S. citizens, including the ability to change jobs at will, to strike, and so on. By assumption, therefore, green-card holders face fewer artificial constraints on their wage bargaining, and they have less of a negative effect on wages. Thus, while the permanent immigration system has not kept pace with the supply and demand of high-skilled labor, permanent immigrants appear to make a greater per capita contribution to U.S. wealth and security, with fewer negative wage effects.

Virtual Migration

A third approach to meeting U.S. demand for high-skilled labor is what Aneesh (this volume) refers to as "virtual migration." Rather than bringing skilled workers to high-technology firms *or* moving high-technology factories abroad, this approach would leave both where they are while sending high-technology *tasks* to the workers. To users of high-technology, this high-tech solution has immediate appeal. Indeed, as Sastri (2000) observes, the Internet was developed with precisely this sort of information exchange in mind. Sastri proposes a virtual marketplace, or "intellectual capital exchange," in which problems and solutions could be posted and traded on-line. Aneesh's case studies—as well as the strong performance of business-to-business e-commerce and of the open-source-code movement—suggest that such a solution is quite feasible within the private sector.

On one level, virtual migration appears to be an ideal way to satisfy the U.S. national interest in immigration. A worldwide intellectual capital exchange would give U.S. firms unlimited access to the best minds in the world. It is still likely that firms would recruit a limited number of individuals when production processes need to be fully internalized, or because certain workers have proved to be especially valuable to the company over time; but wide-scale on-line knowledge exchange would greatly reduce the demand for imported skilled labor. As a result, most of the questions associated with migrant recruitment and integration would be sidestepped altogether.

But a move toward more virtual migration would not be without costs from a U.S. national interest perspective. If bringing in fewer workers promises to limit the downward effect of migration on wages, shipping out more tasks promises to increase it, and the state (as well as national governments around the world) will have no recourse to regulate wages or working conditions. On the contrary, firms will shop for the lowest regulatory bidder—by locating their Web servers and administrative offices in whatever country imposes the least restrictions on their actions—resulting in an international race to the bottom more damaging to U.S. interests than anything seen domestically. Finally, greater transnationalization of firms and of the labor process represents an additional threat to U.S. security interests because the spillover benefits of high-technology innovation will no longer be captured.

Policy Recommendations

In sum, each of the three options discussed has strengths and weaknesses. A system relying on virtual migration is most likely to assure a steady supply of high-skilled labor. But by allowing skilled workers to remain in their countries of origin, this is the least desirable solution from a U.S. national interest perspective because it minimizes domestic job creation. A solution that emphasizes temporary immigration does well at providing a sufficient quantity of labor, but historically it has failed to promote migrant integration and has created unnecessary negative wage effects. For these reasons, a U.S. policy of promoting temporary immigration also probably discourages some elite workers from immigrating. Finally, skills-based permanent immigration has been slow and limited in scope, but it is the most successful at limiting downward wage effects and promoting immigrant integration. Assuming most high-skilled immigrants want the unambiguous *option* of becoming U.S. citizens, then allowing them to enter as legal permanent residents also facilitates higher-quality immigrant recruitment.[25] Thus, if the U.S. interest in high-skilled immigration is to promote the recruitment and integration of the best and brightest high-tech workers in the world, while minimizing the negative wage effects of the expanding labor market, the ideal solution would be to expand and streamline skills-based front-door immigration, while limiting or even doing away with temporary high-skilled immigration.[26]

Four objections may be raised to this proposal. First, the inability of the INS to process visa applications quickly—and the long waiting list for permanent visas—were incentives for creating and expanding the H–1B program in the first place; perhaps it is not possible to process visa applications quickly enough to meet demand. But the same technology and staffing power that allow H–1B visas to be processed in 90 days would surely allow the processing of permanent visas without major adjustments. A second objection is the concern that a radical expansion of permanent skills-based immigration would result in too much permanent immigration to the United States. This may be true, but it should be remembered that most "temporary" high-skilled immigrants to the United States also eventually adjust their status, and all enter with the promise of that option. The only difference is that under the current system they must endure a waiting period of several years before doing so, and this waiting period is detrimental to U.S. and immigrant workers and to the generation of U.S. wealth and security. If it is desirable to lower the level of permanent immigration to the United States, it is not appropriate to do so through the accounting trick of calling hundreds of thousands of (future) permanent immigrants "temporary."

A third objection to replacing the H–1B visa system with a permanent visa system is that the demand for high-skilled labor may change and the H–1B system provides desired flexibility. But it is just as feasible to pass a law that raises skills-based permanent visa quotas for a limited time as it is to raise H–1B caps for a limited time. Given that H–1B visa holders enter with the intent to naturalize, and the promised

---

[25] It is safe to assume that most immigrants would prefer entering on green cards, rather than with H–1B visas, and that none *prefer* temporary status. Regardless of an immigrant's specific preferences, green cards provide more options and a broader set of legal protections, with no disadvantages. More than 60 percent of current H–1B visa immigrants eventually adjust to LPR status despite the high bureaucratic hurdles and long waits to do so.

[26] Donnelly (2000) makes a similar recommendation, though he also raises questions about the fairness of moving skills-based immigrants—temporary or permanent—ahead of the hundreds of thousands of individuals waiting for family-based visas. I assume away this concern by focusing on an economic/security definition of the national interest.

ability to do so, the only sense in which the current program is more "flexible" is that unpredictable numbers of immigrants become frustrated by INS bureaucracy before the paperwork to adjust their status is processed.

The final objection that could be made to the plan I have described is that it does not give sufficient consideration to the needs of migrant-sending countries or to those of poor U.S. residents. In response to the former point, although U.S. policymakers can and should at times consider the international effects of U.S. immigration policy, they have not done so in this policy discussion, and I have attempted to adopt a narrow definition of the U.S. national interest to keep my analysis consistent with the actual policy debate. Regarding the question of distributive effects among U.S. workers, I believe the choice in the high-tech industry is between importing workers or exporting jobs. If I am correct, then all high-skilled immigration policy can do is seek to maximize the positive externalities from the jobs created, and to minimize immigrants' downward effects on wages.

How would a program to replace H–1B visas with greater skills-based permanent immigration function? Given the global distribution of high-tech workers available, this approach would require lifting current per-country caps. Increasing skills-based immigration does not necessarily imply imposing new limits on family-based visas if the former are issued for the economic/security reasons discussed here, and the latter are issued in pursuit of the normative goal of family re-unification. In fact, however, many U.S. legislators and voters will inevitably see a trade-off between skills-based and family-based immigration. If these immigrants do tap the same pool of visas, one rational way to allocate them, as Borjas (1999) argues, is through a "point system," similar to those used in Canada, Australia, and New Zealand. In such a system, immigrants would get a number of points for each desirable characteristic they possess: high-tech skills, years of education, close family member in the United States, and so on. Points could be awarded for specific job skills to retain—or reject—current H–1B visa allowances for fashion models and non-technical administrators. Then the question of how visas are allocated is simply a function of how many points are awarded for each desirable characteristic; and the overall flow level is set by how many points are required for entry.

In sum, if the U.S. national interest is to promote wealth and security without depressing wages, then immigration policy should be guided by the principles of assuring access, encouraging integration, and maximizing skill levels. The most rational policy for pursuing these goals would be to expand permanent skills-based immigration and to limit, or even eliminate, the H–1B visa program. This response would require the reallocation of INS personnel so that permanent skills-based visas could be issued as efficiently as H–1B visas are processed under the current policy regime. A focus on permanent immigration would facilitate the recruitment of the best and brightest high-tech workers around the world; immigrants would have less of a depressing effect on U.S. wages; immigrants would be more able and willing to make long-term investments in the United States, including through job-creating entrepreneurial activities; and immigrants would be more likely to become citizens and thus contribute to U.S. national security.[27]

The 2000 H–1B Reforms

On October 3, 2000, the U.S. Senate passed the American Competitiveness in the Twenty-First Century Act 96-1; the House voted later that night on an unusual voice vote (with fewer than 50 members present) to pass the Senate's version of the bill. The 2000 reforms to the H–1B visa program address some, but not all, of the concerns raised above. First, the bill greatly expands the number of temporary high-skilled visas available, raising the overall cap to 195,000 for each of the years 2000 through 2002, and offering non-quota H–1B visas to thousands of university and non-profit employees as well as recent advanced degree graduates of U.S. universities. Second, the bill takes a small step to reduce the backlog in H–1B adjustment to LPR status petitions by removing some restrictions on the unequal distribution of high-skilled permanent visas; but backlogs will remain for high-flow countries given that the overall cap of 20,000 visas per country per year will remain in place. And third, the bill makes two changes designed to make these long backlogs less onerous: allowing immigrants to extend their temporary visas indefinitely once they have filed for LPR status, and allowing H–1B visa holders to change jobs while an adjustment petition is pending.

In terms of the goals outlined above, the 2000 reforms to the H–1B program took strong steps to ensure that sufficient numbers of immigrants are available—and much weaker steps to promote integration, maximize the quality of immigrants admitted, and minimize negative wage effects. In particular, while expanding H–1B admissions but failing to eliminate per-country caps or to radically alter the INS adjustment bureaucracy, the 2000 legislation guarantees that the number of "temporary non-immigrants" will continue to expand far faster than

---

[27] Promoting the long-term integration of high-skilled immigrants is especially important from a national security perspective given that these immigrants come disproportionately from China and India, the two countries poised to become great powers in the twenty-first century (see Kugler, Tammen, and Swaminathan 2000).

will the LPR visas made available to them. Even though these non-residents will at least be allowed to change jobs, they will remain in a state of limbo, with limited legal rights, a weaker wage bargaining position, and less ability to make long-term plans. Moreover, the legislation missed an opportunity to enhance immigrant quality, rejecting the Clinton administration's proposal to raise fees on H–1B visas (as a deterrent to recruitment of low-end immigrants) and to require that a proportion of H–1B visa recipients hold advanced degrees.

Analysis

What accounts for the difference between my analysis of the U.S. national interest in high-skilled immigration and Congress's actions on the subject? Why was the H–1B program so greatly expanded while permanent immigration remained unchanged? In short, high-tech firms have captured this aspect of the policy-making process, and they do not share my concerns about the distributive effects of high-skilled immigration policy. Indeed, unwieldy and time-consuming adjustment-to-status procedures are a direct transfer from immigrants and the public at large to high-technology firms. Lax screening procedures and low H–1B visa fees may promote a race to the bottom in high-technology wages and lower the overall quality of immigrants admitted, but this, too, is a boon for high-tech employers. Finally, although the largest high-tech firms are able to establish satellite offices and so benefit from virtual migration, most employers prefer the option of bringing individuals into the firm to minimize agency problems. A totally free-market (virtual migration) solution allows high-skilled labor to sell their services to the highest bidder on a job-by-job basis, and this would, therefore, represent a relative transfer of power from firms to labor.

For these reasons, a diverse group of "high-technology firms" was able to overcome potential collective action problems and present a united front to legislators, demanding expanded caps, low fees, minimal screening of immigrants, and few changes to facilitate immigrant adjustment.[28] This unity of preference—along with geographic concentration, substantial financial resources, and access to cutting-edge communication technology—made high-tech firms a perfect example of a privileged group, in Olson's (1964) sense of the term.

---

[28] In game theory terms, the policy outcome weakly dominates all others for all high-tech firms, and so is a stable policy equilibrium. That is, all the firms that have relied on H–1B labor consider this combination of policies to be better than, or at least as good as, any other option discussed above, so opponents of the H–1B reforms had no ability to exploit cleavages within the employer sector.

In contrast, the actors who would benefit from a policy that emphasizes permanent immigration or virtual migration are latent groups without unified preferences, and they face high obstacles to being an effective lobby. In the case of an emphasis on permanent immigration, the most concentrated beneficiaries would be high-skilled immigrants—hundreds of thousands of individuals from dozens of different countries, with a wide variety of skill levels and professional backgrounds, and without peak associations that engage in politics. Moreover, by definition, these immigrants are non-residents of the United States, meaning they are no policymaker's constituents. The other beneficiaries of replacing temporary with permanent immigrants would be the members of the general public, who would benefit from greater productivity and from the contributions that LPRs and citizens make to civil society. It goes without saying that the general public is poorly equipped to influence policy-making in this issue area.

Finally, while large firms are already able to exploit virtual migration without legislative assistance, smaller U.S. high-tech firms that might employ virtual migrants if legislation somehow facilitated such a move would face stiffer competition in a truly global market. A major move to virtual migration would also limit the positive security externalities the United States captures from high-tech production. Thus the main beneficiaries of a move to virtual migration would be foreign high-skilled labor (which is powerless in the policy debate for the reasons discussed above), and the migrant-sending states from which their brains would no longer be drained. Although migrant-sending states often seek to influence U.S. immigration policy, international influence on U.S. immigration policy depends on two factors. First, sending-state influence declines as the domestic salience of an immigration issue increases; and H–1B issues have been highly salient within the mainstream media and for the major political parties. Second, sending-state influence is greatest when it overlaps with the president's foreign policy agenda and his concerns about national security.[29] In this case, the negative security externalities of virtual migration would be a hindrance to the president supporting sending-state lobbying for virtual migration.

---

[29] Thus Mexico was highly effective at influencing bilateral *bracero* agreements during World War II and the Korean War largely because the executive branch perceived a shortage of Mexican labor as a serious national security threat to the United States (see Rosenblum 2000).

In this case, Clinton sought to link migration relief for Central America to the H–1B legislation, largely for foreign policy reasons (see Bach, this volume), but the high domestic salience of immigration and partisan politics during an election year prevented him from doing so.

High-Skilled Immigration and the International System

A final set of issues raised by the chapters in this volume relates to the general phenomena of increasing labor and capital mobility, described elsewhere as "globalization." Given the importance of the high-technology sector, how does high-skilled labor mobility affect the international state system and sovereignty as we know it? Answers to this question include changes in the identity of players and in how the gains from production are distributed.

Globalization theorists have identified three ways in which the increasing density of capital and labor flows threatens traditional international relations thinking about state sovereignty. Soysal (1994) and Jacobson (1996) argue that international human rights norms constrain states that wish to be members of the international system, and that states are being forced by international regimes and national judiciaries to grant immigrants fundamental rights not found in national legal codes.[30] Although Sassen (1998) weakly endorses this normative migrants' rights argument,[31] she makes a stronger assertion about evolving "rights of capital." Sassen argues that the increasing speed and scope of capital mobility undermine the ability of states to perform traditional functions, like regulating national currency markets, and so international financial firms are empowered as "players" in the international system.[32] But given that firms still depend on state-based infrastructure, firms employ their enhanced bargaining power to demand that states protect the interests of capital. To the extent that highly mobile firms are able to play states off each other, these "rights of capital" take on a supra-national quality.

The argument here—that the high-technology sector is strategically important and that high-tech labor determines the limit of high-tech production—updates Sassen's arguments about globalization in two ways. First, if the high-technology sector sits at the center of the third industrial revolution, then all states will be inclined to support these industries. And although Sassen is correct that high-tech production is

---

[30] Joppke (1998) and Hollifield (1992) also emphasize the importance of national judiciaries as checks on the state's ability to regulate flows; but they see these judicial checks deriving from liberal constitutions, not the international system—an argument that receives support from the highly uneven application of these judicial checks across states.

[31] Sassen correctly acknowledges that *enforcement* of supra-nationally derived rights for unskilled immigrants is weak, but she asserts that the presence of formal rights vested in individuals regardless of nationality establishes a precedent upon which immigrants may build.

[32] This portion of Sassen's argument, in particular, is not new. It draws on earlier work by Keohane and Nye (1977), Strange (1988), and others.

limited to *some* "global city" for infrastructural support, production is not site-specific. Thus high-tech firms are even more able to become "actors" in the international system than are the finance firms upon which Sassen focuses, and we should expect high-tech firms to play states off against each other while negotiating for the most generous regulatory and tax packages.

The second implication of my argument is that *individual* cerebreros may also become quasi-players in the international system. Immigrant entrepreneurs are likely to be at the cutting edge of any movement to demand global rights for firms because the are, by definition, mobile. Among non-entrepreneurs, it is already commonplace, as Aneesh argues, for high-end "body shop" workers to set firm policy by redirecting business plans for technical reasons. More noteworthy are Chakravartty's "heroes and anti-heroes of high-tech development"—Linus Pauling, and the mythological "Indian Bill Gates," on the one hand, and Onel de Guzman, the 23-year-old Filipino Robin Hood who released the Love Bug virus in May 2000, on the other. Along with the ability to influence outcomes and to sell their skills to the highest bidder, high-skilled immigrants share with firms the ability to demand new rights.[33] In short, just as the first and second industrial revolutions allowed unskilled labor to demand rights at the national level, the third industrial revolution may eventually allow highly skilled labor to demand a set of global rights. Thus, even if Soysal and Jacobson are overly optimistic about the growing importance of human rights norms, cerebreros may demand global citizenship—albeit only for an elite group—by virtue of their industrial importance.

In addition to increasing the importance of firms and workers as players in the international system, this third industrial revolution may have important distributional consequences, as did earlier periods of significant technological change. The first such likely implication echoes Sassen's unit-level observation that the transformation to a service-based economy within economically advanced states has contributed to growing income inequality: while elite services (that is, high-technology labor) receive inflated compensations, support services (janitors, restaurant staff) are, in Sassen's term, devalorized. Zlolniski (this volume) provides a case study of this phenomenon in Silicon Valley. If I am correct that global citizens will be in a position to sell their services not just to the highest bidding firm but also to the highest-bidding nation, then both of these wage trends are likely to accelerate as nations bid up the packages they provide to high-end labor (migrants and natives) by taking services *away* from low-end service

---

[33] Indeed, the minor pro-immigrant changes included in the 2000 H–1B reforms reflect precisely this dynamic.

workers. Chakravartty has already identified this pattern unfolding in India's Bangalore region, which has an even more bifurcated income structure than does the rest of India.

Two additional distributional issues are located at the systemic level. Here the information revolution appears, in some respects, more "fair" than earlier periods of change in that late developers like India, Pakistan, and China are more important players in the high-technology game than are the countries of Western Europe. Moreover, with labor as the limiting factor of production, a number of additional countries have come on-line as minor players in the 1990s (Mexico, Ireland, and Malaysia, for example), taking advantage of the fact that it is easier to create a cadre of highly literate programmers than it was to suddenly develop wealth in coal or capital 200 years ago. Thus, in the long-term, the third industrial revolution threatens to change the international distribution of resources as fundamentally as did previous transitional periods.

At the same time, however, the demand for specialized infrastructure and for a critical mass of intellectual capital promotes agglomeration. Thus, although "global cities" exist in many less developed countries, the barriers to entry are increasing with each passing day. The window of opportunity during which peripheral countries may develop both the infrastructure and the intellectual capital to join the party may soon close, if it has not done so already. Thus, over time, the same bifurcated wealth structure that followed previous industrial revolutions within and between countries will be reinforced within the international system as well, and the majority of the previous have-nots will find themselves even farther behind.

Finally, these distributional issues raise questions about the possibility of a multilateral skilled-labor migration regime. Although migrant-receiving states have never had a reason to cooperate on an unskilled-labor migration regime given that the supply of labor has outstripped demand, the same is not true of high-skilled labor. For this reason, current members of the high-technology "club" would benefit from lower interstate barriers between them (for example, by granting communal citizenship or through a reciprocal expedited visa process) in an effort to raise entry barriers to new members. (A multilateral regime of this sort would deepen the "global citizenship" rights discussed above, but it would limit their scope to regime members.) For the moment, however, the three leading players all believe they have resources to attract and retain sufficient levels of labor by acting alone, appealing to high quality of life, on the one hand (the United States), and to low cost of living and nationalism, on the other (India and China). Thus a multilateral skilled-labor regime remains unlikely in the foreseeable future.

References

Borjas, George. 1994. "The Economics of Immigration," *Journal of Economic Literature* 32 (December): 1667–1717.

———. 1999. *Heaven's Door: Immigration Policy and the American Economy*. Princeton, N.J.: Princeton University Press.

Donnelly, Paul. 2000. "Indefinitely Temporary: Senate Boost to High Tech Guest Workers Will Block Green Cards," *Backgrounder* (Center for Immigration Studies), March.

Espenshade, Thomas, Margaret Usdansky, and Chang Chung. 2000. "Employment and Earnings of Foreign-Born Scientists and Engineers in U.S. Labor Markets," *Population Research and Policy Review*.

Hollifield, James. 1992. *Immigrants, Markets, and States: The Political Economy of Postwar Europe*. Cambridge, Mass.: Harvard University Press.

Jacobson, David. 1996. *Rights across Borders: Immigration and the Decline of Citizenship*. Baltimore, Md.: Johns Hopkins University Press.

Joppke, Christian. 1998. "Why Liberal States Accept Unwanted Immigration," *World Politics* 50 (January): 266–93.

Keohane, Robert, and Joseph Nye. 1977. *Power and Interdependence*. Boston, Mass.: Little Brown.

———. 2000. "Globalization: What's New? What's Not? (and So What?)," *Foreign Affairs* 118: 104–119.

Krasner, Stephen. 1999. *Sovereignty: Organized Hypocrisy*. Princeton, N.J.: Princeton University Press.

Kugler, Jacek, Ronald Tammen, and Siddharth Swaminathan. 2000. "Power Transitions and Alliance in the 21st Century." Manuscript.

Naughton, Barry. 2000. Comments at the conference "The International Migration of the Highly Skilled," Center for Comparative Immigration Studies, University of California, San Diego.

Papademetriou, Demetrios. 2000. Comments at the conference "The International Migration of the Highly Skilled," Center for Comparative Immigration Studies, University of California, San Diego.

Rosenblum, Marc. 2000. "At Home and Abroad: The Foreign and Domestic Sources of U.S. Immigration Policy." Ph.D. dissertation, University of California, San Diego.

Sassen, Saskia. 1998. *Globalization and Its Discontents*. New York: New Press.

Sastri, Bharat. 2000. "H1B Visas? Use the Internet Instead," *ENEWS*, May 15.

Schuck, Peter. 1998. "The Re-Evaluation of American Citizenship." In *Challenge to the Nation-State: Immigration in Western Europe and the United States*, edited by Christian Joppke. New York: Oxford University Press.

Schumpeter, Joseph. 1976 (1942). *Capitalism, Socialism, and Democracy*. London: Allen and Unwin.

Soysal, Yasemin N. 1994. *Limits of Citizenship: Migrants and Postnational Membership in Europe*. Chicago: University of Chicago Press.

Strange, Susan. 1988. *States and Markets*. New York: Basil Blackwell.

Thurow, Lester. 1999. *Building Wealth: The New Rules for Individuals, Companies, and Nations in a Knowledge-Based Economy*. New York: Harper Collins.

Appendix

Table A.1

U.S. Scientists and Engineers, by Occupation and Non–Native-Born Status, 1995

Occupation	Total	Non-native-born (%)
Total scientists and engi- neers	3,186,000	15
Computer scientists[a]	641,000	12
Mathematical scientists	87,000	16
Life scientists	305,000	16
Chemical and physical scientists	274,000	17
Social scientists	318,000	9
Engineers[a]	1,560,000	17

[a] Totals for engineers and computer scientists differ from totals in other National Science Foundation/Division of Science Resources Studies publications. Here, computer software engineers have been counted as engineers.

Source: National Science Foundation/Division of Science Resources Studies, Scientists and Engineers Statistical Data System (SESTAT), 1995.

Table A.2
U.S. Engineers, by Non–Native-Born Status, Employment Sector, Age, and Highest Degree, 1995

Characteristic	Total	Non–native-born (%)
Total engineers[a]	1,560,000	17
Employment sector[b]		
Private industry	1,151,000	16
Academia	71,000	34
Government (all levels)	199,000	16
Age		
Under 30	213,000	15
30–39	598,000	17
40–49	419,000	17
50–59	226,000	19
60 and over	105,000	15
Highest degree[c]		
Bachelor's	1,042,000	12
Master's	434,000	25
Doctorate	76,000	41

[a] Includes computer software engineers, who are counted as computer scientists in other National Science Foundation/Division of Science Resources Studies publications.
[b] About 139,000 engineers worked in other sectors.
[c] The highest degrees of about 8,000 engineers did not fall into these categories.

Source: National Science Foundation/Division of Science Resources Studies, Scientists and Engineers Statistical Data System (SESTAT), 1995.

Table A.3
H–1B Petitions Approved, by Country of Birth,
October 1999–February 2000

Country of Birth	Total	Percent
Total	81,262	-----
Known countries of birth	80,786	100.0
India	34,381	42.6
China	7,987	9.9
Canada	3,143	3.9
United Kingdom	2,598	3.2
Philippines	2,576	3.2
Taiwan	1,794	2.2
Korea	1,691	2.1
Japan	1,631	2.0
Pakistan	1,508	1.9
Russia	1,408	1.7
Germany	1,261	1.6
France	1,204	1.5
Mexico	1,011	1.3
Brazil	861	1.1
South Africa	838	1.0
Colombia	769	1.0
Hong Kong	738	0.9
Malaysia	722	0.9
Australia	644	0.8
Indonesia	635	0.8
Other countries	13,386	16.6
Unknown country of birth	476	------

Note: Approximately 0.6 percent of total petitions have an unknown country of birth. Percents shown in the table are based on the total number of petitions with known countries of birth.

Source: U.S. Immigration and Naturalization Service, *Characteristics of Specialty Occupation Workers (H–1B): October 1999 to February 2000* (Washington, D.C., June 2000).

Table A.4

H–1B Petitions Approved, by Major Occupation Group,
October 1999–February 2000

Occupation LCA Code (2-digits)	Total	Percent
	81,262	-----
Total		
Known occupations	79,548	100.0
Computer-related occupations (03)	42,563	53.5
Occupations in architecture, engineering, and surveying (00/01)	10,385	13.1
Occupations in administrative specializations (16)	6,619	8.3
Occupations in education (09)	4,419	5.6
Occupations in medicine and health (07)	3,246	4.1
Managers and officials, N.E.C. (18)	2,530	3.2
Occupations in social sciences (05)	1,963	2.5
Occupations in life sciences (04)	1,843	2.3
Miscellaneous professional, technical, and managerial (19)	1,659	2.1
Occupations in mathematics and physical sciences (02)	1,453	1.8
Occupations in art (14)	1,066	1.3
Occupations in writing (13)	548	0.7
Occupations in law and jurisprudence (11)	428	0.5
Fashion models (297)	344	0.4
Occupations in entertainment and recreation (15)	293	0.4
Occupations in museum, library, and archival sciences (10)	146	0.2
Occupations in religion and theology (12)	43	0.1
Unknown occupations	1,714	------

Note: Approximately 2.1 percent of total petitions have an unknown occupation. Percents shown in the table are based on the total number of petitions with known occupations.

N.E.C. = Not elsewhere classified.

Source: U.S. Immigration and Naturalization Service, *Characteristics of Specialty Occupation Workers (H–1B): October 1999 to February 2000* (Washington, D.C., June 2000).

Table A.5

H–1B Petitions Approved, by Highest Degree Earned,
October 1999–February 2000

Highest Degree Earned	Total	Percent
Total	81,262	-----
Known degree	74,205	100.0
No diploma	357	0.5
High school graduate	134	0.2
Less than 1 year of college credit	82	0.1
1 or more years of college credit, no diploma	671	0.9
Associate's degree	357	0.5
Bachelor's degree	41,849	56.4
Master's degree	22,974	31.0
Doctorate degree	6,035	8.1
Professional degree	1,746	2.4
Unknown degree	7,057	------

Note: Approximately 8.7 percent of total petitions have an unknown degree. Percents shown in the table are based on the total number of petitions with known degree.

Source: U.S. Immigration and Naturalization Service, *Characteristics of Specialty Occupation Workers (H–1B): October 1999 to February 2000* (Washington, D.C., June 2000).

Table A.6

H–1B Petitions Approved, by Major Occupation Group and Annual Wage, October 1999–February 2000

Occupation LCA Code (2 digits)	Total petitions	Annual Wage		
		25th percentile	Median	75th percentile
Occupation	74,202	$40,000	$50,000	$65,000
Fashion models (297)	304	$100,000	$130,000	$221,000
Occupations in law and jurisprudence (11)	394	$40,000	$80,500	$101,000
Occupations in architecture, engineering, and surveying (00/01)	9,475	$42,240	$55,000	$68,500
Computer-related occupations (03)	39,214	$45,000	$53,000	$65,000
Managers and officials N.E.C. (18)	2,375	$35,000	$52,000	$85,000
Occupations in mathematics and physical sciences (02)	1,330	$36,000	$47,834	$64,000
Miscellaneous professional, technical, and managerial (19)	1,564	$33,290	$46,473	$75,000
Occupations in medicine and health (07)	2,825	$33,526	$45,760	$88,763
Occupations in administrative specializations (16)	6,151	$31,000	$40,000	$58,000
Occupations in social sciences (05)	1,682	$32,640	$40,000	$58,000
Occupations in museum, library, and archival sciences (10)	121	$28,000	$36,000	$45,000
Occupations in art (14)	1,008	$29,000	$35,961	$50,000
Occupations in life sciences (04)	1,660	$29,000	$34,700	$46,000
Occupations in education (09)	3,998	$27,500	$33,500	$43,620
Occupations in writing (13)	504	$27,045	$33,000	$45,000
Occupations in entertainment and recreation (15)	246	$24,000	$31,200	$48,000
Occupations in religion and theology (12)	30	$25,000	$31,100	$41,000
Unknown occupations	1,321	$36,000	$44,000	$62,358

Note: Approximately 8.7 percent of the petitions do not have annual wage information and have been excluded from the table.

N.E.C. = Not elsewhere classified.

Source: U.S. Immigration and Naturalization Service, *Characteristics of Specialty Occupation Workers (H–1B): October 1999 to February 2000* (Washington, D.C., June 2000).

Table A.7
Leading Employers of H–1B Workers, October 1999–February 2000

Rank	Company	Number of H–1B Petitions Approved
1	Motorola Inc	618
2	Oracle Corp	455
3	Cisco Systems	398
4	Mastech	389
5	Intel Corp	367
6	Microsoft Corp	362
7	Rapidigm	357
8	Syntel Inc	337
9	Wipro LTD	327
10	Tata Consultancy Serv	320
11	PriceWaterhouseCoopers LLP	272
12	People Com Consultants Inc	261
13	Lucent Technologies	255
14	Infosys Technologies LTD	239
15	Nortel Networks Inc	234
16	Tekedge Corp	219
17	Data Conversion	195
18	Tata Infotech	185
19	Cotelligent USA Inc	183
20	Sun Microsystems Inc	182
21	Compuware Corp	179
22	KPMG LLP	177
23	Intelligroup	161
24	Hi Tech Consultants Inc	157
25	Group Ipex Inc	151
26	Ace Technologies Inc	149
	Hewlett Packard Co	149
28	Everest Consulting GR	147
29	Bell Atlantic Network Serv	141
30	Ernst Young LLP	137
31	Agilent Technologies Inc	136
32	Deloitte Touche LLP	130
33	Birlasoft	128
	Global Consultants	128
35	IBM	124

continued

Rank	Company	Number of H–1B Petitions Approved
35 (cont.)	R Systems Inc	124
	Sprint United Mgt	124
	Wireless Facilities	124
39	Cognizant Technology Solutions	123
	Satyam Computer Serv	123
41	Keane	114
42	University of Washington	113
43	Analysts Intl Corp	110
44	Capital One Serv	109
45	Apar Infotech	108
	Modis Inc	108
47	L&T Technology LTD	107
48	Complete Business Solutions Inc	105
49	Techspan	101
50	CMOS Soft Inc	100
51	Renaissance Worldwide	99
52	University of Pennsylvania	97
53	Conexant Systems Inc	96
	I2 Technologies Inc	96
55	AT T	93
56	Jean Martin	91
57	EMC	90
58	Atlantic Duncans Intl	87
	Merrill Lynch	87
60	Unique Computing	86
61	Computer Intl	85
	Indotronix Intl	85
	Nationwide Insurance	85
64	Interim Technology Consulting	84
65	Compaq Computer	80
	GE	80
	MSI Majesco Software Inc	80
68	Data Core Systems	78
69	IT Solutions Inc	77
70	Allied Informatics Inc	76
71	Ciber Inc	75
	Deloitte Consulting LLC	75
	Goldman Sachs	75
74	Baton Rouge Intl	74

continued

Rank	Company	Number of H–1B Petitions Approved
75	Cyberthink	73
	Stanford University	73
77	Cap Gemini America	72
	Infogain	72
79	Ajilon Serv	71
	Allsoft Technologies Inc	71
	Morgan Stanley Dean Witter	71
82	Ericsson Inc	70
	Harvard University	70
	Sabre Inc	70
	Yash Technologies Inc	70
86	Pyramid Consulting Inc	69
87	MSX Intl Inc	68
88	Softplus Inc	67
89	Baylor College of Medicine	65
	Microstrategy	65
	University of Minnesota	65
	Universal Software	65
93	Computer Horizons	64
94	Ramco Systems	63
	Siebel Systems Inc	63
96	Insight Solutions Inc	62
	Synopsys Inc	62
	Texas Instruments Inc	62
99	Infosynergy	61
	Lason Systems Inc	61
	Vanguard GR	61
	Yale University	61
Subtotal for 102 companies listed		13,940
Subtotal for companies not listed		67,322
Grand Total		**81,262**

Source: U.S. Immigration and Naturalization Service, *Leading Employers of Specialty Occupation Workers (H–1B): October 1999 to February 2000* (Washington, D.C., June 2000).

Table A.8
Foreign Workers in Canada, by Type of Employment, 1998

Type of Employment	Total	Percent
Professional occupations in art and culture	9,127	14.0
Professional occupations in natural and applied sciences	7,682	11.8
Professional occupations in social science, education, government services, and religion	5,749	8.8
Professional occupations in business and finance	5,117	7.9
Technical occupations related to natural and applied sciences	3,995	6.1
Intermediate occupations in primary industries	3,669	5.6
Technical and skilled occupations in art, culture, recreation, and sport	3,368	5.2
Intermediate sales and service occupations	3,361	5.2
Middle and other management occupations	2,382	3.7
Trades and skilled transport and equipment operators	1,737	2.7
Other types of employment	18,961	29.1
Total	65,148	100.0

Note: The individuals in the Foreign Worker population are shown in the year in which they received their first temporary authorization.
Source: Citizenship and Immigration Canada, *Facts and Figures*, 1999.

Table A.9

Skilled Workers Admitted to Canada, by Top Ten Source Countries, 1999 (principal applicants)

Country	Total	Percent	Rank
China	10,065	24.26	1
India	3,439	8.29	2
Pakistan	2,239	5.40	3
France	2,134	5.14	4
Iran	1,285	3.10	5
South Korea	1,225	2.95	6
United King-dom	1,210	2.92	7
Romania	1,132	2.73	8
Taiwan	1,109	2.67	9
Russia	1,035	2.50	10
Philippines	925	2.23	11
Hong Kong	731	1.76	13
Total for top ten only	24,873	59.96	
Total other countries	16,609	40.04	
Total	**41,482**	**100.00**	

Source: Citizenship and Immigration Canada, *Facts and Figures*, 1999.

Table A.10

Skilled Workers Admitted to Canada, by Level of Education, 1999 (principal applicant)

Education[a]	Total	Percent
0 to 9 years of schooling	644	1.55
10 to 12 years of schooling	1,098	2.65
13 or more years of schooling	1,695	4.09
Trade certificate	2,288	5.52
Non-university diploma	3,438	8.30
Bachelor's degree	21,458	51.79
Master's degree	8,665	20.91
Doctorate	2,150	5.19
Total	41,436	100

[a] Applies to individuals who are 15 years of age or older.

Source: Citizenship and Immigration Canada, *Facts and Figures*, 1999.

About the Contributors

Rafael Alarcón is an anthropologist and Professor in the Department of Social Studies at El Colegio de la Frontera Norte in Tijuana, Mexico. A specialist on international migration and regional development, he co-authored *Return to Aztlan: The Social Process of International Migration from Western Mexico* (University of California Press, 1987). His recent publications include "Skilled Immigrants and *Cerebreros*: Foreign-born Engineers and Scientists in the High-Technology Industry of Silicon Valley," in Nancy Foner et al., eds., *Immigration and Immigration Research for a New Century* (Russell Sage Foundation, forthcoming).

A. Aneesh is a Ph.D. candidate in the Department of Sociology at Rutgers University. He was recently a recipient of research fellowships from the Population Council and the Social Science Research Council. Author of articles on migration and information technologies, Aneesh focuses his research on the intersection of technology, the nation-state, and international migration.

Robert Bach is Deputy Director of the Working Communities Division of the Rockefeller Foundation. Dr. Bach served in the Clinton administration as Executive Associate Commissioner of the Immigration and Naturalization Service, where he was the senior policy, planning, and program development official. He has also been a professor of sociology at the State University of New York–Binghamton and a Senior Fellow at the Carnegie Endowment for International Peace. He has published on U.S. domestic and foreign policies on migration and is completing two monographs, *Immigration and Legal Services in the United States* and *Market Reforms and Migration in Vietnam.*

Monica Boyd is the Mildred and Claude Pepper Distinguished Professor of Sociology at Florida State University, where she also is a research associate in the Center for the Study of Population. A demographer and sociologist, Dr. Boyd has written numerous articles, books, and monographs on social inequality and international migration, focusing on policy issues, immigrant integration, and immigrant women. She was recently a Visiting Scholar at Statistics Canada, where she conducted research on Canadian immigration and ethnic stratification.

Paula Chakravartty is Assistant Professor in the Department of Communication at the University of California, San Diego. Her research concentrates on the intersections between political economy and cultural studies in the field of international communications. Her areas of interest include labor and gender in the new media and information technology sectors, especially in the context of the emerging economies of Asia and Latin America. She is currently working on a book entitled *The Politics of High-Tech Development in India.*

Wayne Cornelius is the Gildred Professor of Political Science and Adjunct Professor of International Relations at the University of California, San Diego. He is the founding director of UCSD's Center for Comparative Immigration Studies and its Center for U.S.–Mexican Studies. His publications deal with the political economy and sociology of Third World labor migration to industrialized nations (especially the United States, Japan, and Spain) and the Mexican political system. His books include *Controlling Immigration: A Global Perspective* (Stanford University Press, 1995, co-edited with James Hollifield and Philip Martin). He is completing a comparative study of the role of immigrant labor in the U.S. and Japanese economies.

Thomas J. Espenshade is Professor and Chair of the Department of Sociology and Faculty Associate at the Office of Population Research, Princeton University. His previous work includes research on models of undocumented U.S. migration, public attitudes toward contemporary U.S. immigration, the fiscal impacts of immigrants, and the labor market consequences of high-skilled immigration. His recent publications include an edited volume, *Keys to Successful Immigration: Implications of the New Jersey Experience* (Urban Institute Press, 1997), and "Immigration and Public Opinion," in Marcelo Suárez-Orozco, ed., *Crossings: Mexican Immigration in Interdisciplinary Perspectives* (Harvard University Press, 1998).

Jessica Gurcak graduated from Princeton University in 1998 with an A.B. in economics. She is currently working as a writer and editor for a historical reference publisher in Santa Barbara, California.

Mahmood Iqbal is a principal research associate at the Conference Board of Canada. Since joining the Board in 1988, Dr. Iqbal has participated in a variety of research projects related to foreign investment, technology transfer, business linkages, and international tax competitiveness. Recently he completed a major study on brain drain. Prior to joining the Conference Board, he was Assistant Professor of Economics at Concordia University, Montreal.

Magnus Lofstrom is a research associate at the Institute for the Study of Labor (IZA) in Bonn, Germany; he will soon join the University of California, Irvine. His research deals with European and American immigration, focusing on self-employment and labor market performance, assimilation, welfare dependency, and educational attainment. His work has been published in George Borjas, ed., *Issues in the Economics of Immigration* (University of Chicago Press, 2000) and the *Journal of Population Economics.*

B. Lindsay Lowell is Director of Research at the Institute for the Study of International Migration, Georgetown University. He was previously Director of Policy Research with the congressionally appointed, bipartisan U.S. Commission on Immigration Reform. His research interests focus on the international movement of skilled workers. His recent publications include an edited volume, *Foreign Temporary Workers in America: Policies that Benefit the U.S. Economy* (Quorum Books, 1999).

Martha Paskoff is a student in the Woodrow Wilson School of International and Public Affairs at Princeton University, focusing on policies for urban redevelopment and revitalization. She has been an intern at the Brookings Institution's Center on Urban and Metropolitan Policy, where she assisted with a study of welfare reform in the one hundred largest cities in the United States.

Marc R. Rosenblum is Assistant Professor of Political Science at the University of New Orleans. His work focuses on U.S.–Latin American relations, immigration, and Latin American politics. He has published in *Comparative Political Studies* and the *UCLA Journal of Law and International Affairs*. A policy paper by Dr. Rosenblum was recently published by the University of California's Institute on Global Conflict and Cooperation.

Idean Salehyan is Staff Research Associate in the Center for Comparative Immigration Studies at the University of California, San Diego. His research interests include the international political economy of migration and the determinants of immigration and refugee policy. He is the author of *The Domestic Uses of International Law: Refugee Policy in the United States and Canada* (CCIS Monograph No. 5, forthcoming).

AnnaLee Saxenian is Professor of City and Regional Planning at the University of California, Berkeley, specializing in regional economies and the information technology sector. Her current research examines the contributions of skilled immigrants to Silicon Valley and their growing ties to regions in Asia. Her publications include *Silicon Valley's New Immigrant Entrepreneurs* (Public Policy Institute of California, 1999) and *Regional Advantage: Culture and Competition in Silicon Valley and Route 128* (Harvard University Press, 1996).

Aaron Sparrow is a doctoral student in economics at Princeton University. He is currently working on projects evaluating the reintegration of criminals into the labor market and the effect of neighborhood amenities on real estate values in New York City. Prior to his graduate studies, he worked as a research assistant at the Urban Institute and the Brookings Institution.

Margaret L. Usdansky is a graduate student in the Department of Sociology at Princeton University. She previously worked as Special Assistant to Joseph A. Califano, Jr. at the National Center on Addiction and Substance Abuse at Columbia University and as the demography reporter for *USA Today* and the *Atlanta Constitution*.

Christian Zlolniski is an anthropologist and Professor in the Department of Social Studies at El Colegio de la Frontera Norte in Tijuana, Mexico. His research focuses on the role of low-skilled Mexican immigrant labor in high-tech industry in the United States. He is the author of "The Informal Economy in an Advanced Industrialized Society: Mexican Immigrant Labor in Silicon Valley" (*Yale Law Journal*, 1994) and "Etnografía de trabajadores informales en un barrio de inmigrantes mexicanos en el Silicon Valley" (*Revista Mexicana de Sociología*, 2000).